A Certain Amount

Black Critique

Series editor: Anthony Bogues

We live in a troubled world. The rise of authoritarianism marks the dominant current political order. The end of colonial empires did not inaugurate a more humane world; rather, the old order reasserted itself.

In opposition, throughout the twentieth century and until today, anti-racist, radical decolonization struggles attempted to create new forms of thought. Figures from Ida B. Wells to W.E.B. Du Bois and Steve Biko, from Claudia Jones to Walter Rodney and Amílcar Cabral produced work which drew from the historical experiences of Africa and the African diaspora. They drew inspiration from the Haitian revolution, radical black abolitionist thought and practice, and other currents that marked the contours of a black radical intellectual and political tradition.

The Black Critique series operates squarely within this tradition of ideas and political struggles. It includes books which foreground this rich and complex history. At a time when there is a deep desire for change, black radicalism is one of the most underexplored traditions that can drive emancipatory change today. This series highlights these critical ideas from anywhere in the black world, creating a new history of radical thought for our times.

Also available:

Red International and Black Caribbean:
Communists in New York City, Mexico and the West Indies, 1919–1939
Margaret Stevens

A Certain Amount of Madness

The Life, Politics and Legacies of Thomas Sankara

Edited by Amber Murrey

Foreword by Horace Campbell
Afterword by Aziz Salmone Fall

PLUTO  PRESS

First published 2018 by Pluto Press
345 Archway Road, London N6 5AA

www.plutobooks.com

British Library Cataloguing in Publication Data
A catalogue record for this book is available from the British Library

ISBN 978 0 7453 3758 6 Hardback
ISBN 978 0 7453 3757 9 Paperback
ISBN 978 1 7868 0224 8 PDF eBook
ISBN 978 1 7868 0226 2 Kindle eBook
ISBN 978 1 7868 0225 5 EPUB eBook

This book is printed on paper suitable for recycling and made from fully
managed and sustained forest sources. Logging, pulping and manufacturing
processes are expected to conform to the environmental standards of the country of origin.

Typeset by Swales & Willis
Simultaneously printed in the United Kingdom and United States of America

Half of all author proceeds for this book are donated to the June Givanni Pan-African
Cinema Archive (www.junegivannifilmarchive.com). This is the largest archive of
Pan-African filmmaking in Europe, operating to promote Pan-African art and
philosophy to a wide audience, supporting Black artists in a colonial matrix that
otherwise marginalizes their perspectives and cultivating an appreciation for Black life
and art – all causes that were foundational to Sankara's radical Pan-African vision.

For Ndewa Jean (1948–1990)
and all the others who wept
on 15 October 1987

Contents

Foreword
The Life and Legacy of Thomas Sankara
Horace G. Campbell

Thomas Sankara was born in Burkina Faso in 1949, the same year that the Chinese Revolution succeeded in laying the foundations for a transition to socialism. This revolution had succeeded after years of war, sacrifice and ideological struggle. Sankara was killed in 1987, the year of the decisive military change to defeat apartheid militarism in Africa. In the 37 years while Sankara traversed the earth, he was shaped by the political, social and ideological struggles in the anti-imperialist world. Sankara helped to assert the claim of African peoples to be a part of those defining the future of humanity. In his adult years, Sankara served as a soldier in the armed forces of Burkina Faso. This was a branch of the imperial military chain to control the labour power of the producing classes in Africa. He made a decisive break with this tradition.

Burkina Faso was previously called Upper Volta, one of the regions of French colonial plunder and exploitation in Africa. Sankara had been groomed to serve these interests but he wanted to be a decent human being in a society of upright human beings. Hence in the period of his short leadership of Burkina Faso, 1983-1987, he changed the name and orientation of the society to signal a Pan-African assertion of dignity and self-confidence. These two aspects of self-determination have now been inscribed within the project for the unification and emancipation of a socialist Africa. Sankara's life and work as a soldier left many lessons for the African revolutionaries of today, whose task it is to speed the break from imperial domination. The 23 chapters of this book on Sankara remind the younger generation of what a life of dignity can do for peoples everywhere.

BIRTH IN THE SHADOW OF REVOLUTIONARY CHANGES

Thomas Sankara was born in a territory that had been exploited by France in its bid to represent itself as a major force in world politics. Both Britain and France had been diminished by the Second Imperialist war and wars of national liberation from China and Vietnam to Malaysia and Egypt had weakened both colonial powers. The United States had emerged out of World War II as the dominant imperial force and had created the North Atlantic Treaty Organization to defend global capital. France and Britain had mobilised colonial troops to maintain its place at the international table of Global Capital. Colonial armies were deployed in Vietnam and the marginalized elements of colonial societies were recruited as foot soldiers for the dying colonial enterprise. Hence in places such as the Central African Republic and Uganda, soldiers were recruited to fight to save French and British capitalism. Jean Bedel Bokasa of the Central African Republic and Idi Amin of Uganda were two archetype colonial soldiers who fought against freedom fighters in Indo China and in Kenya. It was this tradition of fighting against the forces of self-determination that was drilled into soldiers all across Africa after World War II. Those soldiers who supported the independence struggles, such as Dedan Kimathi of Kenya, had lent their military skills and training to the task of freeing Africa.

By the time Thomas Sankara was ten years old, the Cuban Revolution had sent a message that size was not a barrier in the fight for freedom. The emergence of the military and political ideas of Fidel Castro and Che Guevara had become a new source of inspiration for youths all across the anti-imperialist world. It was this world into which Thomas Sankara grew. Upper Volta, as his home society was called, was a reservoir of workers and soldiers from the French imperial system. The super exploitation of the working poor and farmers in the society was amplified by a system of migration where the poor of worked as cheap, bonded labor in the farms of Ghana and Ivory Coast. Hence the class character of Upper Volta was shaped by the dominance of French capital, with French commercial and trading firms in the interstices of the system. French domination was maintained through the coercive organs of the state - police, military, courts, prison and tsetse fly control. At the ideological level, the French system depended on the reinforcement of ideas of African inferiority.

The local class structure was stymied by the absence of a social force capable of asserting the self-confidence of the producing classes. There was no African bourgeoisie in Upper Volta. There were some chiefs who functioned as landlords and alienated the labor power of poor peasants, but these land-owners did not comprise a class in their own right. These landlords who fluctuated between the chiefly structures of the pre-colonial society and the French administrative structures were timid at the material, cultural and intellectual levels. A few intellectuals who were trained in the metropoles failed to gain support because of this internalisation of the idea that there were differences between commoners and chiefs. Constant reference to the poor as slaves in their discourse meant that even when these intellectuals articulated Pan-African ideas, the reference point for freedom was not the peoples, but the freedom for this stratum to have more room within the hierarchy of French domination.

Below the African landed class was the salariat and the professional classes of doctors, lawyers, journalists, priests and marabouts (healer-diviners). The dominant social force both numerically and politically were the millions of poor workers, small farmers, lower civil servants, small-scale miners, teacher's traders, cultural workers and soldiers. Thomas Sankara was born into this latter social group and as a youth travelled throughout the country, where he saw that the exploitation of these forces covered the entire territory. As a young soldier, Sankara was sent for training in Madagascar and it was there that he saw that the conditions of the exploited African were common throughout Africa. The interaction with workers, poor farmers and soldiers in Upper Volta and Madagascar sent Sankara searching for the ideas and forms of organization that could change the conditions of the peoples.

MEETING AMILCAR CABRAL, JULIUS NYERERE, WALTER RODNEY AND CHE GUEVARA

As a soldier, Sankara read widely both from the classical literature on socialism and the more recent literature from African thinkers and activists. Sankara was particularly drawn to the ideas and social practices of Che Guevara and Amilcar Cabral, as two of the chapters in this volume will bring out. Burkina Faso could not sustain a form of 'parliamentary democracy' because the resistance of the workers and farmers required the deployment of the military and police constantly. After independence protests by students and labor unions became the dominant form of political expression and, from the early years of independence, the military intervened to curb the search for power by the oppressed masses. These stirrings of workers and students in Upper Volta threatened the fragile position of neighbours, such as the Ivory Coast and Togo. It was the energy of the trade unions that shaped the society, but these trade union leaders did not have the ideological training to link their battles to the poor peasantry. Conscious of the exploited nature of the society, the military interveners presented themselves as saviors and hence, in the coup before Sankara became president, the military junta called themselves the Council of Popular Salvation (CSP). The fluctuation between the military and the workers radicalised a section of the military and it was from this radical sector that Sankara emerged. It was a military coup in August 1983 that propelled some of these soldiers to the top of political power.

RADICALISM FROM ABOVE

From the outset, it became clear to Sankara that there were no clear vehicles for popular expression and participation. To remedy this absence of political forum for the most oppressed, there were initiatives such as the Committees for the Defense of the Revolution (CDRs). These Committees depended on the energies of Sankara and did not become institutionalised enough to prevent his murder and the reversals of the gains of the poor. France, the United States and other imperial powers were afraid of the demonstration effect of young soldiers siding with the poor at a moment when the battles against apartheid had ignited tremendous anti-imperialist sentiments in Africa. Sankara's leadership inspired a series of revolutionary programmes which included mass-vaccinations, infrastructure improvements, the expansion of women's rights, encouragement of domestic agricultural consumption and anti-desertification projects. Sankara was one of the principal supporters of the idea of the Great Green Wall across Africa. Imperialism was alarmed at the nationalisation projects along with the clarification that Africa did not need aid, but rather a return of its stolen assets.

The radical foreign policies of Sankara in West Africa had emerged at the same moment when leaders such as Samora Machel were calling for greater mobilisation against imperialism. For this, Samora Machel was killed in October 1986 and Sankara was killed one year later in October 1987.

The Life of Thomas Sankara was one that exemplified sacrifice for freedom and modesty of leadership. However, these personal qualities could not substitute for the more rigorous form of political organisation that were required to shift power decisively into the hands of workers, peasants and soldiers. The collective weight of anti-people elements in France, Liberia, Ivory Coast and Togo was unleashed to kill Sankara and those who rebelled after he was killed. Those forces continue to conspire to ensure that the life of Thomas Sankara does not emerge as the symbol it should be. This book is one modest effort to keep alive the memory and spirit of Thomas Sankara. As rank and file soldiers from Egypt to Ethiopia and from Uganda and Sudan stir under new conditions of super-exploitation, this book can be another instrument in clarifying some of the tasks of revolutionary organisation in Africa.

Imperialism remains aware of the ultimate power of a radicalised soldiery within the movement of a radicalised population. In the thirty years since the killing of Sankara, the end of apartheid, the growth of the reparations movement and the massive organisation globally against neo-liberal capitalism have breathed new life into the ideals of Sankara. The global capitalist crisis of 2007–2008 unleashed new pressures on the poor and, in response, all over Africa there are new uprisings, including the awakenings in 2011 in North Africa, which sent new tremors around the world. In Burkina Faso, the energetic youths finally removed the killers of Sankara and drove them from the society, but the institutional basis for exploitation remains. This book can serve as one other weapon to investigate how the new awakenings can lead to a decisive break with imperial domination and unleash the push for socialist transformation.

1 Sankara's revolutionary vision for an economically independent Burkina Faso included increased efforts to produce and consume Burkinabè products. The locally produced weaved cloth was reclaimed with the new name: the Faso Dan Fani. Sankara is remembered as saying, 'to wear the Faso Dan Fani is an economic, cultural and political challenge to imperialism'. Such developments were symbolic under his government and were designed to build national pride, celebrate Burkinabè achievements and harness the country's economic potential. Sankara promoted this national pride at every level. Here he is wearing a Faso Dan Fani, while welcoming festival guests at a reception during the Pan-African Film and Television Festival of Ouagadougou (FESPACO) in 1987. The Faso Dan Fani is still an iconic fashion product, not only in Burkina Faso but also with fashionistas around and beyond the African continent. (Previously unpublished photo and caption courtesy of June Givanni, 1987.)

2 During my first two visits to the FESPACO Film Festival in 1985 and 1987, festival guests and other dignitaries were invited to participate in solidarity with the social reconstruction campaigns that were being introduced during Sankara's fledgling presidency. In 1985, it was 'La Bataille du Rail' ('The Battle of the Rails') that laid rail-track on the railway construction linking Burkina's major cities of Ouagadougou and Bobo-Dioulasso. In 1987, it was an environmental campaign of countrywide tree planting. I took this photograph of Sankara on the occasion of the tree-planting event that took place during the FESPACO film Festival. He had been bending down digging a hole and planting a tree and just as he stood up, he looked in our direction. (Previously unpublished photo and caption courtesy of June Givanni, 1987.)

Acknowledgements

This book was a collective dream and a collective effort. So many need to be named in gratitude. Thank you to each of the authors for their thoughtful contributions to this project; each provided new insights into Sankara's life and legacy. Thank you to my teachers, comrades and friends, who offered much-needed guidance, encouragement and criticism: Horace Campbell, Patricia McFadden, Patricia Daley, Gnaka Lagoke, Aziz Solomone Fall, Nicholas Jackson, Bruno Jaffré, Adam Elliott-Cooper, Ashok Kumar, Odomaro Mubangizi and the dozens of activists, intellectuals and students who reached out to me over the years, expressing passion and interest in Sankara's story. Thank you to Sharon and Kristy Burnett, who applauded the work from the beginning and demanded the first copies; to Alexandra Reza, whose insights helped give form to early work on this project and whose scholarship on Sankara was instructive throughout; to my editor, David Shulman, whose markedly patient insistence saw the work to fruition. Thank you to Derogy Ndewa, who introduced me to Thomas Sankara and fêted every milestone of the project with me and our daughters, Malicia and Sankara.

Introduction

Amber Murrey

In late October 2014, protests broke out across Burkina Faso in response to a proposed constitutional amendment to extend presidential term limits. Hundreds of thousands of protestors took to the streets, asserting again that 'trop, c'est trop!' ('enough is enough') and demanding that Blaise Compaoré step down after 27 years as the country's president. When tear gas, live ammunition and the declaration of martial law failed to suppress the protestors, Blaise announced his resignation. On 30 October 2014, protestors stormed the Parliament building in Ouagadougou (or as it is more commonly referred to, 'Ouaga'). Popular social media websites, including Facebook and YouTube, were flooded with video clips and photos of some Burkinabè youth connecting this political victory to the heritage and legacy of their former president and revolutionary, Thomas Isidore Noël Sankara (1949–1987). It was a powerful moment for contemporary Pan-Africanism and youth-led political activism (Reza 2016).

Thomas Sankara was one of the most confident and vocal anti-imperialists of the late twentieth century. His life and political praxis continue to be significant in shaping and inspiring anti-imperial and Pan-African youth activism and resistance across the African continent and beyond. *A Certain Amount of Madness* draws together contemporary scholarship on Sankara's life and political praxis with work on the contemporary resistance movements in Burkina Faso and elsewhere that draw inspiration from Sankara's politics. While a growing body of important interdisciplinary and journalistic writing has emerged in the last half decade on Sankara's life and assassination, there have been few serious considerations of his political praxis and relevance for contemporary revolutionary movements today. Part of the intention of this volume is to pay more serious attention to Sankara's legacy (multifaceted, ambiguous and disputed) and afterlives together with reconsiderations of his innovative political praxis. The combining of these previously divergent projects allows for a more complete understanding of Sankara's on-going relevance at the same time that our examinations avoid hagiography or hero worship.

Considering Sankara's own proclamations against panegyric or excessively praising depictions – this was a man who refused to have photographs of himself displayed in public, denounced the popular songs praising himself and famously declared that 'there are 7 million Sankaras' – shows us that he would oppose overly celebratory depictions of himself. He would urge us to have a broader focus when we look at the politics of social justice in Burkina Faso, the 'land of the upright people'. He would demand that we prioritise integrity and people's material and cultural well-being and that we do so in a language legible to many.

The 23 chapters of the volume attest to Sankara's wide appeal: about half of the contributors are Anglophone or predominantly English-speaking and authors come from more than a dozen countries. Contributors are journalists, activists, students, development practitioners, academics and artists. Those authors who are academics are deeply interdisciplinary, representing nearly every discipline in the social sciences and humanities, including political science, political economy, human geography, development studies, sociology, anthropology, communications, comparative literature, history, art history, African studies and philosophy. This unique grouping of contributors makes for a diverse, unapologetically non-uniform and sometimes eclectic conversation on Sankara's politics, philosophies and legacies.

A number of historical and biographical chapters consider Sankara's rise to power in the late-Cold War context, including his leadership style, encounters with labour unions and assassination. Several of the chapters in the volume are critical of aspects of Sankara's political leadership and other chapters emphasise a holistic landscape of activism and resistance in modern day Burkina Faso (referred to here as 'Burkina' or 'le Faso'). Sizeable demonstrations occurred in 1999, 2003, 2006, 2007, 2008 and 2011 as diverse groups from across civil society came together, including youth activists protesting against the unjustly arrested, detained, assassinated or disappeared (see Chapters 17 and 23, this volume; also Harsch 1999; Chouli 2012a, 2012b, 2014). In Chapter 3, British political economist and novelist Leo Zeilig considers the sizeable tasks of the revolution and the ways in which these posed considerable (and ultimately 'deadly') challenges for Sankara's government: to at once cultivate change and empowerment at the grassroots while also initiating large-scale and top-down development projects. Drawing from the research of French activist and writer Lila Chouli in Burkina Faso, Zeilig argues that the National Council of the Revolution (CNR)'s 'authoritarian approach had alienated sections of the Burkinabè population, leaving Sankara and his allies isolated'. In Chapter 4, British labour scholar Craig Phelan documents the tensions between Sankara's government and labour unions in Burkina, arguing that Sankara 'underestimated' the influence of such unions.

Chapters from American historian Brian Peterson and French activist and biographer of Thomas Sankara Bruno Jaffré detail some of this isolation and alienation (Chapters 2 and 6, respectively). Peterson explains, 'it was the Cold War, a zero-sum game, and there were repercussions to every alliance'. Sankara's early relationships with Libya, North Korea, Cuba and Nicaragua, alongside his brazen diplomatic style and refusal to display deference to former colonial powers, meant that he was identified early on as a threat to global capitalist powers. Nigerian scholar Sakue-C. Yimovie (Chapter 12) writes on some of this threat in the form of Sankara's conviction that the countries of Africa unite and refuse to pay odious debt, and his identification of debt as 'a cleverly managed re-conquest of Africa … [in which] each of us becomes the financial slave, which is to say a true slave' (from Sankara's speech at the Summit of the Organisation of African Unity in Addis Ababa, 1987).

Sankara's vocal refusal to model the Burkinabè revolution after those of other nations distanced him from potential allies, among them the USSR and Libya, with both communist powers ultimately allegedly playing roles in incapacitating his leadership (see Chapter 2, this volume). The USSR by backing oppositional communist labour unions and Libya by allegedly arming and training the Liberian mercenaries who would collaborate in Sankara's assassination (see Chapters 2 and 6, this volume). The inadvertent collusion of neoliberal capitalists and anti-capitalist communists in Sankara's death is one of the great tragedies and ironies of the late Cold War in Africa. That Sankara's assassination gave rise to 27 years of presidency by a neoliberal autocrat with close ties to colonial and imperialist powers makes his elimination all the more devastating (as is argued by Nicholas A. Jackson in Chapter 7 of this volume).

While chapters critical of Sankara are important, it is crucial to situate his brief presidency within the systematic decontextualisation and over-generalisation of leadership and politics across the African context, which has given rise to easy dismissals of African leaders like Sankara as merely autocratic, militaristic and/or populist. Jackson, for example, explains in Chapter 20 that the 'central administrators of corporate political science shoehorned Sankara's legacy into the conventional social science categories of anti-hegemonic resistance, populism and totalitarianism'. Indeed, as the editor of this volume, I often found myself cautioning authors against the pervasiveness (even unintentional) of the dismissive language of the academy in regards to African heads of state, wherein presidencies are labelled 'regimes' and decision-makers are dismissed as 'authoritarian', 'putschists' and 'military men' (see Chapters 1 and 5, this volume).

A number of chapters engage with aspects of Sankara's philosophies and praxis, including his particular form of humanist Marxism, affinities and dissimilarities with other Pan-African philosophers and leaders (Tajudeen Abdul-Raheem, Kwame Nkrumah, Walter Rodney and Jerry Rawlings among them) and commitments to gender equality. The chapters authored by American journalist and biographer of Sankara Ernest Harsch and Nigerian scholars of Africana studies and political science Felix Kumah-Abiwu and Olusoji Alani Odeyemi look at Sankara's praxis and its ruptures with Marxist socialism (Chapters 9 and 13, respectively). These examinations offer re-readings of Sankara. The political and economic context in which the Burkinabè revolution emerged required that Sankara develop a nuanced political praxis capable of implementing practical actions to address the combined forces of neo-colonialism, patriarchy, environmental degradation, food justice and more. While Sankara was inspired by strands of Marxist thought, the challenge of reconfiguring the relationship between the people and the Burkinabè state required a nuanced political praxis that necessarily departed from key aspects of Marxism, including, for example, the belief that socialism would arise from worker coalitions in societies characterised by advanced capitalism or that social revolution necessitated the elimination of private property. Setting often-divergent readings of Sankara's praxis and politics side-by-side allows the collection to avoid placing Pan-African political figures – from Sankara to the contemporary activists organising under the Sankarist mantle – into pre-conceived political categories.

Chapters from African feminists Patricia McFadden (Chapter 11) and Namakula E. Mayanja (Chapter 14) emphasise the ways in which gender justice was integral – rather than auxiliary – to Sankara's understanding of revolutionary emancipation. McFadden characterises this aspect of Sankara's revolutionary imperative as the most radical rupture it offered, writing 'Sankara posed an epistemological and foundationally ontological challenge to all black men. The challenge was to politically re-define the meaning and practice of heterosexual gendered identities. He went even further in his use of the notion of "authenticity", arguing that becoming non-patriarchal is the *necessary process by which men will 'become human'* (Chapter 11, this volume; emphasis added). Perhaps more than any other aspect of his radical political philosophy, his unequivocal call for gender justice has gone without contemporary parallel. Again asserting the importance of Sankara's insistence on the emancipation of women for African politics today, Mayanja argues that the neoliberal articulations of gender equality offered through international organizations have failed to address the structural and socio-historical foundations of patriarchy. She argues that Sankara recognised that 'women's emancipation is … the essential … feature for reconstructing Africa's statehood in a way that ensures social and ecological well-being, yet it remains a missing link' (Chapter 14, this volume).

Independent scholar and activist Ama Biney argues in Chapter 8 that

Sankara's political philosophy was an early and powerful form of decolonial thought, asserting black radical thought and praxis as an important point of heritage in what has been described as a predominantly Latin American counter-epistemology. Meanwhile, in Chapter 18, Haitian-American scholar Patrick Delices similarly positions Sankara within movements for decolonisation, most specifically his solidarity with the Saharawi people and the Polisario Front in Western Sahara. Drawing on decolonial scholar Sandew Hira's 'decolonising the mind' framework, Delices evaluates Sankara's multifaceted and internationalist struggle against imperialism in the region. Sankara's solidarity with Western Sahara was 'a powerful socio-cultural, anti-colonial symbol', but according to Delices, Sankara's solidarity lacked economic or material substance given the constraints of Burkina's economy.

One of the book's strengths is the volume of insightful chapters written by African and Black feminists and Pan-Africanists. Ghanaian historians De-Valera N.Y.M. Botchway and Moussa Traore (Chapter 1) look at Sankara's Pan-Africanism alongside nuanced considerations of the role of militarism and culture in African revolutionary movements. Jamaican-British feminist political geographer Patricia Daley (Chapter 10) considers the politics of premature death and assassination of African leaders like Sankara and Abdul-Raheem in the context of pervasive neoliberalism.

Sankara's recognisable intellect, humour and charm have attracted a generation of African youth – the so-called 'conscious generation' that arose out of the 'lost generation' of the 1980s, that generation that suffered price hikes, austerity and joblessness under neoliberal policies. Prominent among these social movements has been Balai Citoyen (or Citizen's Broom), a Burkinabè organisation that emerged powerfully against Blaise Compaoré in October 2014. Burkinabè sociologist Zakaria Soré explains in Chapter 15 that, drawing from a Sankarist orientation, the group 'animates youth through a bottom-up Africanist discourse' including 'the values of integrity, honesty, social justice and accountability in public governance'.

In Part IV of the book, Dutch development practitioner and scholar Fiona Dragstra (Chapter 23), French art historian Sophie Bodénès Cohen (Chapter 21) and Ghanaian-American scholar-activist and development practitioner Celestina Agyekum (Chapter 22) look at the internationalisation of Sankarism through the political lives of activists and (in the case of Agyekum) Peace Corps volunteers who draw upon the Sankara mantle in diverse socio-political landscapes. The focus here is on the ways in which contemporary activists, artists and intellectuals find inspiration (or not) in Sankara's work and praxis. This approach ensures that the volume moves away from a limited focus on the individual – which Sankarist politics would reject – towards a critical framework that brings the 'new Sankaras' (or the 'children of Sankara') into view: the youth who are organising today, often despite great obstacles.

Agyekum's chapter is also an occasion to revisit Sankara's critiques of international development as fostering dependency and perpetuating misunderstandings. In an interview with Jean-Philippe Rapp in 1985, Sankara described aid volunteers from Europe:

> They... are very sincere, but their ignorance about Africa leads them to make mistakes, blunders, that are sometimes insignificant, but that become decisive as time goes on. So after several years they go home completely disgusted with Africa. Yet it's not for lack of noble purpose. It's just that they came here with a patronizing attitude.
>
> (Sankara 1985a: 191)

Sankara would suspend the Peace Corps (PC) programme in 1987. He was not alone in his suspicions of the PC, with Kwame Nkrumah expressing initial reservations with neo-colonial practices within American foreign policy prior to the launching of the PC in Ghana in 1961 (Amin 1999).[1]

By foregrounding contemporary Pan-African collectives and philosophies, the book disrupts the scholarly treatment of Pan-Africanism as a 'historical' movement not only for demonstrating its importance for Sankara during the 1980s (during a period of relative 'hibernation' for Pan-Africanism[2]) but also for social movements today. Jamaican American Pan-Africanist, Horace G. Campbell (2017: 64–65), describes the contemporary global Pan-African movement as having 'grown in the past 25 years and in the process [it has] registered new milestones. One of the most important of these interventions has been the reassertion that *Black Lives Matter* and charting new directions for the repair of the planet earth ... This revolution is unfolding at an exponential pace'. Sankara has been an important figure for this new struggle, particularly on the African continent, as South African author and political commentator Levi Kabwato and South African researcher Sarah Chiumbu demonstrate in their chapter here. Kabwato and Chiumbu argue that the #RhodesMustFall and #FeesMustFall movements for the decolonisation of universities and the Economic Freedom Fighters (EFF) 'draw inspiration from an awareness of international movements and renowned Pan-African figures, including Thomas Sankara' (Chapter 19, this volume).

German political scientist Bettina Engels furthers this task in Chapter 17 by examining oral histories of contemporary worker and labour movement protestors who distinguish their mission from Sankara's politics and offer alternative interpretations for social movement organising in modern day Burkina. Situating these chapters alongside other, more celebratory readings of Sankara's legacy for social movement actors and activists is an important part of this book's refusal to over-inflate Sankara's role and significance in Burkina's complex landscape of resistance and emancipatory projects. While certainly important and central for many Burkinabè and African youth, Sankara's legacy is neither static nor flat – his legacy is as ambiguous and contested as the revolutionary project. Alongside this is the ethnographic work of scholar of African development and politics T. D. Harper-Shipman (Chapter 16), whose dialogues with Burkinabè development stakeholders working predominantly in the health sector in 2015 revealed, for example, the on-going importance of Sankara's vision of development ownership, even in a sector that has been thoroughly neoliberalised since his assassination.

Other chapters consider the visual, literary and artistic homages to Sankara following his assassination. Sankara himself was a musician and guitarist. His enthusiastic support for the arts is a rare aspect of his presidency not erased by Compaoré. In Chapter 21, Sophie Bodénès Cohen gives thoughtful consideration to the visual iconography of Sankara, while also critically evaluating the risks and dangers of hagiography among artists and activists. What happens, Cohen demands that we ask, when a revolutionary leader is reduced to a face on a T-shirt? Is there power in the symbol that reflects the substance of Sankra's life and philosophies? These chapters, including the final contribution from American independent researcher Nicholas A. Jackson, look at the disappearing of Sankara from radical scholarship and consider Sankara's place in contemporary efforts to decolonise knowledge.

A Certain Amount of Madness moves from the cult of the individual towards a holistic approach to Sankara's praxis by centring upon collective and participatory actions for self-emancipation that draw inspiration and guidance from Sankara's political praxis and thought. Even with the wide-ranging focus of the chapters in this book, much remains to be written and said about Thomas Sankara, whose politics and praxis were 'rich with a thousand nuances' (Sankara 1985b: 238). The chapters here open up more questions to be addressed and more studies to be done, including the rich potentiality of further work on Sankara's philosophy of race and racism (see Chapter 11, this volume) and more excavation of the archives on the political context and agents of Sankara's assassination including up-to-date work on the on-going prosecution of those responsible for his death (see Chapter 6, this volume, as well as Aziz Salmone Fall's Afterword). Just as this book goes to press, French President Emmanuel Macron vowed to students at the University of Ouagadougou that he would make public the French archives on Sankara's assassination. While we welcome this development, Bruno Jaffrè reminds us that while this would be 'an important breakthrough ... it would be insufficient ... [as] even when official papers are made public in France, there are still many remaining obstacles on the path to establishing the truth'. In responding to this announcement with poise and calm, Sankara's widow, Mariam Sankara commented, 'This is a good thing. Now, let us wait and see. Because we have wanted this for a long time ... [perhaps] we will finally see where the responsibility of France lies' (2017).

THOMAS SANKARA

Sankara's childhood and young adulthood were marked with experiences of injustices and poverty on a personal level. From Sankara's interviews and speeches, we know that these early experiences marked him deeply. Indeed, Sankara had a keen ability to connect key moments in his childhood with his later political orientation.

Born in December 1949, in the town of Yako in the north of Burkina Faso, Sankara attended primary school in Gaoua. His family lived in the 'normalised rural poverty' of people in the villages and towns of the Sahel (Benamrane 2016: 17). An attentive mother worked diligently to instil in her children a strong moral and ethical code, with modesty and humility high on her list. She urged of her children that each one of them should be proud of themselves and should make efforts to be the best at what they do so that they are among the best of their chosen trade (Pondi 2016). Jean-Pierre Pondi attributes some of Sankara's attention to women's rights to his strong and early relationship with and respect for his mother and older sister, Marie Denise. Marie Denise contracted meningitis as a young child and never fully recovered. To Sankara's great annoyance, his father beat and ridiculed Marie Denise, attributing her disability to 'stubbornness'. In response, by the age eleven, Sankara would refuse to engage with his father for periods of time (Pondi 2016). In Chapter 11 of this volume, Patricia McFadden wonders, 'What was it about his resistance consciousness, his experiences of anti-colonialism and his desire for freedom that created the shift in his perceptions of women's freedoms as crucial to a different African future?' It is possible that the foundations of Sankara's attention to gender justice originated in these early encounters.

He later went to school at Lycée Ouezzin Coulibaly in Bobo-Dioulasso, the second largest city in Burkina Faso. He recalled arriving alone in the new city and being informed that, on the first day, classes were postponed and that the boarding house was also closed until the following morning. He walked the streets with his suitcase on his head ('I was too small to carry it any other way', he remembered), until he came to a bourgeoisie home and a kind man took him in for the night. Sankara never forgot the man's name, Pierre Barry, and was able to meet with him as an adult and thank him again for his kindness. Sankara's penchant for thanking and recognising kindness was one of his lasting attributes (see Jaffré 2007; Pondi 2016).

Thomas and his close childhood friend Fidèle enjoyed watching films. Among those noted as Sankara's preferred were the comedy skits of British actor Charlie Chaplin and the 1960 Italian/French co-production *Morgan, the Pirate* (in French, *Capitaine Morgan*). The latter is a fictionalised and romanticised account of the life of Henry Morgan, a Welsh profiteer and lieutenant governor of colonised Jamaica. Jean-Emmanuel Pondi explains that the film so impacted

Sankara during the Christmas vacation of his fourteenth year that he became known by his friends, premonitiously, as 'Captain'.

When Sankara presented himself with an interest in perusing medicine – at the time, he wanted to be a surgeon – for junior high school (brevet d'études du premier cycle), he was overlooked in favour of children with influential family connections, although many of them had lower class standing than Sankara. This was an early lesson in the significance of family connections and wealth rather than intellect or merit (Pondi 2016). During this period of frustration, Sankara heard a radio announcement for a scholarship at a military high school, Prytanée Militaire du Kadiogo (PMK) at the military base Kamboincè near Ouaga.[4] Founded by the French Army in 1951, the school was recruiting students. Sankara was accepted, although he was unable to convince Fidèle to apply. Sankara, who always enjoyed rigorous intellectual and physical activities, entered a new environment – one that would have a considerable impact on the trajectory of his life. Had his family been able to pay the fees for a superior school, Sankara would most likely have never pursued a military education, might never have travelled to Madagascar, Morocco and France, might not have participated in politics in a similar fashion.

After PMK, Sankara was selected as one of a few handfuls of students to be sent to officer training at l'Académie Militaire d'Antsirabé in Madagascar in 1966. Although his radical politics have often been attributed to his officer training, Sankara's politics were also influenced by the exposure to a culture and place that revealed to him the poverty of Ouagadougou and of Burkina Faso (at the time still The Republic of Upper Volta). Pondi imagines that Sankara might have characterised Ouagadougou as a 'dusty and unworthy village' when compared to the capital city of Madagascar, Antananarivo. In Antsirabé, Sankara is recalled as having prevented conflicts between other trainees while studying military strategy, sustainable agriculture and agro-ecology, writing and editing as well as the guitar (Jaffré 2007). All the while he continued to reflect on the failures of the first decade of African independence (Pondi 2016). After obtaining his diploma as a superior officer at Antsirabé, Sankara remained in Madagascar for another year. During this year, he studied economy with a Malian Professor, Sidibé, and – ever pursuing physical labour and self-sufficiency – planted a field of rice (Pondi 2016). During his studies, he read the work of René Dumont, Amilcar Cabral, Samora Machel and Kwame Nkrumah – each of which seem to have influenced his approach to ecology, Pan-Africanism, humanism and politics in unique ways.

Sankara went on to complete professional training in Pau, France (with the parachutists) and Rabat, Morocco. In Morocco, he became close with Blaise Compaoré, who would be his second in command throughout his presidency (for more on this relationship, see Chapter 6, this volume). In the years before his presidency, Sankara fought in the border war against Mali (although he disagreed with it), was appointed and resigned as secretary of state and, as prime minister, invited Muammar Qaddafi to visit Burkina Faso without authorization from the president, Jean-Baptiste Ouédraogo (for a detailed historical account of his rise to power, see Chapter 2, this volume). Following his arrest in May 1983, massive street demonstrations occured in Ouagadougou to demand his release, after which Sankara was placed under house arrest. In response, Blaise Compaoré and 250 military personnel organised a coup d'état on 4 August 1983 that delivered Sankara to power (see Chapters 2 and 6, this volume). He was president of the country for four years and two months before he was assassinated on 15 October 1987 alongside five of his special cabinet members, Paulin Bamouni, Bonaventure Compaoré, Frédéric Kiemdé, Christophe Saba and Patrice Zagré as well as seven soldiers. Blaise Compaoré assumed power with the support of Jean-Baptiste Lingani and Henri Zongo.

'A CERTAIN AMOUNT OF MADNESS': NONCONFORMITY AND ANTI-IMPERIAL POLITICS

One of the central aims of this book is to look more seriously at aspects of Sankara's political thought and praxis, strands of which are referred to in these chapters as Sankarism, Sankarist(e) thought or burkindlum. It is important to note that Sankara himself was critical of self-aggrandisement and self-promotion and would have been critical of such titles; he never gave a formal name to his philosophical orientation nor published political treatises. Indeed, he was even reticent to reveal his own reading preferences, saying 'I never make notes in a book or underline passages. Because that's where you reveal the most about yourself' (Sankara 1986: 263). Sankara's was a political praxis that was, contributors here argue, distinctive from other forms of Marxism and Pan-Africanism. In terms of revolutionary movements in Africa, Sankara's stands out not only because it occurred well after independence, but also because of the ambition of its vision: Sankara was an economic revolutionary who aimed to achieve social justice at home while recalibrating Burkina Faso's place in the international system. Also, unlike many of the African leaders of his generation and those preceding him, Sankara did not author books that captured or guided his political philosophy in any systematic way our task is to trace Sankara's words and actions to synthesise his radical and comprehensive approach to social transformation, self-sufficiency and freedom.

The title of the book, *A Certain Amount of Madness*, draws from Sankara's interview with Jean-Philippe Rapp in 1985, when he said:

> I would like to leave behind me the conviction that if we maintain a certain amount of caution and organization we deserve victory ... You cannot carry out

fundamental change without *a certain amount of madness*. In this case, it comes from nonconformity, the courage to turn your back on the old formulas, the courage to invent the future. It took the madmen of yesterday for us to be able to act with extreme clarity today. I want to be one of those madmen. ... We must dare to invent the future.

(Sankara 1985a: 141–144; emphasis added)

Although Sankara attributes some of his political philosophies and praxis to an awareness that fundamental change would be *perceived as madness* ('les audaces les plus folles'), the chapters in this collection reveal that much of this apparent madness was part of Sankara coming into power with a commitment to the people of le Faso alongside an understanding of the operations of oppression, imperialism and a colonial global political economy. Sankara understood the immensities and dangers of the revolutionary project before him; he knew that he would be perceived as a 'madman' for fighting against a powerful global economic elite.

Sankara spoke often of radical black leaders who were being assassinated all around him (Maurice Bishop among them). Although he was only 33 years old when he became president, he referred to his wife as 'la veuve' (the widow), a darkly humorous title that nonetheless revealed his awareness of the likelihood of his premature death as well as his absence of fear in regards to it. Sankara's bravery – his 'madness' – would again be echoed in the popular movement of 30 and 31 October 2014, when student protestors would embody some of this 'mad' courage and draw courage from the proverb, 'cabri mort n'a plus peur du couteau' ('a dead kid [i.e. baby goat] is no longer afraid of the knife'), meaning that someone with little to lose also has little to fear. This expression of 'madness' embodied the courage to stand up to the Compaoré government, which had for so long 'instramentalised a feeling of fear to govern' (Ouédraogo 2015: 4).

For Sankara, politics was praxis. He prioritised the politicisation of non-elites and non-specialists in a determination to *do*, *make* and *effect* social change (as opposed to writing about it). As he reminded the audience during one speech, 'What is left for us to do is [to] *make* the revolution!' Revolution, for Sankara, was more than a 'passing revolt' or a 'simple brushfire'. Rather, the political economy of le Faso needed to be 'replaced forever with the revolution, the permanent struggle against all forms of domination' (Sankara 1984a). His praxis was deeply populist and oriented to the grassroots. Sankara's political philosophy shows an undaunted attention to praxis over philosophising, saying that 'singers, dances, and musicians' can equally stand with formal representatives of the revolutionary party to 'explain ... what the revolution should be' (Sankara 1984b: 149). He was a modest but demanding 'organic intellectual' with a preference for easily understandable language.

Nonconformity and brazen courage were central to Sankara's innovative praxis (see Chapter 9, this volume). Sankara combined this awareness with strands of humanist Marxism, an unabashed, pro-women Pan-African populist nationalism, nuanced ecological and gender awareness and a notorious commitment to self-less, humble living that stands as an exceptional illustration of leadership-by-example. Sankara was ambitious, driven and often uncompromising. His presidency offers a glimpse into what it looks like when a militant activist becomes the leader of a country. Sakara's speeches and activities were more like those of radical social justice activists than with heads of state. Sankara maintained his captain's salary of US$450 during his four years and two months as president. He wore cloth spun from Burkinabè cotton, the faso dan fani, and encouraged or demanded that other members of the government to do the same.

Even as president, he would share rations with his troops, as his chauffeur, Sidibé Alassane, recalled in an interview in 2017.[5] Some displays of this sort of radically humble and down-to-earth living were not well received by all government officials. After one particular meeting, Sankara announced to his ministers that they would go and eat lunch together at a nearby restaurant. The group applauded in apparent pleasure, until he named the restaurant: Yidigri, a restaurant serving mostly low-income clientele near the Yalgado Hospital. After lunch, Sankara announced that each minister would pay their own bills, along with the bills of their chauffeurs. The event was intended to be a lesson in collectivism, unpretentiousness and generosity – all pillars of Sankara's political praxis (Pondi 2016) – but not everyone welcomed nor appreciated these public effacements of social privilege. Some journalists and academics have suggested that at least some of his modest lifestyle was a ruse while others have characterised him as 'manipulative' in working to appeal to a popular base. What none of these examinations provide, however, is any indication of what ulterior motive would have prompted Sankara to orchestrate such a persona. This is particularly so considering that he actively worked against his own self-enrichment both in and out of the public eye.

Arguments that Sankara's humble lifestyle was adopted merely for public audiences do not hold up to more thorough considerations of his politics, all aspects of which reflect a radical way of living. His wife, Miriam Sankara, recalls for example that Sankara would sleep on the terrace during warm nights because he did not want to run the air conditioning when others were sleeping without it (Mariam Sankara in the preface to Pondi 2016). At the time of his death, Sankara owned little and was quite possibly one of the poorest heads of state in the world. Among his possessions at the time of his death: four bicycles, a car, three guitars and a refrigerator. Take, on the other hand, Blaise who has an estimated net worth of US$275 million.

Sankara understood his role as that of critical space-maker: he sought to create the socio-economic and political conditions for well-being, integrity and empowerment with the understanding that these were not material goods to be given or passed around. Against neo-colonialism and imperial domination, Sankara demonstrated an insistence on the agency of oppressed peoples. He maintained a conviction in the potential(s) of mass politicisation through a consciousness of race, Pan-African unity and indigenous knowledges for the creation of a new Burkinabè society. His revolutionary orientation was founded upon an insistence that all Burkinabè be free and empowered but that genuine self-empowerment was something to be cultivated through hard-work and seized through struggle rather than allotted by the government or given through international aid.

Indeed, in 1984, his symbolic renaming of Burkina Faso – 'land of the honest/upright people' – and the effacing of the previous, colonially imposed title of 'Upper Volta' (Haute Volta) is indicative of his foundational political philosophy: that of burkindlum (a philosophy explored by Soré in Chapter 15, this volume). Burkindlum is a philosophy of self-esteem, self-care, sacrifice for the community, integrity and love of justice (see Ouédraogo 2015). Upper Volta, on the other hand, mimicked the manner of naming the divisions of the regions of France (Haute-Normandie, Basse-Normandie, etc.) and was titled after the Volta River (itself named by the Portuguese in the fifteenth century) as one of the main tributaries runs through Burkina. Sankara's renaming of the country was a symbolic gesture of unity that honoured local knowledge and language. In the Mossi language *Burkina* means 'integrity', '*bè*' in Foufouldé means people while *Faso* in Diouala means 'homeland'. From these three emerged Burkina Faso and the new Burkinabè.

While working to foster growth in national pride, creativity and self-sufficiency, Sankara simultaneously confronted the material conditions of poverty in one of the world's most impoverished countries. In order to embark upon a series of ambitious countrywide health, sanitation and environmental initiatives, he required funds. At the same time, he rejected the premise of 'aid' for victimising the people of Burkina Faso as well as for stripping them of agency. This stripping of agency occurred on multiple levels: it was both intellectual, through the insinuation that local solutions were unlikely (and, thus, a form of mental colonisation), as well as tangible, through the suppression of an environment in which people's own creativity could lead to innovative responses to local dilemmas.

His 'madness' was evidenced in his 'courage to implement practical policies as well as to make reasonable demands that were nevertheless intolerable to the corporate entities centred in Europe, the United States and elsewhere' (Jackson in Chapter 7, this volume). Sankara's economic and political 'madness' was an ethical and humanistic orientation founded in a rejection of capitalist and imperialist domination and exploitation alongside an insistence on collective responses and sacrifices. This 'madness' included his refusal to witness people suffer and die when there were solutions to the material and political-economic structures that caused such suffering. Speaking powerfully before the United Nations General Assembly in 1984, he said:

> I speak, too, on behalf of the child. The child of a poor man who is hungry and who furtively eyes the accumulation of abundance in a store for the rich. The store protected by a thick plate glass window ... The window protected by impregnable shutters. The shutters guarded by a policeman with a helmet, gloves, and armed with a billy club. The policeman posted there by the father of another child, who will come and serve himself – or rather be served – because he offers guarantees of representing the capitalistic norms of the system, which he corresponds to.
>
> (Sankara 1984b: 163)

In the interview with Rapp in 1985, Sankara explained the origins of his militant activism:

> I started out with a very clear conviction. You can fight effectively only against things that you understand well, and you can't win unless you're convinced your fight is just. You can't wage a struggle as a pretext, a lever, to acquire power, because generally the mask cracks very fast. You don't get involved in a struggle alongside the popular masses in order to become head of state. You fight. Then the need to organize means that someone is required for a given post ... You have to convince yourself that you're capable of fighting, that you're courageous enough to fight for yourself, but above all that you have sufficient will to fight for others.
>
> (Sankara 1985a: 190)

In this fight on behalf of others, he drew upon memories and stories of his family and other people whom he knew well – he was, in this way, grounded in the struggle much like the political philosophy of Guyanese scholar Walter Rodney, assassinated in 1980. One such story:

> I remember a man I knew well. We were right in the middle of a period of drought. To avoid starvation, several families from his village collected the little money they had left and gave him the job of going to Ouagadougou to buy food. He travelled to the capital by bicycle... he had a brutal and painful encounter with the town ...
>
> (Sankara 1985a: 191)

Sankara explained that the bicycle and the money entrusted to the man from the town was stolen:

> In despair, he committed suicide. The people of Ouagadougou didn't lose any sleep over him ... They dug a hole and threw in the body like a useless weight they

had to get rid of ... We have to ask ourselves: Do we have the right to turn our backs on people like this?

(Sankara 1985a: 191)

Refusing to seek foreign assistance if it meant sacrificing autonomy and self-reliance, Sankara moved quickly to radically reorganise public spending in a way that would privilege those least fortunate and those most at risk of illness, premature death, hunger and the struggles of living in poverty and uncertainty. This radical reorganisation of public spending, along with the revolutionary leadership's decision early on to set-up Councils in the Defense of the Revolution (CDRs), would make up part of the internal catalysts for Sankara's assassination.

Perhaps more than ever, Sankara's anxieties about the relationship between knowledge and colonialism are being exposed through massive student mobilisations to decolonise knowledge and the space of the university as well as Southern-led projects within the academy to reorient knowledge creation and circulation. His struggle to validate the indigenous knowledges of le Faso was a subversive one, particularly in the 1980s during the rise of the intellectual dominance of neoliberal economic thinking. For Sankara, externally imposed and directed development initiatives caused the greatest devastation at the scale of human creativity and the distortions of knowledge. His political project stood in opposition to the racialised colonial narrative undergirding mainstream development practice: that idea that Africans required European 'tutelage' and that 'Africans could not overnight become autonomous selves ready to take on the responsibilities of self-government and generally directing their own affairs by their own lights' (Táíwò 2010: 404). Sankara understood the pressures on African intellectuals to reproduce an economic and political status quo and called on them, saying that intellectuals

> must understand that the battle for a system of thought at the service of the disinherited masses is not in vain ... [and that this project] must allow the people to achieve fundamental changes in the political and social situation, changes that allow us to break from the foreign domination and exploitation that leave our states no perspective other than bankruptcy.
>
> (Sankara 1984b: 158)

In this, he had much in common with Joseph Ki-Zerbo, the Burkinabè opposition leader and historian (for examinations of the tensions between Ki-Zerbo and Sankara see Chapters 5 and 7, this volume). Ki-Zerbo (2003: 200) said that, 'without a real African education, we have no hope'. For Sankara, as well as other revolutionary Pan-African scholars, including Frantz Fanon, Amilcar Cabral, Kwame Nkrumah, Walter Rodney, and Ki-Zerbo (2003: 13), colonialism is an intellectual superstructure – one that continues to exist. The global order remains imperialist in nature and therefore a 'Sankarist' inspired resistance is as important as ever. Ama Biney (Chapter 9, this volume) argues that Sankara's 'project is unfinished not only for the fact that he was assassinated in the prime of his life, but in that the existing neoliberal capitalist order and neo-colonialism have reconfigured new forms of "coloniality" or domination in … the economy, knowledge, the environment and the control over women's bodies in reproductive health in a global phallocentric gendered dispensation'. In such a context, Aziz Salmone Fall asserts:

> there is … a noticeable arousal of internationalist citizenship. It is exasperated by the horrors of our mode of production and conception, and the impunity that keeps it incompatible with the survival of the species. Humanity is awaking to the urgency, and the capacity of indignation of the youths testifies to this. In Burkina Faso, Sankarists must transcend obedience and resume the impetus of progressive change.
>
> (Fall 2012: n.p., translated by author)

In articulating the revival of such a 'Sankarist' inspired resistance, we might return to Sankara's address at the UN in 1984, when he identified ignorance, hunger and thirst as equally important for the aspirations of the revolution. His orientation was uniquely grassroots, although he was an unmistakably firm and demanding leader. His role, as he articulated it, was to set in place the economic, political and social structures that would allow all Burkinabès to embrace their own dignity, knowledge and well-being: 'Our economic aspiration is to create a situation where every Burkinabè can at least use his brain and hands to invent and create enough to ensure him two meals a day and drinking water' (Sankara 1984a). While Sankara was resolved in establishing the foundations of the revolution, he worked hard to encourage the people to assume fundamental responsibility and agency:

> I personally maintain unshakable confidence … that, under our pounding blows of the howling anguish of our peoples, our group will maintain its cohesion, strengthen its collective bargaining power, find allies among all nations, and begin, together with those who can still hear us, to organize a genuinely new international system of economic relations.
>
> (Sankara 1984b: 219)

In this project of dignity and liberation, he recognised his limitations and challenges. Again, this reflected his humble approach to politics and life. On the topic of women's liberation, he said, 'we are ready to welcome suggestions from anywhere in the world that enable us to achieve the total fulfilment of Burkinabè women … Freedom can only be won through struggle, and we call on all our sisters of all races to go on the offensive to conquer their rights' (Sankara 1984b: 162).

Sankara was also certain in his stance against the symbolic naming of places as a tactic to erase people and a people's history. He dismissed the titles Upper Volta and the Third World in particular, calling the latter a 'hodgepodge held in such contempt ... invented by the other worlds ... in order to better ensure our intellectual, cultural, economic, and political alienation' (Sankara 1984a). Against the symbolic and representational violence of neo-colonialism, Sankara decried, 'our existence must be devoted to the struggle to rehabilitate the name of the African' (Sankara 1984a: 149). He said:

> everything that is done, said, or organized around the world as part of the commemorative ceremonies should stress the terrible price paid by Africa and the Black world for the development of human civilization. A price paid without receiving anything in return, and which no doubt explains the reasons for the current tragedy on our continent ... It is our blood that fed the rapid development of capitalism, that made possible our current state of dependence, and that consolidated our underdevelopment. The truth can no longer be avoided, the numbers can no longer be doctored. For every Black person who made it to the plantations, at least five others suffered death or mutilation. I purposely leave aside the devastation of our continent and its consequences.
>
> (Sankara 1984b: 172)

Sankara did not assert an ideology of isolationism or exclusion. Rather, the oppressed would have an important role to play in guiding oppressors to fuller articulations of well-being and solidarity. 'As blacks, we want to teach others how to love each other. Despite their meanness toward us, we will be capable of resisting and then teaching them the meaning of solidarity' (Sankara 1984a: 150). The need for decolonisation remains urgent – let us learn from the varied legacies and radical politics of Thomas Sankara as we continue this struggle.

NOTES

1 Ghana would be the first country in the world to receive PC volunteers, most likely because Nkrumah's immediate need for education expansion coincided with the introduction of the programme (Hoffman 1997).

2 Here I draw on the vocabulary of Ivorian scholar-activist and founder of The Revival of Pan-Africanism, Gnaka Lagoke (in an interview with the author, August 2017), who speaks of the 'great hibernation' of Pan-Africanism after the assassinations of key leaders in the mid-1900s, Ruben Um Nyobè (1913–1958) and Patrice Lumumba (1925–1961) among them.

3 Full interview on *DW: Made For Minds* with Mariam Sankara available (in French) at www. dw.com/fr/emmanuel-macron-fait-un-geste-dans-laffaire-thomas-sankara/a-41568289

4 At the time, the school was called École Militaire Préparatoire de Ouagadougou.

5 This interview is available at www.afrikipresse.fr/afrique/militaire-retraite-un-ex-chauffeur-de-sankara-temoigne-toujours-une-peine-d-evoquer-ce-drame-1 (accessed 25 May 2017)

REFERENCES

Amin, J. A. (1999) The Perils of Missionary Diplomacy: The United States Peace Corps Volunteers in the Republic of Ghana. *The Western Journal of Black Studies* 23(1): 35–48.

Benamrane, D. (2016) *Sankara, Leader Africain*. Paris: l'Harmattan.

Campbell, H. (2017) *Perspectives on Culture and Globalization: The Intellectual Legacy of Ali A. Mazrui* (eds K. Njogu and S. Adem). Nairobi: Twaweza Communications.

Chouli, L. (2012a) *Enough is Enough! Burkina Faso 2011: Popular Protests, Military Mutinies and Workers Struggles* (trans. A. Wynne). Botswana: International Socialist Tendency.

Chouli, L. (2012b) Peoples' Revolts in Burkina Faso. In F. Maji and S. Ekine (eds), *African Awakening: The Emerging Revolutions*, 131–146. Nairobi: Fahmu Books.

Chouli, L. (2014) Social Movements and the Quest for Alternatives in Burkina Faso. In N. S. Sylla (eds), *Liberalism and its Discontents: Social Movements in West Africa*, 263–303. Dakar: Rosa Luxemburg Foundation.

Fall, A. S. (2012) Thomas Sankara 25 Ans: 'Prouvez Nous que Cette Tombe Parmi la Dizaine Issue de ces assassinats est bien celle de Thomas'. Interview with Youssouf Bâ. *Burkina24*, 15 October. Retrieved 12 August 2017 from https://burkina24.com/2012/10/15/special-15-octobre-aziz-salmone-fall-prouvez-nous-que-cette-tombe-parmi-la-dizaine-issue-de-ces-assassinats-est-bien-celle-de-thomas.

Harsch, E. (1999) Trop, C'est Trop! Civil Insurgence in Burkina Faso, 1998–99. *Review of African Political Economy* 26(81): 395–406.

Harsch, E. (2014) *Thomas Sankara: An African Revolutionary*. Athens, OH: Ohio University Press.

Hoffman, E. C. (1997) Diplomatic History and the Meaning of Life: Toward a Global American History. *Diplomatic History* 21(4): 499–518.

Jaffré, B. (2007) *Biographie de Thomas Sankara, La Patrie ou la Mort*. Paris: l'Harmattan.

Ki-Zerbo, J. (2003) *À Quand l'Afrique? Entretien avec René Holestein*. La Tour d'Aigues, France: Éditions de l'Aube.

Ouédraogo, B. N. (2015) L'Armée et L'Exercice du Pouvoir Au Burkina Faso: Enseignements De L'insurrection Populaire Du 30–31 Octobre 2014. *Notes Internacionals Barcelona Centre for International Affairs* 106. Retrieved on 1 June 2017 from www.files.ethz.ch/isn/187237/NOTES%20106_OUEDRAOGO_FRAN-1.pdf.

Pondi, J. (2016) *Thomas Sankara et l'émergence de l'Afrique au XXIe Siècle*. Yaoundé: Éditions Afric'Eviel.

Reza, A. (2016) New Broom In Burkina Faso? *New Left Review* 101: 93–119.

Sankara, T. (1984a) Our White House in Black Harlem. Speech at rally in Harlem, 3 October. Reproduced in Sankara, T. (2007): 147–153.

Sankara, T. (1984b) Freedom Must Be Conquered. Speech at UN General Assembly, 4 October. Reproduced in Sankara (2007): 154–176.

Sankara, T. (1985a) Dare to Invent the Future. Interview with Jean-Philippe Rapp. Reproduced in Sankara (2007): 189–232.

Sankara, T. (1985b) There are Attempts to Unleash an Unjust War Against Us. Speech at Mass Rally in Ouaga. Reproduced in Sankara (2007): 189–232.

Sankara, T. (1986) On Books and Reading. Interview with *Jeune Afrique*. Reproduced in Sankara (2007): 261–265.

Sankara, T. (2007) *Thomas Sankara Speaks: The Burkina Faso Revolution, 1983–87*. New York: Pathfinder Press.

Táíwò, O. (2010) 'The Love of Freedom Brought Us Here': An Introduction to Modern African Political Philosophy. *South Atlantic Quarterly* 109(2): 391–410.

PART I

LIFE AND REVOLUTION

CHAPTER 1

Military Coup, Popular Revolution or Militarised Revolution?

Contextualising the Revolutionary Ideological Courses of Thomas Sankara and the National Council of the Revolution

De-Valera N.Y.M. Botchway and Moussa Traore

INTRODUCTION

The view that the events in Upper Volta on 4 August 1983 marked a 'revolution' still provokes debate in academic and public spheres. The Burkinabè Revolution has been perceived as a 'pseudo-revolution' in some circles because it lacked the features of an 'orthodox' revolution which, according to Marx, is produced and conditioned by various stages of class struggles and social transformations with the working class at its centre. The Burkinabè Revolution was a military putsch (or coup) led by a group of charismatic Marxist army officers. This military putsch, however, had considerable popular support and came to power against a pro-imperialist regime.

This chapter revisits the political structure of Sankara's leadership and the historical episode that has come to be known as the Burkinabè Revolution. We look at Sankara's politics and philosophies (what might be called a philosophy of Sankaraism) alongside a consideration of socialism(s), including Nkrumahism and Marxism(s). We scrutinise the features of Sankara's ideas, like anti-imperialism, nationalism and populism, which informed the direction and policies of the revolution at the cultural and political levels through his government, called Conseil National de la Revolution (National Council of the Revolution, hereafter CNR) from 1983 to 1987. Through our analysis, we dismiss easy dualistic interpretations of the revolution as either a repetition of Marxist revolutions or as an imported phenomenon. Rather, we trace the origins of the revolution in order to re-evaluate whether 4 August indeed marked the beginning of a 'popular revolution'. We examine the source and orientation of the Sankara-backed revolution, given that it was informed by a militaristic engagement with Burkinabè politics. We give considerable attention to the role of the military in Sankara's blended populist-Marxist political policies in order to expose some of the complexities, paradoxes and limitations of Sankara's experiment in radical socialist-inspired social change.

Features of Sankara's ideas remain relevant for contemporary politics as they form part of a strategic base of two groups of contemporary actors: both the Sankarists who organise through registered political parties in Burkina Faso as well as the Sankarians who organise through collective and individual actions, demanding for a restructuring of Burkina Faso society and politics that draw on aspects of Sankaraism. Sankara spoke about the need for significant social change and defended it. He brought out the inner logic of that change; in rationalising it, he contributed intellectual views and acted upon them. Such philosophical endeavours and physical efforts were informed and animated by his own set of beliefs, generated from his experiences of Burkinabè society and culture as well as his knowledge of the political ideologies and economic philosophies of African and non-African thinkers.

Sankara's political philosophy as well as his praxis was informed by a plethora of revolutionary and radical ideas, including anti-imperialism, populism, Pan-Africanism, military nationalism, African Socialism and forms of Marxism. He was influenced by the concepts of pragmatism and pacifism. Sankara's philosophies and actions can serve as a social guide and praxis for social change, one that can perhaps be called 'Sankaraism'. The terms Sankarism (Sankaraism), Sankarists and Sankarians emerged after Sankara's assassination. Some have congregated around the political philosophy and praxis of this leader of a government that deemed itself as the spearhead of a process of social change; this political concept and social guide has been called 'Sankaraism'. Sankarism came into popular awareness in 2000 when the Union pour la Renaissance/Movement Sankariste (Union for Renaissance or Rebirth/ Sankarist Movement), led by lawyer Benewendé Sankara – who was no relative of Thomas Sankara – emerged. This party, which claimed to be Sankarist and averred that 'Sankarism' was its ideology, remained marred with divisions and misunderstandings over trivial issues.

People who believe in the populist, easy-to-relate-to revolutionary political leadership of Sankara, and who work to animate a process of sustainable social change in Burkina Faso, might call themselves Sankarists, in reference to forms of political discipleship to Sankara. The aim of Sankarists is to take political power and continue Sankara's work. Conversely, those who idolise him as an icon of social change, see him as a role model in life and admire his charisma and approve his philosopher-king leadership style are Sankarians or Sankariens (Le Jah 2015). Regarding the orientation of the Sankarien or Sankarian, the Burkinabè artiste Sams'K Le Jah explains that:

> The difference lies in the fact that one can embrace Sankara's ideals without getting involved in politics. For instance, women who produce numerous types of indispensable goods, the local tailor who magnifies the value of the 'made in Burkina cloth' are people who can be called Sankarians; they continue Thomas Sankara's mission, even though they do not belong to any political party.
>
> (Le Jah 2015; translation by author)

Sams'K Le Jah argues that one might adhere to Sankara's ideals without formally getting involved in politics. People who continue Sankara's work outside of the umbrella of formalised political parties (such as women who work to transform produces and products and people who make and promote dresses made in Burkina Faso) are Sankarians. Nevertheless, both Sankarists and Sankarians claim inspiration from Sankara, who coached and guided a process of fundamental change through a combination of ideas and deeds. Unlike Kwame Nkrumah (who fashioned concepts like Nkrumahism and Consciencism), Muammar al Qaddafi (who created the Third Universal Theory, which his *Green Book* articulated), Vladimir Lenin (who was the fountain head of Leninism) or Julius Nyerere (who expounded Ujamaa as a social guide), Sankara did not consciously create an ideology or fashion a concept (or social guide) when he was alive. Our task in this chapter is to excavate the complex political philosophy of Sankara within a context of a militarised revolution.

MILITARY COUP, POPULAR REVOLUTION OR MILITARISED REVOLUTION?

We contend that the founding myth of the regime of the CNR, which remained a largely military-led government, has been that it came to power through a popular revolution. This story raises questions about the nature of the revolution: ontologically, as the CNR was produced through a coup d'etat, how much does this shape the form of the revolution? The 'revolutionary' nature of 4 August continues to be debated (see Chapters 3 and 5, this volume). Sankara himself later attempted to rationalise the day as marking the beginning of a revolution that was both popular and democratic in *Discours d'Orientation Politique*, or the Speech of Political Orientation – a kind of manifesto of the revolutionary vision of the CNR on 2 October 1983.

Averring that both soldiers and civilians, 'comrade militants of the revolution', acted to bring into being a government that valued the role and power of the average citizen, Sankara emphasised the need for 'the people' to achieve bigger victories for the revolution. The revolution, he stated, had to progress with confidence to more resounding victories because it had 'logically evolved from the Voltaic people's struggle against long-standing enemies ... imperialism and its national allies; ... [and] backward ... forces. [It] is the culmination of the popular insurrection. [Therefore], simplistic ... analyses limited to repeating of pre-established schemas cannot change the reality' ('The Political Orientation Speech' in Sankara 1988: 30–54). He argued that the revolution 'came as a solution to social contradictions that could not longer be stifled by compromise' (ibid.: 32) in a society with 'feudal traditions' that fostered or encouraged certain forms of oppression.

It is clear from Sankara's first broadcasted radio address that it was military action that brought the CNR into national politics. He asserted that the army and paramilitary forces had intervened to restore independence and liberty to the country (Sankara, 'Struggle for a Bright Future', 4 August 1983: 21–23). The fundamental change in the government was effected through a coup d'etat. At the same time, radicalised soldiers and civilians deemed the episode of the coup as a heralding event, a beginning that only represented the genesis of a process and longer course. In other words, the coup signalled the emergence of a wider continuum of social changes: a revolution. For example, Valère Somé, a close friend of Sankara, saw the day as the ultimate result of the popular insurrection (Le Faso.net 2015). To him, the national political events in May 1983 (including the arrest of two army officers, Sankara and Lingani) drove students and youths to stage popular anti-government protests in Ouagadougou in solidarity with the detained soldiers (prior to 4 August). When Sankara and others were arrested again shortly after their release (because the government continued to deem them a threat), some of their supporters, like Somé, wanted une guerre populaire généralisée, a general popular war. Consequently, some soldiers decided to act to curtail the emergence of such general 'uncivil'[1] popular war by overthrowing the government, with support from civilians, and ushering in a revolution, a process of change, of becoming, and making Sankara the leader of the revolution's CNR (ibid.).

This process of becoming was what the Sankara-led CNR came to represent in what was called the 'revolution'. As a form of social change, the revolution was guided and sustained by certain ideas and policies. Until Sankara was physically eliminated, the social change process had the figure, ideas and deeds of Sankara, guiding, underlying, polarising and operationalising it. Although the CNR was disbanded and the revolution process curtailed in 1987, the revolutionary interval in Burkina Faso embodied a period of high idealism and mass political activism, which, according to Paul Nugent, has seldom been seen in Africa, and has largely been airbrushed out of the official histories (Nugent 2004). Writing about the significance of the revolutionary interval, René Otayek points out that the CNR and its key instigator, Sankara, initiated a genuine historical fracture from centuries of hierarchical and exclusionary politics and social formations in Burkina Faso. The CNR was different from previous governments. In the view of Otayek, the fracture changed what he referred to as 'a multi-polar political landscape' (a landscape which had nurtured a clientelist and neo-patrimonial state system, producing a 'state of strain' from 1960 to 1966 and a 'debonair state' from 1966 to 1980) and 'initiated the establishment of a state quite novel in the history of Burkina, a "strong state", a totalising state' (Otayek 1991[1989]: 15). This 'strong state' was structured according to the politics and philosophies of Sankara and the revolution: a political philosophy that was unwavering in its assertion of a political orientation toward the masses of Burkinabè society, even though it had come to power through military action.

Sankara was a self-proclaimed Marxist and, even though he attested a profound admiration for revolutions that overturned misfortunes of dominated and exploited peoples, especially leftist revolutions (principally the Cuban one, which drew ideological rationalisation and inspiration from Marxism), he did not impose doctrinaire Marxism as the ideology of the revolution. While Sankara maintained that he was Marxist, he did not classify his political views and political actions as communist (see 'Who Are the Enemies of the People?', 26 March 1983, in Sankara 1988). He declared that, 'through discussion … friendship with a few men … my social experience … reading, but above all to discussions with Marxists on the reality of our country, I arrived at Marxism' (Sankara, interview with Claudio Hackin, August 1987, in Sankara, 1988: 230).

NEGOTIATING MARXISM AND MILITARISM FOR SOCIAL CHANGE

A sizeable body of scholarly work considers the relationship between the military, African states and national politics during the numerous coups throughout the 1960s. Other works have also looked at the military in politics from the 1970s to the 1990s, the timeline within which Sankara's politics fall.[2] Peter Karsten condenses this body of scholarship as 'identif[ying] economic distress, rates of capital investment, election frequency, literacy, years of schooling, and other such measures of economic, social or political development variables [as] predictive of the violent intervention of the military into domestic politics' (Karsten 1998: 223).

These studies present varying interpretations of the military in politics. While some hail the military as a political tool within nation building, others deem the military's role in politics to be a wrecker of political systems in Africa.

The personalist (Baptope 1981: 4), corporatist (Welch 1987: 10), manifest destiny (Finer 1988: 21), Marxist and integrative theoretical models are some of the theoretical frameworks that make sense of military interventions across the continent. Sankara belonged to the category of coup-making and government changing African soldier leaders of the post-colonial period that Nugent refers to with the tongue-in-cheek expression, 'Praetorian Marxists' (Nugent 2004). Others in this category included Captain Marien Ngouabi in Congo-Brazzaville (Radu and Somerville 1988: 172–173), General Mathieu Kerekou in Benin (at the time Dahomey), Major Mengistu Haile Mariam in Ethiopia and Flight Lieutenant Jerry Rawlings in Ghana (Nugent 2004: 258).[3] Given the typical apolitical disposition and strictly hierarchical character of the military, the radically egalitarian political agenda of Marxism and its anti-hierarchical orientation does not seem like a natural political philosophy for military actors and yet, Sankara and other trained officers were able to mobilise – albiet not unproblematically – Marxist-leaning social programmes.

The logic of this model, used and articulated by both scholar interpreters and leaders of puschist governments, presents the intervention of the military and their governments – the Praetorian (Soldier) Marxist juntas (military governments) – as part of the larger issues embodied in the crisis of underdevelopment in Africa. This larger crisis emanates from the peripherisation of Africa in the global capitalist system, colonialism and imperialism. Importantly, military intervention is justified under this model as part of or the face of a popular struggle, a revolution of the impoverished masses against a bourgeoisie capitalist ruling class system. The military, then, is the channel through which to create a popular rule and government that is socialist. In this trajectory of thought, African societies are seen to consist of propertied and non-propertied classes wherein state managers use state powers (including the coercive arms of the police and military) to advance and defend interests of the propertied class and their allies and impoverish the rest because of the dominant capitalist mode of production. Thus, this social dichotomy, based on and fertilised by social injustice and inequality, cultivates class antagonisms that delegitimise civilian regimes and create grounds for instability. Amidst these dire general societal conditions, the military, with a membership largely made up of elements of the masses, will thus draw the non-propertied class into the struggle and some military elements may see these horrendous conditions (and therefore a class antagonism) as a reason to intervene in politics. The military's role in a popular revolution becomes justified in such a context to protect the body politic from disintegration and to engineer a socialist social and economic order. Thus, the involvement of Praetorian Marxists in politics is rationalised, especially by soldiers, as a protector of popular will and aspirations as well as a logical outcome of a long period of a class struggle. These leaders drew on Marxism as a spatially, historically and culturally contextualised guiding sociology and philosophy that elucidated how society worked and how society could be changed, to explain their political actions and to frame a path and paradigm of national economic and political advancement.

Civilian governments, such as those of Nkrumah (in Ghana), Nyerere (in Tanzania), Sekou Toure (in Guinea), Modibo Keita (in Mali), Kenneth Kaunda (in Zambia) and Milton Obote (in Uganda, when he turned left), were attracted to African Socialism because they were not comfortable using Western models of doctrinaire socialism (i.e. classical Marxism). Praetorian Marxists, on the other hand, embraced forms of Marxism. These forms could be Marxism–Leninism or Maoism. For either approach, Marxism was the ideological basis to their political and economic policies and it rationalised their mere involvement in politics as part of a radical agenda of the masses. African Socialism – unlike doctrinaire scientific socialism which, according to Nyerere, 'seeks to build its happy society on a philosophy of inevitable conflict between man and man' (Nyerere 1962: 8) – claimed to draw on communitarian, humanist and socialist values in African traditions without strictly adhering to and following the classical and doctrinaire model of scientific socialism (Marxism) from Europe. Praetorian Marxists viewed the concept of African Socialism as rather limited, including limited in both the logics of execution as well as limited in rationalising the involvement of soldiers in politics. African Socialism was closely associated with the quest of economic liberation and social justice, but in practice each country that used it in the 1960s and 1970s ended up less self-reliant. After these earlier weaknesses, soldier Marxists might have percieved it to be unlikely or even incapable of engineering the sustainable social transformation of the kind called for by Marxists.

Hence, Marxism was the preferred political philosophy for Praetorian Marxists. Sankara averred that soldier politicians should be ideologically conscious because 'un militaire sans formation politique et idéologique est un criminel en puissance' (a soldier without political and ideological training and background is a potential criminal). Although Sankara demanded that soldiers should not turn to Marxism frivolously, others did. For those who did, Marxism became or represented a kind of convenient ideological gloss, what Nugent has referred to as 'a form of "signpost socialism" which was reinforced [especially] by pragmatic Cold War alliances' (Nugent 2004: 243). Thus, an element of opportunism drove some of the Praetorian politician soldiers to adopt Marxism, although it does not seem to have been the case with Sankara himself.

A SOLDIER-ADMINISTERED POPULIST MARXISM

The revolution was highly critical of elite privilege(s) and sought to implement various forms of regulation over economic enterprises in an effort to implement policies that would see wealth and health extend to the impoverished masses, particularly those in rural areas. As leader of the CNR, Sankara devised the rationale and proposed appropriate strategies and policies to maintain social control in a society undergoing rapid social change. To significantly challenge and alter the status quo in the conduct of political and economic life, the revolutionary CNR required swift actions against misconduct and a level of coercion to discipline a small petty bourgeoisie. In addition to the challenges posed by local elites, the CNR needed to prevent the continued interference of global forces – those imperialists that Sankara worked so diligently to challenge – in his country. In this context, Sankara was firm in his policies (some have argued that he was perhaps too firm). Within this framework, legal, organisational and administrative life was closely controlled. The autonomous political activities and individualistic opportunities deemed divisive to the common goal of the one popular revolution were prohibited. Within four years, Sankara and the revolutionary government steadily implemented considerable political, cultural and economic structures that had resulted in tremendous improvements in social, cultural and economic well-being (this would end abruptly with his assassination in 1987; see Chapter 7, this volume). While Sankara infused the character of the CNR and the Burkinabè Revolution with socialist commitements, the soldier-administered government became a populist regime (albeit drawing on other regime styles to govern).

Sankara instituted an administrative policy that was populist in orientation, although it was not like the administrative-hegemonial types or party mobilising forms of civilian governments that were popular in the 1960s and 1970s in places like Kenya, Zaire (now the Democratic Republic of Congo), Côte d'Ivoire, Togo, Nkrumah's Ghana, Keita's Mali, Toure's Guinea, Nyerere's Tanzania, and Kaunda's Zambia. The party mobilising forms tended to reflect the organisational choices of the founders and had socialist proclivities. Neither was Sankara's regime a personal-coercive type like those that became popular in the 1970s in places like Idi Amin's Uganda and Jean-Bedel Bokassa's Central African Republic. Sankara's regime preference and administrative orientation was not of the Afro-Marxist party centralist type that became popular from the mid 1970s in places like Benin, Angola, Mozambique, Ethiopia, Congo and Guinea Bissau, where the enforcers and creators endeavoured to wholly apply Marxist–Leninist principles and construct state institutions under firm party control.

The populism of Sankara's government was similar to that of Gaddafi in Libya and Rawlings in Ghana in 1981. Appearing as the face and director of the government and the continuous process of social change, Sankara and the soldiers showed devotion to the cause of the CNR and subordinated the administrative apparatus directly to the scrutiny of the public in Burkina Faso. This would promote a situation of social inclusion outlined in nonelite terms and forms. To accentuate the idea and belief that a revolution had occurred and was going on, public organisations were restructured and the connection between the excutive, the administration and the mass public constituency was altered, with the intention of eliminating waste and undermining the bureaucracy as an emblematic institution of privilege. The hope was that this would protect the public sphere from the excesses of privileged groups (i.e. top politicians, civil servants and Western commercial groups).

The functions of certain civil services, the judiciary and public corporations continued as before. However, alternative people-centred institutions momentarily circumscribed many of their responsibilities. These institutions included public tribunals, national investigative commissions and peoples' vetting committees. Public civil servants and politicians were dismissed or watched by peoples' and workers' vigilante groups known as the Committees for the Defense of the Revolution (CDR). Such reconfigurations were adopted as ways of introducing a direct popular voice in policymaking, improving efficiency, ordering the public sector, building the political machinery and curtailing excessive independence of the bureaucracy by pressuring it to adhere to certain norms dictated as the products of the revolution and popular will and interests.

Sankara had socialist commitments. However, unlike Afro-Marxists like Kerekou or Mengistu (who declared 'hardcore' Marxism–Leninism as the ideology of their regimes and countries), he did not try to enforce Marxist–Leninist principles on the people in Burkina Faso nor did he declare it as the official ideology of the government. In this way, Sankara had political policies but not an ideology per se for the revolution. Political ideologies are not policies. The definition of ideology is a complicated one. However, we agree that ideologies are systems 'of beliefs that serve as a standard of evaluation and guide to action' (Young 1982: 184). As systems that endeavour to deal with material problems, analyse existing conditions and proffer desired courses of behaviour and action, they embody the conceptual and thus the subjective principles of political action for social and economic change and well-being. An ideology, once established, becomes the intellectual base of group cohesion. An ideology can be mobilised in various ways: in the form of myth, without logical consistency, based on empirical and historical facts, in abuses of all claims to truth or through the use of logical ideas to move people to act and build feelings of solidarity. Whatever their form and shape, hegemonic ideologies express the preferences of rulers or masses and provide justifications for group and individual actions.

In his first speech, 'Struggle for a Bright Future', to the people on 4 August 1983, he outlined some preliminary policies and later provided the orientation of the regime and revolution in the *Discours d'Orientation Politique*. In the first speech, where he endeavoured to show the reason for the basic purpose for the birth of the CNR, he argued that the fundamental reason and main objective of the CNR was to defend the interests of the Voltaic people, and make them realise their deepest aspirations to liberty, real independence, and socio-economic progress.

Based on these revelations, Sankara asked only for popular support for the CNR, the coup and its aims, which were 'the defense of the interests of the Upper Volta people, the realisation of their profound aspirations to liberty, real independence, and economic and social progress' (Sankara, 'Struggle for a Bright Future', 4 August 1983). Hence he pleaded with the people of Upper Volta to rally behind the CNR for the great patriotic battle towards the achievement of a prosperous and bright future for the country (ibid.). He requested this devotion to the cause even if they had to give their lives for the achievement of total freedom in democracy and justice.

Sankara and his close advisors, including Valère Somé, deemed the imposition of the soldier-led CNR as the single supra-political administrative body to be pragmatically necessary for political cohesion in the interests of national sovereignty and unity. Indeed, this approach mirrored the strategies of most African Socialist leaders in their own countries. The populism of the government attracted and sustained popular support for the aspirations of the revolution. Including a second (and 'real') independence for the country to build a new society – one that would use local institutions freed from the shackles and negative effects of unproductive and corrupted traditions and institutions and liberated from the intellectual, cultural, material and political inheritances of neocolonialism and imperialism. Thus, the populism of the government emanated from the frustrations, anguish and resistance against those it deemed to be domestic purveyors of neo-colonialism, external exploiters and/or corrupt elite.

MORE THAN PRAETORIAN MARXISM: THE BLENDED APPROACH OF SANKARA'S POLITICS

In practice, Sankara mixed nationalist ideas with notions from socialism to fashion a path of social change that was in favour of self-reliance and anti-imperialism. His revolutionary rhetoric was extracted from a nationalistic impulse, African Socialism, Pan-Africanism (which Nkrumah was also known for) and leftist revolutions that were humanistic, egalitarian and utilitarian. Thus, it was not only Nkrumah – a self-professed non-denominational Christian and Marxist socialist – who gathered political ideologies and theories to pursue social development, anti-imperialism, African unity and self-reliance in Ghana, as 'a squirrel collects and stores nuts', to use Thomas Hodgkin's interpretation of Nkrumah (Martin 2012: 87–88; Austin 1964: 40). Nkrumahism was born through an eclectic philosophical constitution. Its founder vacillated between African Socialism and Marxism (scientific socialism).

Nkrumahism was a plan. David Apter characterises it as '*clearly a language of socialism, progress and development*' (cited in Bretton 1966: 87; emphasis original). Stokely Carmichael described African Socialism as 'scientific socialism applied to countries emerging from colonialism, and specifically African countries where the Marxist capital-labor conflict is only one of a number of fundamental conflicts' (Carmichael 1973: 41). Tibor Szamueli, of the Kwame Nkrumah Ideological Institute in Winneba, Ghana, deemed it as an 'ideology of the New Africa ... free from imperialism, organised on a continental scale, founded upon the conception of [a] one and united Africa drawing its strength from modern science and technology, and from the traditional African belief that the free development of each is the condition for the free development of all' (cited in Bretton 1966: 163). Sankara likewise gathered and drew on different political ideas that were applicable in his country for positive social change and against Western imperialism and capitalism.

Sankara preferred a social change with a socialist commitment. In this way, he was like Nkrumah, who believed that that capitalism was too complicated a system for newly independent African states, including Ghana, hence a socialistic society was imperative (Nkrumah 1959: vii). Nkrumah and Sankara shared a common passion for Pan-Africanism, anti-imperialism, anti-neocolonialism and self-reliance for their countries and Africa as a whole. However, the approach of the two socialist experiments had some fundamental structural and operational differences. The Nkrumah-Ghana one, which was considered a 'textbook example' of African Socialism (Nugent 2004: 167), was civilian, and the other was military-led. Secondly, Nkrumah oscillated between scientific socialism and African Socialism; however African Socialism largely informed his experiment.

Sankara's socialist experiment was inclined to a socialist commitment that was not qualified with or as African. He never called his paradigm of social justice African Socialism. Secondly, he did not restrict his pro-socialism visions and ideals to Burkina Faso or Africa alone. He maintained socialist alliances and shared the socialist visions of anti-imperialism and social justice with like-minded leaders and their countries in South America and Asia. These included Daniel Ortega (Nicaragua), Fidel Castro (Cuba) and Kim Il Sung (North Korea). Nevertheless, he knew that the radical and socialist orientation of his policies and of the revolution in Burkina Faso was and had to be Africa-specific, even if it was enriched and cross-fertilised by the experience of other nations. Thus, while inspirations could be drawn, lessons learned and ideas received from other historical and contemporary revolutions and social changes, revolutions – including that of the Burkinabè – could not be exported or copied.

Before being overthrown in 1966, Nkrumah indicated that although there existed 'a scientific socialism', there were different paths to socialism, dictated by the specific circumstances and conditions of a particular country at a definite historical period (Nkrumah 1970: 165; Nkrumah 2007[1963]: 120).[4] Hence, in terms of execution, form and content, each revolution was necessarily unique. While each approach was unique, Burkina Faso, Ghana and other post-colonies had shared experiences and histories of oppression. They therefore shared a need to overthrow oppression and engineer a process of sustainable positive social change for social justice with socialist commitments.

His personal familiarity with Marxism occassionally compelled Sankara to integrate class theory as an explanation for domestic politics; for example, he argued that the August event was born by the 'sharpening class contradictions of Voltaic society' (Sankara 1988: 32). Sankara believed that revolution was a means to remove the capitalism system of private ownership and the privatisation of the means of production. In describing the Burkinabè Revolution, he said:

> The revolutions that take place around the world are not all alike. Each revolution has its own originality, which distinguishes it … [T]he August revolution, is not an exception. It takes into account the special features of the country, its level of development, and its subjugation by the world imperialist capitalist system.
>
> (Sankara 1988: 40)

Unlike the more dogmatic scientific socialists and Afro-Marxists, Sankara was not committed to apply certain so-called 'universal truths' and transfer them as an entire well-formulated and all-embracing political philosophy to the African continent or Burkina Faso. His pragmatic policies were informed by an eclectic experiment through a pluralism obtained from the applicable ideas and truths of nationalism, socialisms, anti-neo-colonialism and Pan-Africanism.[5]

In this way, Sankara was at once a contradictory and dialectical personality of an overt Praetorian Marxist from Africa, an African socialist, pragmatist, military nationalist, populist and pacifist. Even as someone who claimed to be Marxist, and in some circumstances advocated the use of violence for freedom and right to life – often brandishing his holstered pistol in symbolic gesture of non-compliance (see Chapter 2, this volume) – he was deeply selfless. He revealed himself as a pacifist in the last moments of his life by dying as one. Contrary to his militant side and his better-known image as 'Africa's Che Guevara', he did not take up arms to defend himself (see Chapter 6, this volume). He did not take up arms to defend the revolution from those who, appearing as counter-revolutionaries and neoliberal actors, killed him and dismantled the revolution.

CONCLUSION

This chapter has examined the special character of the Burkinabè revolution through the prism of Sankara's political philosophies (Sankaraism) and how they encounter (and often contradict) what was a military-led government. In so doing, we have shown that what makes this revolution extraordinary was Sankara's ability to combine his analysis of various political philosophies and ideologies to reflect and suit local Burkinabè needs and circumstances – through concrete policies. This novel approach to African politics can be called Sankaraism. Sankara's use of political orientation rather than ideology made this revolution distinct on the continent. Sankara's ability to rationalise social change through a homegrown understanding of the concept of the struggle between the capitalist haves (and their lackeys) and have-nots was different from other popular and traditional conceptions of Marxist revolution. This rationalisation included his ability to navigate a complex landscape of local forces (often forces that clashed internally) without using a Eurocentric Marxist lens. This revolution was a product and event of anti-imperialism – as a class struggle but as a colonial, racialised class struggle in a global political economy. This perspective made it different from events and processes elsewhere which had been called Marxist revolutions.

The Burkinabè Revolution was also not a replication or transplantation of any other Marxist revolution (see Chapter 9, this volume). Rather, it was an event and process of social change anchored in the political dynamics of Burkina Faso and deeply rooted in the country's own share of the problems of underdevelopment as part of post-colonial Africa and changes therein. Even though Sankara's leadership shared some features with other revolutionary anticolonial and Marxist and socialist leaders in Africa and outside Africa (many of whom named their ideologies and/or published philosophical plans of political action), Sankara did not publish written work. Much like his 1987 homage to Che Guevera indicated, he probably knew that his work and ideas would remain if he left the political scene or died. Sensing that he would not live a long life as a leader, he used to call his wife Mariam Serme Sankara 'the widow'.

His short life span was fully packed with profound socio-political transformations and lasting consequences. His brave criticisms of capitalist imperial and neocolonial injustices as well as his critique of corruption in his country and across the globe remain relevant lessons for today. His tailor-made ideas and polices set his country towards national recovery and self-sufficiency. His revolutionary optimism made him a hero for the many who identify with the pains, struggles and hopes of the globally oppressed.

NOTES

1 We intentionally use the term uncivil because we believe that no war is 'civil'.
2 Some of the works about coups of the 1960s through to the 1990s include Austin and Luckham (1975), Jackman (1978), Wiking (1983), Johnson et al. (1984), Young and Turner (1985), Baynham (1986), Allen et al. (1989), Decalo (1990), Tiruneh (1993) and Osaghe (1998).
3 Nugent (2004) shows that the Rawlings-led 'revolution' did not take roots because he later removed the leftists when he lost faith in the radical 'socialist' agenda of the regime. Nevertheless, the Burkinabè Revolution drew inspiration from this radical tradition next door and Ethiopia till the death of Sankara and the CNR.
4 However, after Nkrumah's overthrow he considered any socialism 'derived from communal or egalitarian aspects of traditional African society' as a myth used to deny the class struggle and hence to 'obscure genuine socialist commitment' (see Afari-Gyan 1991: 170).
5 See for example the speeches 'There is Only One Color – That of Africa Unity', 'The Political Orientation Speech' and 'We Must Fight Imperialism Together' (all included in Sankara 1988).

REFERENCES

Afari-Gyan, K. (1991) Nkrumah's Ideology. In K. Arhin (ed.), The *Life and Work of Kwame Nkrumah*, 165–179. Accra: Institute of African Studies and Sedco Publishing.

Allen, C., Radu, M. S., Somerville, K. and Baxter, J. (eds) (1989) *Benin, The Congo, Burkina Faso: Politics, Economy and Society*. London: Pinter Publishers.

Austin, D. (1964) *Politics in Ghana: 1946–1960*. London: Oxford University Press.

Austin, D. and Luckham, R. (eds) (1975) *Politicians and Soldiers in Ghana 1966–72*. London: Frank Cass.

Baptope, E. (1981) *Coups, Africa and the Barrack Revolts*. Enugu, Nigeria: Fourth Dimension.

Baynham, S. (ed.) (1986) *Military Power and Politics in Black Africa*. London: Croom Helm.

Bretton, H. L. (1966) *The Rise and Fall of Kwame Nkrumah*. London: Frederick A. Praeger.

Carmichael, S. (1973) Marxism–Leninism and Nkrumahism. *The Black Scholar* 4(5): 41–43.

Conseil National de la Revolution. (1983) *Discours d'Orientation Politique (DOP)*. 2 October. Ouagadougou: Conseil National de la Revolution.

Decalo, S. (1990) *Coups and Army Rule in Africa*. New Haven, CT: Yale University Press.

Finer, S. (1988) *The Man on Horseback: The Role of the Military in Politics*, 2nd edition. Boulder, CO: Westview Press.

Jackman, R. W. (1978) The Predictability of Coups d'etat: A Model With African Data. *American Political Science Review* 72(4): 1262–1275.

Johnson, T. H., Slater, R. O. and McGowan, P. (1984) Explaining African Military Coups d'etat, 1960-1982. *American Political Science Review* 78(3): 622–640.

Karsten, P. (1998) The Coup d'Etat in Competitive Democracies: Its Appropriateness, Its Causes, and Its Avoidance. In P. Karsten (ed.), *Civil–Military Relations*, 223–250. New York: Garland Publishing.

Le Faso.net. (2015) Révolution du 04 août 1983: Valère Somé raconte tout le processus. *Le Faso.net: L'actualité du Burkina sur Internet*, 5 August 5. Retrieved on 30 October 2016 from http://lefaso.net/spip.php?article66221.

Le Jah, S. (2015) Je ne suis pas sankariste mais un sankarien. Interview with Agence d'Information du Burkina (AIB), Ouagadougou. Retrieved on 4 December, 2017 from http://www.aib.bf/m-4743-%C2%ABje-ne-suis-pas-sankariste-mais-un-sankarien%C2%BB-sams-k-le-jah.html.

Martin, G. (2012) *African Political Thought*. Basingstoke: Palgrave Macmillan.

Nkrumah, K. (1959) *Ghana: The Autobiography of Kwame Nkrumah*. Edinburgh: Thomas Nelson.

Nkrumah, K. (1970) *Class Struggle in Africa*. New York: International Publishers.

Nkrumah. K. (2007[1963]) *Africa Must Unite*. London: PANAF.

Nugent, P. (2004) *Africa since Independence*. Basingstoke: Palgrave Macmillan.

Nyerere, J. (1962) Ujamaa – the Basis of African Socialism. April. Retrieved on 6 July 2017 from https://webcache.googleusercontent.com/search?q=cache:5U8IaPQ5MwgJ:https://studycircle.wikispaces.com/file/view/20102a,%2BJulius%2BNyerere,%2BUjamaa%2B-%2BThe%2BBasis%2Bof%2BAfrican%2BSocialism,%2B1962.pdf+&cd=1&hl=en&ct=clnk&gl=gh&client=firefox-b-ab.

Osaghe, E. (1998) *Crippled Giant: Nigeria since Independence*. London: C Hurst.

Otayek, R. (1991[1989]) Burkina Faso: Between Feeble State and Total State, the Swing Continues. In D. C. O'Brien, J. Dunn and R. Rathbone (eds), *Contemporary West African States*, 13–30. Cambridge: Cambridge University Press.

Radu, M. S. and Somerville, K. (1989) The Congo. In C. Allen, M. S. Radu, K. Somerville and J. Baxter (eds), *Benin, The Congo, Burkina Faso: Politics, Economy and Society*, 148–233. London: Pinter Publishers.

Sankara, T. (1988) *Thomas Sankara Speaks: The Burkina Faso Revolution, 1983–87*. New York: Pathfinder Press.

Tiruneh, A. (1993) *The Ethiopian Revolution, 1974–1987*. Cambridge: Cambridge University Press.

Welch, C. (1987) *No Farewell to Arms?* Boulder, CO: Westview Press.

Wiking, S. (1983) *Military Coups in Sub-Saharan Africa: How to Justify Illegal Assumption of Power*. Uppsala: Scandanavian Institute of African Studies.

Young, C. (1982) *Ideology and Development in Africa*. New Haven, CT: Yale University Press.

Young, C. and Turner, T. (1985) *The Rise and Decline of the Zairean State*. Madison, WI: University of Wisconson Press.

CHAPTER 2

The Perils of Non-Alignment
Thomas Sankara and the Cold War
Brian Peterson

This chapter situates Thomas Sankara's political itinerary and approach to international relations within global and regional contexts. It emphasises Sankara's positions on non-alignment, which took both pragmatic and radical forms, covering the period from 1981 to 1985. In charting Sankara's diplomatic trajectory, the paper explores the complex and perilous balancing act that Sankara performed during the Cold War. Sankara's diplomatic moves took on greater importance because, in late 1983, Burkina Faso was elected a Non-Permanent Member of the UN Security Council for two years. This overlapped with Sankara's one-year term (1984–1985) as president of CEAO (Economic Community of West Africa), through which he actively battled transnational forms of corruption in francophone West Africa. Therefore, Burkina Faso, hitherto viewed as a small and impoverished country lacking diplomatic clout, had an outsize influence on international affairs during the period. Moreover, Sankara's appeal to African youth meant that neighbouring African heads of state could not simply ignore the revolution that he led. Young people were drawn to his charismatic and populist style; they admired his unbridled attacks and outrage against the international 'establishment'.[1]

There were various strands to Sankara's approach to foreign affairs. Officially, he considered the revolution in Burkina Faso as 'part of the world movement for peace and democracy, against imperialism and all forms of hegemonism'. He called for 'mutual non-aggression', 'non-interference in domestic affairs', fairness in trade and for respecting 'each other's independence, territorial integrity, and national sovereignty'. A committed Pan-Africanist, he supported national liberation movements around the world and was devoted to the anti-apartheid struggle. Sankara also advocated for debt non-repayment and disarmament and was far ahead of his times on environmental issues (Sankara 2007: 108–109).

In terms of diplomacy, Sankara called for a true 'democratisation' of international relations, to be based on 'the equality of rights and obligations'. In international fora, he wanted his country to be treated on equal footing; he refused to genuflect to his African political elders. Sankara idealistically held the view that every country was free to choose relations with any other without outside interference or pressure. But he dangerously cultivated relations with countries that were viewed with suspicion by Western governments, such as Libya, North Korea, Cuba and Nicaragua. Indeed, it was the Cold War, a zero-sum game, and there were repercussions to every alliance. Within francophone West Africa, Sankara was equally brazen in his approach to foreign affairs. He routinely challenged Ivoirian president Félix Houphouët-Boigny, the doyen of French neocolonial power in West Africa. Despite his youth, Sankara wasn't willing to 'wait his turn' and demanded respect from his fellow African heads of state. Thus, Sankara became a polarising figure, particularly as he threatened the established political order in Africa. He became a hero for African youth, but for many African heads of state, the Sankarist revolution called into question their modes of governance.

There were often discrepancies between Sankara's rhetoric in public speeches and his more pragmatic approach to diplomacy in private settings. This has led to a misappraisal of Sankara as a political leader, as he is mostly known through his speeches. Indeed, Sankara's passionate and provocative speeches led many to believe that his fiery rhetoric found echoes in his interpersonal dealings or in diplomacy. But Sankara had clearly distinct private and public personas, as documented by his friends, colleagues, journalists and diplomats. This chapter will not delve into this public-private split, but it should be noted that these disparities between his words and actions characterised his approach to foreign affairs while presenting a diplomatic challenge for his contemporaries. As an example, the US Ambassador to Upper Volta, Julius Walker, wrote in a cable: 'In one-on-one situations [Sankara] has tremendous charm and persuasion ... [But] he responds to crowd stimulus like a gospel revivalist and says things he probably wouldn't have considered in quieter moments.'[2]

Ideologically, Sankara was an intellectual and political pragmatist. He eschewed dogma. In far-reaching interviews with *Afrique-Asie*, the quintessential Third Worldist magazine of the era, Sankara observed that it mattered little whether or not a country was communist, socialist or capitalist, so long as it 'considered Africa as its hunting grounds, their closed field, their market, where they unload whatever garbage in order to exploit our sub-soil, our territory'. Regardless of a foreign power's political orientation – socialist France, communist Soviet Union and China, or capitalist United States – all were potential exploiters of Africa. Sankara saw how regimes had used socialist ideology to the detriment of their people. He noted the limits to such political labels: 'One doesn't choose socialism as if it's a product in a supermarket. It's not because someone proclaims socialism that socialism exists ... If tomorrow it is socialism that brings happiness, then it's socialism. But if it's another thing, it will be another thing.'[3] This ideological flexibility was reflected in Sankara's notion of 'true non-alignment' during the Cold War. He cultivated his image as a revolutionary and progressive, and he had a strong sense of kinship with other revolutionary movements, but he always remained open to maintaining and improving relations with Western capitalist countries.

THE COLD WAR CONTEXT OF THE REVOLUTION

Sankara's rise to power took place within a context of global recession. Coming after the economic downturn of the 1970s, the 1981–1982 recession led to a precipitous decline in prices for raw materials produced in African countries. It contributed to worsening terms of trade and indebtedness, in tandem with widespread mismanagement and corruption. It also propelled many African countries into IMF-imposed structural adjustment programs, which further exacerbated the vicious cycle of indebtedness. Concomitantly, China's reorientation toward a market economy had the result of undermining faith in socialism in the Third World. Across Africa, there was growing disillusionment with socialism and Marxist-inspired revolutionary movements, most of which had degenerated into leftist military juntas. Many of the Soviet Union's Third World allies were even defecting from Marxism–Leninism and initiating market-oriented reforms. Despite its costly invasion of Afghanistan from 1979 to 1989, and its continued support for leftist regimes in Angola and Ethiopia, the Soviet Union itself was in the throes of a decade-long process of economic collapse and political disintegration (Hobsbawm 1994: 433–499).

And yet there was a small but significant countervailing wave of revolutionary movements spanning the world from Iran to Nicaragua. In the late 1970s, this wave spread into Central America and the Caribbean, with guerrilla movements in El Salvador and Guatemala, the Maoist uprisings in Peru and the leftist New Jewel Movement in Grenada under Maurice Bishop. The most important and successful revolutionary movement was the Sandinista Front, which took power in Nicaragua in 1979. Backed by Catholic priests espousing 'Liberation Theology', the Sandinista revolution drew on populist, socialist and Catholic ideas. But this revolutionary counter-current, and the Soviet invasion of Afghanistan, prompted a powerful riposte as the Reagan administration initiated its policy of rollback during the so-called 'second Cold War' of the 1980s. With a renewed commitment to interventionism, Reagan moved aggressively to undermine revolutionary movements and governments, initiating clandestine wars against adversaries in such places as Nicaragua, Guatemala, El Salvador, Angola, Libya and Afghanistan. In its policy of 'constructive engagement', the

Reagan administration also fought hard against the African National Congress (ANC) in giving full support to the apartheid regime in South Africa, even as much of the world – including the US Congress – was joining the global anti-apartheid movement (Westad 2005: 331–395; Gleijeses 2013: 166–342). It was in this wider geopolitical context that Sankara rose to power. However, in order to understand Sankara's revolution we must turn to the more proximal causes.

THE RISE OF THOMAS SANKARA

Closer to home, there were developments that created conditions favourable to Sankara's rise. First, the devastating droughts of 1982–1985 caused immeasurable suffering across the Sahel zone and made the population of Upper Volta even more desperate for radical change. This was seen in the series of coups from 1980 to 1983, precipitated by widespread famine, social unrest and government corruption. During this time, Sankara's group of left-wing military officers grew in stature, taking up key positions within the military and committing themselves to the political struggle. Sankara also connected with former students returning from France and leaders in the powerful labour union movement. The labour unions had played critical roles in the overthrow of Lamizana in 1980 and Zerbo in 1982 and would mobilise during the months leading up to Sankara's taking power (see Chapter 4, this volume). Although the wider leftist movement was thrown into disarray by ideological disputes surrounding the Sino-Albanian split, many former students established new political parties, such as the Union of Communist Struggles (ULCR), or joined already existing ones like the Patriotic League for Development (PAI-LIPAD). It was a period of political ferment for the francophone left, which saw French socialists claim important electoral victories, including François Mitterrand's presidential election in May 1981, which buoyed leftists and held out promise for progressive change in West Africa. Finally, on Upper Volta's southern border, Flight Lieutenant Jerry Rawlings, a fellow young military officer, staged a coup in 1979 and initiated a left-leaning revolutionary process in Ghana. Rawlings would provide crucial military aid to Sankara's core of young progressive officers, facilitating the shipment of Libyan weapons via the commando base in Pô. He would also be Sankara's closest African ally on the international front.[4]

Against this backdrop, and after many years in the military, Thomas Sankara entered government as the Secretary of Information (Secrétaire d'État chargé de l'Information) of Upper Volta in September 1981. Reluctantly serving under President Colonel Saye Zerbo and the CMRPN regime, Sankara made it his mission to fight for press and labour union freedoms. But he also engaged in a bit of diplomacy; his signal diplomatic victory was in bringing the live television broadcast of the 1982 World Cup games to Upper Volta. Within this context,

Sankara negotiated with Jean-Pierre Cot – French Minister of Cooperation. In 1982, Cot's advisor for African affairs Hugo Sada met with Sankara several times both in Ouagadougou and Paris. 'The main thing Sankara wanted was for France to help Burkina to set up a system of satellite television so that Burkina could directly transmit the FIFA World Cup', Sada explained:

> It was something that was very expensive. So there was some hesitation on the French side to provide this … Then, at some point during the negotiations, Sankara said bluntly, 'If France does not want to help, then I will ask Qaddafi to help with this.'
>
> (Interview, French adviser, Hugo Sada, 20 April 2013)

Sankara succeeded in getting France to pay for the costs, but word spread quickly within Western diplomatic and intelligence circles that Sankara was reaching out to Muammar Qaddafi, the Libyan leader. At the time, the CIA and the French military were engaged in covert operations against Qaddafi's forces in Chad's civil war. Indeed, France was about to embark on its largest military intervention in post-colonial Africa, by escalating its support for Hissène Habré's forces against the Qaddafi-backed rebels in Chad (Woodward 1987: 87–91).[5]

After resigning in protest over the Comité Militaire de Redressement pour le Progres National (CMRPN)'s repressive measures and enduring a six-month imprisonment in Dédougou, Sankara was liberated and became Prime Minister of Upper Volta in January 1983. Then, in late February, Sankara embarked on an extended international trip, which culminated in his attendance at the summit of the Non-Aligned Countries in New Delhi, India. His trip included controversial visits to Libya and North Korea. Sankara hoped that an alliance with Qaddafi would yield greater economic development in Upper Volta. In interviews and speeches, Sankara stood his ground on Libya, arguing that Upper Volta had the right to cultivate friendships with any country of its choosing. After a week in Libya, Sankara left for North Korea, where he had the chance to see another type of revolutionary experiment. But Western governments were increasingly concerned about visits to such international pariahs (Sankara and Gakunzi 1988: 33–34).[6]

From 7 to 13 March 1983, Sankara was at the summit of the Non-Aligned Countries in New Delhi, India, where he had the chance to meet Fidel Castro, Daniel Ortega, Indira Gandhi, Jerry Rawlings, Maurice Bishop and many others. In his speech, he highlighted the main principles of non-alignment, which in certain ways had lost its way with the slow collapse of the Eastern Bloc. Sankara reminded his listeners that they were free to choose their allies in the world, and their own paths of development. He called for the 'democratisation of international relations based on the equality of rights and obligations'. Sankara also entered the fray of Middle Eastern politics and, in the process, made his first public criticisms of US foreign policy. 'The Israeli government, publically supported by the United States, despite the unanimous condemnation of the entire world, invaded Lebanon with its army, submitted the capital Beirut to ruthless destruction', Sankara said. 'Despite the ceasefire called for by the international community, the Israeli government has allowed the indescribable massacres of Sabra and Shatila, and whose leaders [in Israel] should be prosecuted for crimes against humanity.' He also condemned US imperialism in Nicaragua and El Salvador and expressed solidarity with the people of South Africa, Mozambique and Angola.[7]

Soon after his return from New Delhi, Sankara delivered blistering speeches in Ouagadougou (26 March 1983) and Bobo-Dioulasso (14 May 1983) in which he ratcheted up the anti-imperialist message and called on the youth to mobilise against the internal and external 'enemies of the people'. During this time, Sankara met with ANC representatives to discuss the anti-apartheid struggle just as the Soviets, Americans and Cubans all deepened their involvement in the battle for South Africa and Angola. But it was the Libyan spectre that caused most concern. A CIA report warned that an Upper Volta government led by 'radicals allied with Sankara' would offer Qaddafi 'increased opportunities for meddling in Niger, Côte d'Ivoire and Togo'. Stemming from these concerns, a US diplomatic cable reported that there were 'certain attempts underway to remove Prime Minister Sankara'. Sankara was eventually arrested on 17 May 1983. Indeed, stabilising Upper Volta, and keeping Libyan influence at bay, was a top French priority in Africa. When US diplomats met with Mitterrand's Director of African Affairs Jean Ausseil at Quai d'Orsay, Ausseil placed emphasis on the 'importance France places on Qadhafi's [sic] setbacks in Upper Volta and CAR [Central African Republic]'. The French official went further stating that Libyan expulsion from Upper Volta was 'even more important than recent and current events in Chad'.[8]

SANKARA'S REVOLUTION AND COLD WAR POLITICS

Despite the best efforts of the French government to keep Sankara out of power, Sankara and his fellow progressive military officers mounted a coup d'état on 4 August 1983, and thus launched the 'Democratic and Popular Revolution'. A year into the revolution, Sankara would change the name of the country to Burkina Faso. On the diplomatic front, shortly after taking power, Sankara met with the US ambassador Julius Walker privately. According to the minutes from the 8 August meeting, Sankara wanted to clear up any suspicions of Libyan influence. He was pragmatic and emphasised that he would be taking his distance from Qaddafi, and went so far as telling the US ambassador that Qaddafi 'will be shocked' by some of Sankara's statements and that he was 'not controlled by Libya and will be doing and saying things which Qadhafi will not like'.[9]

But, during this time, Western news reporting placed singular focus on Libya. *Le Monde* highlighted Sankara's ties to Qaddafi. The *New York Times* referred to Sankara as 'a pro-Libyan paratroop captain'. He was characterised as 'a committed Marxist–Leninist', who had 'made several trips to Libya'. These factors, according to the *Times*, were 'expected to fuel fears in Western-oriented African capitals'. Among the neighbouring African countries to express alarm was the Ivory Coast. In fact, Houphouët-Boigny had recently been invited to the White House in June 1983, and according to Herman J. Cohen – Reagan's special assistant and senior advisor on African Affairs within the National Security Council – Houphouët-Boigny had become an indispensable ally in the region, mainly owing to his role in the Angolan civil war, backing the 'pro-West' Jonas Savimbi and UNITA against the Cuba and Russia-backed MPLA (Cohen 2015: 17–30).[10]

Notwithstanding the concerns over Libya, the National Council of the Revolution (CNR) drew most of its influence from the Cuban revolution. 'We had nothing to do with the Libyan model', CNR member Valère Somé explained:

> At the beginning, Qaddafi helped us by sending arms through Ghana, but he soon realised Sankara was not going to be his disciple. Qaddafi thought he could impose his Green Book on us, but we flatly refused. Immediately after August 4, the divergence between Sankara and Qaddafi began because of this refusal. Actually, our revolution drew mostly on the Cuban revolution … There was absolutely no trace of Qaddafi's influence in our revolution and Qaddafi would even have a hand in the assassination of Sankara.
>
> (Interview, Valère Somé, 13 March 2013 and 22 August 2015)

As the revolution deepened, Sankara routinely offered blunt criticism of Qaddafi's involvement in Chad. In early 1984, Sankara even hosted one of Habré's ministers in Ouagadougou and took considerable heat from the Libyans. Sankara was trying to play the role of mediator between the belligerent parties, but Qaddafi refused to accept Upper Volta's neutrality. In response to Sankara's disapproval of Libyan intervention in Chad and Sankara's resistance to Libyan pressure to follow their revolutionary example, Qaddafi began withdrawing support for Sankara while cultivating relationships with other military members of the CNR, such as Blaise Compaoré. A secret US embassy cable ominously reported in 1984 that Compaoré was already working with Qaddafi, and that Compaoré was 'certain to stage a coup in the near future … with the possibility of Libyan support' (Jaffré 2012: 179).[11]

Relations with France were fraught with tension. On 4 October 1983, Sankara was at the tenth annual Franco-African summit in Vittel, France. Those who attended the conference remembered Sankara's controversial presence. LIPAD leader Philippe Ouédraogo recalled the Vittel conference:

> I was there in Vittel with Thomas at the meetings. And Sankara made quite a stir by showing up with his pistol, which he put on the table in front of him. He was so young, and he had just done this coup. And the journalists were curious and drawn to him. He was very controversial and pushing the boundaries, challenging the neocolonial order.
>
> (Interview, Philippe Ouédraogo, 31 August 2015)

Sankara knew that he was 'stirring up the tranquil pond of Franco-African relations'. But he was also painfully aware that his country was dependent on France. Paris was by far Burkina Faso's largest aid donor, providing some $55 million USD in economic aid, which constituted 40 per cent of its annual budget. Burkina's debt to France was roughly $155 million; by this time, the country had fallen into arrears. The public debt consumed one-quarter of state revenue. Even as Sankara pushed ahead with ambitious new projects, the country was facing major fiscal challenges and the CNR was feeling pressure to reach an agreement with the IMF. Thus, despite his public declarations aimed at challenging France, Sankara understood that he couldn't break with the neocolonial power completely (Sankara 2007: 132–133).[12]

Shortly after his return from France, Sankara learned of the killing of Maurice Bishop, the revolutionary Prime Minister of Grenada, on 19 October. Within a week, on 25 October, the US military invaded the island on a 'rescue mission' to protect American students. But as it would later become clear, the Reagan administration had grown concerned about the island's ties to Cuba and the Soviet Union. Reagan saw a golden opportunity to combat communism in the region. According to Cold War historian Odd Westad, the invasion of Grenada was a 'breakthrough for a more offensive strategy against revolutionary regimes'. It contributed to the 'development of a counterrevolutionary strategy that was global in reach'. Sankara took a public stand against the US invasion of Grenada and expressed support for the Sandinistas in Nicaragua. Soon US Ambassador Walker warned Sankara that the US government would be forced to re-examine 'its cooperation agreements and aid programs with the country'. But over the next two years, Upper Volta, as a non-permanent member of the UN Security Council, would be voting with Nicaragua, Cuba, Ghana and others against the United States (Westad 2005: 345).[13] Sankara reasoned:

> Burkina Faso was elected with the votes of more than 104 countries. We had to represent their interests, in particular those of the non-aligned countries. Their interests, as well as those of other peoples in revolt, should be defended every day, constantly and courageously. Otherwise the UN would become an echo chamber manipulated by a few powerful drummers.
>
> (Sankara 2007: 150, 195)

The Reagan administration was growing perturbed by the fact that this 'small and insignificant country' was opposing it at the UN and perceived as being 'up on the stage every place in the world, denouncing US imperialism and siding with Cuba, the Soviets and with Nicaragua', as the new US ambassador Leonardo Neher explained:

> We had very little economic interest in this country. We just wanted to try to wean them away from certain radical ideas, and to moderate the regime. The thing was that Sankara's rhetoric and his posturing just pissed off the Reagan administration … Jeane Kirkpatrick was extremely hostile towards Sankara and wanted me to go out there and tell him off. And the USAID director said that we were going to zero out the AID projects. The Reagan administration was very hostile towards Sankara from the beginning.
>
> (Interview, Leonardo Neher, 23 June 2014)[14]

Faced with the hostility of France and the United States, Sankara was eager to cultivate relations with socialist countries, hoping to counter-balance Burkina Faso's high level of dependence on Western donors. But, a year after taking power, Sankara had yet to draw much interest in his revolution from the communist world. The Chinese built a stadium, but provided little economic assistance. Although the Soviet Union had a foothold in Mali and Benin, Soviet relations remained distant; Moscow offered no economic or military aid program. Furthermore, the August 1984 expulsion from the CNR government of Marxist–Leninist PAI-LIPAD members – who had close links to the USSR – led to a cooling of Soviet interest. The Soviets even publicly stated that the expulsion was unacceptable, to which Sankara responded by expelling the Soviet deputy chief of mission in Ouagadougou. Sankara then refused a paltry Soviet offer of food aid because of conditions that Sankara found insulting. When asked about the refusal of Soviet food aid, he later explained, 'We have our dignity to protect … We could have mortgaged off our country … We are the ones who decided that all forms of outside control should be rejected.' Members of the CNR's Political Bureau thought it was the lack of interest in the Soviet model that kept the Eastern Bloc from supporting the revolution. But Sankara's ties to North Korea and Libya also served to alienate potential supporters (Sankara 2007: 201–232).[15]

In late September 1984, Sankara embarked on a historic ten-day trip to the United States, Cuba and Nicaragua. According to *Carrefour Africain*, the visit to Cuba was in response to Fidel Castro's 'personal invitation'. Sankara was given a reception attended by 'most of Cuba's top ranking officials'. Castro awarded Sankara with the 'Order of José Marti' honour. In accepting the honour, Sankara thanked Cuba for its 'deep feelings of love', citing José Marti with the phrase 'love is repaid with love'. Sankara ruminated on Marti's life and admitted that it was 'no accident at all that our national slogan is captured in one you know so well: Homeland or death, we shall overcome' (Sankara 2007: 136–142).[16]

In Cuba, Sankara had a chance to talk with Castro at length and visit sights around Havana, such as the recently constructed Che Guevara Pioneer Palace and Lenin Park. Sankara travelled to the Isle of Youth, which was known for hosting some 10,000 African and Nicaraguan students who studied at the Cuban government's expense. This kind of cooperation was not unique; Cuba had a history of involvement in Africa during the Cold War, including its support for the MPLA in Angola and Nelson Mandela in South Africa; it had been hosting African leaders and students for decades. All of these experiences profoundly marked Sankara. Soon he would be sending a large group of Burkinabé youth to study in Cuba.[17]

Days later, in New York City, Sankara attended the 39th session of the UN General Assembly on 4 October and delivered the most important international speech of his life. Sankara remained true to his convictions and positioned himself on the international left and in support of the non-aligned movement. He expressed solidarity with all those who suffered in 'the stranglehold of imperialism'. He especially singled out Israel for refusing to grant Palestinians the right to an autonomous existence. But Sankara's most impassioned plea for justice was saved for South Africa (see more of this heritage in Chapter 19, this volume). He described the apartheid system as one of 'terrorism' designed to 'physically liquidate the country's black majority'. He emphasised the need for intensifying the campaign to free Nelson Mandela. Then, in a provocative move, Sankara called for the suspension of Israel and the outright expulsion of South Africa from the UN for their unwillingness to cooperate with the international community (Sankara 2007: 154–175).

Before returning to Ouagadougou, Sankara took a brief sojourn to Nicaragua, where he met the head of the socialist Sandinista government, Daniel Ortega. The visit was sure to raise a few eyebrows in Western foreign policy circles. By 1984, the US–Nicaraguan conflict was at its peak, with the Soviets and Cubans supplying arms to the Sandinistas and the CIA supporting and equipping the anti-Sandinista forces, the Contras, and even mining the harbours of Nicaragua to prevent arms shipments from reaching the government. Two years later, Sankara travelled again to Nicaragua for a celebration of the Sandinista movement. In his 1986 speech, Sankara called for support for the Nicaraguan struggle. He was certainly not alone in condemning the US-backed contras. Many Western leaders opposed Reagan's policy and, on the same day that Sankara spoke in Managua, the US Congress announced its plans to investigate what would become known as the 'Iran-Contra affair'. But Sankara's travels could hardly have helped in his dealings with the United States. In fact, it was around this time that Reagan made his famous statement that Libya, North Korea, Cuba, Nicaragua and Iran constituted a 'confederation of terrorist states ... a new international version of Murder Incorporated' (Sankara 2007: 297–302; Westad 2005: 339–348; Gleijeses 2013: 314).[18]

CHALLENGING FRANÇAFRIQUE

In late October 1984, Sankara was disrupting the regional political order. He flew into Bamako, Mali for the tenth annual CEAO (Economic Community of West Africa) Summit. He was greeted by enthusiastic crowds of youth chanting his name along the roadside. All across West Africa, Sankara was raising the hopes of young people, and now he was being sworn in as the new CEAO president. Sankara promptly used the position to extend his anti-corruption crusade to neighbouring francophone African countries. As it turned out, under his one-year CEAO presidency, the largest financial scandal in the organisation's history erupted. Known as the 'Diawara Affair', it involved the Ivoirian Minister of Planning, Mohamed Diawara, who was charged with embezzling 6.5 billion CFA of CEAO funds that had been earmarked for famine relief. In his speech to CEAO leaders, Sankara stated unequivocally that it was time to 'clean house'. To the dismay of fellow African heads of state, Diawara and his accomplices were arrested and put on trial before a Popular Revolutionary Tribunal in Ouagadougou. They were convicted and imprisoned. The Malian political class was enraged. In a cable to Washington, the US ambassador in Mali reported that the Malian government was incensed by Sankara's words and actions at the CEAO summit. President Moussa Traoré was described as 'furious'. Moreover there was an 'underlying concern of the Malian elite over Sankara's potential appeal to Mali's young, often unemployed urban masses'. The revolutionary threat that Sankara posed would eventually lead Traoré to provoke a senseless border war in late 1985.[19]

By early 1985, Paris was also reportedly 'fed up' with Sankara's public rhetoric. French Ambassador Jacques Le Blanc began toying 'with a strategy of reducing French aid'. In a conversation with Ambassador Neher, Le Blanc discussed plans to 'approach Sankara, point out the value of French aid, and say that France will reduce its assistance'. The US had already begun drastically cutting aid to Burkina in response to Sankara's public statements attacking the Reagan administration. During the meeting, Le Blanc offered his assessment of Sankara as an 'impetuous, childish and inexperienced leader'. He characterised the CNR as a 'simple military dictatorship' and said France was still deeply concerned about Sankara's ties to Libya.[20]

Mali and the Ivory Coast accelerated their efforts to counter the revolution. It was around this time that Houphouët-Boigny began cultivating Blaise Compaoré as a useful ally by arranging a marriage with Ivoirian Chantal Terrasson de Fougères. Then, amid the growing tensions with the Ivory Coast,

Sankara attended a meeting in Yamoussoukro on 10 September 1985. The issue of the day was Libyan efforts to destabilise the region and Sankara was put on the hot seat over Qaddafi's actions. Houphouët-Boigny was reportedly trying to 'burn bridges between Sankara and his neighbours, notably Mali'.[21]

Returning to Ouagadougou on 11 September, Sankara was livid. At a public meeting, amid loud cheering, he protested:

> We know that at the present moment, they are trying to foment plots of all kinds against our people ... They are trying to create, to trigger an unjust and multiform war against our people... The other peoples who are at our borders they also are people who need revolution. To be clear ... I'm talking about Mali ... The revolution of the Burkinabé people is at the disposal of the Malian people if they need it.
>
> (*Sidwaya*, 13 September 1985)

The speech gave a clear *casus belli* and reason to stop the revolutionary contagion from spreading. Within two months, a pretext had been generated to declare war on Burkina Faso: the unresolved border dispute. But the real motivation was to teach Sankara a lesson, to humble the young revolutionary, and perhaps precipitate a coup. Leading up to the war with Mali, *Afrique-Asie* reported that 'everything has been undertaken by the Ivoirian president to combat his neighbour: attempts at assassination, financing military and civilian plots, thinly veiled interventions at Élysée, Matignon, Quai d'Orsay and even the Socialist Party headquarters, but also in numerous African and Western capitals in order to strangle the young revolution'. According to a CIA report, the war 'stemmed from Bamako's hope that the conflict would spark a coup in Burkina', and that 'Traoré believed the conflict would give Burkinan [*sic*] dissidents the opportunity to overthrow Sankara', while distracting public attention away from Mali's own dire economic situation.[22]

For Sankara, the war was a tremendous disappointment. It showed that he had few regional allies. Houphouët-Boigny, Traoré, Eyadéma and Kountche all had good reason to distrust Sankara, and so they were content to watch the young captain get humbled. Regarding Libya, as one CNR member recalled, the war with Mali 'allowed us to see who our friends were [and] Libya did not send us a single bullet, nor a single litre of gasoline'. Sankara was even more isolated than he had thought. In his crusade to purify the CEAO, he had taken a tremendous risk. Furthermore, according to Commander Abdoul-Salam Kaboré, there was a growing faction of 'bellicose officers' who were angry with Sankara for not leading a counter-attack. Burkina's military feebleness in the face of Malian aggression diminished Sankara's standing within the military. Soldiers blamed him for the defeat. There was now an anti-Sankara faction coalescing within the military, and opportunistic officers waiting in the wings for their chance to seize power (Andriamirado 1987: 145–151).[23]

CONCLUSION

Relations with France would improve slightly after the war. Even the United States reported that a humbled and more contrite Sankara was now willing to cooperate on a range of issues, including a possible agreement with the IMF. French ambassador Le Blanc indicated that the French government was 'guardedly optimistic' about Sankara and 'thoroughly convinced' that Houphouët-Boigny was saying the right things in support of Sankara. However, on 15 April 1986, all the optimism ended when the Reagan administration launched its bombing of Libya. In response, Sankara decided to take a stand against the US military operation by publically showing his solidarity with the Libyans. Unfortunately for Sankara, his expression of loyalty to Qaddafi was not reciprocated and it won him few favours with neighbouring heads of state. Even an alleged coup attempt in Togo was soon blamed on Sankara. And over the next year, Qaddafi would deepen his ties to Sankara's internal and external enemies as the focus of Libyan destabilisation shifted to Liberia (see Chapter 6, this volume).[24]

Over the final year of his life, Sankara would place emphasis on debt non-repayment as a core issue (see Chapter 12, this volume). He would deepen his support for the liberation struggle in South Africa, reaffirm his ties to Cuba and the Sandanistas in Nicaragua, and maintain his non-aligned position. But he found himself increasingly isolated in West Africa, as the Ivory Coast, Mali, Togo, Niger, Senegal and others grew weary of his challenges to the established system. Even Ghana was coming to terms with the IMF and World Bank, eventually entering into the kind of structural adjustment program that Sankara opposed. Finally, there was evidence of diminished French commitment to Burkina Faso, especially after Mitterrand's visit to Ouagadougou in November 1986 and the return of Jacques Foccart within the cohabitation government. Moreover, Sankara's expulsion of the Peace Corps from Burkina Faso in 1987 served to further alienate the US. In the face of uncertainty, and the on-going anti-imperialist rhetoric, France and the United States were not willing to absorb the recurring costs, and diplomatic headaches, required to support Sankara. And with the rise of a new neoliberal order, and the 'dramatic extension of the Cold War into the global economy', socialist countries were unable, or unwilling, to provide the kind of patronage Sankara needed to stay in power. He would make one trip to the Soviet Union in October 1986, but the visit resulted in no significant Soviet aid. In fact, it was just days before Mikhail Gorbachev's historic meeting with Reagan in Reykjavik. The Cold War was drawing down and 'there wasn't much interest in supporting Burkina Faso', according to the US ambassador Leonardo Neher.[25]

In his final international address, Sankara focused on the theme of indebtedness. With barely three months to live, he warned that African nations had to come together to 'avoid going off to be killed one at a time'. But, by this time, such talk of African unity fell on deaf ears, as most African countries, facing economic collapse, desperately sought out arrangements with the Washington Consensus. Sankara then finished his speech with a bit of gallows humour: 'If Burkina Faso alone were to refuse to pay the debt, I wouldn't be at the next conference' (Sankara 2007: 373–381). And indeed this would be his last.

NOTES

1   This chapter draws on interviews, journalistic sources, and government documents, including US embassy cables and documents acquired through a Freedom of Information Act (FOIA) request I submitted on Sankara for the period 1982 to 1988. In this chapter I draw on only a small portion of these research findings presented in my forthcoming book, *Sankara: A Revolutionary Life in Late Cold War Africa* (Indiana University Press).

2   See Sankara and Gakunzi (1988). *Afrique-Asie* 305, 13 October 1983; AMEmbassy-Ouaga to SecState-WashDC, August 1983, February 1984, FOIA; Interview, US diplomat Robert Pringle, 18 July 2014.

3   *Afrique-Asie* 319, 9 April 1984; *Afrique-Asie* 320, 23 April 1984.

4   For useful background, see Jaffré (2012); Ziegler and Rapp (1986); Englebert (1986).

5   Interview, Fidèle Toé, 14 March 2013; interview, US Diplomat, Thomas Hull, 13 November 2014; *Afrique-Asie* 284, 6 December 1982.

6   *Afrique-Asie* 283, 22 November 1982; interview, Abdoul-Salam Kaboré, 25 August 2015.

7   'Ni Confusion, ni resignation: Thomas Sankara au 7eme sommet des non-alignes', *Afrique-Asie* 293, 11 April 1983; see also 'Discours prononcé au Sommet des Non alignés de New Delhi' on thomassankara.net.

8   AMEmbassy-Ouaga to SecState-WashDC, 6 May, 15, 18 and 27 July 1983, FOIA; 'National Intelligence Daily' (NID), CIA, 24 March and 7 May 1983, FOIA files; *Afrique-Asie* 297, 6 June 1983.

9   AMEmbassy-Ouaga to SecState-WashDC, 9 August 1983, 8 August 1983; SecState-WashDC to AMEbassy-Abidjan, 9 August 1983, FOIA.

10 *New York Times*, 5 and 7 August 1983; *Le Monde*, 9 and 10 August 1983.

11 *Afrique-Asie* 320, 23 April 1984; *Le Monde*, 7 October 1983; interview, Mousbila Sankara, 21 August 2015; AMEmbassy-Ouaga to SecState-WashDC, 13 September 1983, 9 February and 9 June 1984, FOIA.

12 *Le Monde*, 4 October 1983; *Jeune Afrique* 1188, 12 October 1983; AMEmbassy-Ouaga to SecState-WashDC, 7 August 1984, 6 July 1984, 18 June 1984, FOIA; 'Burkina: Pressures on Sankara', CIA-Directorate of Intelligence, August 1986, FOIA.

13 *Carrefour Africain* 805, 18 November 1983; AMEmbassy-Ouaga to SecState-WashDC, 22 and 31October, 8 November 1983, FOIA; AMEmbassy-Ouaga to SecState-WashDC, 22 October, 8 November, 15 February 1983, FOIA; interview, Pascal Sankara, 12 July 2015.

14 AMEmbassy-Ouaga to SecState-WashDC, 6 December 1983, 12 September 1984, FOIA.

15 *Le Monde*, 8 November 1984; AMEmbassy-Ouaga to SecState-WashDC, 28 September 1984, 12 December 1984, FOIA; 'The Soviet Response to Instability in West Africa', September 1985, CIA-Directorate of Intelligence, FOIA; interview, Valère Somé, 10

March 2013.

16 *Carrefour Africain* 850, 28 September 1984.

17 USINT-Havana to SecState-WashDC, 26 September 1984 and October 4 1984, FOIA.

18 *New York Times*, 2 September 1984; *Los Angeles Times*, 9 November 1986.

19 *Carrefour Africain* 856, 9 November 1984; *Afrique-Asie* 335, 19 November 1984; AMEmbassy-Bamako to SecState-WashDC, 20 December 1984, FOIA.

20 *Le Monde*, 16 February 1985; AMEmbassy-Ouaga to SecState-WashDC, 22 April 1985, FOIA.

21 *Afrique-Asie* 358, 7 October 1985; interview, Valère Somé, 12 March 2013.

22 *Afrique-Asie* 365, 13 January 1986; 'Burkina: Pressures on Sankara', August 1986, CIA-Directorate of Intelligence, FOIA.

23 AMEmbassy-Ouaga to SecState-WashDC, 31 December 1985, FOIA; interview, Abdoul-Salam Kaboré, 25 August 2015.

24 AMEmbassy-Ouaga to SecState-Washington 14 April 1986, FOIA.

25 Interview, Leonardo Neher, 23 June 2014.

REFERENCES

Andriamirado, S. (1987) *Sankara, le rebelle*. Paris: Groupe Jeune Afrique, 1987.

Cohen, H. J. (2015) *The Mind of the African Strongman*. Washington DC: New Academic Publishing.

Englebert, P. (1986) *La Révolution Burkinabé*. Paris: l'Harmattan.

Gleijeses, P. (2013) *Visions of Freedom: Havana, Washington, Pretoria, and the Struggle for Southern Africa*. Chapel Hill, NC: University of North Carolina Press.

Hobsbawm, E. (1994) *The Age of Extremes*. New York: Vintage.

Jaffré, B. (2012) *Biographie de Thomas Sankara*. Paris: l'Harmattan.

Peterson, B. (forthcoming) *Sankara: A Revolutionary Life in late Cold War Africa*. Bloomington, IN: Indiana University Press.

Sankara, T. (2007) *Thomas Sankara Speaks: The Burkina Faso Revolution, 1983–1987*. New York: Pathfinder.

Sankara, T. and Gakunzi, D. (ed.) (1988) Oser Inventer l'Avenir: La Parole de Sankara. Paris: l'Harmattan.

Westad, O. (2005) *The Global Cold War*. Cambridge: Cambridge University Press.

Woodward, B. (1987) *The Veil: The Secret Wars of the CIA*. New York: Simon & Schuster.

Ziegler, J. and R., J. (1986) *Sankara: Un nouveau pouvoir africain*. Lausanne: Pierre-Marcel Favre.

CHAPTER 3

Thomas Sankara and the
Elusive Revolution

Leo Zeilig

Thomas Sankara sought a national break from Upper Volta's neo-colonial and imperialist domination. In 1983, he stated the aims of the revolution categorically: this would be 'a new society free from social injustice and international imperialism's century long domination and exploitation' (cited in Sankara forthcoming). Yet, securing such a break was a far from simple aim. The combination of popular and grassroots initiatives, with more classic development projects and support for businesses, expressed a real contradiction. The revolution tried to hold on to a complex (and ultimately deadly) ambiguity. This chapter looks at the limited, hugely constrained, circumstances of reforms under Sankara's military government. Reforms had to be secured in the cracks and fissures that were temporarily available.

At the start of the age of austerity on the African continent, in the early 1980s, Thomas Sankara emerged as a leading figure to challenge the cynical class of leaders who led the new states from independence. Within a very short period, he became the figurehead of the confrontation of a people to the demands of structural adjustment, multinationals, the International Monetary Fund and World Bank, and their local and international accomplices.

The period from 1970 to the mid-1980s held many contradictions for African revolutionaries. There was a combination of new struggles in Africa and a deepening economic crisis that brought to an end the myth of rapid economic development directed by the state. It also marked the end of the long boom that had stretched precariously and unevenly around the world since 1945. By the early 1970s industrial production had slumped in the advanced economies by 10 per cent in one year, while international trade had fallen by 13 per cent (Hobsbawm 1995: 405). The resulting recession had a devastating effect on Africa. Still locked into economic dependency, most African economies relied on the export of one or two primary products. By the mid-1970s, for example, two-thirds of exports from Ghana and Chad were coffee and cotton respectively, while the fall in copper prices meant that by 1977 Zambia, which depended on copper for half of its GDP, received no income from its most important resource (Marfleet 1998: 104). Regions already marginal to international capitalism were further marginalised, impotent to resist the violence of these slumps.

The struggle for independence from Portugal represented, for some, a renaissance of socialism in Africa (Davidson 1978). Since the crisis in the Congo, guerrilla movements had multiplied in Africa, the most effective fighting under the leadership of Amilcar Cabral in the small West African state of Guinea-Bissau. Amilcar Cabral, intellectual and activist, a symbol of the new generation of African socialists, managed to humiliate the Portuguese army. The Portuguese army was also involved in Angola and Mozambique in an increasingly desperate bid to hold on to Portugal's African empire.

Although the new leaders of liberation movements were often committed to 'Marxism-Leninism', they remained critical of the experience of decolonisation. The MPLA in Angola and FRELIMO in Mozambique both faced external invasions from South Africa and internal destabilisation by movements funded by the USA. But these movements still highlighted the upsurge of radicalism on the continent. The Portuguese revolution that followed a military coup in 1975 was both precipitated and inspired by the struggle for national liberation in Africa (Zeilig and Seddon 2009).

If the 'second wave' of political transformation increasingly appeared compromised during the second half of the 1970s and into the 1980s, all paths of autonomous national development adopted by existing African regimes were increasingly undermined as the global economic crisis deepened. Although the economic crisis of the late 1970s and early 1980s was a global capitalist crisis, much of the pain of adjustment was borne by the developing countries, and particularly by those that relied heavily on oil imports and on borrowing from the West (Harvey 2005).

Loans granted in the 1970s turned into debts, as the process of global adjustment and restructuring required for the resolution of the international capitalist crisis proceeded. More and more African states found their options constrained and their macroeconomic policies increasingly shaped by the conditions imposed by the International Monetary Fund (IMF), the World Bank, western governments and the private banks (Walton and Seddon 1994). By the time the free market governments of Thatcher and Reagan had been elected, development policy had shifted to focus on the market and the private sector. The IMF and World Bank became the central players in this policy. As the World Bank reported at the time, 'Africa needs not just less government – [but] government that concentrates its efforts less on direct intervention and more on enabling others to be productive' (Sandbrook 1993).

For most African economies, 'structural adjustment' preceded more far-reaching economic and institutional reform, leading to varying degrees of economic liberalisation. The costs of economic liberalisation and the austerity policies that accompanied it, however, fell unevenly on different social classes. The poor and working class, particularly in urban areas, felt the pain of adjustment most acutely. But they did not just suffer passively, as victims of the crisis; they struggled in various ways, resisted and protested.

The reaction of the working class and poor was not only defensive and geared towards survival; it was also offensive – aimed at resisting, protesting against and changing the policies, and at challenging those interests that so evidently oppressed and exploited them. The targets of popular protest included the international financial agencies (particularly the IMF), the governments that adopted the austerity policies and the representatives of the big corporations (foreign and national) that benefited from liberalisation (Seddon and Zeilig 2005: 9–27). It was from this radicalising, continental moment that Sankara had started to develop his own understanding of political possibilities and transformation.

SANKARA EMERGES

From the devastation of the continent, Sankara emerged as a force promising, at any cost, to break from this pattern, to refuse the inevitability of poverty and misery in West Africa and turn his back on both the 'inevitability' of adjustment *and* the failure of the two waves of independence. The Burkinabè revolution, as it became known, was a complex process, full of contradictions, set-backs, failure and more limited success.

Sankara understood that Africa had to find its own way to development by severing the lines of economic and political slavery with the North. In all of these ways, he was correct and worthy of our celebration and study. In the process of implementing his project for Burkina Faso, he wielded and created institutions and organizations from above – in this, he failed. Sankara's tools for transformation proved too weak. Sankara is a crucial starting point for each of us who seek the same transformation of the continent's skewed political economy in the context of capitalist globalisation. Sankara was more than the speeches and declarations he made at international forums, great as these were. He fought against a world economy that was set-up to crush initiatives such as his, even in poor countries like Burkina Faso. The enemies of the regime were national and international and even such a top-down project – for the Conseil National de la Revolution (CNR), the governing body of the revolution, directed and coordinated transformation from the top of a military command structure – posed too great a threat to many important interests (Martens 1989).

Some of these top-down initiatives were successful and incredibly audacious, and there are thousands alive today as a result. In primary health care, the regime scored some of its greatest successes. A few examples should suffice: infant mortality fell from 208 in every 1000 births, in 1982, to 145 in 1984. Local pharmacies were built in approximately 5,834 of the 7,500 villages (Sankara 1988: 21). Even more impressive was the programme of mass vaccination, between 1983 and 1985, two million children were vaccinated against different illnesses. The achievement was appropriately recognised and celebrated by UNICEF, Sankara's recent biographer writes:

> By most estimates, the greatest triumph was the Vaccination Commando, a child immunization campaign. Previous vaccination campaigns were carried out strictly through the government's regular and very limited health services – and thus reached only a tiny fraction of children, even in Ouagadougou. Reflecting Sankara's typical impatience with slow, bureaucratic procedures, the cabinet decided in September 1984 to launch a commando-style campaign to vaccinate most Burkinabè children against the key childhood killers (measles, meningitis, and yellow fever) – and to do so over a period of only two weeks, just two months later. Foreign donor agencies advised against such a fast and extensive campaign and suggested a more cautious, measured approach … By the end of the two weeks, some 2 million children had received a vaccination, about three times the number in previous campaigns. Rural coverage was almost as high as in the cities. According to a joint evaluation by UNICEF and the Ministry of Health, sensitization of the population to health issues was 'the most spectacular aspect of the operation.' In addition, health worker morale increased significantly, as did greater overall public demand for better health services. Most immediately, the Vaccination Commando meant that in 1985 the usual epidemics of measles and meningitis – which often claimed the lives of between 18,000 and 50,000 children – did not occur.
>
> (Harsch 2014: 77–78)

In addition, tens of thousands were given, for the first time, access to education and literacy, including many poor peasant farmers and women. School fees were reduced, and thousands of classrooms and school premises were built. All of these were achievements, even if they were uneven, that were hard to sustain and suffered also from the regime's own decision to sack striking teachers in 1984, which had a devastating impact on the lives of thousands (Chouli 2012: 6–8).

Despite these achievements, the government was still locked into a deeply unequal relationship with the world economy. The recession that rocked the continent stung and chaffed Burkina Faso's radical government severely. The country's economy was dependent on gold and cotton, with cotton comprising half of all export revenue. Although cotton production increased from 60,000 tons a year from 1980 to 170,000 tons in 1987, the actual income levels, despite this increase, barely rose. Cotton continued its inexorable fall since 1960 – Sankara was powerless to affect this (World Bank 1989).

Cash crop production, as Sankara knew, actually contributed to the country's overall instability. Attempts, valiant though they were, to diversify the economy into production and manufactured goods were important but remained largely symbolic. Food instability – another target for reform of the CNR – deepened in the 1980s, so in 1984 and 1985; the government was forced to import food, triggering a dramatic trade deficit. The sacred cow of contemporary African finance ministers, foreign investment, remained pathetic under the CNR, so the deficit was filled by long-term borrowing which doubled the country's debt burden by 1987. Economic and financial independence remained a dream. The regime's relationship with the World Bank was fraught. The original aim of the government as we have seen was to extend Burkina Faso's potential, to make as much use of the country's resources as possible. Gold mines were opened; there was an attempt to build a railway line in 1985 – which was valiantly undertaken by the regime itself after the World Bank and other donors refused funding – to connect manganese fields in the northeast to the rest of the country; local businesses were subsidised; a poll tax on local farmers was lifted. The project was not so much anti-capitalist as national capitalist development and the World Bank was not always opposed to many of the measures: it found, in 1989, that economic growth in Burkina Faso, between 1982 and 1987, had been 'satisfactory'. A World Bank report noted that, in-particular, agriculture had performed particularly well, with an added value increase annually of 7.1 per cent, the reasons for this were linked to a number of reforms the government had pushed through, including improved land utilisation in the south and south-west and impressive use of technology in cotton production (World Bank 1989).

At a time when structural adjustment, as a condition for accepting IMF or World Bank financing, was being implemented across the continent, Burkina Faso managed to escape much of this adjustment. The reason for this was that Sankara was able to impose his own form of 'restructuring'. There was considerable control over budgetary expenditure with a reduction in public sector employment and attempts to generate private capital investments in manufacturing, in line with imposed 'reform' packages elsewhere on the continent at the time (Sandbrook 1993).

The genuine and committed efforts at agricultural reform included 'austerity' measures designed to lighten the state deficit, while the income levels of state employees, teachers and civil servants, suffered and levies were raised on workers to fund development projects. Nevertheless, these efforts (an attempt to make up for underdevelopment as a result of the country's incorporation into the global economy, less than a hundred years before), were understandable; what other tools were available to achieve such development and to alleviate the country's terrible poverty?

Sankara was nothing if not an enigma. He argued for a radical plan of national self-development, condemning in powerful terms the behaviour of ex-colonial powers, financial institutions and global capitalism. Yet he also made a kind of compromise with these bodies while attempting to build up and diversify the economy. This terrible and dangerous dance, between competing and hostile interests, meant that national capitalist interests overrode all others; the regime was left at the end of 1987 without any powerful domestic allies. Sankara was almost without comrades and some of this was due to how he conducted politics. Left-wing supporters and opponents were condemned and imprisoned and the unions were often silenced. The trade unionist Halidou Ouédraogo was unequivocal in his verdict and it was harsh, 'We do not understand how the foreign revolutionaries can have a positive verdict on Sankara, without having heard the opinion of the unions' (Martens 1989: 28).

Yet – and this is an important, indeed vital, addendum – the appearance and behaviour of the government was impressive. Ministers were no longer overlords and gods, living in the dizzying heights of luxury, extravagance and conspicuous consumption. They received modest wages, while basic health and education was delivered to the poor. In an atmosphere of national austerity, implemented from above but that included the highest office-holders in the executive, there was a genuine commitment in practice to the endeavour. Denunciations were routinely made of imperialism. The role of the big bourgeoisie was regularly denounced.

Still the verdict is mixed. Though Sankara's project was a valiant attempt at radical reform, he was unable to buck the market. He forced through what could be seen as economic restructuring and even launched a systematic attack on trade unions. Some studies have concluded that the position of enterprises was actually strengthened after 1983; wages in the public sector fell and food prices increased. Sankara's project was a self-conscious effort at capitalist modernisation and development, its characterisation as a revolution is confusing and unhelpful (Labazée 1988: 243).

IDEOLOGICAL CLARITY

The appeal for ideological clarity is not to issue orders and directives from a mountain top, from where we can survey and shout instructions to the frenzy and chaos of human society. At the end of 1960 the Algerian revolutionary, Frantz Fanon, travelled through newly independent West Africa. With comrades in the Front de libération nationale (FLN), he sought to find a route to supply the liberation movement fighting the French in Algeria, from the south. Fanon's sub-regional reconnaissance trip in November and December 1960, through Guinea, Mali and into Southern Algeria, was a practical attempt to bring the continent and its struggle for liberation, North and South, together. On the journey, Fanon wrote notes to himself that were never intended for publication.

Among his notes was the apprehension that the continent, with its colonial divisions, must be done away with. But most importantly, Fanon concluded:

> Colonialism and its derivatives do not as a matter of fact constitute the present enemies of Africa. In a short time this continent will be liberated. For my part, the deeper I enter into the cultures and the political circles the surer I am that the great danger that threatens Africa is the absence of ideology.
>
> (Fanon 1967: 186)

Fanon saw the absence of ideology, the confusion of the project for radical transformation on the continent, as an acute danger as the continent reached for liberation. It is in this absence (or rather the lack of clarity on ideological questions) that much of the continent's post-independence history can be written. Sankara and his comrades, including left-wing supporters in the Parti Africain de l'Indépendance (PAI), argued that they stood as revolutionaries in the traditions of the Russian revolution. Yet, all of them were equally infected by a notion of socialism from above, and the revolutionary process as state edict and control. They claimed this politics for socialism, but in reality it was a Stalinist aberration.

Despite Sankara's speeches being replete with references to the people, seeing them as 'leading' the Burkinabé revolution, the actual involvement of these popular masses was tightly constrained. In some respects, the statement of their leading role in the revolution, was a declaration of abstract 'future' intent. Babou Paulin Bamouni, one of Sankara's leading advisors, was clear that the middle class had led the revolution, but that at some later, ill-defined stage the path for the peasantry and working class would be cleared (Bamouni 1986).

Again, these elements of 'substitution' of the military regime for the working class, the heroic guerrilla for the peasantry, the idealised proletariat for the revolutionary agent, have a rich and troubled history in independent Africa. In Guinea-Bissau, the revolutionary leader, Cabral, explained the historical role played by the middle class, in the place of a weak or non-existent working class, 'the stratum which most rapidly becomes aware of the need to free itself from foreign domination':

> This historical responsibility is assumed by the sector of the petty-bourgeoisie which, in the colonial context, can be called revolutionary ... In place of a 'real proletariat' an 'ideal' one would be comprised of a class of students and intellectuals who would help create unity between the oppressed classes and combat ethnic divisions.
>
> (Cabral 1969: 88–89)

The intelligentsia had to commit class suicide to become an ideal proletariat. The radical military coup in Burkina Faso becomes the revolutionary movement *par excellence*.

In 1960s Congo, the greatest 'peasant' fighter of the second half of the twentieth century, Che Guevara, fought in the name of the working class – a class that was not actually 'invisible' in African political economy, but was absent in the projects that were undertaken in its name. Sankara, in different ways, became part of this tradition of radical substitutionism (Cliff 2001: 117–132).

Again and again, it was the military, then the political bureau and then finally the trusted, leading cadre who were charged with leading political transformation in the name of the disempowered and illusive people. The notion of popular movements – and their governments and programmes – involving the self-engagement and emancipation of the poor was lost. The substitute for this power, military rule, enlightened dictatorships and incorruptible presidents may be easier to mobilise (and imagine), but they remain harder to sustain. Such projects built on well-intentioned rhetoric, commitment and revolutionary iron will, survive on a limited popular base. Simply stated there can be no radical, anti-capitalist project on the continent which is not empowered by the poor themselves. Too late, Sankara realised the weakness of his own project and the base of popular support (Sankara 1987).

In the absence of these social forces Sankara is revealed as a heroic, though essentially tragic figure. Perhaps one of the most important critics of Sankara's rule in recent years has been the French activist and writer Lila Chouli. As we have seen, Sankara's social reforms were from the top-down, not the self-emancipation of the working and popular masses – indeed his reforms worked against such popular empowerment. The result of this approach, Chouli tells us, was to bring the regime into conflict with sections of the working class and its organisations. In January 1985, a trade union front was set up against the decline in democratic and trade union freedoms. Though this front remained active throughout the so-called revolutionary period, trade unions and independent organisations would be considerably undermined as a result of repression of union activity. By 1986, less than three years from 4 August 1983, the CNR's authoritarian approach had alienated sections of the Burkinabé population, leaving Sankara and his allies isolated, cut off also from elements within the ruling circles. Yet, paradoxically, these were exactly the forces that could have defended a radical project of social and political change.

As Chouli has argued, 'As a result, the government banned trade unions and the free press as these were seen as obstacles to the CNR's reforms'. Additionally, as an admirer of Fidel Castro's Cuban Revolution, Sankara set up Cuban-style Comités de Défense de la Révolution (Committees for the Defence of the Revolution, CDRs). In principle, all Burkinabès were members of the

CDRs and critics and opponents were branded 'enemies of the people'. The actions of the trade unions were considered subversive and could be punished with 'military sanctions'. The ruling CNR found itself unable to conduct a meaningful dialogue with other groups and the elusive 'people' about its objectives and how to achieve them. There were simply no authentic channels for this dialogue, once critics, trade unions and others had been labelled 'enemies of the people'. Chouli explains:

> In the name of wanting to make a revolution for the mass of poor people, they did it without them. Sankara recognised this in his self-critical speech of 2 October 1987. But he and his allies did not have time to restore the severed lines between the authorities and the mass independent organisations of the poor and the working class.
>
> (Chouli 2012: 6–7)

Nothing could illustrate the crisis of Sankara's project better than what happened under his executioner. Blaise Compaoré, who became the new head of the state, proclaimed that the aim of his government was a 'rectification' of the revolution. To achieve such a goal, a Popular Front was created, diverse enough to include political tendencies, trade unions and popular movements. As a consequence of this 'democratic opening', limited though it was in many ways, the trade unions were able to rebuild. In 1988, the Confédération Générale du Travail du Burkina (General Workers Confederation of Burkina, CGT-B) was formed from the trade union front of 1985. The CGT-B claims to follow revolutionary trade unionism and, in 1989, the Mouvement Burkinabé des Droits de l'Homme et des Peuples (Burkinabé Movement for Human and Peoples' Rights, MBDHP) was established. Since 1989, an alliance between the CGT-B, the MBDHP and the Union Générale des Etudiants Burkinabé (General Union of Burkinabé Students, UGEB) was generally on the frontline of popular struggles throughout the 1990s and 2000s.

CONCLUSION

We have to be extremely cautious in our criticism of Sankara; remaining wary of easy proclamations of revolutionary purism. There is no revolutionary movement that is pure, in fact a condition of a committed and serious revolutionary is the lack of purity. Sankara's project was extraordinarily daring and serious, the sort to orientate the entire state machinery – puny as it was – with its hostile class interests, against the global market. He attempted to wrestle as much autonomy from the world market as possible in an effort to build up Burkina Faso's economic independence.

Sankara's project was state-led development orientated to the poor, as part of a perceived transition to socialism, though a socialism that remained almost completely absent in his official speeches and declarations. Carried out by a military hierarchy and an even smaller political cadre around Sankara – on behalf of the poor – the project was inherently elitist. This is not a criticism, rather a description.

The story of Sankara is one of absences: of other social forces, of radical left organisations, of a social base that could have sustained his project. The presence of an ideological and organisational centre for the radical left in Burkina Faso *and* the region, could have ensured the permanence of a 'project' of delinking from the world market as part of a radicalising movement across West Africa and the continent. This could have developed as a practical and realistic alternative. There was no such tradition. In the dramatic lacuna of the regions left, Sankara's project was a brave attempt to create a strong and independent national economy – but it was also severally constrained by conservative forces in the region and the global economy marching in another direction.

By 1987 the isolation of the ruling military group around Sankara was almost total. Sankara, true to form, refused the option of breaking the regime's isolation (and principles) by incorporating a wider circle of openly establishment parties. But the crisis and isolation was real. Blaise Compaoré, his comrade and friend, had no such compunction and did not want to see his power overthrown with Sankara. Knowing he would fail to persuade his comrade in argument, Compaoré resorted to the murder of Sankara and his loyalists. The murder of Sankara marked the end of incredibly brave, though mislabelled, Burkinabé revolution.

REFERENCES

Bamouni, B. P. (1986) *Burkina Faso: Processus De La Revolution*. Paris: L'Harmattan.

Cabral, A. (1969) *Revolution in Guinea: An African People's Struggle*. London: Stage 1.

Chouli, L. (2012) *Enough is Enough: Burkina Faso 2011*. Botswana: International Socialist Tendency. Retrieved on 1 June 2017 from http://roape.net/site/wp-content/uploads/2016/04/burkinafasopamphlet.pdf.

Cliff, T. (2001) 'Trotsky on Substitutionism' in *International Struggle and the Marxist Tradition*. London: Bookmarks.

Davidson, B. (1978) *Africa In Modern History: The Search For A New Society*. London: Penguin.

Fanon, F. (1967) *Towards the African Revolution*. New York: Grove.

Harsch, E. (2014) *Thomas Sankara: An African Revolutionary*. Athens, OH: Ohio University Press.

Harvey, D. (2005) *A Brief History of Neo-Liberalism*. Oxford: Oxford University Press.

Hobsbawm, E. (1995) *Age of Extremes*. London: Abacus.

Labazée, P. (1988) *Entreprises et Entrepreneurs du Burkina Faso: Vers une Lecture Anthropologique de l'Entreprise Africaine*. Paris: Karthala.

Marfleet, P. (1998) Globalisation and the Third World. *International Socialism Journal* 81.

Martens, L. (1989) *Sankara, Compaoré et la Révolution Burkinabé*. Anvers: EPO.

Sandbrook, R. (1993) *The Politics of Africa's Economic Recovery*. Cambridge: Cambridge University Press.

Sankara, T. (1987) Thomas Sankara: The Speech He Would Have Given on October 15 1987. *Pambazuka News*. Retrieved on 1 June 2017 from www.pambazuka.org/pan-africanism/thomas-sankara-speech-he-would-have-given-october-15-1987.

Sankara, T. (1988) *Thomas Sankara Speaks*. New York: Pathfinder.

Sankara, T. (Forthcoming) The Political Orientation Speech. In J.-C. Kongo and L. Zeilig (eds), *Voices of Liberation: Thomas Sankara*. Cape Town: HSRC Press.

Seddon, D. and Zeilig, L. (2005) Class and Protest in Africa: New Waves. *Review of African Political Economy* 33(103).

Walton, J. and Seddon, D. (1994) *Free Markets and Food Riots: The Politics of Global Adjustment*. Oxford: Blackwell.

World Bank (1989) *Burkina Faso: Economic Memorandum*. Washington, DC: World Bank.

Zeilig, L. and Seddon, D. (2009) Marxism, Class and Resistance in Africa. In L. Zeilig (ed.), *Class Struggle and Resistance in Africa*. Chicago, IL: Haymarket.

CHAPTER 4

When Visions Collide

Thomas Sankara, Trade Unions and the Revolution in Burkina Faso, 1983–1987

Craig Phelan

INTRODUCTION

During the popular uprisings that gathered momentum after 2011 and eventually led to the 2014 overthrow of Blaise Compaoré, the image and name of Thomas Sankara was everywhere. The crowds chanted his name, speech after speech invoked his memory and his face and his slogans were on posters and placards at nearly every rally. Although in power just a few short years at a time well before most of the protestors had been born, Sankara – the 'Che Guevara of Africa' – nevertheless personified the resistance to Compaoré's 27 years of semi-authoritarian rule. For the Balai Citoyen (Citizen's Broom), the protest organisation that captured the headlines in the foreign press and inspired the nation's youth, the image, the symbolism and the rhetoric of Sankara was fundamental (Touré 2014). He was the symbol of radical political change, of national self-sufficiency and pride, of justice, equality and hope for the future. Along with the demand that Compaoré 'dégage' (get out) was the demand that he finally be charged for the murder of Sankara, his erstwhile friend and fellow revolutionary (*Jeune Afrique* 2016). For the country's trade unions (which had been the vanguard in every significant political protest since the nation's birth until 2011, and which also played a major role in the ouster of Compaoré), the legacy of Sankara was not so straightforward.

For the older trade unionists who gathered together at Ouagadougou in December 2009 to celebrate ten years of trade union unity in the fight against Compaoré, Sankara was not remembered as a hero. Nor was he merely a face on a poster or a symbol of national unity and hope. Rather, Sankara represented the fifth and most dangerous authoritarian regime in Burkina

Faso's short history. The trade union movement took tremendous pride in its long-standing political role and its ability to challenge and destabilise every one of the regimes, especially that of Sankara. 'Since independence in 1960', the trade unionists declared in 2009, the movement had battled against each regime and the 'thousand-and-one tricks to militarise, diminish and subjugate the workers and its organisations.'

One after another, trade unions had fought against the governments of Maurice Yaméogo (1959–1966), Sangoulé Lamizana (1966–1980), Colonel Saye Zerbo's CMRPN (Comité Militaire de Redressement pour le Progrès National) (1980–1982), Jean-Baptiste Ouédraogo's CSP (Conseil de Salut du Peuple) (1982–1983), 'and especially the accession to power of the Conseil National de la Révolution (CNR) of Captain Thomas Sankara on 4 August 1983' (Coupé 2009). For trade unionists, the battles against Sankara were little different than those against Compaoré or any other regime, because each had tried to 'liquidate' the trade unions, and, having failed, each sought to 'weaken them, to militarise them, and to control them by repression, corruption, and division' (UAS 2009: 8). On another occasion in 2009, one veteran radical trade unionist recalled that, while the Sankara years were 'often presented as a 'progressive' period', they were in fact 'marked by a very hard authoritarianism' and a virtual ban on the trade unions that resisted 'the confiscation of their power by the CDRs (Comités de défense de la révolution)'. Many of the founders of the CGT-B (Confédération Générale du Travail du Burkina), which emerged from the wreckage of the Sankara years in 1988 and remains Burkina Faso's most radical and influential trade union confederation, 'had been imprisoned, tortured, (and) banned from professional employment during this period' (Coupé 2009).

The 'war' between the trade unions and Sankara's CNR tells us a great deal about the failure of the 4 August revolution. By any measure, Burkina Faso is one of the poorest countries in the world, and its political instability since independence in 1960 has been one among many impediments to economic growth. Its semi-authoritarian military and civilian leadership has pursued a neo-colonial path to economic survival, one based on close relations to, and loans from, France. Yet, Burkina Faso has always been fertile ground for more progressive alternatives, and in the 1980s two powerful radical forces took centre-stage in a struggle for control of the country's destiny. On the one hand was the Afro-centred populism of Thomas Sankara, who took power in a military coup and pursued a revolutionary programme that included a restructuring of the countryside. Sankara's pursuit of agricultural self-sufficiency, economic populism, meaningful independence from France, women's rights, environmentalism and other reforms made him a heroic figure throughout the developing world. On the other hand, the militant trade union movement, which had always been a major political force in the country, pursued a wage-labour centred vision of democratic modernisation, one that privileged the salaried public sector workers rather than the peasants. The struggle between the two forces was both ideological and real, leading to mass sackings and imprisonment of radical trade unionists. The key issue in the struggle was Sankara's creation of 'revolutionary committees' in all workplaces (the CDRs de service), a Leninist strategy to transform autonomous trade unionism into a pliant tool of the ruling party. In the end, trade union opposition to Sankara's revolution was powerful enough to help destabilise the regime and pave the way for Sankara's 1987 assassination and the 'rectification' of the revolution in the years that followed. Equally important, the struggle illuminates the tensions between the populist-agrarian and the wage-labour-centred visions of socialism that play such a vital role in many developing countries.

BURKINA FASO'S TRADE UNION MOVEMENT

On the eve of the 4 August Revolution, the trade union movement in Burkina Faso was the most impressive in all of French-speaking Africa (see Kabeya-Muase 1989a; Sandwidi 1996; Engels 2015; Phelan 2016). As was true of many other African trade union movements, membership was largely restricted to the public sector (education, transport, communication and health services), the state bureaucracy and the handful of parastatals. Trade unionism in Burkina Faso was therefore small in numbers, but it wielded far more influence than its membership would suggest. Unlike all other trade union movements in the former French colonies, le syndicalisme Burkinabè had successfully defended its autonomy since independence in 1960. During the struggle against French colonial rule, trade unions and nationalist movements had been partners. Strikes and labour protests damaged colonial economic interests and therefore aided the push for independence. Once independence was achieved, and nationalist movements became one-party states, trade unions were instantly transformed from allies to enemies. Whether the political leaders pursued radical socialist agendas like Guinea's Sékou Touré or Benin's Mathieu Kérékou, or moderate pro-West agendas such as Côte d'Ivoire's Félix Houphouët-Boigny, all political leaders in francophone Africa recognised the threat that a vibrant, independent trade union movement posed to their political and economic ambitions, and all took steps to neutralise that threat (Phelan 2011).

By legislation or by force, each francophone African state by the mid-1970s had either suppressed the trade union movement or absorbed it into the state apparatus (Martens 1994). Each state, that is, except Burkina Faso. Here, the labour movement remained fiercely combative, autonomous of state control, extremely jealous of its legal right to organise and strike and proud of its victories over the succession of semi-authoritarian leaders who had sought to subdue it.

As Sankara himself put it, 'in Burkina Faso strikes have always been used to make and break governments' (interview with Jean-Philippe Rapp, 1985: 224). Four factors help explain the strength and resilience of the labour movement: the relative weakness of the state in Burkina Faso; the capacity of trade unions to overcome ideological and organisational differences when faced with a crisis; the close alliance between student unions and the labour movement; and trade unionism's ability to identify itself with popular democratic struggles in the urban centres and thereby create mass unrest. For example, when the country's first president, Maurice Yaméogo, sought to force all trade unions into a state-controlled confederation and restrict the right to strike, trade unions created a united front, organised coordinated strikes and protests and led a mass march toward the presidential palace that forced Yaméogo to resign in 1966 (Phelan 2016).

While adept at protecting its autonomy, and powerful enough to undermine any regime, trade unionism was not strong enough to construct and impose an alternative political agenda. When not under threat, trade union unity vanished and the movement was beset by a disheartening pluralism, with confederations and independent unions representing the entire political spectrum. There were moderate trade union confederations (UGTB, CNTB and ONSL) that at times issued radical-sounding propaganda but were largely reformist. There were also two avowedly revolutionary confederations (USTB and CSB) (Sandwidi 1996). Pan-Africanist and defiant, the USTB (Union syndicale des travailleurs du Burkina Faso) pledged itself independent of any political party but dedicated to social justice and the 'elimination' of all forces 'reactionary, imperialist, feudal and neo-colonial' in order to create 'a true independence for Burkina Faso' (Sandwidi 1996: 330). The CSB (Confederation syndicale burkinabé) was equally radical. It, too, declared itself independent of all parties, although its general secretary, Soumane Touré, also served as the head the Ouagadougou branch of the pro-Soviet group, LIPAD (Ligue patriotique pour le développement) (Kabeya-Muase 1989b).

The 4 August revolution was at first nothing more than a military coup, one of several that had already taken place in Burkina Faso's short history. To translate the military takeover into a popular movement, Sankara needed the trade unions. They were the bridge between the military and the 'people' in the urban centres. Sankara had known radical trade unionists from the USTB and the CSB before the revolution because he and his co-revolutionaries from the military – Blaise Compaore, Jean-Baptiste Lingani and Henri Zongo – were part of the radical scene. It had been the left-wing officers and trade unions working together that brought Jean-Baptiste Ouédraogo to the presidency in November 1982 with Sankara as prime minister and after the 4 August revolution, Sankara depended on the trade unions to consolidate his authority among public sector workers and government fonctionnaires. 'Our main support is from the organised workers,' Thomas Sankara explained in a March 1984 interview. 'Without them we couldn't have won, they prepared the masses for us' (*Afrique-Asie* 318, 12 March 1984: 21).

THE OUTBREAK OF WAR

Sankara was a keen student of history who claimed to have read the entire works of Lenin. His favourite book was *The State and Revolution*, which was for him, alongside the Bible and the Koran, the most important book ever written, the one that 'provides an answer to problems that require a revolutionary solution' (Sankara interview in *Jeune Afrique*, 12 March 1986: 262). Yet Sankara was no ideologue. He rejected the label socialist and he was offended by any other label (such as Marxist or Leninist) that suggested Africans were incapable of their own radical traditions and had to adhere to European templates. 'It's a continual practice of Eurocentrism to always uncover spiritual fathers for Third World leaders', he said. 'Why do you want to put us in an ideological slot at any price, to classify us?' (*Genève Afrique* 1986: 39). The multi-faceted programme that Sankara adopted for his revolution (the Discours d'Orientation Politique or DOP) was highly eclectic; it was an anti-imperialist, Pan-African populism, coupled with land reform and women's rights. While the revolutionary programme can in no way be characterised as Marxist–Leninist, Sankara and the CNR nevertheless exhibited a Leninist understanding of trade unions and the role of the revolutionary party.

'The proletariat constitutes the true revolutionary force capable of driving the revolution to triumph', declared Sankara's press secretary, Babou Bamouni. To take its place 'at the head of the revolution', however, the proletariat required education so that it could be 'armed ideologically with Marxist–Leninism'. At present, there existed an 'aristocratic' element among the working class, and there were many workers lacking 'revolutionary consciousness'. Equally dangerous were the 'reactionary trade unions' led by 'petit-bourgeois incapable of accepting their political suicide' (Bamouni 1986: 122–127). Before they could play a leading role in the revolution, therefore, the reactionary trade unions needed to be 'liquidated' and the labour movement brought under the tutelage of the CDRs de service, established in all workplaces, which represented the spirit of the revolution. Once the CDRs de service eliminated the existing 'politically and ideologically eclectic trade unionism', a single state-controlled confederation (une centrale syndicale unique) would emerge 'in the service of the Revolution' (ibid.). Theoretically, the revolution allowed for the continued existence of trade unions, but their autonomy would have to be abandoned and their role redefined.

In practice this meant that, despite peaceful overtures on the eve of the 4 August Revolution, Sankara's CNR pursued an anti-trade union agenda remarkably similar to that pursued by virtually every one-party state in francophone Africa before it. The 'Révolution démocratique et populaire' sought to marginalise the labour movement by creating a state-controlled alternative (the CDR de service in the first instance and a more permanent state-controlled confederation in the future). At the same time, it used the repressive apparatus of the state to destroy the most vocal trade union opposition, to arbitrarily imprison the most charismatic leaders and to undermine the most potent weapon in the arsenal of the movement – the right to strike. For a regime that exhibited revolutionary thinking on so many fronts, there was nothing at all novel in the CNR's approach to trade unionism. Nor was the result novel, at least not in the context of Burkinabè politics.

The ideological cleavages that marked trade unionism since its inception made it far easier for the revolutionary government to ignore it, to suppress it and to set up revolutionary agencies that bypassed it. Trade union disunity could be discerned in the various reactions to the 4 August coup. The more moderate trade union confederations (UGTB, CNTB and ONSL) adopted a wait-and-see attitude. Having seen numerous governments come and go, each one making exaggerated pronouncements, the moderates wanted to make sure that the new government survived before declaring their support or opposition. Many of the autonomous trade unions were wary and even hostile to the new regime from the very beginning. Fiercely protective of trade union independence, they looked suspiciously at a takeover of junior military officers determined to remake society in the name of the people. They rightly regarded 4 August as a military coup and not a genuinely popular uprising and they feared that the new regime, despite its promises, would seek to undermine trade union autonomy just like every regime before it. The radical CSB was the only trade union confederation to unreservedly endorse the coup. Led by Soumane Touré, the CSB threw itself wholeheartedly behind Sankara and the CNR. It applauded the coup as a revolutionary insurrection that had liberated the people from neo-colonial oppression. The CSB called for the unification of the entire labour movement to better serve the revolution. The CSB, of course, expected to be the organisation into which all other confederations would merge and those who failed to do so would be exposed as reactionaries and imperialists (Sandwidi 1996: 336–337).

The most significant trade union to declare its opposition to the CNR from the outset was the powerful teachers' union, SNEAHV (Syndicat national des enseignants africains de Haute-Volta). This opposition was anticipated, since this union alone had endorsed the hated CMRPN regime (1980–1982) and was allied with the political party FPV (Front progressiste voltaïque) of Joseph Ki-Zerbo. As were all political parties, the FPV had been banned and the progressive and popular Ki-Zerbo had gone into exile. The CNR, the teachers' union declared, was 'just another name for the fascism' that the country had experienced under the CSP (1982–1983) and it warned that the new regime would soon implement 'anti-worker' measures (Kabeya-Muase 1989b: 50–51). This attack sparked a ferocious war of words between the CNR and SNEAHV, with the former blasting the latter as 'anti-revolutionary', 'rotten state employees' and 'the last bastion of reaction' (Kabeya-Muase 1989a: 199). Words turned to repression when, on 9 March 1984, the CNR arrested three leaders of SNEAHV, accusing them of plotting against the state in collusion with the FPV (Englebert 1986: 153). In response, the union called a strike on 20 March. The members of the union showed impressive organisational discipline and most members heeded the strike call. Sankara and the CNR immediately and imperiously sacked all 1380 striking teachers. The dismissed teachers at once lost both their jobs and their pensions. Sankara later justified this action by claiming this was not simply a labour dispute, but rather an act of treason. The teachers 'were fired for waging a strike that was, in reality, a subversive movement against Burkina Faso ... We aren't against the teachers but against the plot that was using the teachers' (interview with Jean-Philippe Rapp, 1985: 223–224).

The mass sacking of 1380 teachers in March 1984 was an unmitigated political blunder. True, SNEAHV's leaders were hostile to the regime, but the union had already marginalised itself in the wider labour movement due to its collaboration with a previous government (that of Zerbo), the despised CMRPN. The mass dismissal of striking teachers was the act of an autocrat and it accomplished what had occurred only twice before in Burkina Faso's history: the unification of the country's fractious labour movement. As had happened in 1966 and again in 1975 (and later in 1999 in an effort to oust Compaoré), a grave political threat to trade union autonomy inspired the movement to overcome its ideological pluralism and band together in a united front (Front syndical). Hoping to divide and conquer his political rivals, Sankara had in fact antagonised and unintentionally unified the only force capable of challenging his one-party rule. In February 1985, the Front syndical could point to a litany of systematic infringements of trade union autonomy: the firing of 47 militants; the arrest of 200 trade union leaders; 47 cases of torture; more than 20 cases of armed prevention of trade union assemblies and incessant intervention in the leadership and functioning of trade unions (Sandwidi 1996: 344).

The second political blunder of Sankara's regime was the refusal to abandon the CDRs de service. While the geographical CDRs were necessary to carry the revolution beyond the cities to the villages, the effort to establish CDRs in all workplaces needlessly made enemies of erstwhile trade union supporters. Another strong teachers' union, SUVESS (Syndicat unique voltaïque des enseignants du secondaire et du supérieur) publicly declared its opposition to the attempt to 'substitute the CDRs for the trade unions' and 'refused all efforts to make a vassal of trade unionism' (*Carrefour Africain*, 13 January 1984: 23).

The CNR's insistence on CDRs de service also cost the revolution the support of the most influential of the trade union confederations, the CSB. Soumane Touré had declared the support of his confederation from the outset of the revolution. He was fully prepared to allow Sankara to use the CSB as the official state-controlled labour movement. Touré thus proposed what all leaders of one-party regimes in francophone Africa had sought: the absorption of the trade union movement into the apparatus of the state. Sankara's refusal of this offer was a mistake. His single-minded determination to use the CDRs de service to displace trade unionism in the workplace and to undermine the movement's role as interlocutor between the government and the salaried workers can only be explained by a dictatorial drive that precluded any deviation from the revolutionary plan. Rather than an ally, Soumane Touré was deemed an enemy of the state. The result was to drive the CSB into the Front syndical in January 1985, marking a major escalation of the war between the regime and trade unionism (Englebert 1986: 152–155).

Having needlessly created an enemy of the trade union movement, Sankara showed no willingness to compromise. His regime tried to weaken the confederations from within through paid informants and infiltrators who sought to destroy unity, capture elections, hold rival congresses and provoke illegal activity. His regime imprisoned the most outspoken trade unionists and tortured many, dismissed others from employment, labelled many enemies of the state and characterised the entire movement as petit bourgeois. In this, Sankara's behaviour toward the trade unions was no different than previous heads of state in Burkina Faso and other francophone African states. The decision to co-opt the May Day celebration was Sankara's one novel anti-union strategy. By high-jacking this symbolically and organisationally significant annual event, so vital to trade unionists' sense of identity, and by turning it into an affair of peasants rather than salaried workers, the regime sought to impose its dominance (Sandwidi 1996: 343–345). Yet none of these tactics worked. The spirit of defiance among trade unionists ran deep. Despite all his revolutionary fervour, his charisma and the nobility of his vision to transform every facet of life in Burkina Faso, Sankara's brutal and clumsy attempts to destroy the country's proud and militant trade union movement was no more idealistic and no more effective than previous efforts had been.

To his credit, Sankara remained true to his word and never passed legislation restricting the right to strike. This issue was critical to trade unionism and Sankara understood how the CMRPN's effort in that direction had undermined that regime. Yet the dismissal of 1380 teachers made the right to strike largely null and void in practice. Even without resorting to strikes, however, the trade union movement never succumbed to the systematic effort of the CNR to repress it. Its resolve never wavered even when its resistance was reduced largely to propaganda attacks against the regime. Most notably, even the CNR's menacing decree of April 1987 which outlawed all trade union propaganda that was 'incompatible with the institutions and the interests of the nation' failed to stem the tide of opposition. The CSB refused to replace Soumane Touré as its leader even after his arrest on 30 May 1987 and his imprisonment as a 'counter-revolutionary' (Kabeya-Muase 1989a: 217–222).

THE COSTS OF WAR

The unsuccessful war against trade unionism weakened the Sankara regime by denying it the support of the educated, the salaried, the urban and the students. To be sure, there were many true believers in the CDRs de service who honestly believed that the trade union movement constituted an internal enemy – a reactionary fifth column that needed to be eliminated or absorbed. Many activists in the CDRs de service were not motivated by any promise of reward to infiltrate and undermine the CSB and other confederations of the Front syndical. Rather, they were motivated by the revolution itself and by unflinching loyalty to Sankara. There is much to admire in this political commitment, just as there is much to admire in the revolution itself. However, the war against the trade unions pitted the only two viable progressive forces in the country – radicals in the ranks of the military and trade unionists – against each other. It was a weakness that manifested itself in growing discontent within the revolution itself. When the opposition began to coalesce around Blaise Compaoré, he became convinced that a coup would succeed and the revolution could be 'rectified'. It is not a coincidence that among Compaoré's first actions as the new head of state was to re-employ all the teachers of SNEAHV who had been dismissed and to release all trade unionists from prison (Kabeya-Muase 1989a: 224).

The Sankara years revealed yet again the tenacity and the fierce autonomy of the Burkinabè trade unions, highlighting their unique strength among all other trade union movements in francophone Africa. Yet, the Sankara years also exposed the movement's limitations. Although powerful enough to survive in a hostile environment, and, when unified, capable of weakening both civilian and military governments that dared to oppose it, trade unionism in Burkina Faso was neither sufficiently unified nor powerful enough to reshape politics by itself. Its power was wielded within the confines of that triumvirate of forces that has always dominated politics in the country: a semi-authoritarian civilian political elite; a politicised military that regards itself as the final arbiter of political power and a trade unionism strong enough and belligerent enough to topple unpopular regimes (Phelan 2016). The revolution of 4 August successfully eliminated, albeit temporarily, the civilian political elite as well as the traditional chiefs who still held sway outside the cities, but the revolution was not powerful enough to silence the trade unions. With the rectification of the revolution under Compaoré, the civilian political elite was revived and the triumvirate was restored.

Given the initial promise of the revolution and its progressive goals, one might ask why the labour movement did not commit itself more wholeheartedly to it at the outset. Radicalism in the military overlapped with radicalism in the trade union movement in Ouagadougou. In the small radical circles, they debated and discussed Marx, Lenin, Mao and the Cuban Revolution together. The 4 August revolution seemed to be a radical rupture, a momentous transition in Burkina Faso's politics, a chance for this poverty-stricken nation to build a more egalitarian society, to defy the neo-colonialist control of France and to build a better future based on a socialist vision steeped in African traditions (Harsch 2013). The promise of true independence and national unity came in the form of a young military officer charismatic enough to possibly make that dream a reality. For a trade union movement to oppose the revolution, to undermine it through a propaganda war, to challenge many of its initiatives – seemingly places that movement on the wrong side of the struggle for justice. And that is the peculiar legacy for a movement that stood alone – before and after Sankara – as the only progressive institutional force on the national scene.

Perhaps the Sankarists were correct. Perhaps the failure of trade unionism to take a more positive role in the revolution illustrates Lenin's critique of trade unionism. They were manifesting a limited 'trade union consciousness' while Sankara and his regime had elevated to 'revolutionary consciousness'. Whereas the former meant a fixation on the conditions of labour and the amelioration of the worst aspects of capitalist society, the latter implied a clear understanding of the global forces at work and the need to displace capitalist production altogether. It is true that trade unions did not generally appreciate the salary and benefit reductions imposed by the CNR, or the cost-saving shrinking of the civil service that meant job loss for some trade unionists and anxiety for students who aspired to work in the civil service. The wage bill of the public sector represented an enormous slice of the national budget (almost 75 per cent), and the revolution proposed to reduce that slice and shift national resources to agricultural development. In the long run, Sankara's drive for agricultural self-sufficiency posed a serious threat to the public sector and the state bureaucracy, which were the backbone of Burkinabè trade unionism. Thus, to a certain extent, trade union defiance of Sankara's agenda reflected a desire to protect its own members, to secure their jobs and their salaries and to prevent a major redistribution of resources that would have spelt doom for their movement. Viewed from this perspective, the trade union movement appears as another privileged sector of the old society – along with the political elite and the traditional chiefs in the countryside – that had to be swept away for the revolution to proceed (for a Marxist–Leninist analysis of the revolution, see World to Win 1980).

Trade union consciousness manifested itself in an even more fundamental way, one that has been an impediment to African trade unionism since its inception: the failure to organise the non-salaried unorganised workers who made up the clear majority of the population. Even today, as African trade unionism is disappearing after decades of neo-liberal structural adjustment has decimated the public sector, African trade unions find it exceptionally difficult to organise the self-employed majority in the informal sector. The labour movement in Burkina Faso remained trapped in an essentially European conception of trade unionism, in which the working class was the vanguard of change. Trade unionists imagined themselves – the salaried, formal workforce that comprised no more than four per cent of the population – as the working class. Seldom did those in the movement conceptualise the peasants as the vanguard in a Maoist sense, or the self-employed informal sector workers as the true Africa working class. Sankara incorporated the peasants in his vision of the future in a way that trade unionists never did. Sankara may have been extremely clumsy in his efforts to transform the countryside. His public works projects may have been reminiscent of the colonial system of forced labour and the CDRs in the countryside often provoked resentment rather than enthusiasm for the revolution. Yet, Sankara at least realised that agricultural self-sufficiency was a critical first step and that any revolution needed to address the issue of peasant poverty. The trade unions never came to that realisation. They clung to self-serving ideas about who constituted the working class and they resisted the shifting of the nation's resources to the countryside.

The war against the trade unions exposed the dictatorial, one-party mentality of Sankara and the CNR. They exhibited the same intolerance of dissent, the same arbitrary, authoritarian impulse and the same refusal to engage in any meaningful social dialogue that characterised every other regime that has ruled Burkina Faso. The insistence on distinguishing between the true and the false revolutionary, the readiness to find subversion everywhere and the recourse to arbitrary violations of civil liberties created a 'democratic deficit' (Guissou 1995: 91–94) and a 'spiral of violence' (Lejeal 2002) that was at once ineffective and made a mockery of the name 'Révolution démocratique et populaire'. Sankara undermined his own regime by fighting the same opponent in the same way as the political elite who came before him. Most of the labour movement responded to him in the same way that it had responded to each previous regime. A wait-and-see attitude became transformed into an oppositional stance when it became clear that, despite the early promises of dialogue, and despite Sankara's refreshingly progressive perspective on a host of issues, his insistence on one-party rule and a war against the trade unions showed him to be part of the political continuum rather than a complete break from it. Consequently his regime suffered the same fate as those that came before.

CONCLUSION

The war between the trade unions and the Sankara regime greatly undermined the latter and exposed the weaknesses of both. Sankara grossly underestimated the political power of Burkina Faso's trade unions. That is surprising, given the fact that the combativeness and fierce autonomy of Burkina Faso's labour movement had led to major confrontations with every government since independence. Sankara seemed not to recognise that the very fighting capacity of the trade unions had destabilised the CMRPN and made possible the success of his own 4 August Revolution. Nor did Sankara foresee that the same trade union bellicosity could easily weaken his own regime and pave the way for the success of a coup against him. Sankara failed to appreciate the central role that trade unions played in Burkina Faso's politics. They were the expression of political opposition on the streets of the urban centres, in the schools, in every public building and in the state bureaucracy. The trade unions were the interlocutors between the salaried minority and the young, educated people who hoped to join their ranks. Trade unions were the voice of the educated, the radical and the urban. While trade union membership was small, the trade unions had always possessed the ability to organise mass protest, to shut down the capital and to topple governments. Sankara should have known better than to underestimate them.

REFERENCES

Bamouni, B. P. (1986) *Burkina Faso: Processus de la Révolution*. Paris: L'Harmattan.

Coupé, A. (2009) Les 20 ans de la CGT-B. *La Revue: Solidaires International* 4(1): 19–24.

Engels, B. (2015) Trade Unionism in Burkina Faso. *Revue Tiers Monde* 224(2): 67–82.

Englebert, P. (1986) *La Révolution Burkinabè*. Paris: L'Harmattan.

Guissou, B. (1995) *Burkina Faso: Un espoir en Afrique*. Paris: L'Harmattan.

Harsch, E. (2013) The Legacies of Thomas Sankara: A Revolutionary Experience in Retrospect. *Review of African Political Economy* 40(137): 358–374.

Jeune Afrique (2016) La justice Burkinabè a annulé les mandats d'arrêt contre Compaoré et Soro. *Jeune Afrique*, 29 April. Retrieved on 1 December 2017 from www.jeuneafrique.com/321756/societe/justice-burkinabe-annules-mandats-darret-contre-compaore-soro.

Kabeya-Muase, C. (1989a) *Syndcalisme et démocratie en Afrique Noir: L'expérience Du Burkina Faso*. Paris: Karthala.

Kabeya-Muase, C. (1989b) 'Un pouvoir des travailleurs peut-il etre contre les syndicats?', *Politique Africaine* 33(2): 50–58.

Lejeal, F. (2002) *Le Burkina Faso*. Paris: Karthala.

Martens, G. (1994) French-Speaking Africa. In A. Trebilcock et al. (eds), *Towards Social Dialogue: Tripartite Cooperation in National Economic and Social Policy-making*, 297–329. Geneva: ILO.

Phelan, C. (2011) West African Trade Unionism Past and Present. In C. Phelan (ed.),

Trade Unions in West Africa: Historical and Contemporary Perspectives, 1–22. Oxford: Peter Lang.

Phelan, C. (2016) Plus ça change: Trade Unions, the Military and Politics in Burkina Faso, 1966 and 2014. *Labor History* 57(1): 107–125.

Sandwidi, K. (1996) Syndicalisme et pouvoir politique: De la répression a la résistance. In R. Otayek, F. M. Sawadogo and J.-P. Guingané (eds), *Le Burkina entre révolution et démocratie, 1983–1993*, 325–352. Paris: Karthala.

Sankara, T. (1985) Dare to Invent the Future. Interview with Jean-Philippe Rapp. Reproduced in Sankara, T. (2007), 189–232.

Sankara, T. (1986) On Books and Reading. Interview with *Jeune Afrique*, February. Reproduced in Sankara, T. (2007), 261–265.

Sankara, T. (2007) *Thomas Sankara Speaks: The Burkina Faso Revolution, 1983–1987* (2nd edn), Pairie, M. (ed.). New York: Pathfinder.

Touré, I. (2014) Jeunesse, mobilisations sociales et citoyenneté en Afrique de l'Ouest: etude comparée des mouvements de contestation 'Y'en A Marre' au Sénégal et 'Balai Citoyen' au Burkina Faso. Conference paper. Tunis: Council for the Development of Social Science Research in Africa.

UAS (2009) *L'Unite D'action Syndicale Au Burkina: Bilan Critique De Dix Ans De Lutes Unitaires (1999–2009)*. Ouagadougou: UAS.

World to Win (1980) The Fall of Captain Sankara, or Why You Can't Make Revolution without the Masses. *A World to Win* 10: 26–34, 56, 80.

CHAPTER 5

Africa's Sankara
On Pan-African Leadership
Amber Murrey

In the pages of many popular media outlets, online forums and academic venues, Thomas Sankara is referred to as 'Africa's Che Guevara'. Like the Argentine revolutionary, Sankara was informed by Marxist struggles, a knowledge of the history of colonialism and imperial domination of the so-called 'Third World', a steadfastness against the powerful status quo as well as military training. Both shared a focus on agrarian reform and a commitment to promoting collective well-being through a reformation of the person: Guevara encouraged people to auto-adopt new, more collective characteristics to become 'el Hombre Nuevo' (the New Man) necessary for a more egalitarian society. Sankara similarly spoke of the importance of a transformative education that would allow all Burkinabè to become new people capable of pursuing projects for 'une société nouvelle' (a new society; see Sankara 1983d). Both shared an affinity for military garb: Guevara for olive-green military fatigues and black beret and Sankara for his captain's uniform and red beret. There are many additional similarities between the two that are not captured by the somewhat glib and insufficient tag line, 'Africa's Che Guevara', and which have not been sufficiently explored.

Guevara was radicalised during his time traveling throughout South America as a medical student, when he witnessed the human costs of economic exploitation: hunger, thirst, disease and death. Sankara wanted to pursue a medical specialisation and eventually become a surgeon but his family did not have the funds necessary to pay his school fees – his experience of being rejected based on his family's poorer economic status was an early source of radicalisation for Sankara. Consequently, he won a scholarship to attend a military school (see Introduction, this volume for more on Sankara's early life). Patricia McFadden (Chapter 11, this volume) reminds us that Sankara, like Amilcar Cabral, was assassinated 'shortly after [a] critical episode of revolutionary solidarity with the Cuban revolution'. His last public speech, now titled 'You Cannot Kill Ideas', was delivered on 8 October 1987, honouring Che Guevara, who had been killed precisely twenty years before. Che's son, Camilo Guevara March, attended the speech in Ouagadougou to mark the opening of an art exhibition honouring Che. When asked about the significance of the street in Ouagadougou named after Che, Sankara responded with a statement that reflects his strong personal admiration for Che, 'This man, who gave himself entirely to the revolution, with his eternal youth, is an example. For me the most important victory is the one conquered deep inside yourself' (Sankara 1987b: 384). Before Sankara became known as 'Africa's Che' in the global revolutionary consciousness, Sankara pre-emptively described Che as 'African'. He said, Che is 'a citizen of the free world—the free world that we're building together. That's why we say that Che Guevara is also African and Burkinabè' (1987c: 422).

While this popular nomenclature – 'Sankara is Africa's Che' – facilitates a contextualisation of Sankara politically, it nonetheless situates Sankara as a mimicry of another, external leader and, in so doing, unconsciously casts him as less important. In this global popular revolutionary narrative, Sankara becomes an imitation of another figure. The implication is that to understand Sankara we begin with an understanding of Guevara. This popular labelling of Sankara mirrors the situating of the continent of Africa within a racialised discourse in which African leaders are the caricatures of other, better, more authentic leaders. Although his revolutionary commitment to radical social justice shared elements with Guevara's politics and philosophies, the chapters in this volume show that Sankara is *Africa's Sankara*. Asserting and demanding that we recognise Sankara as Africa's Sankara is more than a superficial political statement. It is part of the exigent project of decolonising the idea of 'Africa' (Mudimbe 1988) as well as the dominant idea of politics and political leadership in Africa.

In the two and a half years that it took to pull this volume together, I had countless conversations with students, activists and politically-minded Africans and Pan-Africans about Sankara's legacy and contemporary importance. One of the most commonly repeated concepts during these exchanges was that of the so-called 'leadership crisis in Africa'. Indeed, this thesis is often so unproblematised that we might refer to it officially as a mechanism of contemporary politics: 'the African Leadership Crisis' and abbreviate it as ALC. Dozens of academic and journalistic articles have been written on the seeming paradoxes of this so-called 'crisis' in leadership.[1] This one-dimensional characterisation of 'African leadership' over-simplifies 'Africa' as something uniform while pessimistically over-inflating the negative in African contexts. This is reflected in the language used to describe African governments: 'regime' and 'power' are used rather than tenure or government. Other off-handed and often un-defined terms include: Authoritarian, Autocratic, Praetorian, Putschist, Militaristic, Dictatorial, Propagandistic. Consider, on the other hand, the fact that 26 of America's 44 presidents have served in the military[2] or that its government spends more than half of its annual budget on the military (far more than any other country on the planet) and yet the US is not predominantly characterised as a 'military state' but as a 'representative democracy' and a 'constitutional republic'.

The scholarship on the 'ALC' has claimed to identify some key features and origins of the 'crisis' as: greed and the desire for personal enrichment; moral bankruptcy and corruptibility; 'pernicious ethnic and religious' animosities (Agulanna 2006: 255); an aging political cadre with a lack of interest in the general well-being of their countries; inefficient bureaucracies and more. This literature has often been less assertive regarding the origins of current African state formations and institutions. Namakula E. Mayanja's chapter in this volume draws on the scholarship of Cheikh Anta Diop and Basil Davidson to provide a richer history of the post-colonial 'burden' of the nation-state inherited by African states, which retained colonial relations and mechanisms of power and domination in the post-colonial period. Mayanja's distinction between 'leader' and 'ruler' is instructive in this context. She writes, 'rulers dominate, govern states as personal businesses and are not accountable to people', suggesting the need for more nuanced distinctions between different heads of state. In such a reading, we see that among Sankara's powerful leadership capacities was his fundamental self-sacrifice and leadership through *love* (Chapter 14, this volume).

The popular resentment against the 'leadership crisis' came to the fore in 2010, as noted by Burkinabè anthropologist and sociologist (2014), Boureïma N. Ouédraogo, when 17 African countries celebrated 50 years of independence but the celebration was subdued by popular resentments vis-à-vis an economic and political situation of on-going colonisation. Lila Chouli (2014: 265) recounts the form and scope of some of these resistance sentiments across Burkina in 2011: 'Compaoré heard the sound of marching boots and smelled the reek of smoke. The "riot" phenomenon – complete with the burning of police stations and other symbols of power ... reached proportions never before equalled'. So much so that national Independence Day celebrations were cancelled entirely that year. Ouédraogo argues that this oxymoronic marking of 50 official years of independence with the realities of violence, assassination, domination, election manipulation, poverty and coloniality planted the seeds for the jasmine revolution in Tunisia, which would overturn the presidency of Zine El Abidine Ben Ali and inspire the subsequent mobilisations against leaders of across the Middle East and Africa.

In the context of a widely proliferated and untroubled idea that there is a 'leadership crisis', Sankara's legacy emerges as an important historical figure against such a trend – as Sophie Bodénès Cohen argues in her chapter in this volume, his memory becomes a 'pacifist symbolic weapon' for contemporary resistance. French-Nigerien Anthropologist Jean-Pierre Olivier de Sardan explains some of the recent turn toward political figures like Sankara in Niger:

> the qualities that are attributed to Sankara all over Africa, rightly or wrongly, thirty years later, draw in a hollow what everyone would wish an elected president would finally dare to do and the correlative disappointment that ensues when it turns out to be no different from the others, [when it is also] so powerless to move the walls [of global economic and political hierarchy].
>
> (de Sardan 2016: n.p.)

This turning toward figures like Sankara for hope inspires both rage and despair regarding our current political moment. When young people feel like they are 'in abusive relationships' with their states and with their governments (see Fungai Machirori's 2014 reflection on her relationship with Zimbabwe), Sankara's political trajectory offers a reprieve and evidence that another political leadership is possible.

While we find reason for optimism in his life, his trajectory was equally tragic. Sankara's autopsy, only released to the public in October 2015, indicates that his body was riddled with 12 bullet holes. The bullet hole under one armpit corroborates Halouna Traoré's first-hand account of the assassination: Sankara went peacefully and knowingly to his death. Sankara most likely had his hands up in surrender when he was shot (see Chapter 6, this volume).

Sankara's assassination fits within a larger landscape of the assassinations of dangerous – indeed, 'mad' – anti-imperial leaders (see Chapters 6 and 8, this volume). Carina Ray put together a sketch of just some of the assassinations of Pan-Africanists between 1961 and 2005, including Patrice Lumumba, Amilcar Cabral, Steve Biko, Maurice Bishop, Walter Rodney and Chris Hani. *Wikipedia* now has a 'List of People Assassinated in Africa' page. While not comprehensive, it lists the killing of some 150 leaders and activists. The list does not mention the deaths of countless journalists or lesser-known protestors, including journalist and peace activist Norbert Zongo in Burkina Faso, whose body was found along with three others in a burned out car while he was investigating the torture and murder of David Ouédraogo (the former driver of François Compaoré, Blaise's brother; see Chapter 23, this volume).[3] The leadership 'crisis' thesis fails to acknowledge this larger geopolitical context, which nurtures certain leaders while actively suppressing and eliminating others.[4] I was asked recently if 'Sankara was in the wrong place at the wrong time'. This reading infers that he was too radical and too isolated – and too 'mad' – and that, therefore, his death might have been avoidable. Yet, Sankara's assassination is the norm within the historical geopolitical context of imperialism in the South in the Cold War, indeed non-aligned socialist leaders who survived, like Fidel Castro or Jerry Rawlings, were the exceptions to the norm. In his chapter in this volume, Bruno Jaffré argues, 'The contextualisation of Sankara's assassination within the political and economic events at the time underlines *the narrow path that Burkina Faso was allowed to follow'* (emphasis added).

Apart from the crude conglomeration of 'Africa' as if it were a homogenous entity, the 'African leadership crisis' tends to overlook probably the most important detriment to other kinds of leadership on the continent: economic and political imperialism and the propping up of leaders content to orchestrate and perpetuate direct domination, coercion, repression and political assassination (see Chouli 2014; Ouédraogo 2015; Chapter 6, this volume; Afterword, this volume). Benamrane (2016: 12) describes those nurtured leaders as 'skeletal elites, inaudible because already domesticated by the masters of the world of yesterday, today and tomorrow'. Against this malleable leader swayed by promises of security and wealth and intimidated by threats of violence, Sankara offers a generous leadership. In his 1985 interview with Jean-Philippe Rapp, Sankara described his nuanced attention to creating a society with tangible improvements in people's everyday lives:

> ... Other leaders have had the chance to immerse themselves in the daily lives of the people. That's where they find the necessary reserves of energy. They know that by making such-and-such a decision they'll be able to solve such-and-such a problem, and that the solution they've found is going to help thousands, even millions of people. They have a perfect grasp of the question without having studied it in a sociology department. This changes your perception of things ...
>
> (Sankara 1985: 191)

Sankara had the 'madness' to pursue a radical revolutionary agenda that fixed mental emancipation, agrarian justice and people's agency front-and-centre. Yet, the spectre of death haunted his presidency. After the death of Mozambique's President Samora Machel in October 1986, Sankara reasserted a pragmatic and unbending focus on the revolutionary aims of well-being and liberation, saying:

> With sentimentalism one cannot understand death. Sentimentalism belongs to the messianic vision of the world, which, since it expects a single man to transform the universe, inspires lamentation, discouragement, and despondency as soon as this man disappears ... Samora Machel is dead. This death must serve to enlighten and strengthen us as revolutionaries ...
>
> (Sankara 1986b: 315)

For Sankara, Machel's death revealed another suppression tactic used by counter-revolutionary forces; he explained that imperialism 'organises and orchestrates' the arming and training of mercenaries, the organisational capacity needed for large-scale surveillance and the manufacture and circulation of knowledge, information, equipment, arms and ammunitions.

Olivier de Sardan (2016) argues that Sankara is admired today because he symbolises a refusal of economic privilege, a rehabilitative politics and the courage to do politics differently. He wonders:

> What head of state will have the courage to disappoint, at least in some respects, his [*sic*] financiers, his militants, his allies, his officials … his donors? What head of state will dare to 'do politics differently', even if he has to put down many of his classical supporters? What head of state will be able to develop strategies of rupture with a whole set of established habits at the very heart of the state? What head of state will be able to assume reforms against his courtiers?[5]
>
> (de Sardan 2016: n.p.)

When we consider Sankara as a figure of promise for politics today, we cannot fail to speak to Sankara's near-explicit premonition of his own death. Does Sankara's brief presidency illustrate that another politics is possible or, given the context of his assassination, does it confirm the clout of the global capitalist system, neo-imperialism and counter-revolution?

The question shows us that, in celebrating Sankara's life as evidence of a more grounded, radical and pro-people leadership for today, we must also speak to the on-going threat of imprisonment, disappearing and death for such political leaders. The Ivoirian Pan-Africanist scholar Gnaka Lagoke asks, 'What leader has the willingness to die?' (interview with author, June 2017). A week before his own assassination, Sankara declared:

> It's true, you cannot kill ideas. Ideas do not die. That's why Che Guevara, an embodiment of revolutionary ideas and self-sacrifice, is not dead … Let's draw closer to Che … not as we would a god, not as we would an idea – an image placed above men – but rather with the feeling that we're moving toward a brother who speaks to us and to whom we can also speak … Every time we think of Che, let's try to be like him, and make this man, the combatant, live again … by rejecting material goods that seek to alienate us, by refusing to take the easy road, by turning instead to education and the rigorous discipline of revolutionary morality …
>
> (Sankara, inauguration of exhibition honouring Che Guevara in Ouagadougou, 1987b: 421–422)

We might take his words about Che as an invitation to our engagement, thirty years later, with his own life, politics and memory. His assertions against consumerism and his rejection of hagiography require similarly critical readings of the proliferation of mass produced T-shirts with his face emblazoned on the cloth.

RESPONDING TO CRITIQUES OF SANKARA

In responding to critiques of Sankara, it is first important to sketch the precarious and inherently challenging context of the revolution.[6] Again and again Sankara characterised the revolutionary project – one that holistically brought together an attention to gender, health, knowledge and education, housing, food, water, sanitation, ecology, agriculture and culture with an unbending insistence on self-sufficiency, sovereignty and dignity – as ambitious, enormous and prolonged. In response to the problem of food production alone, Sankara asserted (in the 1985 interview with Jean-Phillippe Rapp), 'we confront a combination of physical, social, and political problems that must be resolved simultaneously' (Sankara 1985: 209). When he became president, he described the state of the country:

> [We have] 7 million inhabitants, with over 6 million peasants; an infant mortality rate estimated at 180 per 1,000; an average life expectancy limited to 40 years; an illiteracy rate of up to 98 percent, if we describe as literate anyone who can read, write, and speak a language; 1 doctor for 50,000 inhabitants; 16 percent of school aged youth attending school; and finally, a per capita Gross Domestic Product of 53,356 CFA francs, or barely more than 100 US dollars ... The root of the problem was political. The solution clearly needed to be political.
>
> (Sankara 1984c: 159–160)

Sankara had a holistic understanding of transformative social change and sought to engage with all generations and genders, across all regions of the country, for a more thorough and meaningful mode of governance. He described the opening of an institute for the study of Black culture in le Faso as a 'gigantic task before us' (1984a). These words can be extrapolated to the revolution itself. The enormity of the revolutionary project cannot be overstated. As with all great social, economic and political changes, some resistance (often also in the form of counter-revolution or counter-insurgency) is unavoidable: turbulence, friction and loss are unavoidable during massive structural transformations. The challenges for realising this vision of a society were many; Sankara faced a context of considerable social heterodoxy and near-constant pressures from many different groups: from the proliferation of leaflets critical of the Comités de Défense de la Révolution (CDR) financed by Houphouet-Boigny (in Côte d'Ivoire), to the boycotts, economic sabotage and fiscal strategies to under-value Burkinabè agro-products and 'strangle' the Burkinabè economy by the French (Sankara 1985: 212), to the drafting of articles 'hostile' to Sankara by French diplomats for media and journalistic outlets (see Chapter 6, this volume).

While he pushed hard and moved quickly, with an impatient and sometimes unsympathetic efficiency, he knew that these revolutionary projects were 'ambitious'. He said, 'On the level of economic management, we're learning to live modestly, to accept and impose austerity on ourselves in order to be able to carry out ambitious projects' (Sankara 1984c). For such an immense project to be realised, there would undoubtedly be sacrifices and collateral damage. He stated bluntly that the administrative apparatus that served the status quo would be 'shattered' before being rebuilt (Sankara 1984c: 160). Against mental colonisation, Sankara called for a popular refashioning or 'reconditioning' that would encourage the cultivation of a sense of self-worth, integrity and pride for and in each person. He said, 'We have to recondition our people to accept themselves as they are, not to be ashamed of their real situation, to be satisfied with it, to glory in it, even' (Sankara 1985: 197). This shattering and refashioning would give rise to a new cultural identity, including more equitable gender relations and endogenous knowledges that would respond to the real problems and material needs of Burkinabès (Sankara 1984a, 1984b). For Sankara, this endogenous knowledge and action needed to be actively cultivated in the face of the imperialist interests that profited on the suppression of sovereignty and the perpetuation of an idea of 'Africa' as underdeveloped.[7] Much like for Amilcar Cabral, Sankara held that cultural emancipation was fundamental in the long struggle for freedom (see also Chapter 11, this volume, for more on the comparisons between Cabral and Sankara). Recognising this long struggle speaking before 1,300 delegates at the Fist National Conference of the Committees for the Defense of the Revolution (CDRs) on 4 April 1986, Sankara urged his collaborators to re-focus. Against internal and external threats, including selfishness and irresponsibility by some CDR delegates, he said, 'We must now move on to a much more conscious level of organization... we must organize ourselves a lot more scientifically, a lot more methodologically, and we must correct ourselves at every step in order to advance' (1986a: 288).

The Burkinabè historian and founder of the Parti Pour la Démocratie et le Progrès (Party for Democracy and Progress) Joseph Ki-Zerbo was one of Sankara's most well-known and also well-respected critics. Surprisingly, perhaps, Ki-Zerbo's understanding of both revolution and Pan-African unity reflects much of Sankara's own approach, although with noted distinctions. Both maintained a focus on Burkinabè values and cultures for a transformation of Bukinabè social relations. While Sankara remained vigilant of the tendency to romanticise pre-colonial institutions and relations and called for a transformation of the social system that would rise out of contemporary realities (rather than return to pre-colonial relations), Ki-Zerbo has been critiqued for sometimes citing 'pell-mell' indigenous or African practices, including 'the conception of the traditional practice of power, the existence of the notion of [a] 'public thing' (the 'foraba' in the dyula language), or the institution of palaver as a mode of consensual decision-making[8] – each of which are historically, anthropologically and sociolinguistically debatable (Ouédraogo 2014: 10).

On revolution, Ki-Zerbo seems to agree with Sankara concerning the immensity of change at stake for revolutionary social change, but not with the pace of this change:

> Revolution is a structural process that makes things progress in an invisible way until the moment when the structure of these structures is such that one must necessarily make a qualitative leap ... The revolution is against the grain of what exists. It's not just turning the page, but a changing of the dictionary.
>
> (Ki-Zerbo 2003: 16)[9]

In a series of interviews with René Holenstein, Ki-Zerbo recalled the one occasion in which he met Sankara in person: an hour-long meeting in 1983, shortly after Sankara became president. After returning from France, Ki-Zerbo had been placed under house arrest because, according to his wife Jacqueline, he was considered a political 'reformist' (Jaffré n.d.).[10] During their brief meeting, Ki-Zerbo described Sankara as 'direct and frank':

> I was struck by the [bluntness] of his remarks ... [his words were] a presentation of the revolution of 4 August 1983 and a warning in the event that some decided to oppose them. I also responded directly, saying that we had never exercised power [in support of the coup and] that we had a program, an ideal that we defended without sidetracking for many years.
>
> (Ki-Zerbo 2003: 135)

After his death, Jacqueline Ki-Zerbo described her husband as 'reading between the lines' of this exchange and opting to leave and remain in exile during Sankara's presidency (Jaffré n.d.). Sankara would appeal to him repeatedly to return and 'commit himself' to his country. Ki-Zerbo recalled Sankara's words, 'You should come back; this is your country, it needs you.' To this, Ki-Zerbo replied:

> in principle, there was no problem, but not in the immediate future, it would take some time. Sankara was a sincere and selfless patriot, a voluntary idealist. He did not realise soon enough that the objective conditions of the revolution were not met. Moreover, the context was opposed to the realisation of his program.
>
> (Ki-Zerbo 2003: 136)[11]

While Ki-Zerbo was not directly forced into exile, he was suspected of opposing the revolution – if not before his departure, then certainly after it. Both Joseph and Jacqueline Ki-Zerbo were sentenced in absentia to two years of detention for tax fraud in 1985. The Supreme Court later overturned the sentence. Before attempting a coup d'état in 1984 (along with Colonel Didier Tiendrébéogo), Amada Ouédraogo met with Ki-Zerbo briefly in Dakar (according to testimony from Gérard Dango Ouédraogo, Amada Ouédraogo's uncle). Ouédraogo was executed on 11 June 1984 along with six others for orchestrating the attempted coup. The execution of these seven political opponents has been held up as evidence to support the thesis that Sankara was an authoritarian. In his chapter in this volume, Nicholas A. Jackson asks, 'was Sankara right to distrust the Ki-Zerbo-led teacher's unions, given that they repudiated him immediately after he took power? How best can one separate grassroots movements from faux-destabilizations?' Sankara made no claims to certainty or perfection, preferring pragmatism to address urgent socio-political and economic issues, saying, 'I know I don't have the perfect solution. But even if this decision were only 60 per cent right, I would stick by it' (1985: 215).

Questions regarding to the frictions between Ki-Zerbo and Sankara aside, Sankara was certainly (and necessarily) a firm and often-demanding president. Pursuing an 'audacious' revolutionary programme and refusing to collaborate if it meant compromising the sovereignty of Burkina, Sankara faced constant threats. Bruno Jaffré (Chapter 6, this volume) and Nicholas A. Jackson (Chapter 7, this volume) capture some of the murkiness of these simultaneous and relentless aggressions and tensions: France, the US, Côte d'Ivoire, Mali, Libya and Liberia were among the international cadre hesitant toward or openly hostile to the revolutionary project. Concurrent with this international context, Sankara faced local criticisms and frustrations (see Chapter 3, this volume), most prominently from labour unions (see Chapter 4, this volume), the urban petite bourgeoisie and state officials, whom were being asked to make personal sacrifices in income and lifestyle for the immediate material needs of the country's poorest people. Modest vehicles replaced the preferred status-connoting Rolls Royce for government officials – Sankara himself was notorious for riding a bicycle to work. Government salaries were reduced in 'self-enforced' austerity measures (Sankara 1985: 200). These measures were not taken to repay the country's inherited 3 billion CFA francs of debt from structural adjustment (in the neoliberal trend) but to contribute to the projects of becoming food self-sufficient, promoting rural well-being through the building of irrigation canals and cultivating a new Burkinabè citizen – one with the knowledge and confidence to live in modest dignity.

SANKARA AND THE CDRS

The uncompromising nature of the revolution was perhaps no better expressed, nor more acutely critiqued, than through the setting up of the Committees in Defense of the Revolution (CDRs). These councils mirrored some of the distinctive revolutionary logic of the Cuban Revolution of 1959, after which Fidel Castro set up the Comités de Defensa de la Revolución (CDRs – with leaders called 'CeDeRistas') to foster grassroots support for the revolution while also watching out for (and reporting on) counter-revolutionary coordinating. Similarly, in Ghana, between 1981 and 1984, Jerry Rawlings set up People's Defence Committees fashioned after Muammar Qaddafi's Basic People's Defence Committees (PDCs). In *The Green Book*, Qaddafi sketched an understanding of the PDCs as fundamental to his populist philosophy of *jamahariyah* (or the 'state of the masses'). Political scientist Jeff Haynes explains the importance of the PDCs in Libya – a context that echoes some of what transpired in Burkina:

> all political parties ... were banned on the grounds that they merely represented different class interest and were, therefore, divisive. They were replaced with a pyramidal structure of political decision-making committees, known at the grassroots level as Basic People's Congresses, which was an attempt to create a communal as opposed to a party-political democracy.
>
> (Haynes 1990: 58)

In this order, political participation is collectivised. In Burkina, the Conseil National de la Revolution (CNR)'s 'ultimate ambition was to achieve an original social renaissance, which made it imperative to revolutionise all sectors of the [Burkinabè] society'.[12] To achieve such an ambitious project at such a considerable scale the CNR needed a structural apparatus to guide different sectors of society at the local-level. Unfortunately, as Marcel Marie Anselme Lalsaga notes, the CNR did not immediately have clear statutes to organise the function and regulations of the CDRs. The absence of written protocols instigated adaptations that 'caused various problems and intrigues' (Lalsaga 2012: 52). Prominent among these structural and practical issues in the functionality of the CDRs were the lack of horizontality and the concentration of power and responsibilities in the hands of a few individuals, the absence of consensus prior to making a decision, a slowness to action, poorly defined prerogatives as well as low female representation (ibid.). The later is disconcerting given Sankara's own commitments to women's emancipation (Sankara 1987a). In addition to the weaknesses noted by Lalsaga were the tensions of achieving radical populism while maintaining a system of national unity and coherent national economic and political policies both domestically as well as in the late Cold War context of constant enemies everywhere (see Chapter 2, this volume). In his chapter in this volume, Leo Zeilig is direct in his criticism of Sankara's ultimate inability to navigate this dangerous and uncertain landscape, writing, 'This terrible and dangerous dance, between competing and hostile interests, meant that national capitalist interests overrode all others; the regime was left at the end of 1987 without any powerful domestic allies'. While Brian Peterson (Chapter 2, this volume) likewise characterised Sankara as a 'polarising figure', he also reminds us that 'there were often discrepancies between Sankara's rhetoric in public speeches and his more pragmatic approach to diplomacy in private settings'.

Although the CNR and the CDRs are often attributed to the political leadership of Sankara (and, as such, equated with it[13]), the organisation was not conceived spontaneously after 4 August 1983 but predated the revolution, albeit clandestinely (Lalsaga 2012: 37). In May 1983, progressive officers and left-leaning organisations came together with the provisional intention of coming to power and ousting then President Jean-Baptiste Ouédraogo. The president of the political party, Patriotic League for Development (Ligue Patriotique pour le Dévelopment, LIPAD) an association with considerable ties to the labour union movement, Adama Toure (who would later serve as Minister of Information under Sankara), recalled a final meeting on 25 July 1983, only months before taking power:

> Mainly, the meeting decided on the creation of the governing body of the next power under the name of the Conseil National de la Révolution (National Council of the Revolution, CNR), which was to proclaim revolution as soon as [Ouédraogo and the government in power] was overthrown and, at the same time, call on the people to create immediately, wherever they could, the Committees in Defense of the Revolution (CDR).
>
> (Quoted in Lalsaga 2012: 38)[14]

Shortly after, carried by the enthusiasm of and for the revolution, the CNR emerged publicly and encouraged the creation of CDRs at the grassroots. In a radio diffusion on 4 August 1983 the call was made:

> People of Upper Volta the National Council of the Revolution calls every Voltaics – men and women, young and old – to mobilize and remain vigilant, in order to give the CNR their active support. The National Council of the Revolution invites the Voltaic people to form Committees of Defense of the Revolution everywhere, in order to participate in the CNR's great patriotic struggle and to prevent our enemies here and abroad from doing our people harm.
>
> (Sankara 1983b: 67)[15]

Lalsaga describes the revolutionary leaders of the CNR as 'politically orphaned', explaining that these leaders

> ... did not have a political organisation peculiar to them ... [At the same time,] they did not want to be prisoners of the revolutionary organisations ... therefore, they thought of creating structures that depended solely on them. Under these circumstances [and drawing inspiration from Cuba, Ghana and Libya], the initiative for the creation of the CDRs was born, an idea that had been endorsed by the leaders of the other leftist organisations.
>
> (Lalsaga 2012: 40–41)[16]

Tracing the origins of the CNR and the CDRs is useful for understanding the larger context of the revolution. These were not structures unilaterally imposed by 'Sankara-as-authoritarian' but were collectively decided upon by a revolutionary and militant cadre made up of radical factions of the military, student and labour unions and civil society. This group, however, did not immediately sufficiently anticipate the disappointments that would come to characterise the roles played by the CDRs in the revolution. Yet, just two and a half years into the revolution, Sankara reminded delegates at the First National Congress of the CDRs of previous failures of CDRs in other revolutionary contexts and urged them to

> correct ourselves at every step in order to advance. We have examples in other places of the failures of certain organisations similar to CDRs—revolutionary committees. Wherever such failures have occurred, it's been because the forces of reaction have successfully laid traps for these other organizations in some countries. We must be conscious of our weaknesses.
>
> (Sankara 1986a: 288)

The grassroots collectives of CDRs, originally embraced by key trade unionists, would become the very instruments to suppress some trade union activity (see Chapter 4, this volume). In this same speech, Sankara invited 'self-criticism' and critiqued the CDRs for being 'riddled with incompetent people' (1986a: 283).

Opposition groups secretly circulated anti-CNR literatures in the country. One such leaflet included an illustration of a gun-carrying soldier covering a civilian's mouth with his hand had the inscription '*Sois Burkinè et tais toi!*' ('Be a Burkinabè and keep quiet'; see Chapter 1, this volume); this was part of a series of pamphlets funded by Côte d'Ivoire and possibly the USSR (see Chapter 6, this volume). Possessing this sort of literature was an offence punishable by the CDRs. On the issue of freedom to criticise, Sankara was firm in his defense of the aims of the revolution and his insistence that neo-imperial forces not have a public platform, saying, 'freedom for sincere men should not mean freedom for dishonest men' (Sankara 1983a: 58).

Some of the initial friction between Sankara and the heterodox labour union movement in Burkina was a result of pre-existing tensions between factions of the labour union itself, most notably between the Ligue Patriotique pour le Développement (LIPAD) and the Union des Luttes Communistes – Reconstruite (ULC-R), both of which were affiliated early on with Sankara's government and both of which held important ministerial posts (LIPAD had five and ULC-R had three). Craig Phelan explains the threats posed by the CDRs to the largest and most influential trade union confederation in Burkina, the CGT-B (Confédération Générale du Travail du Burkina; see Phelan 2016: 114).

Sankara often declared that appropriation and mimicry would be avoided by the Burkinabè revolution and that an indigenous path would be the most suitable for its people and context. Sankara sought to adapt the structure of the Committees in ways that suited the needs of Burkinabè society - but he was engaged in this seizable and risky projects alongside many other revolutionary endeavours and projects. Sankara understood revolution as a process of social change that proceeded through different stages of transition and it is possible that the inadequacies in CDRs procedure, direction and guidance would have ameliorated with time. The CDRs, designed to be participatory and to decentralise authority, were ultimately critically unsuitable for the revolution and facilitated criticisms of the revolutionary government in an already precarious geopolitical context. Haynes explains,

> Although initially created as a means of 'defending' the revolution from internal attack, the CDRs largely became autonomous groups of the un- and under-employed, members of which were frequently armed with guns which they used to arrest perceived opponents. Shortly before his own assassination, Sankara was reported to 'fear their power', and to admit his inability to control them.
>
> (Haynes 1990: 65)

In 1987, Sankara urged and encouraged, with his usual energetic bluntness, the CDR leadership to ease the pressures, in particular, on labor unions. This included his insistence that the 1,300 sacked teachers be reinstated and that civil servants receive a raise in salary. The raise went into effect on 16 October 1987, the day following Sankara's assassination and Compaorè took credit for the action.

SANKARA AND THE MILITARY

As Ki-Zerbo reminds us, Sankara came to power in a military coup. This invariably informed his presidency, while also seeming to invalidate it to some of his critics. Ki-Zerbo (2003: 3) argued that a 'better *coup d'état* is still, nonetheless, a *coup d'état*. What was needed was a system of governance that did not perpetuate a cycle of military coups'. In Chapter 1 of this volume, De-Valera N. Y. M. Botchway and Moussa Traore argue that the 'founding myth' of the CNR was that 'it came to power through a popular revolution'. While Sankara was openly critical of militarism, speaking often in distain for a global proliferation of arms and scientific research in support of warfare, he perhaps did not speak sufficiently enough of the implications of his coming to power through a military operation – even though he tried to avoid it and did not actively participate in the events of the coup itself. In his biography of Sankara, Harsch explains some of the context of Sankara's reluctance to engage in a coup d'état:

Sankara continued to negotiate with President [Jean-Baptiste] Ouédraogo in the hopes of arranging a peaceful political transition and avoiding bloodshed. At a meeting with Sankara on August 4, Ouédraogo reportedly indicated his willingness to resign as president ... [However,] Somé Yorian was preparing a decisive initiative of his own: to assassinate Sankara, [Jean-Baptiste] Lingani, and [Henri] Zongo; push President Ouédraogo aside; and assume power in his own name. That prompted the [progressive] rebels to strike first.

(Harsch 2014: 50)

Prior to the military operation that ousted Ouédraogo, the youth of Ouagadougou marched in the streets for three days to protest Sankara's imprisonment, shouting, 'Libérez Sankara! Libérez Sankara! Libérez Lingani! A bas Jean Baptiste! A bas l'impérialisme!' (Lalsaga 2012: 35). These mobilisations reveal a strong popular base in support of Sankara prior to his presidency. More than this, the 'ease' with which the progressives seized power from Ouédraogo revealed close collaborations between Leftist parties, labour unions, student groups and the dissident soldiers at the time (Lalsaga 2012). This progressive collective belies claims that Sankara seized power without popular support (indeed, civilian groups collaborated to effect the coup d'ètat by serving as guides, cutting off power to areas of the city and remaining at the command base in Pô), although certainly the Burkinabè political landscape was complex and highly fractured prior to the August Revolution (see Chapters 3, 6, 7 and 17, this volume).

In regards to the role of the military in society, Sankara spoke harshly about the need for political and ideological training, saying, 'a military man [or woman] without a political education is a potential criminal'. On the other hand, because he was not voted into office, our speculation on the nature of and extent of his popular appeal is reduced to just that: speculation. As a result, some have dismissed Sankara out-of-hand as 'just another' leader to come to office through military means. Indeed, the revolution was dismissed early on in the international and Western media as 'just another' coup; Sankara responded at a press conference on 21 August by articulating a distinction between types of coups, 'It is not a question of the military taking power one day and giving it up the next. It is about the military living with the Voltaic people, suffering with them, and fighting by their side at all times' (Sankara 1983c: 75).

Boureïma N. Ouédraogo (2015) reminds us that the army has dominated the exercise of power in Burkina Faso almost uninterruptedly since independence in 1960 – including in the 27 years that Blaise Compaoré (himself a captain in the military) was president.[17] Considering the popular movement of 30 and 31 October 2014, Ouédraogo (ibid.: 2) highlights some of the ambivalence of the roles played by the army in the country, remarking that the army is at once a force capable of being 'blindingly coercive' and 'liberating'. Ouédraogo (ibid.) explains that the perpetuation of the power of the army, particularly at the level of the head of the state, is not the product of direct domination but rather 'the result of a process of normalising the charisma of the army' in Burkina. Tracing the history of the 'charisma of the army', Ouédraogo (ibid.) argues that, before Compaoré, the army often intervened on behalf of the people against civilian elites and that military commanders did not 'function in an authoritarian way' nor did they demonstrate ethnic or regional favouritism. Indeed, the Sankara years 'boosted' the army's association with charisma – and this sentiment was later instrumentalised by Compaoré's presidency (ibid.).

Some of the critiques of Sankara on the basis of his military training and militaristic rise to power might well be balanced with a more serious critique of liberal democracy, too. Senegalese political economist Ndongo Samba Sylla (2013), echoing (in part) the scholarship of Samir Amin (2004) in *The Liberal Virus*, demystifies the celebratory language of 'free and transparent' elections for 'liberal democracies' in Africa as fictitious systems that benefit the economic elite in-so-much as they create an impression (rather than a reality) of an emancipated collective. Such a system, according to Amin (2004), amounts to little more than 'low-intensity democracy': a fixed constitutional formula imposed from the West and designed to ensure continued dispossession and accumulation. Drawing from Sankara's example, Sylla explains:

> ... democracy is not ... a gift that can be received from elsewhere. The very idea that there would be a democratic model valid everywhere and at all times was unacceptable ... [Sankara's] conviction was that democracy is a historical construct, a set of tinkering here and there that makes sense for the community and which, more fundamentally, allows the people, in their multiple determinations, to express themselves freely and to emancipate [themselves from] different forms of subordination or dependencies.
>
> (Sylla 2013: n.p.)[18]

Others have dismissed Sankara as an autocrat, who imposed policies from above and harshly condemned those who did not 'fall in line' with the revolution. That Sankara banned multipartism has been thoroughly critiqued (sometimes instinctively and un-thinkingly so) and has contributed considerably to the castigation of Sankara as a 'despot' and 'autocrat', particularly in Anglophone scholarship. Again, however, Sylla's consideration of the revolutionary context is helpful in rethinking some of these too-easy dismissals of Sankara's approach to radical politics in Burkina Faso. Sylla writes that the

> revolutionary instinct is different from the instinct of the despot who seeks to maintain himself at all costs ... Sankara was opposed to multipartism, not because he wanted to pursue a career as a tyrant, but because he saw it as a major obstacle to the emergence of a genuine democracy. *The multiparty system is not revolutionary enough for him or at least it was not in keeping with the exigencies of the moment.* In fact, it seemed to him that it was a lure that reinforced the misery of the populations and the neocolonial dependence of his country.
>
> (Sylla 2013: n.p.; emphasis added)

Sankara himself explained precisely this view at length in a 1983 interview with Mohamed Maïga of *Afrique Asie*, describing the multiparty system as a 'quantitative' illusion. He argued that greater and greater numbers of registered political parties had no bearing on the concrete practice of politics and held up the Upper Volta of 1978 to demonstrate his point. At the time, the country had 'no fewer' than nine contending political parties; Sankara explained:

> For many, especially for those who, through ease or ignorance, *wanted to perceive it like this*, it was the very model of democracy. A general in power, who was questioning himself, with eight adversaries freely organized! ... it is tempting to stick the label 'democratic' to Voltaic politics. It was written, celebrated and sung everywhere ... For us it was only a masquerade. Nothing else. A masquerade that ... was very expensive.
>
> (Sankara, interview with *Afrique Asie*, 1983e: n.p.; emphasis added)

For Sankara, the multiparty system operated as a colonial deception: it created a quantitative illusion in public all the while obfuscating that these nine parties, Sankara explained, were made up of

> Twenty-seven persons with the same interests, intimately linked by the politico-financial affairs of the comprador, bureaucratic and political bourgeoisies and by their role as intermediaries of some large foreign commercial companies. Twenty-seven individuals linked by their infiltration to the same neo-colonial forces, who spoke of democracy because they controlled nine parties... these individuals received their 'electoral' funds from abroad. They bought ... the consciences through notables, feudals and many other dignitaries of the country. Millions of Voltaic *people voted by order* ... for me, it is not democracy.
>
> (Sankara, interview with *Afrique Asie*, 1983e, emphasis added)

Sankara's critics who have described him as authoritarian on the basis of his banning of opposition parties have not addressed this superficiality and co-optation in multiparty politics.

Other critics of Sankara have asked: how much were his populist policies and populist speech-making a representation of *his own* version of Pan-Africanism and how much were they versions of populist grassroots desires from the bottom? In addressing these questions, however, we might consider the near impossibility of actually measuring 'popular support' for any leader – let alone a leader whom has been assassinated and subsequently nearly erased from historical record (until the last decade or so; see Chapter 20, this volume).

When we take as context, however, Sankara's own words, we begin to understand how he situated himself and his role in the struggle for the '*bolibana* of imperialism' (for imperialism's 'end of the road') and the struggle for social, gender, racial and ecological justice (see those chapters in Section II of this volume).

CONCLUSION

Sankara understood that part of his role as a leader for the grassroots would be a rejection of silence in the face of widespread hunger, thirst and neo-colonialism. He used his international platform to address the historical foundations of poverty and to reject to contribute, even through silence, to the perpetuation of such a system. He said:

> I protest ... on behalf of all those who vainly seek a forum in this world where they can make their voice heard and have it genuinely taken into consideration. Many have preceded me at this podium and others will follow. But only few will make the decisions ... I am acting as a spokesperson for all those who vainly seek a forum in this world where they can make themselves heard. So yes, I wish to speak on behalf of all 'those left behind', for 'I am human, nothing that is human is alien to me'.
>
> (Sankara 1984c: 165)

Sankara was a man who wore many hats – who played many difficult and dangerous roles – simultaneously: He was, among other things, an educator and a wise man, an unflinching encourager of the people, a militant activist informed by a no-nonsense pragmatism, a president with military training and agro-ecology education as well as a feminist Pan-African Marxist. While we evaluate Sankara based on his role as president – as president who came to power during a coup d'état – we must also judge his actions against other Burkinabè presidents and against other presidents in general. Many leaders are co-opted by the power that they obtain, not so with Sankara. This was a man who refused power, money and privilege. When his name was first put forward for the presidency, after the coup on 7 November 1982 that overthrew Saye Zerbo, Sankara refused (Harsch 2014: 44).

I am not moved by the argument that, had he lived, he would have been corrupted at some later date. We see nothing in his character, philosophy or actions to indicate that this would be so. Sankara remarked often that he had the privilege of having access to a global stage and used it to mobilise for the people. He understood the limitations of the military, encouraging soldiers to undergo political training at the risk of becoming the hand of empire, protecting private capital.

Are we waiting for an ideal? In terms of presidents, whom do we look to if we do not look to the actions and philosophies of Sankara, who achieved so much in four years and two months and in the face of such overwhelming obstacles? States are collections of peoples too diverse to expect or demand that any one leader would be uniquely popular among all or that any one leader would be uniquely responsible for all of the actions of the state. Certainly Sankara had weaknesses – his ambition, uncompromising nature and urgency are among those identified in the chapters in this collection – but these are also the same markers that we respect and admire in activists (see the Introduction, this volume). He stands out as a distinctively pro-people leader, willing to make an almost unimaginable level of self-sacrifice for his abiding belief that he was acting with the people and for the people – even if his policies were novel, new, 'mad' and untested and uncertain (recall his own modest and pragmatic admission that 60 per cent likelihood of success was sufficient in the search for solutions to the problems of hunger, thirst and inequality).

Sankara's political leadership is a powerful example of how governments might re-orient to support the people as the people work to achieve their own fulfilment and well-being. His legacy shows that another politics is possible. Yet, this brazen pro-people political orientation remains so dangerous a challenge to the established economic order that it continues to be dismissed as 'a certain amount of madness'.

NOTES

1 Against this trend, the blog 'African Development Successes' archives and recognizes stories of 'effective leaders from across the continent'. The list is available at https://africandevelopmentsuccesses.wordpress.com (accessed 1 May 2017).

2 Also, importantly, American presidents are not commonly referred to by their military title (General, Sergeant, Captain, etc.) like their African counterparts. Again, there was a conscious decision in this volume not to refer to Sankara as 'Captain Sankara' throughout (as is the academic trend with African leaders with military backgrounds).

3 The government classified the death of Zongo in 1998 a 'car accident'. His murder sparked a resistance movement under the umbrella of 'trop, c'est trop!'. See Chapter 23 of this volume for a consideration of the important of this movement in informing subsequent social movement activism in Burkina.

4 The examples for this argument are many. To name but one: Ivorian President Houphouet-Boigny, when asked why he did not build a cocoa factory in the country responded, 'The French would not have let me'.

5 Passage translated by author.

6 Here again we can draw comparisons between Guevara and Sankara as both have ignited polarised readings of their lives and struggles: they are either militaristic autocrats or fearless leaders struggling against the interrelated forces of classism, capitalism and empire.

7 This idea is also reflected in the approach of Joseph Ki-Zerbo (2013: 8), 'Without identity, [Burkinabès] are ... object[s] of history ... instrument[s] to be used by others: a utensil'.

8 Passage translated by author.

9 Passage translated by author.

10 Bruno Jaffré's analysis of the relationship between Ki-Zerbo and Sankara is available in French at http://thomassankara.net/ki-zerbo-et-sankara (accessed 12 May 2017).

11 Passage translated by author.

12 Passage translated by author.

13 See, for example, Phelan (2016: 108): 'Sankara's authoritarianism, his hostility to strikes and trade unionism and his creation of the Committees for the Defense of the Revolution... prompted increasingly strident trade union opposition to the regime ...'.

14 Passage translated by author.

15 Passage translated by author.

16 Passage translated by author.

17 Until the uprising in 2014, Maurice Yaméogo was the only civilian to be president (1960–1966) of the country. After the 2014 ousting of Blaise, Lieutenant-Colonel Yacouba Isaac Zida took power briefly but was quickly replaced by Michel Kafando, who served as the transitional president until November 2015. At which time another civilian, Roch Marc Christian Kaboré, was elected.

18 Translated from French by author. Original text available at www.pambazuka.org/fr/pan-africanism/repenser-la-démocratie-avec-thomas-sankara (accessed 12 May 2017).

REFERENCES

Agulana, C. (2006) Democracy and the Crisis of Leadership in Africa. *On Africa* 31(3): 255–264.

Amin, S. (2004) *The Liberal Virus: Permanent War and the Americanization of the World*. New York: Monthly Review Press.

Benamrane, D. (2016) *Sankara, Leader Africain*. Paris: L'Harmattan.

Chouli, L. (2014) 'Social Movements and the Quest for Alternatives in Burkina Faso' in Sylla, N. S. (ed.) *Liberalism and its Discontents: Social Movements in West Africa*: 263-303. Dakar, Senegal: Rosa Luxemburg Foundation.

de Sardan, J. P. (2016) Niger : Les Quatres Prisons du Pouvoir. *Le Républicain* (Niamey) 2059: n.p. Retrieved on 12 August 2017 from www.marianne.net/debattons/tribunes/niger-les-quatre-prisons-du-pouvoir.

Harsch, E. (2014) *Thomas Sankara: An African Revolutionary*. Athens, Ohio: Ohio University Press.

Haynes, J. (1990) Libyan Involvement in West Africa: Qadhaffi's 'Revolutionary' Foreign Policy. *Paradigms* 4(1): 58–73.

Ki-Zerbo, J. (2003) *À Quand l'Afrique ? Entretien avec René Holestein*. La Tour d'Aigues, France: Éditions de l'Aube.

Lalsaga, K. M. M. A. (2012) *Pouvoir et Société sous la Révolution au Burkina Faso: Le Rôle Des Structures Populaires dans la Gouvernance Révolutionnaire de 1983 à 1987*. Saarbrücken, Germany: Éditions Universitaires Européennes.

Mudimbe, V. Y. (1988) *The Invention of Africa: Gnosis, Philosophy, and the Order of Knoweldge*. Bloomington, IN: Indiana University Press.

Ouédraogo, B. N. (2014) *Droit, Démocratie et Développement en Afrique : Un Parfum de Jasmin Souffle Sur le Burkina Faso*. Paris: L'Harmattan.

Ouédraogo, B. N. (2015) l'armée et l'exercice du pouvoir au Burkina Faso: Enseignements de L'insurrection Populaire Du 30–31 Octobre 2014. *Notes Internacionals Barcelona Centre for International Affairs* 106. Retrieved on 1 June 2017 from www.files.ethz.ch/isn/187237/NOTES%20106_OUEDRAOGO_FRAN-1.pdf.

Phelan, C. (2016) Plus ça change: Trade Unions, the Military and Politics in Burkina Faso, 1966 and 2014. *Labor History* 57(1): 107–125.

Sankara, T. (1983a) Who are the Enemies of the People? Speech at Mass Rally in Ouagadougou, 26 March. Reproduced in Sankara (2007): 51–64.

Sankara, T. (1983b) A Radiant Future for our Country. Proclamation of 4 August. Reproduced in Sankara (2007): 65–68.

Sankara, T. (1983c) Power Must be the Business of a Conscious People. Press Conference, 21 August. Reproduced in Sankara (2007): 69–75.

Sankara, T. (1983d) Building a New Society, Rid of Social Injustice and Imperialist Domination. Political Orientation Speech, 2 October. Reproduced in Sankara, T. (2007): 76–109.

Sankara, T. (1983e) Douze Heures avec Thomas Sanakra, interview with Mohamed Maïga, *Afrique Asie*. Retrieved on 1 December 2017 from thomassankara.net/douze-heures-avec-thomas-sankara-exclusif-mensuel-afrique-asie-1983.

Sankara, T. (1984a) Asserting Our Identity, Asserting Our Culture. Speech at Burkinabè Art Exhibit in Harlem, 2 October. Reproduced in Sankara (2007): 143–146.

Sankara, T. (1984b) Our White House in Black Harlem. Speech at rally in Harlem, 3 October. Reproduced in Sankara (2007): 147–153.

Sankara, T. (1984c) Freedom Must Be Conquered. Speech at UN General Assembly, 4 October. Reproduced in Sankara (2007): 154–176.

Sankara, T. (1985) Dare to Invent the Future. Interview with Jean-Philippe Rapp. Reproduced in Sankara (2007): 189–232.

Sankara, T. (1986a) The CDRs' job is to Raise Consciousness, Act, Produce. Speech at First National Conference of CDRs, 4 April. Reproduced in Sankara (2007): 270–296.

Sankara, T. (1986b) A Death that must Enlighten and Strengthen Us. Speech on death of Samora Machel, October. Reproduced in Sankara (2007): 313–321.

Sankara, T. (1987a) The Revolution Will Not Triumph Without the Emancipation of Women. On International Women's Day, 8 March. Reproduced in Sankara (2007): 335–372.

Sankara, T. (1987b) 'We Count on Cuba'. Interview with Radio Havana, August. Reproduced in Sankara, T. (2007): 382–387.

Sankara, T. (1987c) You Cannot Kill Ideas. A Tribute to Che Guevara, 8 October. Reproduced in Sankara (2007): 420–424.

Sankara, T. (2007) *Thomas Sankara Speaks: The Burkina Faso Revolution, 1983–87*, 2nd edition. New York: Pathfinder Press.

Sylla, N. S. (2013) Repenser la Démocratie avec Thomas Sankara. *Pambazuka News*. Retrieved on 1 June 2017 from www.pambazuka.org/fr/pan-africanism/repenser-la-démocratie-avec-thomas-sankara.

CHAPTER 6

Who Killed Thomas Sankara?

Bruno Jaffré[1]

WHAT HAPPENED ON 15 OCTOBER 1987?

The initial accounts of Thomas Sankara's assassination were reported by Sennen Andriamirado in the pages of *Jeune Afrique* as early as November 1987 (Andriamirado 1989). Valère Somé, a close associate and friend of Sankara, would complete these first reports through the publication of his book, *Thomas Sankara, l'Espoir Assassiné* (Somé 1990), soon after. The only survivor of the assassination, Halouna Traoré, has been frequently interviewed; he has always confirmed the same version of the events of that day.

According to Traoré, Thomas Sankara had just begun a meeting with his collaborators when armed soldiers arrived at the Conseil de l'Entente headquarters (an office of the CNR). He declared, 'It's me they are looking for' and went outside to face his assassins. The findings of the autopsy – only made public in Ouagadougou in October 2015 – corroborated that he had indeed been assassinated while holding up his arms. His body was riddled with bullets, with one entering just under his armpit. The soldiers shot at him, then at those taking part in the meeting. Valère Somé identified three members of the commando unit: Corporal Maïga (bodyguard of Blaise Compaoré), Hyacinthe Kafando and Corporal Nadié, who was the first to hit Thomas Sankara with a hail of bullets.

In November 2001, an article in the weekly journal *Burkinabè Bendré* published the initials of six members of the commando unit, all servicemen. In 2002, Mariam Sankara's lawyer, Mister Dieudonné Kounkou, in *L'affaire Sankara Le Juge Et Le Politique*, disclosed their names: Ouédraogo Arzoma Otis, Nabié N'Soni, Nacolma Wanpasba, Ouédraogo Nabonsmendé, Tondé Kabré Moumouni and Hyacinthe Kafando (Nkounkou 2002). They were all under the order of Gilbert Diendré, who led Pô's commandos at the time. Gilbert Diendré would later be promoted to the rank of Knight of the Legion of Honour during a visit to France in May 2008 and would serve as Compaoré's chief of staff. In October 2015, Diendré would be arrested after an attempted coup.

Following the popular uprising in October 2014, a judicial investigation began, conducted by the honourable François Yaméogo (of the military judicial system). As this chapter went to press, the trial was still underway and the current French President, Emmanual Macron, vowed to make the French archives of Sankara's assassination public (during a visit to Burkina in late November 2017). Compaoré, after fleeing to Côte d'Ivoire, is currently being tried in absentia. Yaméogo has thus far presided over dozens of hearings and the persons charged have now been publicly named. A few names (previously mentioned) do not appear on the court's list as they have since died. Other soldiers have been added to the list of members of the commando, including General Diendéré, second in command in Blaise Compaoré's regime. Also named are those responsible for falsifying the death certificate of Thomas Sankara, which claimed Sankara had 'died of natural causes'. All of the accused have been arrested, with the exceptions of Blaise Compaoré and Hyacinthe Kafand (the latter was allegedly the chief of the commando unit). However, both are under an international warrant. At the time of this writing, the trial is ongoing and many of the precise circumstances are, as of yet, unknown.

'THE WESTERN IMPERIALIST CAMP': THE GEOPOLITICAL CONTEXT OF THE 1980S

The wave of independence movements across the African continent alarmed what Sankara referred to as the 'Western imperialist camp'. There was considerable apprehension that these newly independent countries would move towards communist ideologies. In each country desires for political and economic independence were quickly subjected to destabilisation attempts. This was the case in 1956 when the Egyptian President Gamal Abdel Nasser decided to nationalise the Suez Canal and, in the Democratic Republic of the Congo (DRC), the first Prime Minister Patrice Lumumba (democratically elected) was assassinated in 1961.

In the French-speaking former colonies, the United States subcontracted the fight against 'communism' to the French, as progressive movements were leading to revolts and popular wars for independence, as in Algeria, Cameroon and Madagascar.[2] After a protracted war in Algeria, France (under the stewardship of de Gaulle), 'granted' independence to French 'possessions' in Northern and Sub-Saharan Africa in an attempt to retain some of their political-economic dominance in the region. Paris installed subservient regimes in order to continue the exploitative extraction of raw materials as well as retain influence in African markets – and thus to maintain its political domination and its status as a world power. At the time De Gaulle entrusted Jacques Foccart with the mission of holding the region under French influence. Nicknamed

'Monsieur Afrique' under de Gaulle and Pompidou, Foccart set up a large network of contacts, which organised surveillance and collected information across the francophone African region. It is well known that he also ordered covert actions and so-called 'dirty tricks' (i.e. destabilisation efforts).

This shadow network would later be termed 'la Françafrique'. La Françafrique was still operational when Thomas Sankara was killed. A number of similar networks, military, financial or supporting various businesses were created, sometimes with competing agendas. Most of them did not hesitate to act illegally, including organising assassinations, destabilisations and 'buying consciences' (i.e. bribery and blackmail). Both Guinea, which had refused to ally itself with France, and Mali, which had good relations with the Soviet Union, were the targets of economic sabotage. On 16 January 1977, the government of Benin, which claimed to be Marxist–Leninist, had to repel a commando raid led by Bob Denard, whose links with the French secret services are common knowledge. In most other French-speaking countries, these networks have imposed and promoted regimes aligned to France with the complicity of local elite by placing advisers at the highest echelons of the state – people who are willing to stifle any aspiration for political independence and sovereignty.

In the mid-1980s the Cold War compelled each country to choose a side. The acrimonious competition between the so-called socialist countries (i.e. those allied to the Soviet Union) and the West under the umbrella of NATO (from which France has formerly withdrawn, albeit is still an active player[3]) had transformed the planet into trench warfare. At stake was access to raw materials and the markets in Central and South America, Europe, Asia and Africa. For many years Latin America was 'the preserve' of the US, which supported bloody dictatorships, resorting to massive arbitrary arrests, tortures and targeted killings. They had to contain recurrent unrest in this part of the world, which has a rich history of struggle for independence. The victory of Cuban *guerilleros*, led by Fidel Castro, was followed by numerous destabilising attempts. Cuban leadership received strong support from the Soviets, causing one of the worst crises in the early 1960s. An exhaustive list of murders, disapperings or other attempts to destabilise countries and movements would be too long to enumerate. Rather, I have described them here to provide an understanding of the geopolitical context of neo-colonialism, including the Cold War conflict that emerged from the colonial struggle for power and domination, as it is within this much broader context that Sankara was assassinated.

INTERNAL POLITICS

In the 1970s, African youth had gone to study in France, joining in great numbers the Fédération des Étudiants d'Afrique Noire. It was here that many discovered

Marxism. In Burkina Faso, the communist ideology in all its variants – Chinese, Soviet or Albanian – spread among the middle class intellectuals. They later constituted the managerial elite of the Revolution.

In the first months of the Revolution, dissenting views appeared within the CNR (Conseil National de la Révolution) as well as outside. The PAI (Parti Africain de l'Indépendance) – which was connected to international communist movements and was the best organised political party and the largest of the two that had taken part in the coup – had misgivings about the frequent changes in the composition of the National Council, the dominance of army officers, the lack of debates and the insufficient preparation for various initiatives launched by the government. This sometimes arose as a consequence of Sankara's insistence on immediate actions to meet immediate needs. A former UNDP collaborator acknowledged that, for the sake of speed, Sankara dismissed extensive studies prior to the construction of water reservoirs, for example (Benamrane 2016).

Another party, the ULCR (Union des Luttes Communistes Reconstituées) lead by Valère Somé, opposed the preponderance of the PAI in the executive bodies and sets up a strategy to challenge it. The setting up of Comités de Défense de la Révolution (CDRs) in the workplace only increased tensions. At the time that they were created in November 1983, the general secretary Pierre Ouédraogo said, 'No union is ready to make sacrifices which the CDR would gladly accept, unless CDR and unions merge for the best – provided that the former has eaten the latter' (quoted in Jaffré 1989: 181).

A prominent member of PAI, Touré Soumane, led the CVS (Confédération Syndicale Voltaïque) and made several defiant declarations to the media. His critics accused him of aspiring to the position of general secretary of the CDR. This first political crisis triggered the resignation of PAI members from the CNR and government, depriving them of their expertise. The ULCR was the only party left sitting on the CNR. Many opportunists and neo-revolutionaries then came to the fore and took on responsibilities. Very quickly they created several organisations under the banner of Marxist-Leninism. The objective conditions for a new political crisis were in place.

Political infighting would resume during the fourth year of the Revolution. The launch of a public debate on the forming of a political party was the pretext. In May 1986 four organisations, UCB (Union des communistes burkinabè), ULCR, GCB (Groupe des Communistes Burkinabè) and OMR (Organisation des Militaires Révolutionnaires), in a common communiqué, pledged to work within the CNR 'for the edification of a unique avant-garde organisation'. However, differences soon surfaced. On one hand, Sankara recommended the prior dissolution of these organisations; on the other hand, he wished to incorporate the PAI but also the PCRV (Parti communiste révolutionnaire voltaïque), which had refused to collaborate with the authorities deemed illegitimate. All civil organisations were opposed, except ULCR on the second point.

More differences arose. At the start of 1987, after the release of Touré Soumane, unions led by members of PAI and PCRV, until then harshly dealt with, resumed their activities. Some CDR activists, close to UCB, attempted to take control of several unions by force. Union leaders again were arrested in late May. In the CNR, members of UCB, GCB and OMR demanded the execution of Touré Soumane. Thomas Sankara and members of ULCR were opposed. On 4 August 1987, the fourth anniversary of the Revolution, Thomas Sankara delivered a keynote speech, urging a 'put[ing to] right' of errors, saying:

> The democratic and people's Revolution needs a people who believe in the Revolution, not a defeated people, a people with convictions, not a people subjugated [and] resigned to its fate … But we must take care to avoid that unity becomes one dry, obstructing and sterile voice. On the contrary, one should promote multiple, diverse and productive viewpoints and actions; nuanced thinking and actions, bravely and genuinely aiming at accepting differences, acknowledgement of criticism and self-examination, towards a bright future which cannot be anything else than the happiness of our people.[4]

He sent a letter that circulated to all the ministries, asking for the reinstatement of sacked staff. Thomas Sankara was aware of a sense of weariness. He offered a pause to slow down the pace of reforms. A pay rise was approved by the Council of Ministers on 14 October. Those who took over on 15 October 1987, the day after, would claim credit for it.

The struggle for power resumed apace. Many discontented rallied round Blaise Compaoré, including those who had been criticised by Sankara, for behaviours he deemed unworthy of revolutionaries, those opposed to opening up the government and calling for new purges as well as those who wanted at last to take advantage of their positions to enrich themselves. A war of leaflets, which comprised more insults than substance, highlighted the tension between the two groups. Blaise Compaoré controlled most of the army and was plotting to attract to his side all these opponents who knew they needed the support of the military forces. His supporters had taken control of many CDRs via activists from UCB, with the complicity of Pierre Ouédraogo, the general secretary of the CDR.[5]

The draft of a speech he was due to make at a meeting in the evening of 15 October 1987, written by himself and authenticated by his relatives, was found a few years ago.[6] Thomas Sankara asserted that those who were hiding behind so-called 'dissensions' did not put forward any argument when engaged in a political discussion. Actually, according to him, their only motive was the lure of power. They were the political guarantors of the plot. Some who sincerely believed that the coup against Sankara was about changing the course of the

Revolution were assassinated when they realised that his death put an end to the Revolution. Those loyal to Sankara, who could not flee, were arrested, often tortured, sometimes until death as several witness accounts, recently made public, reveal (including testimonies from Mousbila Sankara, Guillaume Sessouma and Basile Guissou, to name a few).

THOMAS SANKARA AND BLAISE COMPAORÉ: AN INTENSELY CLOSE FRIENDSHIP OR A RIVALRY?

It would be easy to hide behind political determinism in order to dismiss questions regarding the relationship between Thomas Sankara and Blaise Compaoré. For some, this relationship was the main explanation for the assassination of Thomas Sankara. But one could also presume that Compaoré's state of mind and this extraordinary relationship constituted the weakest link of the leadership – one which the backers of the assassination plot used to their advantage so as to organise Sankara's assassination.

The two young officers, Sankara and Compaoré, allegedly met during the so-called 'war of the poor' between Burkina Faso (then Haute-Volta) and Mali in 1974. But their friendship deepened during a military training in Morocco in 1978. At the time some close to Sankara were surprised by his sudden friendship with Blaise Compaoré. Until then, every new member of the clandestine organisation (that the revolutionaries in the army had created) had to get through various stages before being admitted. But Thomas Sankara asked his comrades to allow Blaise Compaoré to skip the normal procedure. Sankara seemed to have absolute confidence in Compaoré, to whom he entrusted the most secret missions.

Thomas Sankara's father, Joseph Sankara, came to consider Blaise Compaoré, an orphan whose family background was uncertain, as his own son. He had his meals with the family nearly every day and he even asked him to search for a wife on his behalf. When Thomas Sankara was assassinated, his father expected a visit from Blaise Compaoré – a visit that never materialised. Later he said that he lost two sons on that day.[7]

Thomas Sankara recalled his strong friendship in the film, *Capitaine Thomas Sankara* (2012), directed by Christophe Cupelin. The film captures a fascinating and striking account, depicting a fusional but very unequal relationship. In one scene Sankara explained,

It's great to have a man to whom one can tell everything, well almost everything. Letting him guess what you did not dare to tell him yourself ... It's great and very unusual ... But it can be painful because it implies huge efforts from the other to be always responsive. When I call Blaise at 4 o'clock, to ask him to come and see me he has to accept to spend the entire night until dawn making me relax, laugh, boosting me, in order to help me in carrying out my work. We spend night after night discussing. That means he must have no worries. He ought to live to attend to a sick person or I don't know ... to look after. It's unique. When I reflect on this, I am asking myself, who is going to support him? Because he has to have someone to lean upon, to keep [him] sane.

In each of the photographs and scenes depicted in the film, Blaise Compaoré is seen in the background, behind Sankara. Critics say that Sankara did not spare his friend, even publicly.

Their rivalry became apparent when they seized power on 4 August 1983. Blaise Compaoré confided to Vincent Sigué that he wanted to be the 'top man' given his central role in the events that day (an account that was widely believed).[8] Compaoré's wife, Chantale Terrasson de Fougères – herself a well-connected protégée of Ivorian president Houphouët-Boigny[9] – had allegedly pushed him not only to claim the 'top job' but also to claim the traditional chief of Mossi (the largest ethnic group in Burkina), to which Blaise Compaoré belongs. Rule in this group is centralised and is led by an emperor, the Morgho Naba. Thomas Sankara, whose parents were Peulh and Mossi, was deemed to be inferior. Of course, I am not emphasising an ethnic angle to explain the rivalry that developed between the two men. It is simply one possible interpretation – or one potential dynamic – among many.

THE PRESENCE OF SEVERAL LIBERIANS AT THE SCENE

The involvement of Liberians in the assassination has been suspected for many years. The academic and writer Stephen Ellis did research on the war in Liberia; he cites several sources to support this conjecture in his book (published in 1999). Referring to the presence of Liberian refugees in Burkina Faso, he writes:

> These were the men Blaise Compaoré had contacted and whom he asked for help to topple the Burkinabè president Thomas Sankara. According to a former aide of Compaoré, the Ivorian president, Houphouët-Boigny, was aware of the plan of the ambitious Compaoré. On October 15 1987, Burkinabè soldiers under the command of Compaoré with the support of a small group of Liberian exiled, including Prince Johnson, killed Sankara.
>
> (Ellis 2006: 68)[10]

In an interview, Ellis indicated that Liberians had secured the place where Thomas Sankara and his entourage were killed (telephone interview with the author, 3 May 2001).

In 2008, Prince Yormie Johnson confessed to the Liberian Truth and

Reconciliation Commission that he was involved in the killing of Thomas Sankara (*Radio France Internationale* 2008a). He confirmed it again later to a RFI (Radio France Internationale) journalist. Johnson said, 'The only option for our group, to stay in Burkina, then go to Libya, was to positively respond to the request of Blaise, that is to get rid of Thomas Sankara who was hostile to our presence in Burkina' (*Radio France Internationale* 2008b). He also indicated that they had the support of Houphouët-Boigny.

An American researcher, Carina Ray (2008), quoting from the Liberian Democratic Future (LDF) via several media outlets,[11] further confirms this version of events. Sankara was killed in an agreement that Burkina and Libya would help Charles Taylor and his men seize power in Liberia. Libya provided finances, arms and training for the Liberian Future Fighters. Another version has also surfaced: Sankara was murdered before the arrival of Taylor in Burkina. At the Special Court for Sierra Leone during the trial on 25 August 2009, Charles Taylor stated that he did not take part in the assassination because at the time he was detained in Ghana. During the trial, he claimed that the country archives could prove this (Jaffré 2009). Several Liberians have since stated the opposite (discussed further below). Ernest Nongma Ouédraogo, the Interior Minister, during the Revolution, indicated that Taylor was indeed in Ougadougou *before* 15 October 1987 and was living under an assumed name. In my discussion with him, Ouédraogo claimed that he could show me the house where Taylor was living at the time. In July 2009, the Italian TV channel RAI 3 broadcast a documentary, *Ombre Africane* (directed by an investigative journalist, Silvestro Montanaro), about Liberia. In the film, several of Charles Taylor's former close associates, including Momo Jiba (the ex-aide-de-camp of President Taylor), Cyril Allen (the former leader of Taylor's party and ex-chairman of the national oil company), Moses Blah (the ex-vice-president of Liberia) and Prince Yormie Johnson (the former warlord, already mentioned), speak at length about their involvement in the assassination of Thomas Sankara. In this testimony, they indicate that Sankara had refused to help them.[12] It was in this context that they agreed to kill Sankara at the request of Blaise Compaoré. There was an understanding that they would receive assistance following Sankara's assassination and Compaoré's ascension.

Momo Jiba and Cyril Allen claimed that it was Blaise Compaoré himself who had 'fired the first shot' that killed Sankara around 4:30pm. Diendré, on the other hand, said that Blaise Compaoré arrived at the house much later, around 6.00 p.m. The precise timeline of Compaoré's arrival remains unknown.

THE INVOLVEMENT OF THE UNITED STATES

In the book recently published by Herman Jay Cohen (former Assistant Secretary of State for African Affairs), he writes that, as a member of the American

Executive, 'I accused Sankara of trying to destabilize the entire region of West Africa. Houphoüet dismissed my concerns with the flippant remark, "Don't worry, Sankara is just a boy. He will mature quickly." Since we were alone, I insisted that Sankara was hurting the image of the entire French community in West Arica and would eventually hurt Houphouët himself' (Cohen 2015: 23).[13]

The Liberians interviewed in Silvestro Montanaro's documentary, quoted supra, all similarly mentioned the American participation in the plot to kill Sankara. What was the reason? 'The Americans did not like Sankara, he talked about putting in public ownership the country's resources for the benefit of the people: actually he was a socialist. And they decided to get rid of him', as Cyril Allen put it.

The Liberians were willing to tell a bit more, provided that they believed they were not being filmed. To these ends, they made two important disclosures, which were confirmed later on. Firstly, they affirmed that the American Central Intelligence Agency (CIA) helped Charles Taylor escape an American jail, where he was serving a prison sentence. Secondly, Charles Taylor was tasked to infiltrate African revolutionary movements.

Pure coincidence? Charles Taylor recounted the incredible improbability of his escape during his trial before the Special Court for Sierra Leone (SCSL). According to an AFP report dated 15 July 2009: 'For me I have been freed because I did not escape from prison'. In 1985, he was detained in the jail of Plymouth County while waiting to be extradited to Liberia, where he was charged with embezzling US$90,000. The accused explained that, on 15 September 1985, a prison officer rushed into his cell in the high security unit. This officer led him to another wing with less supervision. 'Two other inmates were there', added Taylor. 'We stepped closer to a window. They took a sheet and tied it to the bars. We climb[ed] down outside. A car was waiting … I did not pay anything. I did not know the people who collected me', the accused told. Another AFP report, dated 22 December 2008, reveals that

> An American congressman visiting Monrovia acknowledged … during a press conference that the United States had taken part [in] 'the destabilisation' of Liberia before and during the civil wars and had been 'wrong' to do so … Americans have supported the toppling of William Tolbert [assassinated in 1980 during a bloody coup by Samuel Doe] because he was not doing what they [i.e. the Americans] wanted.

In his testimony at the Truth and Reconciliation Commission of Liberia (TRC), Simpson stated, 'Samuel Doe and Charles Taylor … met the same fate because they refused to carry out orders from Washington'.

More recently, *The Boston Globe*, in its 12 January 2012 issue, revealed that Charles Taylor might have worked for the Central Intelligence Agency and the

Pentagon as early as the beginning of the 1980s (the CIA neither confirmed nor denied these charges, see Bender 2012). The American connection(s) warrants more research.

AND FRANCE?

France had several reasons to see Thomas Sankara as a danger to their interests. Not the least was his growing popularity, his youth, his straight-talking manner and the achievements of the Revolution, in particular against corruption. All of this meant that Burkina was looked at in the region with sympathy and that Thomas Sankara was an admired leader. Sankara's achievements pointed to possibilities of choosing an alternative development model: this model was one opposed to the neo-colonial model that favoured French interests in the region. More than this, there was a fear that Sankara would become a regional example; therefore he threatened to destabilise neighbouring countries, where the elite's rampant corruption was cultivated and instrumentalised by neo-colonial actors. On a very public and international level, Sankara's Burkina Faso was no longer aligning itself with French positions at the United Nations, unlike France's other former colonies.

A series of events increased the tension in 1986. At a reception during President François Mitterrand's visit to Ouagadougou, Thomas Sankara lashed out at French policy in Africa. On his feet, looking defiantly at François Mitterrand (who appeared impassive, gazing in front of himself), Sankara delivered a very undiplomatic speech:

> We cannot understand why bandits like Jonas Savimbi, killers like Pieter Botha, have been authorised to travel to France, so beautiful and decent a country. They stained her with their hands and feet covered with blood. Those who allowed them to commit such actions will bear responsibility here and elsewhere in the world, now and forever![14]

That day, François Mitterrand attempted with his customary sagacity to respond to each point, at times in fatherly manner, 'I admire his great qualities, but he is too forthright; in my opinion he goes too far. Let me tell me out of experience'.[15] This verbal sparring was regarded as an insult by Mitterrand's entourage. According to many commentators, the final decision to 'get rid of' Sankara was taken after this incident.

Other policies of Burkina poisoned relations further. A few months later, another event (one that was far more serious for French diplomacy) earned a more overtly aggressive response. On 2 December 1986, Burkina Faso voted against France in support of New Caledonia's right to self-determination, which was discussed by the UN's Special Committee on Decolonisation. In paragraph 3 of resolution 41/41, the General Assembly 'proclaims the inalienable right to self-determination independence of New Caledonia people'. In Paris, at the National Assembly, the right wing MPs were enraged and the Prime Minister wrote to the Minister for Coopération, demanding economic retaliation against Burkina Faso (Guissou 1995: 107).

French authorities were too often slow to make good on their past errors. After a four-year campaign by the international network 'Justice for Sankara, Justice for Africa', the president of the French National Assembly finally accepted a motion for the setting up of an investigative committee on the assassination of Thomas Sankara (tabled by members of the Green and Front de Gauche parties). Claude Bartelone pretended to ignore that its remit would be precisely to investigate in France and not in Burkina. The questions phrased by the MPs were focused on specific points:

> We have to answer the following questions: why was Thomas Sankara assassinated? How was his assassination made possible? What roles did the French intelligence agencies and the French leaders at the time did play? Did the DGSE know some people were plotting and did it allow them to carry on?
>
> (Assemblée Nationale, 10 June 2011)[16]

The process stalled.

Momo Allen, one of the witnesses in the aforementioned documentary asserted: 'The piano was tuned both by the Americans and the French. There was a CIA agent at the American embassy in Ouagadougou, who was liaising with the representative of the secret services in the French embassy, they took the most important decisions' – the director cut in, saying, 'Then the CIA and the French intelligence services ... decided to get rid of Sankara. These are facts'.

On 23 February 2012, on *France Inter*, the programme 'Rendez-vous avec M.X' focused on the death of Thomas Sankara. Mr X (introduced as a former French intelligence services agent) claimed that after the victory of the right at the parliamentary elections in 1986, which lead to a period of 'cohabitation' with the socialist president, some African leaders called upon Jacques Foccart to take action. They asked him to get rid of Thomas Sankara. The most prominent of them was Houphouët-Boigny, the president of the Ivory Coast, neighbouring Burkina-Faso and a close ally with France in the region. When asked, 'Have the French agencies played a role?', Mr X answered, 'How could it be otherwise? Africa abounds with agents and former ones who work directly for African leaders or companies. They ensured our [i.e. French] interests over there are protected'.

The French journalist, François Hauter, a reporter at large with *Figaro*, recalls a troubling conversation during a panel discussion at Cheikh Anta Diop

University as part of events organised by the Prix Albert Londres in May 2008. During the panel, he informed the audience that he had been contacted by a special adviser to François Mitterrand for Africa, Guy Penne, who asked him to write an article hostile toward Thomas Sankara. More than this, Penne helped connect the journalist with Admiral Lacoste, who called the DCRG (Direction Générale des Renseignements Généraux) and suggested that he meet the Chief of African Operations. The journalist ended by adding, 'That was the biggest attempt at spinning I have ever seen in my entire career as a journalist'.

Ellis informed me in 2001 that 'Charles Taylor was also in contact with Michael Dupuch, former adviser to the President Jacques Chirac, when he was ambassador to the Ivory Coast. A French businessman, Robert de Saint-Pai was acting as an intermediary. He died some years ago'. Jean-Pierre Bat further emphasises France's support to Charles Taylor in his 2012 book, *Le Syndrome Foccart*.

The networks of la Françafrique were not just satisfied with these efforts to destabilise the regime – they also needed to imply that Blaise Compaoré would have the support of the new French government. In 1998, *Jeune Afrique* alluded to these overtures to Blaise Compaoré before October 1987: 'At the time number two of a revolution he did not believe in anymore, ever closer to Houphouët-Boigny, through whom he met his future wife, the handsome Blaise met his French counterpart, then Prime minister, via the Ivorian president and Jacques Foccart who introduced him to the leaders of the French Right, in particular Charles Pasqua'. A few years later, in 1992, Blaise Compaoré awarded the highest distinction in Burkina Faso, *l'Etoile d'or du Nahouri*, to Jacques Foccart.

CONCLUSION

This complex landscape constituted the conditions for an assassination – made up of the converging interests of the United States, France, several French-speaking countries in the region (notably Côte d'Ivoire) and Libya via Charles Taylor associates. Although complex and sinister, the historical geopolitical context described in this chapter is not a mere flight of fancy, as the French ambassador to Burkina declared in 2005. Rather, multiple sources reveal that many geostrategic actors supported, in some form, Sankara's assassination. Togo was also rumoured to have sent a general of gendarmerie with a group of men to Ouagadougou.

When looking for support in the West African region, Compaoré's trip to Côte d'Ivoire was a great occasion. During a party, he met Chantale Terrasson de Fougères, who was a member of a group of girls at the Yamoussoukro Lycée, who were often called upon to make Heads of State's visits to Côte d'Ivoire 'pleasant occasions'. She was the daughter of Jean Kourouma Terrasson, a well-known doctor in Côte d'Ivoire, who had close ties to President Houphouët-Boigny. After their initial meeting, Compaoré, deeply in love, travelled regularly to Côte d'Ivoire to join her. Their relationship progressed quickly and the wedding took place on 29 June 1985, six months after their first encounter. Houphouët-Boigny seemed to want the wedding to be successful. He lent his private jet to transport the couple and gave them numerous presents, including a large sum of money (rumoured to be 500 million FCFA or US$900,000) to ensure that his Franco-Ivorian protégée could maintain her lavish lifestyle – this, of course, was in the context of the political and economic revolution in Burkina Faso, as people were being encouraged to live according to their means, to count on themselves and to abstain from lavish lifestyles.

The geopolitical conditions were in place to prepare the coup. Bernard Doza, a political journalist, former adviser to Blaise Compaoré (August 1987 to July 1988) asserted, 'Houphouët Boigny provide[d] funding – the general secretary to the presidency, Coffie Gervais, estimate[d] the sum to 5 billion CFA francs – in order to finance a campaign of divisive leaflets [that would tear] apart Burkina during June 1987' (Doza 1991). The feud between revolutionary leaders deepened and the Liberians eventually set the assassination into action. Tripoli was alleged to have given intelligence equipment. Blaise Compaoré was confident that he could rely on Diendré to carry out the coup.

As we have seen from the discussion above, grey zones remained. The French media, which had been quiet on the subject, finally seized on the so-called 'Sankara affair' only after Blaise Compaoré was toppled following the popular uprising in October 2014. For the first time, they now widely mention versions of the plot theory outlined here. Yet, there had been no official response from the French government prior to the presidential election in May 2017. Mr Bartolone, the President of the National Assembly, during a visit to Burkina Faso in March 2017, declared in an interview: 'We are in favour [of] the French justice deal[ing] with all the demands [of] Burkina judiciary so [that] there will not be any suspicions in [the] relations between our two countries, including [in] this affair' (Belemviré 2017). This was a different tone than his previous responses in September 2015, when, during a parliamentary inquiry, he stated that the Sankara affair did 'not concern France'.

If a rogatory commission were created, it would entail the appointment of a French judge to lead the investigation in France. As per the declassification of documents (as President Macron has recently indicated France will do), such a commission would constitute an important breakthrough, but it would be insufficient. This is because similar incidents in the past have shown that even when official papers are made public in France, there are still many remaining obstacles on the path to establishing the truth.

In Burkina Faso, Judge François Yaméogo appears to be investigating thoroughly, including looking into the theory that there was an international coup. He asked for judicial assistance from the French authorities so that a judge might conduct hearings. He requested the declassification of related official papers. Nonetheless, no one has yet had any access to the necessary archives (as the date of the assassination goes back further in time than what has been made available). Gradually, we might have new revelations and hopefully compelling documents will be revealed, particularly if journalists and researchers press to open new avenues of investigation into aspects of the case as-of-yet insufficiently explored.

In this chapter, I set out to examine some of the many variables that might have played a part in the murder of Thomas Sankara. Some would like to dismiss his assassination as a rivalry between two men in a deeply complex friendship; others see his death as the consequence of internal politics and others as the result of a complex international plot involving many geopolitical actors. The contextualisation of Sankara's assassination within political and economic events at the time underlines the narrow path that Burkina Faso was allowed to follow.

Contemporary history shows that countries that try to resist the dominance of major global superpowers are subject to thorough destabilisation attempts, including military aggressions. In this case, political differences led to a serious conflict precisely because Blaise Compaoré was able to turn them to his own advantage in order to create the political conditions for his presidency as an alternative. Without political allies, he never could have contemplated seizing power. On the other hand, the civilians who closed rank behind him could not contemplate taking over without the support of the army. The fact that the country quickly returned to the Western fold demonstrates that these so-called 'political opponents' against Sankara (whom they criticised for being too reformist), were interested, first and foremost, in their own enrichment. Personal enrichment is precisely what happened under Blaise Compaoré's regime. Thomas Sankara was too dangerous an obstacle for this enrichment. He had to be eliminated and conditions were met to do it. This remains the most plausible hypothesis. Most of the world's coups, which set out to topple leaders whom have become 'hindrances' to global capitalism, are organised with accomplices among the direct entourage (see Afterward, this volume). Thus they most often arise within internal political situations with deep contradictions. This is precisely what happened in Burkina Faso when Thomas Sankara was assassinated.

The murder of Thomas Sankara stands as one of the most shocking political assassinations in world history. To this day, the exact circumstances are not elucidated. Although some of the victims are forgotten, the prestige of Sankara has continued to increase over the years. In Africa, Europe and the United States, the former leader of Burkina Faso has inspired many creative people, including writers, poets, choreographers, painters, visual artists and playwrights (see Chapters 21 and 23, this volume). Many citizens' movements and political parties now claim that Thomas Sankara's ideas guide their actions (see Chapters 15, 19 and 23, this volume).

Several documentaries, most of them made by European directors, have contributed to his renown.[17] Screenings are generally followed by discussions, allowing activists from the international network 'Justice pour Sankara, justice pour l'Afrique' to remind us of the campaign for truth and justice about the killing of Thomas Sankara. They provide detailed information on what we know and ask the audience to sign petitions. Commemorations on the anniversary of his death are organised everywhere in Africa as well as in many European countries, in the US and in Canada. Videos of Sankara's speeches (particularly that delivered on national debts) are available with subtitles in several languages. International networks against the burdens of debts in poor countries hold events around 15 October in order to pay homage to Thomas Sankara. These actions contribute to prevent what is termed 'l'Affaire Sankara' from being forgotten. Hopefully one day the full truth of Sankara's assassination will come to light.

NOTES

1 Translated by Jean Jaffré with Amber Murrey.

2 These two colonial wars, still mostly unknown in France, resulted in the deaths of tens of thousands of anti-colonial insurgents.

3 French President Nicolas Sarkozy reinstated France in NATO in 2009.

4 See the original in French at http://thomassankara.net/nous-preferons-un-pas-avec-le.

5 However, Pierre Ouédraogo did not appear on the side of the Popular Front (which assumed power on 15 October 1987).

6 The journalist, Denis de Montgolfier, originally located the text in 2001. The full text is available at http://thomassankara.net/lintervention-que-devait-faire-thomas-sankara-a-la-reunion-du-15-octobre-1987-au-soir.

7 See the full interview, in French, at http://thomassankara.net/interview-de-joseph-sambo-sankara-je-nai-pas-mon-fils-thomas-je-nai-pas-mon-fils-blaise-jai-perdu-tous-les-deux.

8 This story was first retold to me by one of Sankara's aide-de-camp, who had also been a friend of Vincent Sigué, who had told him personally. Sigué was killed shortly after Sankara, when he was close to the border of Ghana. A former legionary, whose military qualities impressed his entourage, he remains a controversial character, notably for the ill treatment or the tortures that he would have inflicted on prisoners while he was temporarily in charge of internal security. Thomas Sankara later had him removed from this position and planned to entrust him with the direction of the FIMATS (*Force d'intervention du ministère de l'Administration Territoriale et de la Sécurité*) after an internship in Cuba. The project of creating this security force, sought after by Sankara's entourage in order to better ensure his safety, would never see light. Thomas Sankara would be assassinated before its realisation.

9 After a short courtship, the couple was married on 29 June 1985.

10 Stephen Ellis met several times with Charles Taylor's former companions to realise this work.

11 Among these sources is the on-line news magazine, *The Perspective or the Liberian Mandingo Association*, a New York-based online journal.

12 See transcripts of these interviews and film extras at thomassankara.net/assassinat-de-thomas-sankara-des-temoignages-dun-documentaire-de-la-rai-3-mettent-en-cause-la-france-la-cia-et-blaise-compaore.

13 In an earlier draft of Cohen's manuscript (originally reported in the pages of La Lettre du Continent and confirmed by the author just as this book goes to press), he recalls insisting to Houphouët-Boigny that he '"rid" West Africa of the influence of the captain Thomas Sankara, "to prevent the region from sinking into revolution and subversion"'. This passage was later edited in a way that attempts to minimize US pressure to assassinate Sankara.

14 Jonas Savimbi was the leader of UNITA (Angola's National Union for the Total Independence), a movement supported by both the CIA and South Africa, which was waging war against the Angolan government of the MPLA (The People's Movement for the Liberation of Angola).

15 The entire exchange is available in French at http://thomassankara.net/seul-le-combat-peut-liberer-notre.

16 The transcript of the Assemblée Nationale is available at www.assemblee-nationale.fr/13/propositions/pion3527.asp

17 For example, Robin Shuffield's (2006) *Thomas Sankara, l'Homme Intègre* and Christophe Cupelin's (2012) *Capitaine Thomas Sankara.*

REFERENCES

Andriamirado, S. (1989) *Il S'Appelait Sankara: Chronique d'une Mort Violente*. Paris: Jeune Afrique.

Belemviré, M. (2017) Coopération: Le Président de l'Assemblée Nationale Française en Visite au Burkina. *Burkina Online*. Retrieved on 1 December 2017 from www.burkinaonline.com/wp/cooperation-le-president-de-lassemblee-nationale-francaise-en-visite-au-burkina/Benamrane, D. (2016) *Sankara, Leader Africain*. Paris: L'Harmattan.

Bender, B. (2012) *Former Liberian Dictator Charles Tayler Had US Spy Agency Ties. The Boston Globe*. Retrieved on 14 July 2017 from www.bostonglobe.com/metro/2012/01/17/mass-escapee-turned-liberian-dictator-had-spy-agency-ties/DGBhSfjxPVrtoo4WT95bBI/story.html.

Capitaine Thomas Sankara. (2012) Directed by Christopher Cupelin [Film]. Switzerland: Laïka Films.

Cohen, H. (2015) *The Mind of the African Strongman: Conversations with Dictators, Statesmen and Father Figures*. Washington, DC: New Academia Publishing.

Doza, B (1991) *Liberté Confisquée, Le Complot Franco-Africain*. Paris: BibliEurope.

Ellis, S. (2006) *The Mask of Anarchy: The Destruction of Liberia and the Religious Dimension of an African Civil War* (2nd edn). London: Hurst & Co.

Guissou, B. (1995) *Burkina Faso, Un espoir en Afrique*. Paris: L'Harmattan.

Jaffré, B. (1989) *Burkina Faso, les Années Sankara, de la Révolution à la Rectifrcation*. Paris: L'Harmattan.

Jaffré, B. (2009) Que Sait-On Sur L'Assassinat de Sankara? *Pambazuka News*. Retrieved on 12 July 2017 from www.pambazuka.org/fr/pan-africanism/%C2%AB-que-sait-sur-l%E2%80%99assassinat-de-sankara-%C2%BB.

Nkounkou, D. (2002) *L'affaire Thomas Sankara, le Juge et le Politique*. Paris: NK.

Ombre Africane (2009) Directed by Silvestro Montanaro [Film]. Italy: RAI 3.

Radio France Internationale (2008a) Vérité, Réconciliation et Revelations. Retrieved on 14 July 2017 from www1.rfi.fr/actufr/articles/104/article_71763.asp.

Radio France Internationale (2008b) Prince Johnson: C'est Compaoré qui a Fait Tuer Sankara, avec l'Aval d'Houphouët-Boigny. Retrieved on 14 July 2017 from www1.rfi.fr/actufr/articles/106/article_73998.asp.

Ray, C. (2008) Who Really Killed Thomas Sankara? *Pambazuka News.* Retrieved on 14 July 2017 from www.pambazuka.org/pan-africanism/who-really-killed-thomas-sankara.

Somé, V. (1990) *Thomas Sankara, l'Espoir Assassiné.* Paris: L'Harmattan.

Thomas Sankara, l'Homme Intègre. (2006) Directed by Robin Shuffield [Film]. France: ZORN Production.

CHAPTER 7

'Incentivised' Self-Adjustment

Reclaiming Sankara's Revolutionary Austerity from Corporate Geographies of Neoliberal Erasure

Nicholas A. Jackson

INTRODUCTION

In their 1989 annual report, World Bank analysts commented that since 1984, Burkina Faso's government had 'been taking ... a number of adjustment measures. While it is premature to assess the impact of these programs on economic growth, measures to improve incentives, combined with favourable weather conditions, are beginning to bear fruit' (World Bank 1989: 108). At best, this passage was inserted as a throwaway line, part of a report whose authors desperately sought to justify the then-struggling Structural Adjustment Plan (SAP) framework of development. SAPs had attained hegemonic status within research and high-level administrative departments of the international financial institutions (IFIs) only two years before, when Anna Krueger's (1974) views were largely concretised in the 1987 World Development Report. Despite this short timeline, World Bank scholars and researchers were already preparing the documents to compel strong government facilitation (i.e. what has since become known as 'governance') to address the clear failures accumulating within structural adjustment (World Bank 1987; Krueger 1974).

When held up against the actual words and policies of President Sankara, the World Bank report statements almost attain the status of nonsense syllables, disconnected with any semblance of reality. However, when one moves beyond the formal written discourses of the IFIs into larger geographies (represented, governed and lived) of global corporate exploitation, anti-hegemonic resistance and corporate response, the World Bank statements make much more sense (albeit geographic more than discursive). In this chapter, I look at (a) the ideological roots of Sankara's ideas followed by an explication of the 'revolutionary self-adjustment' that he put in place; (b) the reasons why (beyond the dissention within Burkinabè government power centres that is often blamed), as long-time BBC reporter for Burkina Faso Joan Baxter (2008: 97) commented, 'Sankara could not simply be overthrown ... he had to be permanently eliminated'; and, finally, (c) the flexian networks that underpin Burkinabè power within global geographies of corporate exploitation.

My epistemological approach to power derives from John Allen's (2003: 97) notion that '[While] power is not some "thing" or attribute that can be possessed, I do not believe either that it can flow; it is only mediated as a relational effect of social interaction.' Allen provides important examples of the diversity of modalities through which power is exercised: domination, authority, coercion, seduction, inducement and manipulation (ibid.). For a very long time, certainly since Europeans began exploiting resources from Africa and other eventual colonies, small groups of people have used already appropriated, controlled, 'justified' and 'legitimised' resource wealth to create corporate entities (Apter 2005; see also Jackson 2009). I define these entities as bundles of representation, location and governmentality, ones that are able to exercise power as if by one body.[1] Developers of corporate entities compose these entities of people, rules, habits, symbols, narratives, buildings, boundaries, rhythms, walls and much else besides. Corporate entities include not only business, but also government, academies, churches, non-governmental organisations and so on. They exercise power dynamically and collectively through social interaction – above all to control the production of space to their benefit. That is, these corporate entities are built to gain hegemony over exploitation.

Corporate entities have long exploited 'producing margins' through instability and barely controlled violence – instability that has then been judged to their developers' benefit (Mantz 2008). Such 'fragmented stability,' enhanced by occasional spectacular episodes of brutal violence, is not only effective but also less costly than ever-present violence (Jackson 2009, 2016). However, every condition of such corporate exploitation generates resistance and more brutal conditions or stronger opposition movements often bolster anti-hegemonic resistance, whereby people attempt to overturn existing configurations of power. Corporate entities respond to anti-hegemonic resistance with the lowest cost option possible. More potent and effective resistance necessitates more costly responses: ranging from strategic silence and disregard at the local level, to perception and risk management, to the very rare transformation of the corporate suite along with the industry and perhaps the entire configuration of power. Sankara understood very well these regimes of resource mobilisation and control, particularly as they attempted to position Burkina Faso within a global, colonial political economy: 'From imperialism's point of view, it's more important to dominate us culturally than militarily. Cultural domination is more flexible, more effective, less costly ... to overturn the Burkinabè regime ... [you] just need to forbid the import of champagne, lipstick and nail polish' (Sankara 2007: 197).

Corporate entities commonly attempt to hide the realities of resource exploitation by presenting commodities 'in such a way as to conceal almost perfectly ... the social relations implicated in their production' (Harvey 1990: 300). That way, the violence of direct exploitation can be implemented behind layers of representation and disconnected governance, what Apter (2005: 89) calls 'a basic inversion of simulacrum and original ... whereby an exhibited "people" became more real and authentic than the lands and people themselves' (see also Mitchell 1991). The corporate academy plays a key role in these projects because universities are authorised by states to bestow credentials of 'learning in wisdom', as befit the assumptions and expectations that states are containers of fundamental legitimacy. However, in my framework, the academy is not simply a space (however internally contested) where 'wisdom is learned' (i.e. where doctors of philosophy are credentialed and domiciled) and debated. Rather, corporate entities separate worlds of production and consumption in part through creation and sustenance by senior scholars and administrators within the corporate academy (centred in universities like Harvard, Stanford and MIT) of legitimising narratives that are valid because they 'presume to the status of science'. These narratives are propagated by students, whose training makes them amenable to these hegemonic creations (Peet 2007, 2009). In a self-appraising closed loop, students taught at these institutions then become highly remunerated scholars themselves, recruited by major and minor schools throughout the country. These students enter the research and high-level policymaking departments of the IFIs, where they write governing documents that justify corporate exploitation (Jackson 2017).

The spectacle that is neoliberalism grew out of neoclassical economics, a set of narratives based on the notion of *homo economicus* or rational, self-interested, relatively autonomous individuals (Jackson 2011). This 'economic man' is an example of 'the birth-to-presence of a form of being that pre-exists' and yet requires expert intervention at every turn to bring it – him? – to fruition (Rose 1999: 177). 'Trustees do not direct or dominate; yet they always have work to do' (Murray Li 2007). The 'expert intervention' in this case is structural adjustment: a set of governing policies underpinned by debt service requirements that justify the systematic exercise of power (defined as authority and the inducement of coercion when necessary) to direct productive resources (away from local needs) to the service of global corporate exploitation (George 1988). The 'presuming to the status of science' makes resistance unreasonably eccentric at best and a global (terrorist?) threat at worst (ibid.). As Margaret Thatcher notoriously commented, 'There is no alternative'. Sankara's project represented a significant challenge because he might have actually succeeded and, even in failure, his legacy might have weakened the legitimising narratives and associated governance mechanisms that justified corporate exploitation itself (for a detailed examination on disappearing in the academy see Jackson, this volume).

'REVOLUTIONARY SELF-ADJUSTMENT'

As a child of an Upper Volta colonial official, as one of the relatively few graduates from a *lycée* (state secondary school) in the commercial centre of Bobo-Dioulasso, and as a graduate of Kadiogo military school, Sankara was able to both benefit from some of the best educational opportunities available in the colony and to have ample latitude for internalising what he would later demonstrate was a no-holds-barred militant dedication to the rights of oppressed peoples in opposition to corporate imperialism. Discussion of his broad philosophical underpinnings has been conducted at length in other chapters in this volume (see chapters from Biney, Murrey, Daley, Harsch, Abiwu and Odeymi as well as Botchway and Traore), but here it is important to recognise how Sankara was able to come into power with a deep awareness of the spatiotemporal location of Burkina Faso and, more importantly, the courage to implement practical policies as well as to make reasonable demands that were nevertheless intolerable to the corporate entities centred in Europe, the United States and elsewhere (and who had the resources and desire to exercise power in every space of the globe; see Chapter 6, in this volume). His witness of the 1972 uprisings in Madagascar, and associated contact with participants in the 1968 French uprisings, gave Sankara important insights into theory and praxis of corporate exploitation, anti-hegemonic resistance and corporate response. Martin describes Sankara's thought as clearly influenced by Marxism-Leninism but he was first and foremost 'an ardent nationalist and convinced pan-Africanist'. Minister of external affairs Guissou supported this in a 1985 letter to Martin, 'According to its economic content, our Revolution is a bourgeois revolution. It does not aim at the elimination of private property or private economic initiative and entrepreneurship' (Martin 2012: 112–113).

The French colonialists had created the Burkina Faso that Sankara grew up in as a landlocked area on the margins of French colonial Africa, notable for the tax-compelled colonial appropriation of cotton, livestock and migrant labour to the 'Gold Coast' (Englebert 1996: 79). Throughout colonial and neocolonial periods it remained marginalised, with some of the worst social welfare (literacy, infant mortality, life expectancy, and so forth) indicators in the world. Sankara was thus faced with the crisis and backhanded opportunity of a land and people already at the bottom in their material quality of life, with relatively few dollar-denominated variable interest debts (the presumed justifications for structural adjustment) to repay but, on the other hand, very little surplus wealth to cushion the re-distribution of resources toward social welfare. Sankara used his experience to embark on a program that, while invigorated by Marxist–Leninist anti-imperialist language, was more akin to social democracy. The means of production were not universally socialised but rather were strongly directed and influenced to serve the needs of Burkinabè people (more than the needs of global capital).

To do so, Sankara refocused the economy toward endogenous development and away from debt, migrant labour, export crops, urban concentration and a corrupt civil service glut (Dembele 2013). Sankara's administration nationalised land and then leased it out with preference for rural subsistence and other local products. Sankara famously demanded, 'Where is imperialism? Look at your plates when you eat. The imported rice, maize and millet; that is imperialism' (Sankara, speech at First National Conference of CDRs, 4 April 1986). Burkina refocused cotton production to the domestic textile industry, with Sankara requiring every government official to wear tunics (Faso dan Fani) made from local cotton by local manufacturers. They also revitalised private mining concerns (gold, zinc and others) with public money, to assist with state revenues (Savadogo and Wetta 1992: 59). These changes then supported the administration's strong mobilisation of resources and people toward social welfare programs. While many neighbours were cutting education, health, infrastructure and other public programs for human development, Sankara's administration administered millions of long-overdue vaccines (see Chapter 16, this volume); placed a health centre in nearly every community; increased the literacy rate the most that it had been since colonisation; made tree planting a national and cultural tradition and began massive public mobilisation projects to impede desertification, build dams and lay a railroad from Ouagadougou to the manganese mine in Tambao.

To support these programmes and to increase the power of 'the masses', Sankara confronted many of the traditional civil society elite, including teachers and other largely urban-based trade unions, academics, civil servants ('bureaucratic bourgeoisie') in state administrative organs, and cultural or traditional elite of the countryside, whom he labelled petty bourgeoisie opportunists and counter-revolutionaries attempting to retain their entrenched interests (Sankara 2007: 382ff). In particular, Sankara sought to increase the power of the peasantry and workers, and especially to achieve the full emancipation of women, who 'hold up half of the sky' (ibid.; see Chapters 8, 11 and 13, this volume). These new configurations of power and decision making were mobilised through the Committees for the Defence of the Revolution

(CDRs), charged with spreading the ideological foundations of Sankara's revolution, directing labour for public works, and providing organs through which peoples' voices could be heard at all levels.

Outside of the 'sovereign' space that became Burkina Faso, Sankara strengthened alliances with those international leaders whom he felt were the strongest supporters of his revolution. The Cuban and Nicaraguan leaderships, always under the gun from representatives of their own feudal neo-colonial elite within the United States, were perhaps the most consistent in their alignment with Sankara's revolution. However, they faced similar resource deficiency issues and so their support was primarily moral. Sankara also had a strong though contested relationship with Qaddafi (in Libya), whom he emphasised did not determine Burkinabè policies: 'When it comes to ideology, we're not virgins' (Sankara 2007: 382ff). The fact that Qaddafi quickly became a strong ally of Compaoré, and perhaps even encouraged Compaoré to murder Sankara in order to pave the way for Charles Taylor's invasion of Liberia, lends a note of caution regarding the strength of the alliance with Sankara (French 2011; see also Chapter 6, this volume). Perhaps Sankara's closest friend was Jerry Rawlings in Ghana. Even this friendship, however, was coloured by the fact that Rawlings had already implemented a coercive form of structural adjustment early in his term (Hutchful 1989, 2002). Perhaps because Burkina was a non-aligned country, Sankara's relationship with the Soviet Union seemed always to be at arm's length, with Sankara refusing food aid and the Soviet leadership never completely supporting Sankara's revolution (Sankara 2007: 189ff).

Sankara understood, however, that the global nature of corporate exploitation (imperialism) made it impossible for one state, especially one as small as Burkina Faso, to go forward alone. In addition, transitory alliances were not enough. As a result, Sankara assumed a prophetic role (as befit his strong religious, especially Catholic but also Muslim, sensibilities) and spoke most forcefully, particularly in the fourth year of his term and last months of his life, about the need for all countries in Africa to speak together against odious, illegitimate, neocolonial debt. A critical analysis for our purpose has to do with the character of debt as a governance-based justification for exploitation (see Chapter 12, this volume). As Sankara remarked, '[T]he colonialists have transformed themselves into technical assistants ... [turning] each of us into a financial slave ... of those who had the opportunity, the craftiness, the deceitfulness to invest funds in our countries that we are obliged to repay' (Sankara 2007: 189ff). Sankara was well aware of these implications and, unlike almost all of his contemporaries, he was willing to take on the enormous risk of bucking that debt, while trying to convince his fellow leaders that it was in their people's best interest to do so as well.

ERASING SANKARA AND 'RECTIFYING' THE REVOLUTION

As so often happens with prophetic voices, Sankara would be murdered less than three months after delivering this speech, likely at the command of his erstwhile childhood friend Compaoré. Many reasons for his assassination have been given, including the alienation of teachers, leftist organisations and other groups inside Burkina; the move to create a single party; nominally internal economic pressures;[2] and alliances with particularly adversarial or grasping external leaders, including Compaoré's wife's patron, President Houphouet-Boigny of the Ivory Coast, Charles Taylor of Liberia and Qaddafi in Libya (Jaffré 2007). However, Compaoré's almost immediate 'rectification' of the revolution (that is to say, his reversion to the global corporate status quo) in nearly every manner seems to buttress the argument that Sankara was killed because his policies and philosophies threatened global corporate exploitation. Civil service, professional and 'traditional' elites were 'relieved' to see Sankara go, but the poor and urban and rural youth expressed opposition through 'sporadic protests, overt hostility to the new authorities, and the virtual collapse of most mobilisation efforts' (Harsch 1998: 628). As Hilgers describes it, 'Under the cover of some kind of democratisation, Blaise Compaoré's regime has developed the capacity of using and transforming institutions with the aim of keeping power' (Hilgers 2010: 352).

Compaoré very quickly restored the veto power of global corporate financial organisations over internal economic governance. Soon after Sankara was killed, the Compaoré regime began accessions to the IFI structural adjustment loans (SALs), not because the country had unsustainable debt (though Compaoré's use of public largess to seduce local power elite did further increase government outlays) but simply because, in the words of Prime Minister Youssouf Ouédraogo, Burkina Faso saw 'no other option' (note the parallels to Thatcher's 'no alternative') except for SAL to ensure external financing. Demonstrating how far the Compaoré administration had departed from Sankara's self-adjustment, Ouédraogo was comfortable making the 'common sense' statement that 'there are even financing possibilities [e.g. external Paris Club loans] that [a country] can no longer benefit from [if] it cannot implement a package of conditions which the international community, at a given time, has come to regard as compulsory' (Foreign Broadcast Information Service, 26 June 1992). More than this, though, 'Burkina's trade unions and opposition parties [much like Sankara during his lifetime] see the conditionalities as a loss of national sovereignty. "We take our instructions from the IMF and World Bank like the good pupils we are", opposition leader Joseph Ki-Zerbo bitterly commented' (Harsch 1998: 629).

With the SAL in process, the Compaoré administration had effectively completed two key initiatives. First, the Burkinabè government needed to control anti-hegemonic opposition. They did so through various combinations of insincere negotiations, the repeated institutionalisation of 'commissions' (the proverbial committees to quash opposition) and violence when necessary (Chouli 2011: 145). Secondly, the newly authoritarian government needed to demonstrate their loyalty to global corporate entities, which Compaoré did by implementing SAL. With debt service reactivated, the regime was restored to 'normal status' within a global colonial political economy: an impoverished African state with an authoritarian government and a tenuous lifeline to development (through export crop production).

RETURNING TO BASELINE: FLEXIAN CORPORATE EXPLOITATION JUSTIFIED BY DEBT-DRIVEN STRUCTURAL ADJUSTMENT

With neoliberal and minimalist polyarchic (i.e. elite competitive party) baselines restored (i.e. some opposition parties existed but no transfers of power occurred until his overthrow in 2014), Compaoré's administration was not only able to undertake 'the right kind' of austerity – that is to say, cutting public services such as health, education and water; privatising public industries; redirecting sovereign resources outward – but was also able to build an impressive network of flexians (Wedel 2009, 2014). These flexians move between national and global as well as public and private corporate entities. Compaoré led the way by restoring and revitalising elite relationships wherever they could be found, from the ever-present French networks to his close relationship with the Ivorian president (whose niece he married) to his connections with Taylor in Liberia, Qaddafi in Libya and eventually the United States' 'counter-terror' actors in the Sahel (Kedo and Goodman 2015):

> This national elite comprises several components, some long established, others relatively new. Their interests are far from uniform, but many of the most influential members are linked together through complex webs of personal, family, ethnic, and social ties, often under direct state patronage ... the more successful Burkinabè entrepreneurs generally are those who have forged alliances with foreign capital.
>
> (Harsch 1998: 634–635)

The relationships transcend, and are arguably sustained by, lines of nominal political opposition. Joseph Ki-Zerbo offers a particularly good example. As the leader of the teachers unions that struck against Sankara from the beginning of Sankara's term, Ki-Zerbo then became part of the elite opposition to Compaoré, being particularly critical of structural adjustment. However, one of Ki-Zerbo's allies among 'traditional' chiefs was a cousin of Compaoré's prime minister;

these sorts of relationships 'demonstrate[e] yet again the multiple links among various elite sectors' (Harsch 1998: 637).

Of particular interest to this chapter is the career of Justin Damo Baro. '[Baro], briefly a finance minister under Sankara, later revealed that he had tried on four occasions to persuade Sankara to ask for IMF assistance' (Harsch 1998: 628). In 1987, Damo Baro became a financial analyst with the World Bank, after which he was appointed by Compaoré as an 'adviser in charge of monitoring the economic reforms of Burkina Faso', before eventually becoming vice-governor and then interim governor of the Banque Centrale des Etats De L'Afrique De l'Ouest (BCEAO; Ecodufaso 2015). It is likely that Baro would have influenced the language (e.g. portraying the time of Sankara as a case of 'matching incentives') of World Bank reports about Burkina Faso as well as the governance documents underlying structural adjustment loans. The depths of possible influence become clearer when reading Morten Jerven's (2013) ethnographic research among ministries of finance across Africa, exposing the ways in which data (regardless of its reliability) is fundamental to supposedly 'objectively economic' analysis, especially the gross domestic product.[3] Might Baro have not only contributed to bringing the land and people of Burkina Faso into the orbit of structural adjustment governance, but also influencing the numbers and 'evidence-based policy' that led to Sankara being hidden under 'improved incentives'?[4]

CONCLUSIONS: DEPOLITICISE IF POSSIBLE, ERASE IF NECESSARY

Thirty years after Sankara's murder, former president Compaoré resides comfortably in the Ivory Coast, where he was given citizenship presumably to prevent his extradition to Burkina Faso, after escaping Burkina Faso with the assistance of the French government (BBC 2016). Meanwhile, Sankara's close friend 'in revolution' Jerry Rawlings continues as a highly respected and wealthy elder politician for Ghana, Africa and the world. The flexians whom they supported, or at least accommodated, have reason for continued confidence that Sankara has disappeared *enough*. Rawlings helped by adopting the expected debt service projects imposed (and 'justified') by inter-governmental 'development' organisations, thus promoting and being enriched by the depoliticised story of debt, economic opening, institutional correction and the endless 'not like the West' that is the Africa of legitimising narratives within academies, governments, inter- and non-governmental organisations. Compaoré and his associates in government (Baro) and opposition (Ki-Zerbo) helped by either murdering Thomas Sankara or assisting with writing him out of a history that is now dominated by 'a typical corrupt, long-lived and now deposed dictator' (to characterise in aggregate a long list of standard examples) in Compaoré.

Left out of this dismal account is the fact that Sankara still lives. His words, when spread, are at least as powerful now as when he uttered them. Furthermore, the 'land of upright people' never ceases resisting and transforming, even with the same scarcity of material resources that Sankara encountered 34 years ago. When the 'Africa as it always has been' is upended within the academy and outside the conference rooms of governance organisations by Sankara's 'revolutionary self-adjustment' and other legacies covered in this volume, then we have a much better chance of replacing status quo corporate exploitation with the 'noisy conversations' that ultimately might bring lasting transformation (Giroux 2014).

NOTES

1   For reasons of simplicity, I speak as if 'corporate entities act' when in fact corporate entities are nothing more than the resources, modalities of power and social interaction that comprise and form them. Those who control the resources are the actors. Debates about the agency, structural embeddedness, consciousness or other qualities of these actors is crucial, but beyond the scope of this chapter. For a brief review in the context of neoliberalism as spectacle, see Jackson (2011).

2   Englebert and others concentrate largely on 'internal economic pressures'. However, 'internal' and 'external' pressures are inextricably linked (Englebert 1996: 60–61; Kandeh 2004: 128; Otayek 1989: 13–30).

3   'The buzzword in the development community is "evidence-based policy" and scholars are using increasingly sophisticated economic methods ... The impression of measurability and accuracy is misleading, and that has broad implications across social science disciplines that deal with issues of African development' (Jerven 2013: 9).

4   Jerven (a white European), for his part, did not suffer death for his insights. However, there was evidence that Jerven was dis-invited from meetings of the United Nations Economic Commission on Africa (UNECA) and that his research credibility was questioned. See Taylor (2013).

REFERENCES

Allen, J. (2003) *Lost Geographies of Power*. RGS-IBG book series. Malden, MA: Blackwell.

Apter, A. H. (2005) *The Pan-African Nation: Oil and the Spectacle of Culture in Nigeria*. Chicago, IL: University of Chicago Press.

Baxter, J. (2008) *Dust from Our Eyes: An Unblinkered Look at Africa*. Hamilton, ON: Wolsak and Wynn).

BBC. (2016) Burkina Faso Ex-leader Blaise Compaore becomes Ivorian. *BBC News*, 24 February. Retrieved on 23 December 2016 from www.bbc.com/news/world-africa-35650193.

Chouli, L. (2011) Peoples' Revolts in Burkina Faso. In Firoze Manji and Sokari Ekine (eds), *African Awakening: The Emerging Revolutions*, 131–146. Oxford: Fahamu.

Dembele, D. M. (2013) Thomas Sankara: An Endogenous Approach to Development. *Pambazuka News*, 23 October.

Ecodufaso. (2015) Damo Justin Baro: Le défenseur des Pme/Pmi au Burkina Faso. *Ecodufaso News*, site. 27 July. Retrieved on 1 October 2016 from www.ecodufaso.com/damo-justin-baro-le-defenseur-des-pmepmi-au-burkina-faso.

Englebert, P. (1996) *Burkina Faso: Unsteady Statehood in West Africa*. Boulder, CO: Westview Press.

French, H. W. (2011) How Qaddafi Reshaped Africa. *The Atlantic*, 1 March.

George, S. (1988) *A Fate Worse than Debt*. New York: Grove Press.

George, S. and Fabrizio S. (1994) *Faith and Credit: The World Bank's Secular Empire*. Boulder: Westview Press.

Giroux, H. A. (2014) *Academic Madness and the Politics of Exile. Truthout*, 18 November. Retrieved on 24 December 2016 from www.truth-out.org/news/item/27501-henry-a-giroux-academic-madness-and-the-politics-of-exile.

Harsch, E. (1998) Burkina Faso in the Winds of Liberalisation. *Review of African Political Economy* 25(78): 625–641.

Harvey, D. (1990) *The Condition of Postmodernity: An Enquiry into the Origins of Cultural Change*. Oxford: Blackwell.

Hilgers, M. (2010) Evolution of Political Regime and Evolution of Popular Political Representations in Burkina Faso. *African Journal of Political Science and International Relations* 4(9): 350–359.

Hutchful, E. (1989) From 'Revolution' to Monetarism: The Economics and Politics of the Adjustment Programme in Ghana. In B. K. Campbell and J. Loxley (eds), *Structural Adjustment in Africa*, 92–131. New York: St Martin's Press.

Hutchful, E. (2002) *Ghana's Adjustment Experience: The Paradox of Reform*. Geneva: UNRISD.

Jackson, N. A. (2009) The Spectacle of Neoclassical Economics: The Chad–Cameroon Petroleum Development Project and Exploitation in the Niger Delta and The Chad Basin. Doctoral thesis, University of Denver.

Jackson, N. A. (2011) Neoliberalism as Spectacle: Economic Theory, Development and Corporate Exploitation. *Human Geography* 4(3): 1–13.

Jackson, N. A. (2016) Fragmented Stability: Neoliberalism and the Politics of Belonging in Anglophone Cameroon. In T. Falola and W. S. Nasong'o (eds), *Contested Politics in Africa: Identity, Conflict, and Social Change*, 239–258. Durham, NC: Carolina Academic Press.

Jackson, N. A. (2017) 'Social Movement Theory' as a Baseline Legitimizing Narrative: Corporate Exploitation, Anti-Hegemonic Opposition and the Contested Academy. *Human Geography* 10(1): 36–49.

Jaffré, B. (2007) Burkina Faso's Pure President. *Le Monde diplomatique*, November.

Jerven, M. (2013) *Poor Numbers: How We are Misled by African Development Statistics and What To Do About It*. Ithaca, NY: Cornell University Press.

Kandeh, J. D. (2004) *Coups from Below: Armed Subalterns and State Power in West Africa*. New York: Palgrave Macmillan.

Kedo, A. and Goodman, C. (2015) US Military Aid to Presidential Guards a Risky Venture. LobeLog. Retrieved on 21 December 2016 from http://lobelog.com/u-s-military-aid-to-presidential-guards-a-risky-venture.

Krueger, A. O. (1974) The Political Economy of the Rent-Seeking Society. *American Economic Review* 64(3): 291–303.

Mantz, J. W. (2008) Improvisational Economies: Coltan Production in the Eastern Congo. *Social Anthropology* 16(1): 34–50.

Martin, G. (2012) *African Political Thought.* New York: Palgrave Macmillan.

Mitchell, T. (1991) *Colonising Egypt.* Berkeley, CA: University of California Press.

Murray Li, T. (2007) *The Will to Improve: Governmentality, Development and the Practice of Politics.* Durham: Duke University.

Otayek, R. (1989) Burkina Faso: Between Feeble State and Total State, the Swing Continues. In D. B. Cruise O'Brien, J. Dunn and R. Rathbone (eds), *Contemporary West African States,* 13–30. Cambridge: Cambridge University Press.

Peet, R. (2007) *Geography of Power: The Making of Global Economic Policy.* London: Zed Books.

Peet, R. (2009) *Unholy Trinity: The IMF, World Bank, and WTO.* London: Zed Books.

Rose, N. S. (1999) *Powers of Freedom: Reframing Political Thought.* Cambridge: Cambridge University Press.

Sankara, T. (2007) *Thomas Sankara Speaks: The Burkina Faso revolution, 1983–1987* (ed. M. Prairie). New York: Pathfinder Press.

Savadogo, K. and Wetta, C. (1992) The Impact of Self-Imposed Adjustment: The Case of Burkina Faso, 1983–9. In G. Andrea Cornia, R. van der Hoeven, and P. Thandika Mkandawire (eds), *Africa's Recovery in the 1990s: From Stagnation and Adjustment to Human Development,* 53–71. Basingstoke: Macmillan.

Taylor, M. (2013) Poor Numbers: Why Is Morten Jerven Being Prevented From Presenting His Research At UNECA? *African Arguments.* Retrieved on 1 October 2016 from www.africanarguments.org/2013/09/19/poor-numbers-why-is-morten-jerven-being-prevented-from-presenting-his-research-at-uneca-by-magnus-taylor.

Wedel, J. R. (2009) *Shadow Elite: How the World's New Power Brokers Undermine Democracy, Government, and the Free Market.* New York: Basic Books.

Wedel, J. R. (2014) *Unaccountable: How Elite Power Brokers Corrupt Our Finances, Freedom, and Security.* New York: Pegasus Books.

World Bank. (1989) *Annual Report.* Washington, DC: World Bank.

World Bank. (1987) *Industrialisation and Foreign Trade, World Development Report.* Washington, DC: World Bank.

PART II

POLITICAL PHILOSOPHIES

CHAPTER 8

Madmen, Thomas Sankara and Decoloniality In Africa

Ama Biney

*You cannot carry out fundamental change without a certain amount of
madness. In this case, it comes from nonconformity, the courage to turn
your back on the old formulas, the courage to invent the future. Besides, it
took the madmen of yesterday for us to be able to act with extreme clarity
today. I want to be one of those madmen.*
Thomas Sankara at Burkinabè art exhibition in Harlem, 1984[1]

INTRODUCTION

Thomas Sankara was a revolutionary and he committed himself to revolution.
His definition of revolution and fundamental change is alluded to in the
epigraph above. Sankara committed the Burkinabè people – as active
agents in their awareness of implementing a social, economic and political
transformation of both society and themselves as human beings – in a quest
for a different kind of world and society. He wanted the Burkinabè people to
commit to 'nonconformity' and possess 'the courage to turn [their] back on
the old formulas'. In the drastically short time that Sankara led Burkina Faso
(from 1983 to 1987), he demonstrated a boldness of political vision and sought
to 'carry out fundamental change' and would be called a madman for doing
so. In these four years, his small country initiated inspiring endeavours to
arrest the deforestation of his landlocked country and a 10 million tree planting
campaign was introduced in 1985. Literacy programmes were rolled out in
1986. Cuban volunteers assisted with a 15-day mobilisation campaign aimed
to vaccinate all Burkinabè under the age of 15 against meningitis, yellow fever
and measles. Land was nationalised alongside mineral wealth and the allocation
of small plots to farmers. Traditional chiefs were denied tribute payments and

the system of obligatory labour for peasants was discontinued. The philosophy foundational to many of these efforts and changes bears striking resemblances to contemporary 'decolonial' thinking.

'Decolonial' thinking emerged from Latin American scholars such as Walter D. Mignolo (2011), Ramón Grosfoguel (2007), Anibal Quijano (2007), Nelson Maldonado-Torres (2006, 2007, 2011), Santiago Castro-Gómez (2010), Chela Sandoval (2000), Bouaventura de Sousa Santos (2014) and from South Africa in the work of Sabelo J. Ndlovu-Gatsheni (2013a, 2013b, 2016a, 2016b). Broadly, a decolonial position asserts that reconfigurations of domination of the economies, subjectivities, bodies, politics and minds of the former colonised peoples of the world have taken place in the twenty first century which continue the legacies of the plunder, rape and pillage of the so-called 'New World' that was allegedly discovered by Christopher Columbus in 1492. The writings of Kwame Nkrumah, Frantz Fanon, Ngugi wa Thiong'o, Chinweizu and Claude Ake also advocate the necessity of Africa and Africans to decolonise African minds, institutions and practices from a Euro-American mindset ingrained by centuries of colonial and neo-colonial domination and aspirations.

Thomas Sankara, as this chapter will argue, sought to lead Burkina Faso in a decolonial direction through both his radical vision and thinking before the body of decolonial thinking emerged in Latin America in the last two decades of the twenty-first century. It is the argument of this chapter that Sankara's radical Pan-Africanist thinking called for a fundamental break in epistemic dependency, economic dependency on the West and contributes to a transformation in gender relations. He sought for Burkina Faso to rely on its own resources and believed that, vital to this achievement, was the genuine democratisation of society – as opposed to the periodic election of individuals in so-called democracies that inadequately engage the masses in daily meaningful political and social participation in the affairs of their community and society.

Other equally important strands of his vision for a new Africa were his: interrogation of the meaning of development in Africa in which he called for a rupture from existing models of development; an end to aid dependency; the elimination of the intellectual bankruptcy of Africa's ruling class; and a fundamental restructuring and democratising of the UN. Finally, Sankara was courageous in declaring that the Burkinabè revolution was 'establishing new social relations' between men and women which would 'upset ... the relations of authority between men and women' (interview with Jean-Philippe Rapp 1985: 202).

Sankara was the embodiment of a new paradigm of social, political, economic and ecological justice. This chapter acknowledges that the initiatives, policies and intellectual thinking of Sankara remain a major unfinished project. Since 'decoloniality is not a singular theoretical school of thought but a family of diverse positions that share a view of coloniality as the fundamental problem in the modern age' (Ndlovu-Gatsheni 2015: 492), this chapter will seek to enunciate Sankara's thinking as a contribution to decolonial thinking, gender relations and Pan-Africanism as well as an unfinished project of decolonisation. This project is unfinished not only for the fact that he was assassinated in the prime of his life, but in that the existing neoliberal capitalist order and neo-colonialism have reconfigured new forms of 'coloniality' or domination in the forms and spheres of the economy, knowledge, the environment and the control over women's bodies in reproductive health in a global phallocentric gendered dispensation. Equally, the corollaries to these new forms of oppression are the unfolding forms of resistance to oppression waged by human beings all over the globe.

In order to situate and expand upon the connections between Sankara's political thought and decoloniality, it is useful to first interrogate the distinctions between colonialism and coloniality. Maldonado-Torres distinguishes between coloniality and colonialism:

> Coloniality is different from colonialism. Colonialism denotes a political and economic relation in which the sovereignty of a nation or a people rests on the power of another nation, which makes such nation an empire. Coloniality, instead, refers to long-standing patterns of power that emerged as a result of colonialism, but that define culture, labor, intersubjective relations, and knowledge production well beyond the strict limits of colonial administrations. Thus, coloniality survives colonialism. It is maintained alive in books, in the criteria for academic performance, in cultural patterns, in common sense, in the self-image of peoples, in aspirations of self, and so many other aspects of our modern experience. In a way, as modern subjects we breathe coloniality all the time and every day.
>
> (Maldonado-Torres 2007: 243)

Integral to this coloniality of being is the implicit and binary assumption of the superiority of people of European descent who populate countries of the North alongside the belief in the inferiority of brown and black people who populate countries of the South (and North). Grosfoguel (2007: 219) contends that 'we continue to live under the same colonial power matrix', which manifests itself in the current international economic division of labour dominated by the old colonial Euro-American system or the core (made up of countries of the North and the periphery that constitute the countries of the South). It also extends into political, epistemological, environmental exploitation and control over non-European peoples around the globe, despite the fact that the majority peoples in the world are black and brown people. Anibal Quijano contends that, 'Coloniality of power was conceived together with American and Western Europe, and with the social category of "race" as the key element of the social classification of colonized and colonizers' (Quijano 2007: 171). Decolonial thinking embraces the long-term processes of divesting the bureaucratic, cultural, linguistic, epistemological, psychological, and economic manifestations of coloniality in the twenty-first century, recognising that manifestations are rooted in five hundred years of colonialism and imperialism with their present-day articulations in 'coloniality'.

This chapter evaluates Sankara's intellectual thought in light of the fact that he was murdered on 15 October 1987 and three decades since his assassination, the tentacles of coloniality or 'the colonial power matrix' remain deeply entrenched in all spheres of life. This chapter delineates decolonial thinking in Sankara's intellectual vision in regards to his position on colonialism and neo-colonialism; Africa's petty bourgeoisie and Africa's epistemological dependency on the West; his thoughts on Africa's economic dependency on countries of the North; his internationalism; his thoughts on relations between African men and women; and finally his thinking on ecological imperialism.

SANKARA ON COLONIALISM, NEO-COLONIALISM AND THE AUGUST REVOLUTION

The master's tools will never dismantle the master's house.
Audre Lorde, 1981

In his address entitled 'The Political Orientation Speech', given on 2 October 1983 in a radio and television broadcast, Sankara gave both a summary and analysis of the 'immediate and medium-term revolutionary tasks' (Sankara 2007: 30), as well as a class analysis of Burkinabè society. In short, the speech outlined the programmatic vision of the August Revolution. For Sankara the so-called independence in 1960 evolved into twenty-three years of neo-colonialism, culminating in the insurrection of 4 August 1983. He believed that, 'The task of constructing a new society cleansed of all the ills that keep our country in a state of poverty and economic and cultural backwardness will be long and hard' (ibid.: 33).

Sankara understood the historical and material circumstances of his people and country when he declared:

Our revolution is a revolution that is unfolding in a backward, agricultural country where the weight of tradition and ideology emanating from a feudal-type social organisation weighs very heavily on the popular masses. It is a revolution in a country that, because of the oppression and exploitation of our people by imperialism, has evolved from a colony into a neo-colony.

(Sankara 2007: 40)

For Sankara it was imperative that those who sided with the revolution understand the realities confronting them 'so as to be able to assume their role as conscious revolutionaries, real propagandists who, fearlessly and tirelessly, disseminate this perspective to the masses' (ibid.: 41). The 'dual character' of the August revolution he declared is 'to liquidate imperialist domination and exploitation and cleanse the countryside of all social, economic, and cultural obstacles that keep it in a backward state' as well as to secure 'the full participation of the Voltaic masses in the revolution and their mobilisation' (ibid.: 40–41). Key to the achievement of the participation of the Burkinabè people, Sankara asserted that, 'The democratic character of this revolution requires that we decentralise administrative power and bring the administration closer to the people, so as to make public affairs a concern of everyone' (ibid.: 42–43).

Sankara envisioned that the neo-colonial state machinery would be replaced by 'a new machinery capable of guaranteeing the people's sovereignty' (Sankara 2007: 42). The Committees for the Defense of the Revolution (CDRs) were the organs in which popular sovereignty and mobilisation were to be exercised.

Sankara spelled out that 'the philosophy of revolutionary transformation' would apply to the national army, policies concerning women and in relation to economic development (Sankara 2007: 47). In his speech to the 39th Session of the UN General Assembly on 4 October 1984, Sankara critiqued the conservative elements of the African petty bourgeoisie, whom he considered to be allies of imperialists or neo-colonialists since their mind-sets were aligned to Euro-American/Western aspirations, values and perspectives and were among the fundamental stumbling blocks to Africa's future progress. It is this aspect of his thinking that we shall now examine in order to illustrate how his thinking contributed to a decolonial critique.

SANKARA, AFRICA'S PETTY BOURGEOISIE, IMPERIALISM AND 'EPISTEMIC APARTHEID'

... we cannot be conscious of ourselves and yet remain in bondage ...
Steve Biko, *I Write What I like*, 1987

Sankara referred to the Burkinabè petty bourgeoisie as 'the parasitic classes' who were the enemy of the people (Sankara 2007: 37). They constituted several sub layers of classes: the state bourgeoisie, the commercial bourgeoisie and the middle bourgeoisie (ibid.: 37–38). Similar to Amilcar Cabral, Sankara recognised that,

> the petty bourgeoisie, which constitutes a vast social layer that is very unstable and that *often vacillates between the cause of the popular masses and that of imperialism.* In its great majority, it always ends up taking the side of the popular masses. It is

composed of the most diverse elements, including small traders, petty-bourgeois intellectuals (government employees, students, private sector employees, and so on), and artisans.

(Sankara 2007: 39; emphasis added)

Similar to Fanon (1961: chapter 3, 'Pitfalls of National Consciousness'), Sankara was correctly contemptuous of the ideological affiliation of Africa's petty bourgeoisie because he believed 'they are attached by an umbilical cord to international imperialism and will remain so' (ibid.: 37). Before the UN General Assembly in 1984 he characterised this class as being unwilling to relinquish its privileges,

either because of intellectual laziness or simply because it has tasted the Western way of life. Because of this these *petty bourgeois forget that all genuine political struggle requires rigorous, theoretical debate, and they refuse to rise to the intellectual effort of conceiving new concepts equal to the murderous struggle that lies ahead of us.* Passive and pathetic consumers, they *wallow in terminology fetishized by the West* as they wallow in Western whiskey and champagne in shady-looking lounges.

(Sankara 2007: 87; emphasis added)

Sankara was profoundly contemptuous of Africa's bankrupt intellectual elite who slavishly borrowed 'vocabulary' and 'ideas' from 'elsewhere' – that is, from Europe and America. He believed, 'It is both necessary and urgent that our trained personnel and those who work with the pen learn that there is no such thing as neutral writing. In these stormy times *we cannot give today's and yesterday's enemies a monopoly over thought, imagination, and creativity*' (Sankara 2007: 87; emphasis added).

Sankara was therefore discerning in firstly identifying the necessity for an end to intellectual dependency of the African petty bourgeoisie on the West, and secondly, in recognising that 'there is no such thing as neutral writing'. These two themes in his thought have been considerably expanded upon by not only the aforementioned decolonial writers, but also in the works of Ngugi (Wa Thiong'o 1981), Chinweizu (1987), Ake, Linda Tuhiwai Smith (2012) and Fidelis Allen (2016: 181–192), among others, who interrogate not only the pernicious impact of neo-colonialism, or contemporary forms of 'coloniality' on the minds of African and Indigenous people, but who also put forward the case for an end to epistemic dependency on the Western world and a move towards centring the African experience as the continent grapples with its myriad problems. Sankara was also opposed to what Reiland Rabaka aptly defines as 'epistemic apartheid' (Rabaka 2010) and what Lewis Gordon characterises as 'disciplinary decadence' (Gordon 2006). It is also referred to by Castro-Gómez as 'epistemicide' (de Sousa Santos 2016). Common to all these aforementioned authors is a critique of Western epistemological traditions and practices that erases, silences, undermines, exploits, dominates other epistemologies from the South. For Rabaka:

> *Epistemic apartheid* is not simply about institutional racism and racial colonization. It includes and seeks to raise critical consciousness about the ways in which knowledge is... *conceptually quarantined along racially gendered,* religious, sexual orientation, and economic class lines, which ultimately and truculently translates into the dim disciplinary borders and boundaries that Gordon contends cause 'disciplinary decadence'.
>
> (Rabaka 2010: 16; emphasis original)

For Gordon, narcissistic entrapment characterises 'disciplinary decadence' in which each academic or intellectual discipline fails to see beyond its own. Ultimately 'such work militates against thinking' (Gordon 2006: 5). Sankara's condemnation of those who monopolised 'thought, imagination and creativity' (Sankara 2007: 87) concurs with the positions of Rabaka and Gordon, as well as that of Grosfoguel and other decolonial thinkers. Sankara did not believe there was such a thing as objective writing, which much Western scholarship claims to be – but that Western scholarship concealed an agenda to advance its interests and continues to do so.

Grosfoguel (2007: 214) contends that Western epistemology parades itself as separating the mind from the body and mind from nature. It 'hides and conceals itself as being beyond a particular point of view, that is, the point of view that represents itself as being without a point of view' and in doing so dismisses non-Western knowledge as particularistic. Through this dismissal, Western knowledge thereby becomes universal consciousness (ibid.). In the words of Castro-Gómez:

> a single way of knowing the world, the scientific-technical rationality of the Occident, has been postulated as the only valid episteme, that is to say the only episteme capable of generating real knowledge about nature, the economy, society, morality and people's happiness.
>
> (Castro-Gómez 2007: 428)

Linda Tuhiwai Smith concurs with Ake in relation to the ways in which imperialism is embedded in disciplines of knowledge. Ake writes:

> Every prognostication indicates that Western social science continues to play a major role in keeping us subordinate and underdeveloped; it continues to inhibit our understanding of the problems of our world, to feed us noxious values and/ false hopes; to make us pursue policies which undermine our competitive strength and guarantee our permanent underdevelopment and dependence.
>
> (Ake 1979: ii)

Tuhiwai Smith argues that not only do the various disciplines share philosophical foundations, but 'they are also insulated from each other through the maintenance of what are known as disciplinary boundaries' (Tuhiwai Smith 2012: 70), meaning those such as anthropology, sociology, politics, economics, etc., allowing them to develop independently but also allowing for what she characterises as the 'disciplining of the colonized' maintained 'through exclusion, marginalization and denial' (ibid.: 71). Ake also emphasises that Western social science is a critical domain in which the battle for the mind of African people and the economic domination of Africa by the West was being fought out (Ake 1979: 139).

Sankara challenged Africa's intellectual elite to 'rise to the intellectual effort of conceiving new concepts equal to the murderous struggle that lies ahead of us' (Sankara 2007: 87). His position embraces decolonial thinking, which insists on the necessity for a political and epistemic delinking in order to build democratic, just, and non-imperial/non-colonial societies.

Sankara saw the necessity for 'educational reform ... to promote a new orientation for education and culture ... One of the missions of schools in the democratic and popular society will be to teach students to critically and positively assimilate the ideas and experiences of other peoples' (Sankara 2007: 51). This vision of a critical education (necessary also in higher education) and the end of intellectual/epistemological dependency on the West remains an ongoing struggle for Africa and Africans as the twenty-first century unfolds. It is also critically linked to Africa's economic subordination to the North, which Sankara saw as a central problem confronting the African continent. As Mignolo succinctly argues, 'Epistemic dependency was and is parallel to economic dependency' (Mignolo 2011: 119).

SANKARA AND ECONOMIC DEPENDENCY

After all, socialism has still to be built.
Samir Amin, 1985

Sankara addressed the Burkinabè people with no illusions as to the economic reality of the country on 2 October 1983. Agricultural backwardness in which 90 per cent of the people were active in the rural sector accounted for only 45 per cent of the country's GDP and 95 per cent of the country's total exports (Amin 1985: 36). He believed this economic impoverishment was the consequence of imperialist domination and exploitation, which had to end.

At the 39th Session of the UN General Assembly on 4 October 1984, Sankara denounced models and concepts imposed on African countries that perpetrated their economic subjugation to their former colonial masters. He said:

We must state categorically that *there is no salvation for our people unless we turn our backs on all the models that charlatans of all types have tried to sell us for twenty years. There is no salvation outside of this rejection. There is no development separate from a rupture of this kind.*

(Amin 1985: 86–87; emphasis added)

Sankara called for a 'New International Economic Order' (Sankara 2007: 93) and while he did not provide details of how he envisioned this new order would operate, it is likely it would have been modelled on the need for African nations to practice self-reliance in food production, as his small nation attempted to do. It is also likely to have been premised on the need for greater intra-African trade as well as centring the provision of goods and services around the needs of African people in congruence with his belief that ordinary people needed to be active agents in mobilising and democratising their societies in order to fulfil basic needs. In advancing Sankara's thinking on this front, his early death has robbed us of his deeper thinking on worker's self-management and how the Burkinabè state would have transitioned from a neo-colonial society to a more egalitarian socialist society in which ordinary people are active decision makers and participants in all spheres of society.

In his famous address to the heads of government at the July 1987 Organisation of African Unity (OAU) summit, Sankara spoke without notes in a passionate condemnation of debt, which he considered another enemy of the African people (see Chapter 12, this volume). Sankara lamented that debt had led to the 're-conquest of Africa aimed at subjugating its growth and development through foreign rules' and making Africans 'financial slaves' guaranteed to die on account of an inability to repay the debt (Sankara 1987).

It is evident that following the 1987 OAU summit, Sankara's call 'to create an Addis Ababa united front against debt' did not materialise, despite the fact that his contemporaries at the summit heartedly applauded him. Furthermore, Sankara said, 'That is the only way to assert that refusing to repay is not an aggressive move from our part, but a fraternal move to speak the truth' (Sankara 1987).

Thirty years since the murder of Sankara, Africa's debt has not only increased but a corollary of this coloniality of economic power has been the simultaneous rise in illicit financial flows from Africa that continues to haemorrhage Africa's abundant mineral and agricultural resources. Hence, coloniality in the twenty-first century is manifested in the continued pillaging, plunder and rape of Africa's resources via unscrupulous neo-colonial companies in Africa and transnational corporations; state officials who collaborate in the mispricing, misinvoicing, tax evasion, tax avoidance and tax havens around the world that are involved in such practices. The direct impact of illicit financial flows is the continued economic and technological underdevelopment of the African continent (UNECA undated; Africa Focus 2016; Hickel 2017). This aid in reverse (i.e. that is from the poor countries of the South – including Africa – to the rich countries of the North) has amounted to US$13.4 trillion since 1980 (Hickel 2017). The other more human impact of illicit financial flows is illustrated in the words of Tajudeen Abdul-Raheem:

> Indeed, we should regard public officials and their private sector collaborators as mass murderers, killing millions of our peoples through inadequate public services compromised by corruption. Monies meant for drugs, roads, hospitals, schools and public security are siphoned away, making all of us vulnerable to premature death and our societies more unsafe and insecure for the masses.
>
> (Abdul-Raheem 2010: 22; see Chapter 10, this volume)

Hence, debt, illicit financial flows of Africa's wealth and corruption, and their adverse impact on African economies are issues that Sankara – if alive today – would not have remained silent on.

Not only did Sankara consider debt to be a shackle on the African continent, but he argued that aid was as well. He argued:

> Of course, we encourage aid that helps us to overcome the need for aid. But in general, the policy of foreign aid and assistance produced nothing but disorganization and continued enslavement. It robbed us of our sense of responsibility for our own economic, political and cultural territory.
>
> (Sankara 2007: 89)

With these sentiments, Sankara believed that Africans should be wholly economically self-sufficient.

Before the UN General Assembly, Sankara had the boldness of political vision and commitment to declare that his country and people had 'chosen to risk new paths to achieve greater happiness' in order to also create 'the conditions for a dignity worthy of our ambitions' and in doing so 'to dare to invent the future' (Sankara 2007: 89). Hence, Sankara's thinking may suggest he was committed to an unorthodox Marxism (but this is debateable; see Chapters 1 and 9, this volume).[2] His ideological frame of thinking leant itself to a praxis that was continually engaged in appraising the world and society to find meaningful solutions and engagements with human beings that was committed to 'nonconformity' in order to 'carry out fundamental change' (Sankara 2007: 144).

The epigraph that begins this chapter suggests Sankara's 'madness' – and not in the pathological sense, but a meaning of madness in the sense of undaunting audacity, preparedness and enthusiasm for decisive and radical action to overturn existing ways of doing things and thinking – is critical to decolonial thinking and for the future of the development of the African continent. Integral to this is the need to interrogate thinking itself and old formulas and paradigms. As Ake contends, 'The question is not whether one wants economic development but what kind of economic development' (Ake 1979: 151). Furthermore, he points out that there is an implicit assumption in Western societies that all economic development and models are equated with capitalist economic development. Yet, 'there is a world of difference between socialist economic development and capitalist economic development. And these two types of development do not exhaust the possible varieties' (ibid.). Consequently, it is incumbent on human beings to dare to invent better lives in which their economic needs will be fulfilled in a system that ceases to unfairly exploit their labour, environment and their bodies.

Sankara's call for a new economic path for Burkina and a 'New International Economic Order' suggests that if Sankara had lived, he would have been sympathetic to the concept of 'delinking'. Samir Amin defines delinking as associated with a 'transition – outside capitalism and over a long time towards socialism' (Amin 1985: 55). He contends that it does not mean 'autarky' – that is, withdrawal from external commercial, financial and technological exchanges. Delinking means the 'pursuit of a system of rational criteria for economic options founded on a law of value on a national basis with popular relevance, independent of such criteria of economic rationality as flow from the dominance of the capitalist of value operating on a world scale' (ibid.: 62). Clearly there is no blueprint for delinking but, according to Amin, it also requires 'three axes of action' (ibid.: 61) that Sankara is likely to have endorsed given his public echoes of these sentiments. Firstly, 'strengthening of the unity of the Third World;' secondly, 'progress for democracy and respect for collective rights' and finally, a recognition and exercise that 'the peoples of the periphery must be self-reliant' (ibid.: 61–62).

SANKARA'S INTERNATIONALISM IN A PLURIVERSAL WORLD

Our revolution in Burkina Faso embraces the misfortunes of all peoples.
Thomas Sankara, 1984

Sankara's internationalism was evident in his speech to the 39th Session to the UN General Assembly as well as his visit to Cuba in September 1984 where he received Cuba's highest honour, José Marti Order; his visit to several African countries including Ethiopia, Angola, the Congo, Mozambique, Gabon and Madagascar in 1984. He also visited Grenada and met with a close ideological comrade, Maurice Bishop. He stood resolutely with the oppressed people of Ireland, East Timor, South Africa, Namibia as well as 'the Saharaoui people in their struggle to recover their national territory' (Sankara 2007: 54). He had personally visited the regions liberated by the Saharoui people and had full confidence in their organisation, the Polisario Front. He condemned the US invasion of Grenada and intervention in Afghanistan.

Under Sankara's leadership, Burkina Faso withdrew from the 1984 Olympic Games held in Los Angeles in fierce opposition to the apartheid policies of South Africa and demanded the release of Nelson Mandela from prison.

Sankara described himself as 'belonging to a tricontinental whole and to acknowledge as a Nonaligned country and with the full depth of our convictions that a special solidarity unites the three continents of Asia, Latin America, and Africa in a single struggle against the same political gangsters and the same economic exploiters'. (Sankara 2007: 86). Furthermore, he said, 'Therefore, recognizing that we are part of the Third World means, to paraphrase José Martí, "asserting that our cheek feels the blow struck against any man in the world"' (ibid.).

Sankara did not believe in exporting revolution. He believed that:

> Exporting revolution would mean in the first instance that we Burkinabè think we can tell others how to solve their problems. This is a counterrevolutionary view, the view of pseudo-revolutionaries, proclaimed by the bookish, dogmatic petty bourgeoisie. If it were true it would mean that we ourselves think we imported our revolution, and as such, we must continue the chain.
>
> (Sankara 1983: 72)

This particular theme of Sankara's thinking – that is, a genuine belief in the right to think and act differently (or nonconformity to the prevailing ideology) – reflects the 'pluriversal world' of decolonial thinkers such as Mignolo, who argues that, 'Pluriversality means unlearning, so to speak, modernity, and learning to live with people one does not agree with, or may not even like' (Mignolo 2011: 176).

Sankara was aware that there were opponents to the revolution who were residing in neighbouring Ivory Coast. In a news conference marking the first anniversary of the revolution he reflected this belief in 'pluriversality' when he expressed the following:

> But as revolutionaries we understand that whereas we became revolutionaries, the world we have to live with is not revolutionary, and we live with a reality that is not always to our liking. We must be prepared to live with regimes that are not making a revolution of any kind or that perhaps even attack our revolution.
>
> (Sankara 2007: 62)

Sankara illustrated that he was aware of individuals with opposing ideologies that contradicted the ideologies of the Burkinabè revolution and that the world must live with the right of the Burkinabè people to make their revolution.

In essence, decolonial thinking conceives of different futures, different possibilities and options open to human beings – that is, the coexistence of diversity. Decolonial thinking conceives of a pluriversal world in which different paths or what Mignolo calls 'trajectories' have the right to exist (Mignolo 2011: 175–176). This vision would later be reflected in the perspective of Subcommandante Marcos of the Zapatista Army of Liberation (EZLN), when the Zapatista uprising, in early 1994 in Mexico, attacked the North American Free Trade Agreement (NAFTA). Marcos declared, 'We seek a world in which there is room for many worlds' (cited in Sandoval 2000, on page preceding table of contents).

This is a world that genuinely respects all nations, both large and small, and their right to choose their own forms of economic and political development as well as the collective and individual social and political rights of peoples. Inherent in this vision is a genuine democracy based upon the recognition of the diversity of alternatives that a decolonial world promotes. Sankara considered the UN as an organisational body that advanced the social, economic and political rights of all peoples on the earth, as also having an important role to play in creating greater economic and social justice in the world.

However, he was forthright in his address to that body in 1984 that 'the structures of the UN be rethought and that we put a stop to that scandal known as the right of veto' (Sankara 2007: 98). He believed that 'Africa's absence from the club of those who have the right to veto is unjust and should be ended' (ibid.). In an interview with a Swiss journalist, Sankara was candid in revealing that while his country was temporarily a member of the Security Council (SC), he was aware of countries falling into 'international complicity' and thought that the UN member states outside the SC must wage a constant battle 'if the UN is not to become an echo chamber manipulated by a few powerful drummers' (ibid.: 116).

Thirty years since Sankara's death, the authority of the UN has been eroded by the imperialist powers, who have used their right to veto to control other member states and to side-line actions they disapprove, such as condemning Israel and lifting sanctions against Cuba. Samir Amin contends that the UN has been substituted by the G8, NATO and the 'collective triad of imperialism' (i.e. the US, Europe and Japan; Amin 2006: 112). He also argues for the 'reform of the UN as part of multipolar globalisation' (ibid.). In this way, we can again connect the delinking of Amin with Sankara's orientation that future struggles within the South for a multipolar world must be organised around international social and economic justice that incorporates a struggle for disarmament (which entails the removal of US military bases around the globe) with struggles to dismantle the SC and its replacement by the General Assembly with the powers to make resolutions. In addition, solidarity among the peoples of the South must revolve around struggles to end the illicit financial flows of wealth and for ordinary farmers around the world to gain access to land.

SANKARA'S APPROACH TO GENDER: 'UPSETTING THE RELATIONS OF AUTHORITY BETWEEN MEN AND WOMEN'

Patriarchy has no gender.
bell hooks, 2014[3]

Integral to the revolution that Sankara undertook was a revolution in the relationship between men and women. He was clear that 'this task is formidable but necessary' (Sankara 2007: 202). However, as I show in this section, Sankara's commitment to gender justice is unfinished.

On 8 March 1987, International Women's Day, he spoke to thousands of women in the capital, Ouagadougou. He addressed some of the root causes of the subordination of African women, such as 'the system of slavery to which they have been subjected for millennia' (Sankara 2007: 203) and stressed the need to contextualise the struggle of the Burkinabè woman as 'part of a worldwide struggle of all women, and beyond that, part of the struggle for the full rehabilitation of our continent' within a Marxist theoretical framework. The limitation of this analysis is that Sankara believed that 'it was ... the transition from one form of society to another that served to institutionalize women's inequality' (ibid.: 204). For Sankara, 'inequality can be done away with only by establishing a new society, where men and women will enjoy equal rights, resulting from an upheaval in the means of production and in all social relations. Thus, *the status of women will improve only with elimination of the system that exploits them*' (ibid.: 205; emphasis added). While Sankara was correct in declaring that 'the revolution cannot triumph without the genuine emancipation of women' (ibid.: 219) and in focusing on the specificities of the oppression of women, the limitation in his thinking lies in the Marxist tendency to subordinate gender or male sexism to class considerations. Sankara stated that, 'it is for women themselves to put forward their demands and mobilise to win them' (ibid.: 216). More importantly, he identified the problems of low literacy and political consciousness as paramount problems that were obstacles to revolutionary development. Sankara was revolutionary in envisaging that the waging of revolution would indeed 'establish new social relations' between men and women. It would also 'upset the relations of authority between men and women and force each to rethink the nature of both' (ibid.: 216).

The unfinished aspect of this particular strand of Sankara's political thinking is fundamental to a decolonial turn in Africa. The focus must not only be on the current manifestations of African women's oppression but, more critically, gender discourse in the academy and in mainstream African society, which tends to be associated with women – as if men, were not a gender. Therefore, the ongoing struggle against patriarchy[2] also calls for a fundamental rethinking of the nature of African masculinities and femininity, for present definitions are oppressive and harmful to both men and women. Decolonial thinking also needs to seriously grapple with patriarchal constructs, thinking and paradigms in its unfolding praxis if it is not to appear as radical fashionable critique that fails to meaningfully engage with eradicating patriarchy but simply perpetuates it.

Both hegemonic masculinity and femininity embody ideal traits in which the former upholds men/boys to be strong, active, aggressive, dominant, competitive and in control. In capitalist patriarchies, femininity embodies the less socially valued traits of weakness, passivity, receptiveness, emotion, nurturing and subordination. As bell hooks contends, 'When culture is based on a dominator model, not only will it be violent but it will frame all relationships as power struggles' (hooks 2004a: 116). Furthermore, 'Before the realities of men can be transformed, the dominator model [that hierarchy embedded within coloniality] has to be eliminated as the underlying ideology on which we base our culture' (hooks 2004a: 116). Sankara envisioned 'upsetting the relations of authority between men and women' (Sankara 2007: 202), which entails rethinking how we bring up a new generation of men/boys and women/girls to challenge gender stereotypes, values, expectations and roles will necessitate radical men/boys openly and at times privately challenging other men/boys on their patriarchal ideas and practices. It will also involve creating a society and world in which boys and men are taught to authentically communicate their emotions and empathetically listen to others, rather than conceal them in the belief that they are upholding the stereotype of a 'strong' African male, as required by 'rituals of patriarchal manhood [in which they] surrender their capacity to feel' (hooks 2004b: 137–138).[4]

SANKARA'S RECOGNITION OF COLONIALITY IN RELATION TO THE ENVIRONMENT

The White Man's burden is becoming increasingly heavy for the earth and especially for the south.
Vandana Shiva, 2014

Sankara's position on the need to protect and live in harmony with the natural environment made him a forerunner of the environmental movement of the twenty-first century. He said:

African societies are living through an abrupt rupture with their own culture, and we adapt badly to our new situation. Completely new economic approaches are required. Our populations are growing as well as our needs. In addition, our natural habitat and the spontaneous development to which we are accustomed, such as the natural expansion of the forests and crops, exists less and less. We have become great predators.

(Sankara 2007: 130)

He believed that 'draconian measures' were necessary to arrest deforestation in the country in the form of 'three battles' (Sankara 2007: 130). They constituted a ban on the 'unplanned, anarchic cutting of wood' (ibid.: 130); a ban on the random wandering of livestock' which would entail 'imposing rigorous changes in people's mentalities;' and finally, a 'program of reforestation' in which millions of trees would be planted in groves.

For Sankara, 'the battle against the encroachment of the desert is a battle to establish a balance between man, nature, and society. As such it is a political battle above all, and not an act of fate' (Sankara 2002: 89). He had a profound belief in the capacity of human beings to change their realities. He lambasted 'fallacious Malthusian arguments' (ibid.: 90) that the African continent was overpopulated and insisted that the continent remained an under-populated one. To cite Sankara at some length, to illustrate his thinking on the environment, he declared:

Explained in this way, *our struggle for the trees and forests is first and foremost a democratic and popular struggle.* Because a handful of forestry engineers and experts getting themselves all worked up in a sterile and costly manner will never accomplish anything! Nor can the worked-up consciences of a multitude of forums and institutions – sincere and praiseworthy though they may be – make the Sahel green again, *when we lack the funds to drill wells for drinking water a hundred meters deep, while money abounds to drill oil wells three thousand meters deep!*

(Sankara 2002: 90–91; emphasis added)

Sankara's conception that 'the problem posed by the trees and forests is exclusively the problem of balance and harmony between the individual, society, and nature' (ibid.: 91) aligns with recent scholarly developments in eco-feminism and decolonial thinking, as well as movements in Latin America and India that challenge capitalist and Western concepts of nature as a commodity to be conquered, pillaged and plundered in the onward march of infinite modernisation and progress. Such scholarly approaches and movements resist belief in the inexhaustible potential of Mother Earth and consider that at the root of the ecological crisis in the South and the North lies the fixation with pillaging the earth for natural resources such as fossil fuels via the logic and expansion of the market economy. Vandana Shiva claims that following the white man's burden to 'civilise' the non-white peoples of the world (which entailed exploiting their resources), came the need to 'develop the Third World', which necessitated the deprivation of the rights and resources of Third World communities. For Shiva, 'we are now on the threshold of the third phase of colonization, in which the white man's burden is to protect the environment, especially the Third World's environment – and this, too, involves taking control of rights and resources' (Shiva 2014: 264). This ecological imperialism is played out today in the various large gatherings of the Copenhagen Climate Change Conferences in which the big players, who are often the worst pollutants (namely, the USA and China) make promises to commit to the long-term goals of limiting the maximum global average temperature increase to no more than 2 degrees Celsius above pre-industrial levels, but fail to make meaningful and profound changes in the lifestyles and consumption patterns of their peoples (and militaries and corporations) to reduce greenhouse gas emissions.

The deforestation that Sankara was proactive in seeking to arrest has since his death become a more acute issue related to not only the climate crisis in Africa but, as Nnimmo Bassey highlights, forms of 'destructive extraction' across the African continent. Underlying the extraction of minerals (such as coltan, gold and casserite) is an insidious racism in which the environmental impact of such resources is one in which local populations are subjected to toxic waste that seriously undermines the health of communities; criminal negligence on the part of a neo-colonial elite and opportunism on the part of national and transnational corporations who operate below industry standards on the continent (Bassey 2012: 99). Hence, while Sankara recognised coloniality in the environment, the issues at stake since his death have profoundly deepened. There also remains unfinished business in regards to Africans controlling their local environment and living in harmony with it in a planet that is fast diminishing in its natural resources as result of the continuing corrosive logic of imperialism and capitalism.

CONCLUSION

All that comes from man's imagination is realizable for man.
Thomas Sankara, 1985

If Sankara were alive today, he would be 66 years old. His lifespan gave us sufficient insight to extrapolate that if he were alive in our times he would align with progressive forces in Africa and globally against new configurations of coloniality in the twenty-first century. The legacy of Sankara lies – no matter how short lived – in his practical policies in which he sought to overturn a neo-colonial reality in Burkina Faso. His denunciation of debt and aid illustrates his unmasking of the invisible global imperial designs that operate to maintain Africa's subjugated position in the international world order, of which Sankara sought to reimagine as one constructed on the principles of genuine justice, dignity, equality and freedom for all human beings on the earth.

Sankara's intellectual vision embraces a decolonial turn and restores dignity to human beings. He saw such a transformation as imperative for Africa. The creation of a just, egalitarian, pluriversal world as envisioned by Sankara remains an unfinished struggle.

NOTES

1 Unless noted otherwise, quotations from Sankara in this chapter are available in Sankara (2007).

2 It is debatable as Sankara adopts Marxist language such as in his 'Political Orientation Speech' he employs Marxist terms. However, I would argue Sankara was not an orthodox Marxist in that he demonstrated he was prepared to be a non-conformist and did not believe revolutions should be exported to other peoples and societies. See also Chapter 9, this volume.

3 hooks declares, 'patriarchy has no gender' in her conversation with Gloria Steinem at The New School in 2014, the discussion is available at blogs.newschool.edu/news/2014/10/bellhooksteachingtotransgress/#.WipkD7aB2Ax

4 In 'Understanding Patriarchy', bell hooks defines patriarchy as 'a political-social system that insists that males are inherently dominating, superior to everything and everyone deemed weak, especially females, and endowed with the right to dominate and rule over the weak and to maintain that dominance through various forms of psychological terrorism and violence' (hooks undated).

REFERENCES

Abdul-Raheem, T. (2010) *Speaking Truth to Power Selected Postcards of Tajudeen Abdul-Raheem* (ed. by A. Biney and A. Olukoshi). London: Pambazuka Press.

Africa Focus (2016) Africa/Global: 'Stop the Bleeding' Updates. *Africa Focus Bulletin*, 22 June. Retrieved 28 January 2017 from www.africafocus.org/docs16/stb1606.php.

Ake, C. (1979) *Social Science as Imperialism: The Theory of Political Development.* Ibadan, Nigeria: Ibadan University Press.

Allen, F. (2016) Decolonising African Political Science and the Question of the Relevance of the Discipline for Development. In S. J. Ndlovu-Gatsheni and S. Zondi (eds), *Decolonizing the University, Knowledge Systems and Disciplines in Africa.* Durham, NC: Carolina Academic Press.

Amin, S. (1985) *Delinking.* London: Zed Books.

Amin, S. (2006) *Beyond US Hegemony? Assessing the Prospects for a Multipolar World.* London: Zed Books.

Bassey, N. (2012) *To Cook A Continent Destructive Extraction and the Climate Crisis in Africa*. London: Pambazuka Press.

Biko, S. (1987) *I Write What I Like: Selected Writings*. London: Heinemann.

Castro-Gómez, S. (2010) 'The Missing Chapter of Empire: Postmodern Reorganization of Coloniality and Post-Fordist Capitalism'. In W. D. Mignolo and A. Escobar (eds), *Globalization and the Decolonial Option*, 428–448. London: Routledge.

Chinweizu. (1987) *Decolonizing the African Mind*. Lagos: Pero Press.

de Sousa Santos, B. (2016) *Epistemologies of the South Justice Against Epistemicide*. London: Routledge.

Fanon, F. (1961) *The Wretched of the Earth*. London: Penguin.

Gordon R. L. (2006) *Disciplinary Decadence Living Thought in Trying Times*. London: Routledge.

Grosfoguel, R. (2007) The Epistemic Decolonial Turn. *Cultural Studies* 21(2–3): 211–223.

Hickel, J. (2017) Aid in Reverse: How Poor Countries Develop Rich Countries. *The Guardian*, 14 January. Retrieved on 28 January 2017 from www. theguardian.com/global-development-professionals-network/2017/jan/14/ aid-in-reverse-how-poor-countries-develop-rich-countries.

hooks, b. (2004a) *The Will to Change Men, Masculinity, and Love*. Washington, DC: Washington Square Press.

hooks, b. (2004b) *We Real Cool Black Men and Masculinity*. London: Routledge.

Lorde, A. (1981) The Master's Tools Will Never Dismantle the Master's House. In C. Moraga and G. Anzaldúa (eds), *This Bridge Called My Back: Writings by Radical Women of Colour*, 94–101. New York: Kitchen Table Press.

Maldonado-Torres, N. (2006) Césaire's Gift and the Decolonial Turn. *Radical Philosophy Review* 9(2): 111–138.

Maldonado-Torres, N. (2007) On the Coloniality of Being. *Cultural Studies* 21(2–3): 240–270.

Maldonado-Torres, N. (2011) Thinking through the Decolonial Turn: Post-continental Interventions I Theory, Philosophy and Critique – An Introduction. *Transmodernity: Journal of Peripheral Cultural Production of the Luso-Hispanic World* 1(2): 1–25.

Mignolo, D. W. (2011) *The Darker Side of Western Modernity Global Futures: Decolonial Options*. Durham, NC: Duke University Press.

Ndlovu-Gatsheni, J. S. (2013a) *Empire Global Coloniality and African Subjectivity*. New York: Berghahn Books.

Ndlovu-Gatsheni, J. S. (2013b) *Coloniality of Power in Postcolonial Africa Myths of Decolonization*. Dakar: CODESRIA.

Ndlovu-Gatsheni. J. S. (2015) Decoloniality as the Future of Africa. *History Compass* 492: 485–496.

Ndlovu-Gatsheni, J. S. (2016a) *The Decolonial Mandela Peace, Justice and the Politics of Life*. New York: Berghahn Books.

Ndlovu-Gatsheni, J. S. (2016b) *Decolonizing the University, Knowledge Systems and Disciplines in Africa* (eds S. J. Ndlovu-Gatsheni and Siphamandla Zondi). Durham, NC: Carolina Academic Press.

Quijano, A. (2007) Coloniality and Modernity/Rationality. *Cultural Studies* 21(2–3): 168–178.

Rabaka, R. (2010) *Against Epistemic Apartheid: W. E. B. Dubois and the Disciplinary Decadence of Sociology*. Baltimore, MD: Lexington Books.

Sandoval, C. (2000) *Methodology of the Oppressed*. Minnesota, MN: University of Minnesota Press.

Sankara, T. (1983) Power Must be the Business of a Conscious People. Press conference, 21 August. Reproduced in Sankara (2007): 69–75.

Sankara, T. (1984) Asserting our Identity, Asserting our Culture. At Burkinabè art exhibit in Harlem, 2 October. Reproduced in Sankara (2007): 143–153.

Sankara, T. (1985) Dare to Invent the Future. Interview with Jean-Philippe Rapp. Reproduced in Sankara (2007): 189–232.

Sankara, T. (1987) Against Debt. Speech to the African Unity Organisation Summit. Retrieved on 20 November 2017 from www.youtube.com/watch?v=DfzoToJEnu8.

Sankara, T. (2007) *Thomas Sankara Speaks: The Burkina Faso Revolution, 1983–1987.* New York: Pathfinder Press.

Shiva, V. (2014) Decolonizing the North. In M. Mies and V. Shiva (eds), *Ecofeminism*, 264–276. London: Zed Books.

Tuhiwai Smith, L. (2012) *Decolonizing Methodologies Research and Indigenous Peoples.* London: Zed Books.

UNECA (Undated) *Illicit Financial Flows: Report of the High Level Panel On Illicit Financial Flows from Africa.* Addis Ababa: UNECA. Retrieved on 20 November 2017 from www.uneca.org/publications/illicit-financial-flows.

Wa Thiong'o, N. (1981) *Decolonizing the Mind The Politics of Language in African Literature.* London: James Currey.

CHAPTER 9

With The People
Sankara's Humanist Marxism
Ernest Harsch

Visitors to Thomas Sankara's office did not find the usual symbols of an African president: no overstuffed furniture, expensive rugs or rare paintings. There were, instead, bookcases groaning with new and old volumes and books and papers scattered across the desk – signs of intellectual curiosity and a passion for work. Also on the desk was a small bust of the Russian revolutionary Vladimir Ilyich Lenin and on the shelves numerous writings of Lenin, Karl Marx and Frederick Engels. Sankara was open about his ideological leanings.

Decades after his assassination in an October 1987 military coup, many of Sankara's contemporary admirers agree that he was a man of ideas and action: ideas for a better society in Burkina Faso and the world, and action to dethrone Africa's entrenched elites and break the bonds of subordination to the former colonial powers. Many revolutionary thinkers before him had similarly ambitious goals, and Sankara readily acknowledged their influences. Although the insights that guided Sankara came from many different perspectives, his core beliefs were grounded in revolutionary Marxism.

Many contemporary assessments of Sankara's legacy, however, touch only lightly, if at all, on that aspect of his outlook. Even among the generally small 'Sankarist' political parties that are active in Burkina Faso today, few leaders have drawn attention to their hero's communist beliefs. One went so far as to deny that Sankara was ever a Marxist (*Sidwaya*, 17 October 2007). It is possible that they regard Marxism as an outmoded viewpoint ill-suited to the realities of today's world or to the exigencies of electoral politics. So they gloss over Sankara's Marxist views in favour of other elements of his outlook, such as his Pan-Africanism and overall commitment to social justice.

Yet the full range of Sankara's beliefs warrants a careful and frank examination. Such an examination can help clarify how he confronted the complex challenges of trying to bring progressive change to such a poor and underdeveloped society. The way in which he anchored seemingly utopian visions to the daily realities of his country draws attention to his ability to mobilise ordinary people to overcome the 'impossible' hurdles of the present so as to achieve what they did not initially think was attainable. Moreover, focusing on Sankara's particular understanding of Marxism better distinguishes his approach from the dogmatic views and practices of some of his comrades – those who ultimately initiated the coup that claimed his life. It also differed fundamentally from the approaches of the leaders of the Soviet Union and other countries who, in the name of Marxism, committed countless human rights abuses. Against their repressive perspective, Sankara adhered to a conception of Marxism that was profoundly humanist, guided above all by the fundamental interests and needs of the Burkinabè people.

In addition to Sankara's reputation for self-sacrifice and incorruptibility, his humanist outlook and practice undoubtedly contributed to the lasting attraction of his example and ideas. Despite decades of official silence (if not outright vilification) under the authoritarian regime of Blaise Compaoré, many Burkinabè, especially among young people, readily cite his legacy as an inspiration for their own struggles. That was especially evident in the numerous Sankara portraits and slogans that featured in the huge anti-government demonstrations that culminated in Compaoré's ouster and flight from the country at the end of October 2014 (Harsch 2015). Admittedly, the persistence of that legacy had less to do with Sankara's Marxism as such than with the open-minded, practical ways in which he tried to move his country forward.

One of Sankara's most prominent contemporary enthusiasts is the rapper Smockey, a founder of the Balai Citoyen (Citizens' Broom) activist group that helped spearhead the October 2014 popular insurrection. As Smockey told me, Sankara inspired them on several levels:

> On the personal level, his simplicity, modesty and integrity were a model for anyone aspiring to manage public property. On the level of political struggle, we recall his courage and his determination to build a Burkina Faso of social justice and inclusive development that takes into account both the environment and future generations.
>
> (Serge Bambara 'Smockey', interview with author, 28 April 2016)

FROM REFLECTION TO ACTION

In 1987, four years after becoming president, Sankara was asked by a reporter for Radio Havana how he became a Marxist. 'It was very simple,' he replied, 'through discussion, through friendship with a few men ... Gradually, thanks to reading, but above all thanks to discussions with Marxists on the reality of our country, I came to Marxism' (Sankara, interview with Radio Havana, August 1987[1]).

Although a couple of his childhood acquaintances were introduced to Marxist ideas through the student and labour movements, Sankara's own encounter began in the army, when he attended a military academy for officer trainees in the late 1960s. One of the civilian professors employed there, Adama Touré, was secretly a member of the clandestine African Independence Party (PAI), a regional Marxist group. Touré organised after-class gatherings with some students, including Sankara, to discuss imperialism, neocolonialism, socialism, communism, the Soviet and Chinese revolutions and other questions. Later, while undergoing further military training in Madagascar, France and elsewhere in the 1970s, Sankara met other instructors who were Marxist or provided Marxist literature and also established contacts with radical activists his own age (Jaffré 2007: 97).

One friend, Soumane Touré, worked closely with the PAI and in the 1970s founded the country's most militant labour organisation, the Voltaic Union Confederation (CSV). Sankara retained close ties with Touré and other PAI members and participated in a Marxist education course run by the party. From its origins, the PAI was politically aligned with the Soviet Union, although it also worked with activists from other left-wing currents. Sankara himself held frequent discussions with young radicals who belonged to groups influenced by the political orientation of China or Albania, including his close friends, Valère Somé and Fidèle Toé (Jaffré 2007: 85, 96–98). Although he valued and learned from their debates and discussions, Sankara avoided joining any of the organised groups. Nor did he limit himself to Marxist literature. He read widely. Asked later what books he would want if he were stranded on a desert island, Sankara replied that he would 'certainly' want to have Lenin's *State and Revolution*. 'But on an island, I would also take the Bible and the Koran' (Sankara, interview with *Jeune Afrique*, February 1986).

Sankara's political education came not just from books and debates. The second half of the 1970s were a turbulent time in Upper Volta (as the country was then called), reflected in frequent workers' strikes, student protests and other popular discontent prompted by poverty, widespread hunger and the limited opportunities available to young people under the regime of General Sangoulé Lamizana. Those developments gave a sharper edge to political discussions over *how* to bring about progressive change, especially in a society that differed so much from Russia, China and the other countries that the revolutionaries studied so diligently.

One notable characteristic of the political agitation sweeping Upper Volta was its impact *within* the armed forces. Sankara was not the only 'comrade in uniform' to feel the attraction of revolutionary ideas. Blaise Compaoré, Henri Zongo, Jean-Baptiste Lingani and other junior officers also adopted radical perspectives, with some joining leftist organisations and many working with Sankara in clandestine military networks. As the strains within Lamizana's government and army hierarchy deepened under the pressure of economic crisis and social upheaval, other military factions embarked on a series of coups in the early 1980s. Their goals and political orientations were diverse and the military juntas they set up failed to find a stable footing. Recognising the popularity of Sankara and his comrades among the ranks of the armed forces and within the student and labour movements, some dissident senior officers tried to draw them into their plots. Sankara usually spurned such overtures, citing the conservative politics of the plotters or his belief that real change would not come through a strictly military takeover but also had to involve civilian social movements and revolutionary political organisations (Jaffré 2007: 106; Harsch 2014: 38–43).

Despite misgivings about premature military action, Sankara's current of radical officers took advantage of the political instability to advance their views publicly, including by accepting governmental posts. That was particularly the case with the military-led government of President Jean-Baptiste Ouédraogo, which included several PAI ministers. In late 1981 Sankara was himself named prime minister, providing him with a platform to speak out strongly against imperialist domination and meet with several international revolutionaries, including Cuba's Fidel Castro.

Sankara's fiery declarations outraged the more conservative officers in Ouédraogo's government. In May 1983 – with the evident backing of France – they mounted a palace coup that deposed Sankara. The move precipitated widespread protests and plunged the government into crisis, initiating a chain of events that drew together an alliance of radical military and civilian activists. As recounted in detail elsewhere (Andriamirado 1987; Jaffré 2007; Harsch 2017), the crisis was ultimately resolved on 4 August 1983 when the revolutionaries seized power, proclaimed a National Council of the Revolution (CNR) and placed Sankara in the presidency.

CHARACTER OF THE REVOLUTION

The CNR's revolution, Sankara repeatedly affirmed, was 'democratic' and 'popular'. Despite his own ideological views, he took care to not tag the labels of 'socialism' or 'communism' onto that process. He was not being evasive or trying to hide his government's true orientation. The conditions of the country would simply not support any attempt to arbitrarily impose a course followed by revolutionaries elsewhere. In his interview with Radio Havana, Sankara explained:

In our country the question of the class struggle is posed differently from the way it's posed in Europe. We have a working class that's numerically weak and insufficiently organized. And we have no strong national bourgeoisie either that could have given rise to an antagonistic working class. So what we have to focus on is the very essence of the class struggle: in Burkina Faso it's expressed in the struggle against imperialism, which relies on its internal allies.

(Sankara, interview with Radio Havana, August 1987)

In the CNR's main programmatic document, Sankara's October 1983 'Political Orientation Speech', the process was characterised as 'an anti-imperialist revolution' that was 'still unfolding within the framework of the limits of a bourgeois economic and social order'. He was nevertheless highly critical of that order, calling into question the entire post-colonial era in terms that drew liberally from both Marxism and dependency theory. There was little difference between colonial domination and 'neo-colonial society', Sankara emphasised in the speech, except that nationals had taken over as 'agents for foreign domination and exploitation'. To free society of that external dependence meant fiercely combating those elite strata that most strongly defended it, principally the commercial bourgeoisie that relied on foreign trade, the 'political-bureaucratic bourgeoisie' that occupied state offices and plundered the public treasury and the 'traditional, feudal-type structures' in the countryside, that is, customary chiefs (Sankara, 'Political Orientation Speech', 2 October 1983).

The process envisioned by the CNR required not only major economic and social reforms, but also a drastic restructuring of the state. At the lower levels, new Committees for the Defence of the Revolution (CDRs) provided avenues for ordinary citizens to begin organising themselves. At the summit, weakening the grip of the 'political-bureaucratic bourgeoisie' meant launching a determined struggle against corruption. The notion of integrity was in fact woven directly into the state's new identity. On the first anniversary of the takeover, the CNR renamed the country from Upper Volta – a colonial-era designation – to 'Burkina Faso', which roughly translates as 'land of the upright people'.

That name change was simultaneously part of a broader effort to forge a new national identity, one that sought to move away from a loose collection of ethnic groups dominated by the Mossi, the largest among them, towards one in which all had a comparable claim. 'Burkina Faso' itself reflected the society's polyglot identity, with *burkina* coming from Mooré, the language of the Mossi, and *faso* from Dioula. The '-bè' suffix in Burkinabè came from Fulfuldé, the language of the Peulh (Englebert 1996: 1).

Through various policies and initiatives, the CNR pursued a consciously inclusive approach, to open up social and political life to more ethnic groups. The CNR had numerous Mossi in it, but also Bobo, Gourounsi, Peulh and others. Sankara himself was from a marginal sub-group known as the Silmi-Mossi (of mixed Mossi and Peulh ancestry). Whether he and his comrades drew their ideas from Marxism or revolutionary nationalist traditions, they saw the construction of a unified nation as an essential corollary to the building of a modern state. That effort was arguably one of the most successful of the revolutionary era. Years after Sankara's death, significant sectors of the population, including those critical of the CNR, have come to readily accept their identification as citizens of Burkina Faso, as Burkinabè.

In a country as underdeveloped as Burkina Faso, even measures as seemingly mundane as ensuring more food and water for its poorest citizens were revolutionary. Beyond energetic programmes to improve health and education for all, there were particular initiatives to advance women's conditions. Women were encouraged to organise themselves through the CDRs and a new Women's Union of Burkina. Sankara appointed more women to his cabinet than any other government did in Africa at the time – and more than most elsewhere in the world. In the 1980s such a gender composition was new and dramatic (see Chapters 8 and 11, this volume).

Reflecting the economy's continued external dependence, Sankara welcomed foreign aid, but tried to reduce reliance on aid by boosting domestic revenues and diversifying the sources of assistance. Although some of his advisers recommended an agreement with the International Monetary Fund (IMF), Sankara refused. He feared that an IMF programme would compromise Burkina Faso's interests. All across Africa at the time, the IMF and World Bank were imposing structural adjustment programmes that mandated major cutbacks in social spending as well as sweeping liberalisation and privatisation.

The CNR's development policies pointed in a different direction. To benefit ordinary citizens, it insisted on *increasing*, not cutting, spending on health and education. It also shifted from a narrow focus on urban areas to the priority needs of poor villagers in the countryside: irrigation, fertilisers, incentives for small-scale farming and the construction of hundreds of rural schools and health clinics.

Sankara was ahead of other African leaders in favouring environmental sustainability. At the time, most African governments were reluctant to focus on environmental conservation, with some not seeing its importance among many other priorities and a few even regarding it with suspicion as part of a Western plot to obstruct Africa's industrialisation. Only later, after the 1992 Earth Summit in Rio, did more come to understand that development had to be sustainable. Years before then, Sankara argued that, especially in a country where rainfall was so scarce, developing agriculture *necessarily* meant preserving the soil, harnessing what little water there was and planting millions of trees. Burkinabè, Sankara said, simply had to 'struggle for a green Burkina' (Sankara, International Conference on Trees and Forests, 5 February 1986).

What would be the major levers for economic growth and development more broadly? At the local level, Sankara's ruling council, usually acting through the grassroots CDRs, encouraged self-help initiatives by villagers and urban residents. Tens of thousands participated in repeated community mobilisations to clean up refuse, build schools, dig irrigation canals and water reservoirs, contour the soil and accomplish other development efforts. From October 1984 through the end of 1985, a national campaign known as the People's Development Programme mobilised people across all provinces in a more systematic way. By its conclusion, it saw the construction of 351 schools, 314 dispensaries and maternities, 2,294 wells and boreholes, and 274 water reservoirs – not counting the many others facilities built outside that programme.

The results were significant locally and provided very visible evidence of the CNR's commitment to the well-being and participation of ordinary citizens. But much greater efforts and resources were needed to stimulate the economy nationally. The state emerged as the central driver for raising the financing needed to expand social services and increase productive investment. It is likely that the ideological outlook of Sankara and his comrades contributed to such an emphasis, but it also reflected the realities of Burkina Faso.

Whether labelled as 'national' or 'comprador', the country's business classes were small and fragmented, even by African standards. The CNR tried to court manufacturers engaged directly in production. 'Private property is a normal thing at this stage of our society', Sankara noted shortly after coming into power. 'It is normal that it should be protected' (*Afrique-Asie*, 24 October 1983). But hobbled by some of the region's highest energy and transport costs and the absence of suitable physical and commercial infrastructure, few Burkinabè entrepreneurs were in a position to increase their activities. That left the state as the dominant source of investment finance.

Unfortunately, the CNR inherited a state sector and civil service that were inefficient and corrupt. To eliminate waste and enhance the functioning of the government's scores of state enterprises, incompetent managers were replaced and rigorous campaigns fought to root out corruption. While the operations of some state firms appeared to improve, for most of the public sector such efforts, even under the best of circumstances, would necessarily take time.

The CNR's agrarian reform, proclaimed with great fanfare in 1984, also did not have enough time to make a major impact. It nationalised all land, with the aim of halting private land appropriation by a few wealthy farmers and, more commonly, urban functionaries. Since the nationalisation also covered lands held under customary communal tenure, it sought to undercut the powers of traditional chiefs to allocate land and gave authority to designate tenure rights to new commissions that included members of village CDR bureaux. The ultimate goal was to make land rights more secure for poor, small-scale farmers. Unfortunately, implementation of the agrarian reform bogged down in confusion, since chiefs were often the only ones who could sort out conflicting land claims. It took until 1987 for the authorities to draft plans for new land management commissions (which that time included local land chiefs), but the October 1987 coup intervened before they could begin functioning.

Despite the economy's shortcomings and handicaps, real economic growth during 1983–1987, the years of Sankara's CNR, averaged 4.6 per cent annually, notably above Upper Volta's 3.8 per cent average in 1970–1982. Proponents of sweeping market liberalisation at the World Bank and IMF had difficulty explaining such results.

FOR PERSUASION OVER COERCION

Sankara was not tender with perceived 'enemies of the revolution'. Beyond the hundreds of former political leaders and high-level bureaucrats tried, imprisoned and fired for pilfering state coffers or engaging in other abuses, many ordinary civil servants also lost their jobs. Some were probably incompetent, but some were also suspected of little more than insufficient political loyalty. In early 1984 a primary school teachers' union, SNEAHV (Syndicat National Des Enseignants Africains De Haute-Volta) which was aligned with an opposition political current and openly hostile to the CNR, launched a strike. The Council responded by promptly firing 1,380 of the teachers (Muase 1989: 198–201). Although Sankara later ordered the reinstatement of hundreds of them, their initial dismissal was nevertheless quite shocking to many Burkinabè.

Stern pronouncements by Sankara and other CNR figures encouraged some of their followers to go to extremes. The offices of an independent newspaper were mysteriously burned down in 1984, an act for which no one was ever charged. Armed activists of the CDRs sometimes used strong-arm tactics to enforce curfews or compliance with various government directives.

Sankara expressed alarm over such excesses. As early as 1985 he sharply criticised CDR members who acted arbitrarily and sought to 'exercise authority as a dynastic right' (*Carrefour Africain*, 9 August 1985). At the first national conference of the CDRs in 1986, he denounced the 'veritable despots' within the CDRs who did 'unspeakable things' in the name of the revolution. 'Abuse of power must be considered alien to our struggle', he declared (Sankara 2007: 281–285). Most the CDRs' armed vigilance brigades were subsequently dissolved and many of the worst offenders were replaced. Some were tried and imprisoned.

Time and again, Sankara urged supporters to favour methods of persuasion towards Burkinabè who did not fully understand or accept the revolution. After ordering the release of several detained politicians, Sankara explained that the revolution was for everyone: 'It's better to count the number of its adherents than to count the number of its victims' (*Sidwaya*, 7 January 1986). In 1987, on the fourth anniversary of the revolution, he declared: 'The democratic and popular revolution needs a convinced people, not a conquered people – a convinced people not a submissive people passively enduring their fate'. While repression should be reserved strictly for 'exploiters' and 'enemies', the revolution 'must mean only persuasion for the masses – persuasion to take on a conscious and determined commitment' (Sankara, on fourth anniversary of revolution, 4 August 1987).

Sankara developed such views, in part, by drawing lessons from the flaws of revolutions elsewhere in the world. He often praised the Russian Revolution. 'The great revolution of October 1917 transformed the world, brought victory to the proletariat, shook the foundations of capitalism, and made possible the Paris Commune's dreams of justice', he said in his 1984 address to the UN General Assembly. But he then immediately added that while Burkinabè were open to all the world's revolutions, they also 'learned from some terrible failures that led to tragic violations of human rights' (Sankara, United Nations General Assembly, 4 October 1984).

Sometimes he was even more direct. Paraphrasing discussions with the Burkinabè president about his views on a variety of African and international topics, the journalist Sennen Andriamirado wrote that, according to Sankara: 'Stalin killed Leninism by stifling the soviets [elected workers' and soldiers' councils] and making all-powerful the Cheka [secret police], the military' and other repressive bodies (Andriamirado 1987: 116).

Tragically, many of Sankara's contemporaries did not share such views. The PAI, which was most closely aligned with the Soviet Union, participated in the CNR's first government, until it was ousted in 1984. The rift, however, had little to do with the party's ideological orientation and several of the organisations that subsequently joined had more dogmatic conceptions. Foremost among them was the Burkinabè Communist Union (UCB). The UCB and other groups cited as their heroes Joseph Stalin and Enver Hoxha (the avowedly Stalinist leader of Albania). They quoted Stalin in articles on ideology in their periodicals and displayed his portrait on their official logos. At a time when Blaise Compaoré was the CNR's minister of justice, a large portrait of Stalin hung in the Palace of Justice, the main courthouse in Ouagadougou.

Asked in 1984 to explain the Leninist concept of 'democratic centralism', Compaoré said 'it is the top, the leadership, which decides and the grassroots have to submit' (Foreign Broadcast Information Service, Daily Report: Sub-Saharan Africa, 18 June 1984). Valère Somé, who was politically close to Sankara, later questioned whether that particular conception of 'democratic centralism' actually conformed to Lenin's understanding. The way it was often implemented in Burkina Faso 'in fact resembled the practice of bureaucratic centralism', and, as a result, 'the revolutionary structures could not be a place for creative initiatives or free discussions' (Somé 2016: 52).

Neither the UCB nor the other dogmatic organisations had many members outside the universities, government ministries or officer corps. Yet rather than reach out to new people, they remained inward-looking, hostile to anyone who raised the slightest critical question. Beginning in early 1986, this 'Stalinist current' – as the academic Pascal Labazée termed it – argued that it was time for a 'radicalisation' of the revolution. These groups disagreed with Sankara's proposals to grant clemency to political opponents and acted to undermine the influence of Somé's Union of Communist Struggle-Reconstructed (ULCR), which generally backed Sankara's more open approach (Labazée 1986: 119–120; Sennen Andriamirado 1989: 56–58).

This current within the CNR also moved to block Sankara's efforts to reconcile with the PAI, which had a notable base in the unions (unlike the other groups). Because Soumane Touré – a prominent PAI figure, leader of the CSV union federation and personal friend of Sankara – was critical of certain government policies, he was detained several times. In May 1987 UCB supporters within a Ouagadougou defence committee arrested him yet again, but that time they also called for his execution. At a subsequent meeting of the CNR, several UCB leaders and army captains came out in favour of Touré's execution. According to Somé, only his ULCR and Sankara opposed it. Sankara's intervention 'was decisive in saving Soumane Touré's life' (Somé 1990: 89).

Although they often bickered with each other, the political groups that participated in the CNR maintained a public posture of unity and claimed they wanted to build a single 'vanguard' organisation. Sankara, while in principle agreeing with the need for unity, nevertheless opposed cobbling together a dominant party through a simple amalgamation of existing groups. With the examples of other official parties in Africa or the Eastern bloc in mind, Sankara stressed the danger of establishing a 'nomenklatura of untouchable dignitaries' (*Sidwaya*, 7 August 1986). 'Nomenklatura' is the Russian word for a Soviet-style list of state positions that can be filled only by approved party appointees. Sankara generally advocated the creation of a wider front, perhaps including the PAI but also drawing in many of the young activists of the CDRs and other mass organisations. Sankara said that he was against any party that was monolithic and politically stultifying. He was for an organisation that would be 'pluralist, diverse, and enriched by many different thoughts and actions, thoughts and actions rich with a thousand nuances' (Sankara 1991: 267–277).

Sankara was aware that revolutions usually did not go astray simply because of erroneous ideas or inappropriate policies. Often real material interests were also involved, the unspoken social reality that lay beneath the public polemics. In Africa, he told me in an interview, many revolutionaries only went after the top elites, the 'big bourgeoisie'. They then gave big salaries and prestigious posts to the 'petty bourgeoisie' who predominated within their own camp. However, he went on:

> Every revolution that starts out with the petty bourgeoisie comes to a crossroads where it must choose what road to take. To take on the petty bourgeoisie means keeping the revolution radical, and there you will face many difficulties. Or you can go easy on the petty bourgeoisie. You won't have any difficulties. But then it won't be a revolution either – it will be a pseudorevolution.
>
> (Sankara, interview with *Intercontinental Press*, 17 March 1985)

As the differences among the political factions sharpened, the most strident 'radicals' tended to line up behind Compaoré. They also quietly expressed discomfort with Sankara's austere vision of public service and his strong anti-corruption measures. In fact, during the last year of his life, Sankara sought to intensify the struggle against corruption, including within the revolutionary camp itself, by obliging all top officials to publicly declare their incomes and properties. Some failed to declare all their assets, including Compaoré and his wife – who was an adopted daughter of the conservative pro-French president of neighbouring Côte d'Ivoire. Sankara commented to some journalists: 'Today there are people in power who live better than the population, who engage in small-scale trade with Syrian and Lebanese merchants, who find positions for their families, their younger cousins, yet all the while speaking in very revolutionary language' (*Le Matin*, Paris, 17–18 October 1987).

Sankara's efforts to ensure leadership integrity and a more open revolutionary process thus came up against a deadly mix: an alliance of a corrupt wing of the CNR and its hard-line ideologues with powerful regional forces tied to France. The result was Sankara's assassination and the end of the revolution.

Some sympathetic observers have cited the inordinate influence of the military within the CNR as another shortcoming. Oumou Zé (2014), a Burkinabè researcher working with a Belgian development organisation, commented: 'The Sankara regime was certainly military and of a Marxist orientation, and one could reproach him for the military rigor and discipline of the barracks.' Despite this militaristic rigor, Zé noted the continued attraction of Sankara's basic ideas among many of today's activists 'at a moment in history when a good number of people are beginning to strongly express their discontent with a system of exploitation of the country's natural resources by foreign interests, with the complicity of the local oligarchy' (ibid.). In essence, she wrote, Sankara's legacy offered 'a vision centred on the Burkinabè people, its pride, its integrity' (ibid.).

That vision is a timeless one. It has inspired new generations of Burkinabè as well as activists and thinkers across the continent, not only to better understand the political and social ills they confront, but also to try to change them.

NOTE

1 Unless noted otherwise, quotations from Sankara in this chapter are available in Sankara (2007).

REFERENCES

Andriamirado, S. (1987) *Sankara le rebelle*. Paris: Jeune Afrique livres.

Andriamirado, S. (1989) *Il s'appelait Sankara*. Paris: Jeune Afrique livres.

Englebert, P. (1996) *Burkina Faso: Unsteady Statehood in West Africa*. Boulder, CO: Westview Press.

Harsch, E. (2014) *Thomas Sankara: An African Revolutionary*. Athens, OH: Ohio University Press.

Harsch, E. (2015) Resurrecting Thomas Sankara. *Jacobin*. Retrieved on 1 May 2017 from www.jacobinmag.com/2015/05/thomas-sankara-burkina-faso-assassination.

Harsch, E. (2017) *Burkina Faso: A History of Power, Protest and Revolution*. London: Zed Books.

Jaffré, B. (2007) *Biographie de Thomas Sankara: La patrie ou la mort ...* (2nd edition). Paris: L'Harmattan.

Labazée, P. (1986) Une nouvelle phase de la révolution au Burkina Faso. *Politique africaine* 24 (December): 114–120.

Muase, C. K. (1989) *Syndicalisme et démocratie en Afrique noire: L'expérience du Burkina Faso (1936–1988)*. Paris: Editions Karthala; Abidjan: INADES Edition.

Sankara, T. (1991) *Oser inventer l'avenir: La parole de Sankara*. Paris: Pathfinder and L'Harmattan.

Sankara, T. (2007) *Thomas Sankara Speaks: The Burkina Faso Revolution, 1983–87* (2nd edition). New York: Pathfinder Press.

Somé, V. D. (1990) *Thomas Sankara: l'espoir assassiné*, Paris: L'Harmattan.

Somé, V. D. (2016) *Recueil de textes politiques*. Ouagadougou: Editions du millennium.

Zé, O. (2014) Le Burkina Faso Veut Tourner La Page. *Antipodes* 207. Retrieved on 1 May 2017 from www.iteco.be/antipodes/harmattan-africain-au-burkina-faso.

CHAPTER 10

Thomas Sankara and Tajudeen Abdul-Raheem

The Untimely Deaths of Two New Generation African Visionaries

Patricia Daley

How long shall they kill our prophets while we stand aside and look?
Bob Marley, 'Redemption Song', 1979

Thomas Sankara was assassinated at the age of 37 in 1987. Twelve years later, on African Liberation day, 25 May 2009, Tajudeen Abdul-Raheem died in a car crash under mysterious circumstances at the age of 49 (Manji 2009). Their untimely deaths were like wounds of the spirits for African people worldwide.

In a time when the continent of Africa was being dominated by dictatorial and neo-liberal forces, when young people were being encouraged to abandon socialism and equality for economic entrepreneurialism and opportunism, two young men, rather than joining the ranks of rent-seekers, pursued African liberation through socialist Pan-Africanism. Sankara and Abdul-Raheem represented a generation of young people who dared to persist in dreaming revolutionary thought, despite the neo-liberal turn. Both were visionaries: both used Marx's dialectical materialism and internationalism to understand the power dynamics and the conditions of the oppressed. They were taken from this world far too early, but left a legacy that has outlived them. As Sankara noted a mere week before his death: 'You can kill revolutionaries. You cannot kill ideas'. Their legacy is the unshaken belief in the ability of African people to liberate themselves from neo-colonial, capitalist imperial domination. In this chapter, I discuss their unshakeable belief in the power of African people to overcome imperial and domestic oppression. True to his conviction in the importance of human agency, Abdul-Raheem's motto was: 'Don't agonise, organise!'

As much has already been written on Sankara in the pages of this volume, the next section will provide a brief introduction to Tajudeen Abdul-Raheem. This will be followed by a comparison of three themes that pre-occupied both Sankara and Abdul-Raheem: the revolutionary imperative as a mechanism for liberation, feminism (that is, their belief in full equality for women and the centrality of women to Africa's liberation) and a people-centred internationalism and Pan-Africanism.

INTRODUCING TAJUDEEN ABDUL-RAHEEM

Abdul-Raheem was born on 6 January 1961 in Funtua, Katsina State, in Northern Nigeria. He gained a first class honours degree in Political Science from Bayero University in Kano, where there was a vibrant intellectual culture of critical debates. As the Trinidadian scholar David Johnson notes in his obituary of Abdul-Raheem:

> From Calabar to Lagos, Ife, Ibadan, Zaria, Bayero and many other sites, there was present a cohort of students who read widely, theorized, debated, fought, and intervened regularly on imagining and making a Nigeria and Africa that transcended the debilitating greed and politics of the power elite and their friends abroad.
>
> (Johnson 2009)

Abdul-Raheem's talent as a student was recognised by the award of a Rhodes scholarship to study at St Peter's College, Oxford University (1983–1987), where he obtained a Masters and Doctorate in Political Science, under the supervision of the Marxist political scientist, Gavin Williams. Abdul-Raheem would revel in the fact that he had managed to capture some of Cecil Rhodes' loot and used the space of Oxford to campaign for the oppressed everywhere. At Oxford, Abdul-Raheem co-organised lunchtime discussions on the politics of Africa and the diaspora, at which students from across the Africa continent and the diaspora would meet in what was then known as 'the barn' in Queen Elizabeth House to discuss a current publication or event in Africa. Abdul-Raheem possessed a razor-sharp intellect, political astuteness, energy, fearlessness, immense warmth, and 'that most deadly weapon of struggle: humour' (Johnson 2009). The latter was almost always accompanied by an infectious laugh. His immense oratory skills became evident when he took over as President of the Oxford University Africa Society. Johnson writes:

all who knew him understood the cause of global African liberation could not be separated from his work as scholar. He was not the first student to think this way and would not be the last, but there is no finer exemplar of the tradition in his generation.

(Johnson 2009)

Abdul-Raheem moved to London in 1989 to work as a researcher at the Institute of African Alternatives (IAA), which relocated to South Africa after the end of apartheid. In 1990, he and a group of London-based Pan-Africanists founded the Africa Research and Information Bureau (ARIB). As Yusuf Abdullah writes: 'ARIB was in praxis in ways that were unimaginable at IAA; it ministered to the needs of the swelling ranks of West Africans in the 1990s and was an intellectual rendezvous for both continental and diaspora Africans' (quoted in Zack-Williams 2009: 638). ARIB gave Abdul-Raheem, Abdullah writes, 'the intellectual space to think through the African condition in close proximity with battle-tested comrades fresh from the barricades with rich experiences to reflect upon' (Johnson 2009).

Abdul-Raheem was keen that Africans should take the lead in producing research and knowledge about the continent and on Africans in the diaspora. In 1996, ARIB launched a successful semi-academic magazine, *Africa World Review*, with Abdul-Raheem as the editor prescribing over an Editorial Working Committee with members from across the continent and diaspora. ARIB's mission was to research, facilitate discussion, and engage Africa-based groups to participate in the democratic struggles that were taking place all over the continent. Abdul-Raheem's incisive grasp of African politics soon resulted in him becoming a regular commentator on the BBC World Service Programmes on Africa and other news outlets in Hausa and English. Through such platforms he became well known across Africa.

Abdul-Raheem's most prominent role was as the Secretary General for the Secretariat of the 7th Pan-African Congress that was held in Kampala in 3–8 April 1994. In 1990, ARIB members started to participate in discussions on the organisation of the 7th Pan-African Congress. He was encouraged to take on the post of Secretary General by A.M. Babu, the former Tanzanian politician, for which Abdul-Raheem had to relocate to Uganda, where the Pan-African Secretariat was opened in 1992. The 7th PAC took place on 3–8 April 1994, and had some 5000 delegates from 30 countries. Abdul-Raheem was instrumental in the decision to have a women's pre-congress meeting on 2–3 April. It was here that Pan-African women launched the Pan-African Women's Liberation Organization (PAWLO).

While maintaining his role at the Secretariat as it sought to plan the 8th PAC, Abdul-Raheem continued to support a number of Pan-African organisations. He chaired a host of Pan-African social justice organisations, including the Pan-African Development Education and Advocacy Programme, the International Governing Council of the Centre for Democracy and Development, the Pan-African Development Education and Advocacy Programme, and Justice Africa. He established Hawa Memorial College in his home town of Funtua, in memory of his mother, and personally funded the education of numerous school and university students across Africa.

At the time of his death, Abdul-Raheem was contracted as deputy director of the UN's Millennium Development Goals (MDGs) campaign based in Nairobi, yet he was not mainstreamed, he was a fighter in the struggle to get the campaign to support meaningful development programmes.

Abdul-Raheem lived a Pan-African life. Speaking several Nigerian languages, he eschewed narrow Nigerian sectarian politics. For him, Pan-Africanism as a lived experience was facilitated by his employment in Uganda and Kenya and extensive travel. He was welcomed across the continent for his incisive criticism of African leaders and his strong belief in the ability of African peoples to triumph over adversity. He had a unique ability to speak truth to power, as well as to engage with the downtrodden. There is no doubt that he was inspired by Sankara's revolution in Burkina Faso. Sankara's influence is evident in Abdul-Raheem's writings and speeches. He died in a car crash in the early hours of the morning on his way to Nairobi airport to catch a flight to Rwanda for a UN meeting with the head of state. Those who saw the body said his injuries were not consistent with driving at a high speed and there was no other vehicle involved. There was no formal inquiry into his death as car crashes are ubiquitous in Kenya and Africa.

REVOLUTIONARY ZEAL

Both Sankara and Abdul-Raheem advocated revolutionary change as the only way in which Africans could liberate themselves from imperialism, elite domination and mental oppression. In an interview in 1985, Sankara stated:

> I would like to leave behind me the conviction that if we maintain a certain amount of caution and organization we deserve victory ... You cannot carry out fundamental change without a certain amount of madness. In this case, it comes from nonconformity, the courage to turn your back on the old formulas, the courage to invent the future. It took the madmen of yesterday for us to be able to act with extreme clarity today. I want to be one of those madmen. ... We must dare to invent the future.

> (Sankara, interview with Jean-Philippe Rapp, 1985[1])

In 1991, Abdul-Raheem mirrored Sankara, when he commented: 'Maybe it is ambitious on our part and perhaps even audacious, however, I do not think we can all claim to be revolutionaries if we are not ambitious and ready to dare, sometimes where others may fear to tread' (Abdul-Raheem quoted in Biney and Olukoshi 2010: xix).

Abdul-Raheem supported movements for the oppressed; while in the UK, these included the African National Congress, South West African Political Organization (SWAPO), the Save the Sharpeville Six campaign, and the anti-Apartheid Movement. In his turn, Sankara supported the Western Saharawi freedom fighters and other anti-imperialist movements and governments around the world, including those in Cuba, Nicaragua, and Grenada.

Both men were critical of the leaders of the post-liberation governments in certain African states. Sankara blamed the failure of the revolution on the petty bourgeoisie outlook of the leaders of the revolution, who overturn the big bourgeoisie only to replace them. How much Abdul-Raheem saw the effectiveness of the use of armed struggle or *coups d'état* as achieving the goal for transformation is difficult to see. Yet, in private, he was certainly critical of the actions of the post-genocide Rwandese Patriotic Front and the anti-Mobutu movement he witnessed in Rwanda and in the DRC. He supported initially the Rwandese Patriotic Front (RPF) in their struggle to end the genocide, but quickly became critical of the leaders whom he said 'rode on the bandwagon of liberation, only to abandon their people once power is captured'.

In public, Abdul-Raheem challenged revolutionaries who sought to prolong their term in office, such as Muammar Qaddafi of Libya, who said that 'revolutionaries don't retire'. Abdul-Raheem wrote:

What happens to revolutionaries when they get in power: they have stayed so long in power that they have forgotten their previous jobs, values and visions. From heralding 'fundamental change' they have become apostles of 'no change'. They have become reactionaries exhausting the country they claim to have liberated. The challenge now facing Zimbabweans, Ethiopian, Eritreans, and other post liberation societies: how to liberate themselves from their liberators.

(Abdul-Raheem 2008)

In a Postcard dated 19 February 2009, entitled, 'Respect Term Limits for Democratic Change', Abdul-Raheem wrote: 'the world has changed and so must revolutionaries'.

The impetus for revolution, for both men, should and would come from the oppressed. In one of Abdul-Raheem's first journal papers (co-authored with Adebayo Olukoshi), addressing the history of the left in Nigeria, they considered 'how the left can learn from its past [by] drawing on the traditions of the 'radical trade union movement, the radical political legacy among the peasantry and rural poor, and the work of the Women in Nigeria in the struggle for the emancipation of women from gender oppression and the pool of progressive opinion among radical intellectuals, youths and the student movement' (Abdul-Raheem and Olukoshi 1986: 79).

Both saw consciousness-raising as a key element of any revolution. For them, neo-colonialism and neo-colonial way of thinking was a great hindrance to emancipation of the African peoples. A key difference between Abdul-Raheem and Sankara was that, as a head of state and coup leader, the latter argued that he 'took the leadership of the peasant revolt, the brewing revolt of the urban masses, and the just struggles of our masses as we mobilise against imperialism and their domestic allies'. Through the Committee for the Defence of the Revolution, Sankara sought to mobilise workers, farmers and youth. Through his leadership, power would be increasingly democratised.

Abdul-Raheem, on the other hand, sought to help raise consciousness through non-military means. Unlike Sankara, Abdul-Raheem was not schooled in militarism. He did National Youth Service in Nigeria and sported military attire while at Oxford – but this was in solidarity with the liberation struggles of Che Guevara, Fidel Castro and Sankara himself. Abdul-Raheem sided with the dispossessed, the poor, women, students, farmers, market women (*mama mbogas*) and street traders. In his final Postcard of 2009, entitled 'City Beautification Should Not Destroy Livelihoods', he championed the right of informal traders to sell their wares on the streets of African cities.

AFRICAN MEN AS FEMINISTS

Emancipation like freedom is not granted, it is conquered.
Thomas Sankara, United Nations General Assembly, 1984

Sankara and Abdul-Raheem were representatives of a new breed of Pan-Africanists: Pan-Africanists who were feminists. Both envisaged a progressive involvement of women in the struggle for liberation beyond the domesticated activities that were deemed women's spheres. Sankara sought not to organise women in 'folkloric groups, where they sewed uniforms and sing and dance' (*Intercontinental Press* interview, 17 March 1985), nor did he seek to speak for them or organise their liberation. Instead, he supported their developing consciousness. He stated, 'You cannot free slaves who are not consciousness of their situation of slavery' and 'women had to liberate themselves' (Sankara, on International Women's Day, 8 March 1987).

International Women's Day (8 March) provided key moments when both men were able to articulate their feminism. Both challenged the cultural and social constraints that prevented women's full emancipation. Sankara saw the fight against circumcision and polygamy as well as the fight for economic power as central to women's liberation. In a speech given on 8 March 1987, Sankara noted how the Burkinabè revolution was a 'de-personalising darkness for women', while being 'a reality for men' (Sankara, on International Women's Day, 8 March 1987). And yet the authenticity and the future of the revolution depend on women' (ibid). He continued, 'to win the battle for men and women, we must be familiar with all aspects of the women question on a world as well as on a national scale' (ibid).

In 2006, Abdul-Raheem argued that 'every day should be women's day'. In 2009, he advocated not just changes in laws to end violence against women, but general public education and mass awareness. 'This will not just be about laws but also confronting certain received wisdoms, and cultural and social practices that encourage violence against women and disempower them from voicing their pain, let alone seeking legal redress' (Abdul-Raheem 2009b).

Abdul-Raheem's feminism began early when, as a young boy, he helped his mother to give birth. When working on the MDGs, he used his bureaucratic position in the United Nations to challenge states to improve the maternal health care for women. He wrote: 'It is not morally or politically right and it cannot be acceptable that mothers die giving life' (Abdul-Raheem 2009a).

As Secretary-General of the Pan-African Congress, Abdul-Raheem was instrumental in facilitating the incorporation of Resolution 8 of the 7th PAC. The Resolution drew on the recommendations arising from the Women's Pre-Congress meeting. Resolution 8 on Women and Pan-Africanism, in its preamble, notes that 'women make up more than half of the Pan-African world and are therefore an important constituency for Pan-Africanism' and 'that women, individually and collectively, are part and parcel of the Pan-African movement. Consequently, the 7th Pan-African Congress resolved to support women's demand for (i) equal partnership in the Pan-African movement; (ii) the setting up of a women's section in the Secretariat; (iii) a '50% allocation of the financial and other resources at the various international, regional, and sub-regional and local structures of the Pan-African Movement' and (iv) the convening of a women's summit to 'evaluate progress made so far, consolidate networking and together with their brothers lay new strategies for the future'.

While Abdul-Raheem supported the development of the PAWLO movement, many men paid only lip-service to Resolution 8. On International Women's Day in 2017, Biney questioned the persistence of men in the Pan-African movement who harbour patriarchal views. She demanded to know where the contemporary Sankaras and Cabrals were, describing both as 'radical feminists'. I would add Abdul-Raheem to her list of 'anti-sexist, anti-heterosexist, caring, conscious, empathetic men who will develop organisations and institutions that serve African people' (Biney 2017).

INTERNATIONALISTS AND PAN-AFRICANISTS

Both Sankara and Abdul-Raheem were varyingly internationalist and Pan-Africanist. Sankara was a socialist and anti-imperialist who forged alliances with other socialist movements and governments worldwide. He was an advocate for the oppressed of the world and of the non-aligned movement. While Sankara saw Pan-Africanism as a 'problem', he recognised both its inspirational role at a historical juncture (as part of the national liberation struggles) and the potential of the idea, demonstrating an awareness of the difficulties in the realisation of African unity. This may partly account for the strength of his internationalist outlook.

Abdul-Raheem started off as a Marxist, maintained his socialist principles and internationalist outlook against injustice, but became more of a Pan-Africanist as time progressed. In 1996, Abdul-Raheem argued, 'Pan-Africanism as a counter force to imperialism is a necessary tool of analysis and organisational format for the whole Pan-African World' (Abdul-Raheem 1996: 2). He wrote in a Postcard: 'Our optimism is based on the concrete reality of our lived experiences and the brutal reality of the condition of many Africans today both in the continent and in the Diaspora. These have made Pan-Africanism a precondition for our survival instead of it just being a dream.' It is within this context that the 7th PAC called for a second liberation front to defeat re-colonisation, dictatorships, and genocidal practices across the continent. The theme of the Congress was 'Facing the Future in Unity, Social Progress and Democracy – Perspectives towards the 21st Century'. The urgency of these principles was brought to the fore when the Rwandan genocide began on the last day of the conference.

Both Sankara and Abdul-Raheem were associated with a new brand of people-centred Pan-Africanism, and were not afraid to criticise African leaders. Abdul-Raheem (2007a) wrote: 'It is now widely recognized that Pan-Africanism needs to leave the confines of [the] conferences and executive mansions of our leaders and become part and parcel of all our lives building from the down-up.' Abdul-Raheem and Sankara both believed in the unity of Africa peoples but not the one that was being sought by the then leadership of the Organization of African Unity/ African Union. Abdul-Raheem (2007b) argued:

> In spite of the intrigues and manoeuvres by the various camps they share a basic weakness: they are state led and are projecting this vision without the involvement of the broad masses of their own peoples. They do not even involve their own parliaments let alone ordinary citizens. In many cases it is only the Presidency that is involved with Foreign Affairs Ministers playing guessing games.

For Abdul-Raheem (2006b), the Pan-Africanism of the leaders promotes a 'narrow' national identity that is not historically rooted and exclusionary, that does not reflect the realities of people's lived experiences, especially that of 'peasants [and] petty traders who carry their wares across the [international] boundary on *panya panya* roads parallel to the formal border roads'. While Sankara saw borders as administrative devices, Abdul-Raheem called for their abolition and freedom of movement for African peoples. At a meeting of the OAU in Addis Ababa, Abdul-Raheem criticised Ethiopia for having entry visa requirements that make it difficult for ordinary Africans to visit Ethiopia or to get near the meetings of the African Union. Abdul-Raheem became especially critical of the Pan-Africanism of leaders represented by Qaddafi of Libya, who was spearheading a movement for the formation of the United States of Africa (and, as Chapter 6 of this volume argues, who may have played a role in Sankara's assassination plot through his support of Charles Taylor and the group of Liberian mercenaries that implemented the assassination at the behest of imperial-backed Blaise Compaoré). While asking Africans to unite against colonialism, Qaddafi signed pacts with European leaders to imprison African migrants on Libyan soil, in order to prevent them from crossing the Mediterranean, and ignored the killing of 500 African migrants in Libya in September 2009. In May 2009, Abdul-Raheem (2009c) wrote: 'Gaddafi needs to lead by example. Libya must politically educate its own citizens and stem anti-African xenophobia in the country and stop pursuing immigration policies and pacts that make it a gatekeeper for Europe'.

Sankara's ambivalence towards open borders may have been a reaction to the conservative anti-revolutionary forces that had aligned against Burkina Faso in Francophone West Africa, in Côte d'Ivoire and Mali – the very forces that would ultimately conspire with former colonisers to carry out his assassination (see Chapter 6, this volume). While he supported the movement of ideas and people across borders, he saw borders 'as necessary to limit each country's sphere of activity and enable it to see things clearly' (Sankara, on return from Africa tour, August 1984).

Both Sankara and Abdul-Raheem had non-racialised visions of Africa and African liberation. They eschewed the division of Africa into north and sub-Saharan, and attempts, whether by Mobutu (of Zaire) in the case of Sankara, or Lagos-based Pan-Africanists in the case of Abdul-Raheem, to divide Africans along colour lines. For Abdul-Raheem (1996: 3), 'while the majority of Africans are of Negroid origin, it is not true historically, factually or even politically that blackness is the only condition of Africanness'. Sankara, critiquing then President Mobutu's call for the establishment of a league of black states, contended; 'It's not a question of colour. With regard to how we conceive the OAU, there is no room for the colour-sensitive. There is only one colour – that of African unity' (Sankara, on return from Africa tour, August 1984).

CONCLUSION

Progressive forces in Africa mourned the untimely deaths of two young African men who had the potential to transform their societies and inspire others. Both were optimistic in the capacities of the people to bring about meaningful change. Sankara, as President of Burkina Faso, was subjected to far more criticism than Abdul-Raheem, who operated largely within a progressive political sphere. Some close to Abdul-Raheem thought that with his Pan-Nigerian outlook, he would have had difficulty participating in the sectarian politics of Nigeria, even though he had a desire to return home and facilitate changes there.

While Abdul-Raheem respected Sankara's revolutionary praxis in Burkina Faso, one can speculate as to whether this would have continued if Sankara had survived. At the time of his death, his people's revolution was already being undermined, including by the forces that plotted his assassination. According to Justice Africa's Memoriam to Abdul-Raheem, at the time of his death, he was turning his criticism 'of the record of liberation movements in power' into a manuscript of a 'historical account and political analysis of the liberators and where they had gone astray' (Justice Africa 2009). He may well have written about the failure of the Burkinabè revolution.

In the era of neo-liberal individualism and the free market, it is often seen as outmoded to think in revolutionary ways. In modernity, revolutionary thought has been closely bound up with the political project of socialism. By seeing the liberation of the African peoples as only possible through revolutionary transformation, Abdul-Raheem and Sankara drew on the theoretical articulation of socialism's resistance to capitalist modernity, yet their thinking was rooted in indigenous ontologies in which the collectivity is paramount over the individual. This is why a people-centred internationalism and Pan-Africanism remains vital to the liberation struggle from exploitation. Eschewing gendered hierarchies and local and modern forms of patriarchy, they positioned women's equal rights as central to the collective struggle for Africa's liberation from past and present conditions of coloniality and imperial domination. Abdul-Raheem and Sankara paved the way for a new generation of African feminist men, whose actions and words can inspire young African men and women to work together in their struggle for a better future.

NOTE

1   Unless noted otherwise, quotations from Sankara in this chapter are available in Sankara (2007).

REFERENCES

Abdul-Raheem, T. (1996) *Pan-Africanism: Politics, Economy and Social Change in the Twenty-first Century*. London: Pluto Press.

Abdul-Raheem, T. (2006a) Pan-African Postcards: Every Day Should Be a Women's Day. *Pambazuka News* 245.

Abdul-Raheem, T. (2006b) Pan-African Postcards: Africa Must Unite – NOW. *Pambazuka News* 281.

Abdul-Raheem, T. (2007a) Pan-African Postcards: Pan-African Perspectives on the African Union. *Pambazuka News* 289.

Abdul-Raheem, T. (2007b) Pan-African Postcards: Don't Let Them Shave Our Heads from Behind. *Pambazuka News* 303.

Abdul-Raheem, T. (2008) Pan-African Postcards: 'Liberation from "Liberators"? Uganda and the NRM'. *Pambazuka News*.

Abdul-Raheem, T. (2009a) Mothers Should Not Die Giving Life. *Pambazuka News* 422.

Abdul-Raheem, T. (2009b) Pan-African Postcards: Ending Violence Against Women. *Pambazuka News* 423.

Abdul-Raheem, T. (2009c) Pan-African Postcard: Addis Summit Putting Brakes on Progress. *Pambazuka News* 418.

Abdul-Raheem, T. and Olukoshi, A. (1986) The Left in Nigerian Politics and the Struggle for Socialism: 1945–1985. *Review of African Political Economy* 13(37): 64–80.

Biney, A. (2017) Letter to 'Man-Africanists' on International Women's Day. Retrieved on 1 November 2017 from www.pambazuka.org/pan-africanism/letter-%E2%80%9Cman-africanists%E2%80%9D-international-women%E2%80%99s-day.

Biney, A. and Olukoshi, A. (eds) (2010) *Speaking Truth to Power*. Oxford: Pambazuka Press.

Johnson, D. (2009) Tribute to Tajudeen. *Pambazuka News* 434.

Justice Africa (2009) In memoriam: Tajudeen Abdul-Raheem, 1961–2009. Retrieved on 1 December 2017 from http://africanarguments.org/2009/05/25/in-memoriam-tajudeen-abdul-raheem-2.

Manji, F. (2009) Tajudeen Abdul-Raheem – a Giant is Lost on African Liberation Day. *Pambazuka News* 434.

Sankara, T. (2007) *Thomas Sankara Speaks: The Burkina Faso Revolution, 1983–87* (2nd edition). New York: Pathfinder Press.

Zack-Williams, A. B. (2009) 'Tributes to Tajudeen Abdul-Raheem (1961–2009). *Review of African Political Economy* 36(122): 637–640.

CHAPTER 11

Women's Freedoms are the Heartbeat of Africa's Future
A Sankarian Imperative
Patricia McFadden

We must dare to invent the future.
Thomas Sankara, interview with Jean-Philippe Rapp, 1985

This chapter seeks to show, through an African feminist political economy perspective, why Thomas Sankara is 'special' as an African revolutionary thinker, military personality, advocate for freedoms – particularly women's freedoms – and as the former leader of an African country, who actually implemented radical policies (although they were short lived) through which he mobilised the working people at large, and women in particular, towards a different vision of the future. As a Pan-Africanist, Thomas Sankara was a radical nationalist who passionately resisted imperialism and colonialism. He also critically understood the depth of patriarchal oppression and its devastating impacts on the lives of Burkinabè woman across class and social location. Nonetheless, the challenges of militarism as an anti-revolutionary weapon remained largely unresolved, and they proved to be the 'Achilles heel' to his demise. He continues to serve as a vibrant and contemporary role model for younger Africans, particularly in giving an example for how to bring radical courage to the creation of gender- and class-inclusive societies on the continent.

SANKARA'S POLITICAL PHILOSOPHY AND AFRICAN
FEMINIST THOUGHT

Let me begin by declaring that I have a personal/political interest in the ideas and courage that Thomas Sankara represented during the brief episode of his presence as a thinker, military leader and advocate for social justice in the first half of the 1980s. His incorrigible belief in the best in human beings, an ethos whose potency and relevance could not be silenced by a hail of bullets thirty years ago this year, continues to resonate with radicals of all ages and genders – those who know of him, that is. Indeed, he has remained largely 'unknown' to many Africans (see Chapter 20, this volume). As a radical contemporary feminist who lives and struggles for feminist justice on the African continent, my interest in Sankara stems both from having personally participated in anti-colonial resistance across southern Africa, as well as from my identity as an African feminist that is unreservedly critical of nationalism and its constraining influences on African women's politics as gendered struggles against patriarchal power. I share many of the same traditions of radical political economy and critical gendered thinking which influenced Sankara's ideas and ideals concerning the African revolution, as I too dream of a different future and life for Africans generally, but especially for African women.

Thomas Sankara is distinctive in ideological and political terms. It is in these two spheres of intellectual and activist engagement that he made his greatest impact. Whilst he was a nationalist in the resistance traditions of the most outstanding African anti-colonialists (having been born in 1949 during the French colonial occupation of his country, Burkina Faso, then Upper Volta, in West Africa), he differed in that he drew from a very particular radical nationalist ideological tradition, in Africa and internationally: a radical nationalism which pushed for revolution instead of neo-colonial settlement. According to Mary-Alice Waters, he shared anti-imperialist courage and unabashed humanism with Fidel Castro and Che Guevara (quoted in Sankara 1988: 8).

RADICAL ANTI-COLONIAL RESISTANCE AND AN ETHOS OF HUMANISM

His views and ideas, his dreams and resilience in the face of a political backlash and imprisonment by the colonial and neo-colonial regimes of France and Upper Volta, reflected the particularity of radical nationalists like Amilcar Cabral, Samora Machel and Patrice Lumumba. These anti-colonial leaders had embraced the necessity of adopting a historical materialist perspective in understanding colonial occupation and repression, in order to pursue a communist program of socialist transformation for their respective societies (Young 2001). Cabral in particular, was deeply influenced by the examples of anti-imperialist resistance and its successes in South America. The Cuban revolution was an intellectual and political beacon for Cabral (Cabral 1969a, 1969b). In the same vein, Thomas Sankara also deeply admired Che Guevara. Indeed, Sankara, like Cabral, presented some of his most radical ideas on the revolutionary transformation that had to occur in Africa during visits to Cuba. His ideas and visions of a new humanism in African societies drew from the radicalism of the Cuban Revolution. Sankara declared: 'Che is Burkinabè' (Sankara, Political Orientation Speech, 1983). Both Sankara and Cabral were assassinated shortly after these critical episodes of revolutionary solidarity with the Cuban revolution. Che had been brutally murdered twenty years earlier, almost to the day, than Sankara lost his life in a military coup.

In terms of situating Sankara among his revolutionary peers, it is clear that, together with Cabral, Lumumba and Machel, these men stood head and shoulders above the rest of their Pan-Africanist counterparts in the anti-colonial resistance movements that swept across the continent during the course of the twentieth century. This was largely because they went beyond the limited and inadequate understandings of freedom as independence from white colonial rule, which invariably resulted in the installation of neo-colonial regimes. They recognised and articulated – in intellectual and propagandist terms – the centrality of the agency of working people in assuring the victory of their struggles in each specific context.

This unwavering belief in the ability of working people to transform their lives from drudgery and socio-economic exclusion to well-being and social consciousness (a belief which forms the essential core of humanism – as an ethos, a movement, and a radical political principle), inevitably led to their removal from the theatre of African anti-colonial struggles. The retrieval of the humanness of people provided the revolutionary dynamic and the foundation for freedom in the time of imperialist repression, domination and plunder, which still persist across Africa to this day. Sankara, like Cabral, Lumumba and Machel, brought this uncompromisingly revolutionary meaning of humanism to their specific revolutionary projects. In Mozambique and Guinea Bissau this was effected through protracted liberation struggles against Portuguese colonial barbarism; in the Congo, against the brutal, impunitous Belgians and the US corporations/state; in Upper Volta, against the supposedly 'civilised' French.

In all four cases, and in many more that are seldom celebrated and or recognised, Africans whose ideological visions for a revolutionary restructuring of the continent (in economic, political, social and cultural terms) have been assassinated. In other cases, their lives have been made a living hell wherever they have tried to live. Eliminating revolutionaries on the continent and in other societies of the majority south is a well-established part of the project to sustain imperialist and capitalist hegemony across the world (Pilger 2001).

Sankara also shared the radical socialist traditions that made Machel, Lumumba and Cabral distinctive. They each either (a) attempted to implement radical socialist programs once they had occupancy of the State or (b) because they were prosecuted during the anti-colonial wars, they unambiguously articulated these radical ideas and visions. Each wrote and spoke about them with deep clarity and honesty, using their ideas to mobilise the working people in the cause of revolutionary transformation.

For Sankara, it would seem that the repression he had suffered as a child (seeing his parents and other black adults humiliated by French colonials) and the kindnesses he experienced from strangers left deep impressions upon him about the value of kindness. These encounters no doubt instilled empathy in terms of understanding humanism as an innate part of being human. This sensibility against de-humanising behaviour provided the impetus for Sankara's strong sense of outrage against colonial arrogance and the blatant disregard for the humanity of African people in his country, across the continent and in the Diaspora.

As with all black people who joined struggles against racist colonial impunity, Sankara expressed the desire for a retrieval of his humanity and the dignity of his people as core elements of the established nationalist discourse of anti-imperialism. Exposure to Marxism, and the radical ideas of Marx and Engels in particular, explain to a large extent the source of his critical posture against exploitation and colonial and neo-colonial repression. Again, these are the same elements that one notes in the radical journeys travelled by Cabral, Lumumba and Machel who, in certain ways, provided the ideological pathways along which Sankara treaded as he assumed the leadership of the Burkinabè revolution.

WOMEN'S FREEDOMS ARE THE HEARTBEAT: AN ANTI-PATRIARCHAL SANKARIAN PHILOSOPHY

Later, when Sankara comes to gendered consciousness, he extends this critical thinking towards an utter rejection of feudalism and ancient African practices of male privileging. He was highly critical of 'child marriage, female genital mutilation, and domestic violence', which, he argued, was too often 'facilitated by "culture and tradition"' (Sankara International Women's Day, 1987). He maintained a scathing critique of prostitution as not only 'a symbol of the contempt that men have for women' but more significantly, in terms of anti-patriarchal critique, as a form of self-hate: 'In the final analysis, prostitution reflects the unconscious contempt we have for ourselves' (ibid.).

Indeed, as soon as he assumed state power, Sankara pushed the notion of humanism even further, beyond its masculine contours and histories, to include women in the idea of human dignity and wholeness. His critique and rejection of patriarchy and male privilege provided a radical alternative to existing masculinist notions of African maleness. Linking the notion of freedom from colonialism with the necessity of Burkinabè men's recognition of women as complete human beings, he asserted that 'The condition of women is therefore at the heart of the question of humanity itself' (Sankara 1987).

This gendered anti-imperialism is another common ideological tread that Sankara shares with radical nationalists, in this instance specifically with Samora Machel and Amilcar Cabral. Cabral, Machel and Sankara insisted that women were a necessary and inevitable part of the revolution and of a different future. For Cabral, women brought their long traditions of anti-patriarchal resistance to the PAIGC (the African Party for the Independence of Guinea and the Cape Verde Islands) and it was this resistance experience and energy that became the undeniable impetus that gave the liberation movement its ultimate power over Portuguese colonialism (Cabral 1969c: 117–118). The same could be said of Machel, who, in the footsteps of Eduardo Mondlane (1969) insisted that the Mozambican revolution would be incomplete without the liberation of women, their organisation and integration into the structures of the new society in the 'liberated zones' of the country as the struggle progressed.

At independence, FRELIMO actively mobilised and integrated women across class lines, into the key sectors of Mozambican society and, for the first few years of independence, women's emancipation ranked high on the post-liberation agenda of that country. In the case of Cabral, because he was assassinated before Guinea Bissau could gain its independence, we will never know how well his leadership would have implemented the powerful programs for women's freedoms that he so courageously articulated in his writings and speeches. Nonetheless, as Robert J. C. Young has argued:

> Whether locally at the level of resistance to a particular colonial power, or globally against the imperialist system, socialist forms of liberation struggles saw their objectives as essentially compatible with those of socialist feminism. Women worked alongside the men, and the women's movements formed an intrinsic part of the struggle.
>
> (Young 2001: 373)

Conventionally, male politicians call for 'gender equality' as part of an appeal to rescue women from their 'victim' status within societies. Sankara, on the other hand, insists that women's freedoms and their emancipation are not something that men give to women out of some sense of kindness or altruism. They are outcomes of struggle against patriarchy, which is practiced and protected by males. Sankara expressed this very poignantly when he spoke of women's agency for their own liberation: 'Emancipation, like freedom, is not granted, it is conquered. It is for women themselves to put forward their demands and mobilise to win them' (Sankara 1987).

It is this resoluteness in critiquing and challenging patriarchy and imperialism in intellectual and practical terms – (a political consciousness that was almost unheard of among African leaders and males in general, and even among women who participated in the anti-colonial resistance) – which not only sets Thomas Sankara apart from the most radical African nationalists of the past half-century, but which also marks him with a uniquely feminist-inspired radicalism that I am deeply curious about and inspired by as a radical African feminist.

As I re-read his writings recently with a more mature understanding of the power and resilience of radical ideas and with a better understanding of how 'before his time' he was, I realised just how courageous Sankara was, as a black man and as a male revolutionary. There is no other black radical man – intellectual or political leader, or both – who has articulated and insisted upon the advanced gender-inclusive ideas and policies that Sankara advocated for *and implemented*. His goal was to initiate the process of emancipation for women in Burkina Faso; he did a commendable job contributing to this project during his short stay at the helm of the national state.

While Cabral declared the inclusion of women as future citizens of Guinea Bissau, 'Men and women will have the same status with regard to family, work, and public activities' (Cabral 1969c: 137) and both Mondlane and Machel lauded the impact of armed female guerrillas in spreading the message of freedom among the people at the village level, Sankara was deliberately and consistently focused on explaining to Burkinabè women that they had to free themselves from both colonial and patriarchal oppression. He went beyond the call to women as 'victims' who needed the State and or men to save them from oppression (usually implying colonial oppression) by encouraging women to be agents of their own freedom through full participation in the Burkinabè revolution. He recognised that women have been enslaved by structural and relational forces for millennia and that there was a need to 'understand how this system functions, to grasp its real nature in all its subtlety, in order then to work out a line of action that can lead to women's total emancipation' (Sankara 1987).

Therefore, in addition to bringing African dreams of freedom to the notion and practice of humanism and opening up this site of struggle and emancipation to women's humanness, Sankara gendered the very notion of revolution by inviting men to transform themselves through their rejection of patriarchy, thereby assuring the revolutionary experience in Burkina Faso. This is the first time that we hear an African male politician define gendered equality as an essential requirement for fundamental social transformation. Throughout his treatise on women's emancipation and its centrality to the Burkinabè revolution, he is adamant that women are their own liberators, just as men are their own.

In revisiting his ideas, I remain intrigued by the circumstances and personal choices that he must have consciously made so as to become the man that he was at the time of his tragic death. Clearly he was deeply touched and transformed by the literature he had read and his exposure to radical nationalist ideas during his trips to Madagascar and France in the earlier part of his military career training. He spoke of the changes in his worldview after reading Engels, Marx and other communist revolutionaries, as well as how the continued exploitation of his country and its people by both the French and local parasitic classes (comprador and feudal elements) led him to participate in protests against the repressive regime of Jean-Baptiste Ouédraogo on 4 August 1983. However, at no point in the articulation of his radicalism does he indicate where his feminist-inspired consciousness comes from. The question then becomes: What was it about his resistance consciousness, his experiences of anti-colonialism and his desire for freedom that created the shift in his perceptions of women's freedoms as crucial to a different African future?

I am of the opinion that Sankara was deeply influenced by the work of European feminists like Simone de Beauvoir and Alexandra Kollontai, for example, who were part of the Marxist intellectual traditions that young radicals were exposed to at the time of Sankara's studies. His analysis of prostitution, for example, clearly indicates feminist critiques of female commodification through marriage and the exchange of women's bodies in the public and private domains as things. He declares that 'Prostitution is a concentrated, tragic and painful summary of female slavery in all its forms' (Sankara 1987). The objectification of women as the core of the patriarchal system – in economic, sexual, social, cultural and reproductive terms – not only reflective of the influence that Frederick Engels had on his understanding of the development of human society as an exploitative class and gender system, but it is clearly informed by the work of radical feminists of the mid-century.

Sankara never really articulates an openly anti-feminist stance in any of his speeches and writings, except on two occasions in his speech on the revolution and women's emancipation, he alludes to feminism as a 'war of the sexes', preferring instead to explain gendered conflicts as 'a war of social groups and of classes', with an emphasis on the complementarity of women and men. He argues that 'it's the attitude of men that makes such confusion possible. That in turn paves the way for the bold assertions made by feminism, some of which have not been without value in the fight that men and women are waging against oppression' (Sankara 1987). Later in the speech, he refers to 'a few petty-bourgeois women' from the town being preoccupied with feminism as a fashionable politics and dismisses it as 'primitive feminism' (ibid.).

This off-handed dismissal of feminism as something that is contradictory to the core of the revolutionary transformation of gendered relationships within Burkinabè society, and the argument for complementary social relationships as an unavoidable inevitability, reflect two very important nationalistic tenets. These tenets persist in defining African gendered relationships as 'naturally hetero-normative' and maintain that this is 'authentically' African.

Sankara never mentions homosexuality in any of his speeches, nor does he, in any perceptible way, articulate any homophobia. However, his insistence upon complementary gendered relationships between men and women as inescapable, smacks of a passive homophobia that is more actively pursued by most African nationalists across the political spectrum.

THE BACKLASH AGAINST SANKARA'S ANTI-PATRIARCHAL PHILOSOPHY

In critiquing the established African patriarchal order, so deeply entrenched within African cultural discourses, conventions and practices that are essentially feudal and violent, Sankara posed an epistemological and foundationally ontological challenge to all black men. The challenge was to politically re-define the meaning and practice of heterosexual gendered identities. He went even further in his use of the notion of 'authenticity', arguing that becoming non-patriarchal is the necessary process by which men will 'become human'. Speaking to the enormity of the task of self-transformation facing both women and men, Sankara explained that, 'This task is formidable but necessary. It will determine our ability to bring our revolution to its full stature ... This will show to what extent the natural behaviour of man has become human and to what extent he has realised his human nature' (Sankara 1987). Key to this retrieval of their humanity is the total rejection of feudalism in all its forms and expressions.

In a deeply feudal society such as that of Burkina Faso, male patriarchal privilege in the domestic and public areas is considered quintessentially 'natural' to being an African man. In such a feudal society, questioning or challenging how males access and exercise power and insisting upon the equality of women and men in every aspect of life would have generated a deep sense of threat and dislike for Sankara, even among his peers. Indeed, he was too far ahead of his society. So, when he came under attack on that fateful day of 15 October 1987, I have no doubt that, in part, his demise brought with it a sense of relief for many men (and women) in Burkinabè society, even though no such sentiment was ever published. After all, he had gone beyond the pale of conservative, reactionary, patriarchal society with his 'mad' ideas of gender equality and social revolution (for more on the 'madness' of Sankara's political philosophies and policies, see Introduction and Chapter 8, this volume).

The outcry against Sankara's assassination by Blaise Compaoré, his close friend and military counterpart, has remained focused on the duplicity of Francois Mitterrand, then president of France, the reactionary forces in the Burkinabè military as well as the local ruling classes and 'land lords' whose land and ill-begotten assets had been nationalised by the Sankara government. While these critiques have been useful in identifying both the class-based and anti-imperial threats of Sankara's policies, an analysis that factors in the gendered ramifications of what Thomas Sankara was most courageous about – the freedoms of women/females of all ages across the class, social, ethnic and locational divides – has barely, if ever, surfaced in any of Africa's revolutionary conversations following Sankara's assassination.

It was the courage to be non-conformist and to reject all the paraphernalia of black male authenticity (which is repressive and dehumanising to all females) and then to dare to become contemporary in new and inclusive ways that posed the greatest threat to Thomas Sankara's existence. 'Yes, you cannot carry out fundamental change without a certain amount of madness. In this case, it comes from nonconformity, the courage to turn your back on the old formulas, the courage to invent the future' (Sankara 1983).

This silencing of his advanced stance on African women's freedoms is typically nationalist. It signals a pretence that such a contentious stance is not sufficiently relevant to Pan-Africanist and revolutionary discussions and that, if it is acknowledged, it is treated as a peculiarity whose annoying existence will eventually pass. The dominant expectation is that gendered relationships of power and the critique of patriarchy are 'issues' that are the preoccupation of gender activists and feminists and not of 'serious' African intellectuals. The persistent lack of interest and/or engagement with feminism in particular (as a serious political discipline, politics of life and revolutionary transformation) is clearly indicative of a dismissive attitude towards the challenges that women's freedoms still pose within the African academy and in the Pan-African community as a whole.

At the same time, I have not recognised a direct influence by Frantz Fanon on Sankara's thought or sense of black racial identity. Although it is very likely that he did encounter Fanon's work, given that he acquired his revolutionary consciousness during a time when Fanon's work and struggle for Algerian independence had come to international prominence. The absence of a direct reference in terms of Sankara's ideas on race and blackness, as these affected African men in particular, points to a gap in Sankara's political understanding of the trauma that racist colonial oppression had on all Africans. Although he alludes to race in his speech in Harlem in October 1984 and the origins of racism in his speech on International Women's Day on 1987 (Sankara 1987: 344), it is rather peculiar that this lacuna would be so obvious in the critical thinking of one who was so ahead of his peers – politically and practically – and it poses an interesting intellectual challenge for radical scholars who might be interested in further exploring and expounding upon what I think of as a Sankarian imperative.

CONCLUSION

Thomas Sankara not only provides African revolutionary thinkers and activists with a refreshing challenge on revolution as an internationalist inevitability – for example, his embrace of Che Guevara in particular speaks to this interface between personal political identity and the powerful resources that other revolutionary experiences offered (see Chapter 5, this volume) – but he also pushes the boundaries on African male gendered identity in heterosexual terms. That is, he insisted that men must change in order for the revolution to succeed in its fullness.

What implications might the Sankarian Revolution have had for a different African future, in terms of the nationalist dispensation for all Africans and for African women's freedoms in particular? Set in a nationalist framework, but understood and appreciated through a feminist analysis of its significance, the Sankarian Imperative of centring women's freedoms reiterated what women generally (and feminists in particular) have insisted upon for as long as women have expressed their political and social interests. Beyond the liberal admission that women are a valuable resource to all societies is the undeniable connection between human freedoms and creativity in all its dimensions and expressions: artistic, technological, linguistic, knowledge production, social reproduction and women as free beings. These intersections have always been central to inventions, expressions and manifestations of human existence, everywhere. Women's freedoms remain the inescapable necessity for human existence and well-being in every society.

REFERENCES

Cabral, A. (1969a) *Revolution in Guinea: An African People's Struggle.* London: Prinkipo Press.

Cabral, A. (1969b) *Practical Problems and Tactics.* London: Prinkipo Press.

Cabral, A. (1969c) *PAIGC Program.* London: Prinkipo Press.

Mondlane, E. (1969) *The Struggle for Mozambique.* Harmondsworth: Penguin.

Pilger, J. (2001) *Heroes.* Cambridge: South End Press.

Sankara, T. (1987) Speech on International Women's Day, 8 March. Reproduced in Sankara (1988), 335–372.

Sankara, T. (1988) *Thomas Sankara Speaks.* New York: Pathfinder Press.

Young, R. J. C. (2001) *Postcolonialism: An Historical Introduction.* Malden, MA: Blackwell.

CHAPTER 12

Re-reading Sankara's Philosophy
For a Praxeology of Debt in
Contemporary Times

Sakue-C. Yimovie

*The debt cannot be repaid; first, because if we don't pay, the
lenders will not die. That is for sure. But if we repay, we are going to
die. That is also for sure. Those who led us to indebting ourselves
had gambled as if in a casino. As long as they had gains, there was
no debate. But now that they suffer losses, they demand repayment.
And we talk about crisis. No, [there's no crisis]… they played,
they lost – that's the rule of the game, life goes on. We cannot
repay the debt because it is not our responsibility.*
Thomas Sankara, Organization of African Unity conference, 29 July 1987[1]

INTRODUCTION

In this chapter, I move in reverse order, to look at what is at stake with 'debt'
and in 'debt crises' before examining the larger meanings of debt. This might
appear to defy logic, but within this non-logical visage lies the logic: the debate
and argument about debt is at once a debate about what is conveyed in the
notion of debt (and all its philosophical groundings) by its exponents, and
what is or what we *experience* through lived realities by such concept, at the
destination or receiving end. Now, what this means is that defining debt flows
from who is doing the defining and what one assumes of or expects from the
concept. Defining debt appears to be a theoretically objective exercise, unless
we interrogate—as Thomas Sankara did—what is at stake first, thus placing
definitions of debt into fuller perspective and bring to fore their underlying
assumptions. Debt has 'already caused several dire economic slumps' and

continues to do so; as such, its meaning is 'not neutral because it hits people directly' in their everyday lives (Davidko 2011: 78). In other words, we need to be grounded in what is at stake before wading into the definitions advanced by those with varying interests – since defining a concept is not a theoretically objective endeavour.

As Thomas Sankara pointed out, the issue of 'whether to pay or not to pay' debt must be answered through the origin of loan's necessity: those who lend us money are the same people who colonised, extracted, exploited and mismanaged our resources. The former coloniser then returns to 'give' donations and loans as though they are doing these societies favour. Thus what is at stake is the unstable economies of the 'poorer' nations left in the wake of these wars of conquest and plunder. What is at stake is the survival of the people of these countries because debt – a continuation of the disarticulation of slavery, imperialism cum colonialism – further extracts the sweat of the poor and sucks the blood of the innocents to pay for what they never owed, bargained for, or benefitted from. Debt therefore is a repackaged form of imperial control. It is a formula 'gone bad', so that the question of repayment needs not even arise. I examine debt as imperialism and the semantics of debt. The chapter centres on excavating Sankara's political philosophy of debt. Doing so offers an understanding of the role of debt in Sankara's anti-imperialist consciousness, with a particular attention to how this consciousness allows us to reframe contemporary debt 'crisis'.

WHAT IS AT STAKE IN THE DEBT (CRISIS) DEBATE?

The debt crisis (as we know it today) is the fallout of several different yet inextricably linked global events. These include, among others: the resource boom resulting from hike in international oil price; over-borrowing by developing countries and reckless lending by IFIs and bilateral and multilateral institutions with a view of soliciting allegiance in the face of mounting tension of the Cold War era; the collapse of world commodity prices (especially petroleum) and the relaxation of tensions between the East and West; the sharp increase in international interest lending rates and sudden attachment of stringent conditions hitherto unknown when support for Cold War was the order of the day; and the increasing financial notoriety of political leaders of developing societies who, by now, are exposed to the vagaries of gluttonous lifestyles and unaccountability (Iyoha 1999).

The prominent oil crisis of the 1970s sent an acute shock and budget deficit to developing countries and had a disparaging effect that resounded heavily in the international market. In fact, this was an oil crisis in 1973 – when the oil producing major and superpowers experienced domestic economic crisis they displaced this crisis onto the economies of the so-call 'developing countries' by calling in debt (so as to manage their own crisis – thus, displacing economic crisis onto the countries of the South). The implication is that oil-producing Gulf countries had excess of 'petro dollars' and had them stashed away in banks in the West. The banks on the other hand, had liquid cash that needed to be turned for a profit – at any rate. Loans were recklessly given to all and sundry and, more dangerously, debts were easily rolled over and new ones approved without much ado. However, more potent in this reckless and seemingly liberal 'granting' or 'giving' of loans was the political motive: to rally and align Third World countries behind the West against the East. Lending becomes a political tool to marshal support for the mounting pressure of the Cold War and secure control and determine the direction of the affairs of the newly bought territories. This was evident in the characteristic manner in which loans were given to dictators as well as kleptocratic and anti-people governments, many of which were propped up by departing colonial governments. This relaxed approach to lending was profitable to lenders in a particular economic context. Subsequently, the definitive turn of events was the appearance of stringent conditions for loans and insistence on repayment for previous ones (again, when it was profitable for lenders to demand loan repayment).

The trend of overly lax lending was upturned with the collapse of oil prices in 1982 (Iyoha 1999). International lending (interest) rates immediately skyrocketed and developing countries could no longer roll over their debts. Debt has to be serviced to avoid its accentuation. The options varied but all were pernicious: Cut spending for health and education or increase export on raw materials (that has hitherto been unfavourable or disadvantageous). The effect was the same: out-source the peasant masses. In the same vein, rescheduling and refinancing only lead to debt pile-up or stock. Debt began to accumulate to unbearable proportions. It out-paced the growth rate of debtor countries. Between 1980 and 1995, the external debt of sub-Saharan Africa rose from US\$84 billion to US\$223.3 billion respectively, at an all-time high average of 6.7 per cent per annum (Iyoha 1999: 10). Furthermore, amidst the rhetoric of 'helping' poor countries, the Jubilee Debt Campaign's estimates for 2008 show that over US\$20 million daily is reaped out of low income countries to rich countries in the name of debt servicing and repayment.

The goal of the loan becomes so devious that the United Nations Economic Commission for Africa (UNECA) concluded its report this way:

> It is increasingly clear that very little progress, if any, can be made in Africa without the resolution of the debt crisis... there is no way in which Africa can service its existing debt and still have resources left for development financing.
>
> (UNECA 1991: 10)

Sankara understood this half a decade earlier than the publication of the UNECA's report. For Sankara, debt was as an impossible burden to bear if Burkina Faso was to make any progress. According to Sankara, debt was clearly a limitation to the exercise of the sovereign right to self-determination. No one could capture the scenario better than the head of a country that also doubled as one of the 'major recipients of aid'. Sankara explained:

> The example of foreign aid, presented as a panacea and often heralded without rhyme or reason, bears eloquent witness to this fact. Very few countries have been inundated like mine with all kinds of aid. Theoretically, this aid is supposed to work in the interest of our development. In the case of what was formerly Upper Volta, one searches in vain for a sign of anything having to do with development. The men in power, either out of naiveté or class selfishness, could not or would not take control of this influx from abroad, understand its significance, or raise demands in the interests of our people.
>
> (Sankara 2014: 64)

The result of millions of US dollars was an infant mortality rate of 180 per 1,000 live births, 16 per cent enrolment rate for school-age youth, 1 doctor for 50,000 inhabitants and a per capita GDP of 53,356 Central African Francs (Sankara 2014: 65). Meanwhile, Burkina's aid *dependence* was on a steady rise, with the ratio of aid to GDP rising from 0.68 in 1960 to 8.72 by 1983 (Savadogo et al. 2004: 3). This, for Sankara, was unacceptable and needed to be dealt with from its roots: political aid and debt. The stakes were too high. With indebtedness, not only does the political state become non-viable, the livelihood of the people hangs on the balance and at the mercy of foreign forces.

The so-called 'debt crisis' is no unpreventable crisis at all. Rather, it is the inevitable consequence of colonial capitalism. What manifests as 'crisis' is resistance to attempts to extract profit from the people and from a relationship that is more or less imperialistic.

THE SEMANTICS OF DEBT

According to Davidko (2011: 81), the word debt entered into English language, through its metamorphosis from Latin and French, with two distinct meanings: 'moral duty and pecuniary obligation'. How do we come to this 'moral' consciousness that one ought to pay one's debt without enquiry of what exactly is meant by debt? The force of the debt maxim sits deep in our consciousness. Graeber aptly dubbed this the 'moral confusion' in his well-researched treatise on debt: thus (like democracy, which is also a darling concept), everyone talks about debt but only few understand precisely what it is.

Graeber's (2011) *Debt: The First 5,000 Years* traces the myth of bartering and the primordial debt theory through history. For him, debt is a myth. Reeled into consciousness over time, barter and state tax theories are but mythical attempts to rationalize the market, money, tax and, by extension, debt. Like John Commons (2005), Graeber shares Sankara's belief that 'debt', in its historic formulation, *cannot be repaid.* Not only because debt is odious (that is, its accumulation does not elicit the consent of the population) but because paying it will cause real physical harm in the debtor countries, even as default will not harm the lenders (cf. Millet, Munevar and Toussaint 2012: 8). Commons distinguished between 'releasable' and 'unreleasable' debts: the former can be discharged but the latter cannot be repaid. He observes, 'historically it is more accurate to say that the bulk of mankind lived in a state of unreleasable debts, and that liberty came by gradually [substituting] releasable debts' (Commons 2005: 390). Commons, however, associated unreleasable debts with taxes requiring regular payments from citizens, from which redemption is tantamount to cessation of one's membership from the community (Saiag 2014: 573; cf. Graeber 2011: 119; Mauss 1967).

Debt is not only ideologically laden but is also social and therefore cannot be considered in isolation of the larger purposes it serves (Foucault 1972; Davidko 2011). Debt is ideological because it is founded on a set of beliefs that gives meaning to and makes meaning of the world: you need money, you do not have it, you borrow from someone and you look for the money to pay back later. This scenario is determined to be 'how the world works', period. The fact that the dominant stance on debt remains largely unchanged, Davidko argues, 'gives us every reason to believe that the meaning ... is not only highly ideological as it is loaded in favour of political, economic, religious interests of institutions which generate these discourses but also conventional since institutions "make a caveat" to treat a given phenomenon in a particular way', and treat them differently from time to time as deem fit by the author of such consciousness (Davidko 2011: 80–81).

Words are couched in such a way that they are reflective of the norm, morality and acceptable forms (Davidko 2011). The norm of imperialism is to expand and its morality is to maximize profit everywhere. Words are social and the meanings they embody are valid only to the extent they make sense of the social context from which or to which they are directed. But the sense which a hearer, or target, gets of words are nothing more than what the speaker say it is or it is about: this is so because the hearer needs not be critical about the word or even have conceptual understanding beyond what it is said to be (by the speaker) and the knowledge perceived of the speaker by the hearer (see Husserl 2001: esp. 189). Thus debt is usually welcomed as something well intentioned. However, beyond that messianic mask of saviour in debt-as-help discourses, lies imperialistic exploitation.

According to Paul Grice (1957), the intentional meaning of utterances are equivalent to effect they create which ordinarily are recognisable by the audience but difficult to grasp because linguistic semantics offers speakers 'sophisticated means of manipulating the intentional states of others' (Grice in Davidko 2011: 80). Thus we must look, as Sankara asserted, beyond the rhetoric to the effects of indebtedness.

WHAT IS AT STAKE: AID, LOAN OR IMPERIALISM?

Debt should be considered holistically and contextually from its origins. Said origins are in the systems of slavery and colonialism that facilitated the exploitation and enrichment of one part of the world through extraction and disempowerment of the other part of the world. The former is the West, who are the lenders, and the latter is the so-called 'Third World' (now the 'global South'). In his famous speech Sankara at the conference of the Organization of African Unity (now African Union) in 1987, Sankara noted that:

> We think that debt has to be seen from the standpoint of its origin. Debts origins come from colonialism's origin. Those who lend us money are those who had colonised us before. Debt is neo-colonialism in which the colonisers have transformed themselves into a form of technical assistant ... Under its current form, that is imperialism-controlled, debt is a cleverly managed re-conquest of Africa, aiming at subjugating its growth and development through foreign rules. Thus, each of us becomes the financial slave, which is to say a true slave.

Not satisfied with its colonial spoils, a new colonial formula was put in place during the period of formal decolonization. This formula was subtler and less conspicuous: lending fulfils these criteria. The reasons for this are twofold. First, it does not appear as a direct assault on the collective progress of a society. Rather, it functions indirectly to undermine growth, investment and the capacity to think and act innovatively and outside of this system of dependency. Second, it is difficult to resist given the disarticulated nature of the indebted state and since lending is usually seen as devoid of specific nationality. Lending in the global South, however, stands in contrast to the concerted efforts of Western Europe to remedy the damage it occasioned on itself during the First and Second World Wars. To these ends, Sankara asserted:

> We hear about the Marshall Plan that rebuilt Europe's economy. But we never hear about the African plan which allowed Europe to face Hilterian hordes when their economies and stability were at stake. Who saved Europe? Africa. One rarely mentions it, to such a point that we cannot be accomplices of that thankless silence. If others cannot sing our praises, at least we must say that our fathers had

been very courageous and that our troops had saved Europe and set the World free from Nazism.

(Sankara, Organization of African Unity conference, 29 July 1987)

Note that even though Africa has been pillaged by Europe, the former still came to her rescue and has never demanded 'debt' payment. It is important that we put this discrepancy into perspective: while no 'Marshal Plan' has been espoused for Africa, to cater for the damages occasioned by Europe through slavery and colonisation, more than five Marshall Plans have been fritted away from poor developing countries to the 'rich' West – all in the name of debt servicing/settlement between 1985 to 2010. The Marshal Plan for the reconstruction of Europe after the Second World War was US$100 billion, while the net transfer of public debt from developing countries to the West stood at an alarming US$530 billion (Millet, Munevar and Toussaint 2012: 10).

It is in this sense that Ake (2012: 9) observes that, regardless of the flag of independence and the decolonisation processes of the 1950s and 1960s, 'the Third World remains a compelling need for the West. To begin with, the Third World remains very useful as an outlet for surplus capital as well as a source of profit. Income from the Third World is generally far in excess of the outflow of capital from the West to the Third World'. In 2010, developing countries received US$455 billion as inflow from the West in the form of Official Development Assistance (including loans and expenses on refugees) of US$130 billion and Emigrant Remittance of US$325 billion, these countries, however, lost US$827 billion as outflow to the West in the form of foreign public debt service (US$180 billion) and repatriation of profits by multinationals (US$647 billion) (Millet, Munevar and Toussaint 2012: 10).

Debt is imperialism in the Leninist sense, inter alia: 'the export of capital as distinguished from export of commodities acquires exceptional importance'. As Ake (2012: 8) aptly puts it, 'the export of capital and the subordination of foreign lands are demanded by the contradictions of capitalism which set severe limits on domestic accumulation', with a view of maintaining these lands in perpetual poverty and dependence on the largess of the imperial overlords. One important point to note here is that capital, much like humans, needs to grow in order to survive. Capital must expand and must not remain idle, and in that case, it must look for new lands to perch, to settle, to fester, and to prey upon, otherwise it dies. This is an implicit logic of imperialism. This logic is captured in Marx's analysis of the contradiction and dynamisms of capital, particularly the tendency for the rate of profit to fall (TRPF). What the TRPF means is that capital, always in competition with itself among capitalist actors, will lead to the lowering of prices of commodities amongst competitors (in the capitalist core) that will ultimately lead to declines in profit. The only way for capital to 'survive' is through export to foreign and 'frontier' lands in order to revitalise, replenish and reproduce itself. In the context of this chapter, capital has to be exported in the form of loans, forced on unsuspecting societies (not yet mired in capitalist contradictions) in the form of help and rescue packages.

Moreover, debt follows a teleological account: a rescuer and a rescued, a civiliser and a savage, a developed and an underdeveloped society. In each case, the latter progresses towards the former (as explicated by Ake in the *Social Science as Imperialism*). The former is the author and finisher of fate while the latter is the ill-fated recipient of help – thus is already doomed for damnation save for the grace of the 'civiliser'. These attitudes are implicit in imperialist logic: an end to all debates and ideas on human progress with the West as the ultimate arbiter and manifestation of that finality. This attitude is aptly represented in some quarters as the 'the end of ideology'. Ake (2012: 6) explains: 'ideological debates are no longer called for because the critical questions have all been settled and a basic consensus exists from which society can now proceed to deal, with dispatch, the essentially trivial problems that still arise'.

Hence, there is no need for industry and innovation anymore, no need for any formula or creative model to improve the lives of the masses so long as it is going to emanate from non-western source/society. One wonders: *why bother?* The West have already done that, after all… there was, 'once upon a time', an 'Industrial Revolution'. What is now important is that we wait on the West to give answers to all the world's problems; this means, of course, spoon-feeding the 'Third World' in the name of 'aid', 'loaning', 'humanitarianism' 'debt', and so on. *No need to worry, then!* The West is always there to come to the rescue and hand out its ready-made formulas. Hence models and typologies of developmental progression, especially debt, have to be imported. Thus, debt is imperialism.

Let me explain this assertion through four critical arguments. First, there is a 'giver' and a 'taker' (which is not an issue in itself) corresponding to the 'haves' and the 'have-nots'. The tendency is to represent the former as 'good' and the latter as 'bad' or 'poor' or as 'undesirable'. Lending, therefore, becomes a pathway of social transformation from 'undesirable' to 'desirable'. Second, the South is represented as a 'moment in time' in some supposedly *universal* movement towards development, wherein development corresponds to the West's current state and underdevelopment corresponds to the South's current realities. Thus to borrow becomes the means to drive the South towards *becoming like the North*. Third, the Third World's underdeveloped is abstracted from the international economic system, particularly the 'effects of slave trade, pillage, colonialism, and unequal exchange' and now, market capitalism. As a result, blame for the underdeveloped conditions of the Third World falls on the South. 'Underdevelopment' is a self-making, owing to an apparent ineptitude and the existence of certain sociocultural and economic attitudes that are 'averse' to development. Fourth, lending is accompanied by memoranda that implicitly seek to convert, transform and pattern the South (i.e. the undesirable) after the West (i.e. the desirable). Let me be clear: indebting the South has an implicit agenda of making it be like the North.

Adam Smith, the avowed 'father of capitalism', wrote in *The Wealth of Nations*: 'we get not our bread through the generosity of the baker but through the baker's mindful egoistic calculations' (quoted in Ake 2012: 10). Smith's text is a classic manual of imperialism. It speaks directly to the logos of a system that necessarily produces lending. In such a system, it is selfishness and not charity, it is profit and not our plight (suffering), that appeals to the lenders. This incentive is no mystery. Neither is it coveted; it is written everywhere as the hallmark of capitalism, euphemistically referred to as 'free market system' – that same 'free market system' that is the contemporary manifestation of imperialism. Debt has all the outward trappings of imperialism.

TOWARDS A PRAXIS OF DEBT

Whether or not we draw a clear line of distinction on who borrows or owes what, or why this or that debt must be repaid, we do not in any way address the fundamentals of debt itself. By this I mean the philosophical rationalisation that presupposes that an individual, a group of individuals, a nation or group of nations is imbued with the authority to watch over others to the extent that it has the capacity to impose 'help', *under any guise*. This 'help' comes with a corresponding 'moral right': the right to demand restitution under any quasi-spiritual-cum-moral-or-historical explication, thereby establishing the basis for the enslavement of the many by the few.

The government does not bear the debt burden; the people do. A glance at recent events in Hungary and Iceland, where the hard-line against creditors (the IMF and Netherland and UK respectively) was greeted with threat, demonstrates that *creditors do not die* in the event of default and *debtors can as well live*. The Icelandic people, in particular, voted in opposition to the prescriptions (which, of course, were the letters of the creditors) of 'apolitical' and terrified state actors. These letters were in clear disregard to explicit threat from the Netherlands and the UK. The point *is*, the people harnessed their residual powers to mitigate the harm already done them by a collaboration of governments (including theirs) and debt entrepreneurs. People demonstrated their willingness to take charge of their fate. This willingness to demonstrate needs to be internalized across the developing world, and especially Africa, in opposition to debt.

That the strong are duty-bound to help the weak does not mean that we lose sight of the more important question of *how the strong becomes strong in the first place*. History has taught that there is nothing charitable about imperialism, rather every move is an attempt to make profit, to; expand, exploit and reproduce more capital. Thus 'help', 'aid', 'loan' and so on, originate from the imperialist camp and do not escape this logic. On this note, Sankara asserts:

> The root of the disease was political. The treatment could only be political. Of course, we encourage aid that aids us in doing away with aid. But in general, welfare and aid policies have only ended up disorganising us, subjugating us, and robbing us of a sense of responsibility for our own economic, political, and cultural affairs. We choose to risk new paths to achieve greater well-being.
>
> (Sankara 2014: 65)

Sankara's position on debt does not oppose taxes or genuine assistance. It nonetheless suggests that any policy sanctioned by the state or championed by non-state actors that does not advance the common good of the people must be read as the handmaiden of imperialism and should be resisted by the people and banished. Debt, taxes, or whatever might have worked or been useful at some point or in theory, but does not advance the good of the masses in practice, then, the people must dare to invent concepts as well as develop practical approaches to build a future they desire while abandoning those notions/practices that have proved irrelevant, no matter how convenient they might have come to be. The people are the ultimate repository of political power. The people must plan and organise themselves and act tactically as opposed to isolated or spontaneous offensives. People must stand upright for themselves instead of waiting for government without a patriotic political orientation. The core of Sankara's philosophy, as it relates to debt, is that if popular democracy is to function in the interests of the people, then the people must summon the courage to stop blind followership of the concepts and ideas emanating from the heart of imperialist West, and be bold and innovative to dump these concepts in the trash can of history.

However, rising up to these realities will not be taken lightly by the oppressive system. To think otherwise is to kill Sankara for the second time; this time, in spirit. The first was allowing him stand alone, leading to his death in flesh. What this is about is to ideologically arm and prepare the people against the illusion that the struggle against imperialism will be a joy ride. Thus Sankara cautions:

> When we are told about economic crisis, nobody says that this crisis didn't come about suddenly. The crisis gets worse each time that the popular masses get more and more conscious of their rights against the exploiters.
>
> (Sankara, Organization of African Unity Conference, 29 July 1987)

Meaning, as consciousness grows the efforts of the benefactors of an exploitative system also intensifies. Hunger, austerity, retrenchment, loss of job, and more are exacerbated. New formulas are unveiled, new theories and rationalisations are articulated, new models are designed and new methods are hatched to hunt and taunt the conscious generation. The task is to remain vigilant in unity and mindful of the actions and efforts of those who will come to the rescue of the masses with sweet talks of assistance. Conscious people the world over must understand the fight is not for African masses alone because African and European masses are not in any way antagonistic. Rather they are in this together and are being exploited by the same forces. Just as Sankara submits, unity 'is the only way to assert that refusing to repay debt is not an aggressive move on our part, but a fraternal move to speak the truth' to power. Unity here is essential; otherwise, alone and disunited, the masses will be singled out and silenced – just as Sankara cautioned of his own demise.

The goal was to ensure a workable and egalitarian state built on and supported by the people themselves. Indeed, Sankara made explicit, through his philosophies and practices, that our faith in the political state is not misplaced. However, the state, as the pivot of the faith of the people, was misappropriated by its lack of political orientation on the part of its operators (politicians, bureaucrats and the military) thereby it functioned in reverse form. The political state, as the vehicle through which the collective will of society is represented and made manifest, was a response to and prevention (precaution) from the uncertainties that surround human idiosyncrasy, especially where power is associated with individuals.

Sankara asserted a consciousness centred on the notion that freedom must be conquered in struggle. This invitation to critical engagement at all levels and in all fronts is opposed to passive mental colonisation. The task is to evolve new ways of doing things: new concepts, new interpretations and alternative models. At the theoretical level this involved interrogating and rejecting theories and concepts that undermine the capacity of the people to aspire to their full emancipation, and reinventing/formulating radically new concepts that set fire to the imagination of the people for productive engagement. At the scientific/technological level, this required critical engagement with available human/natural resources as well as the transformation of the environment in the light of the needs of society.

FROM 'ASSISTANCE' TO COMPULSION

This discussion so far has shown that debt continues to be clothed as 'assistance' to the world's poorer countries. All the while, debt is not assistance or a rescue mechanism. The rhetoric of debt has grown more sophisticated with the passage of time. The propaganda of debt is facilitated through a vast complex of seemingly independent nodes that are, indeed, ultimately and inextricably linked by a shared desire (or common pursuit) to propagate imperialism, in one of its subtlest forms. From international financial institutions (IFIs) to socioeconomic think tanks, from academics to experts to governments, the tales are all too familiar: debt is a viable option out of economic crisis. Indeed, it is presented as morally imperative on the part of the giver to give and for the receiver to aspire for and remain faithful to loan conditionalities regardless of the consequences.

I want to highlight the ways in which propaganda is espoused to imprison the masses to the pervasive effects of debt burden. I draw from Stergios Skaperdas's (2015) work on the seven myths associated with the Greek Debt Crisis as there are important echoes between this scholarship and Sankara's consciousness. Sankara said, 'there can be no salvation for our people unless we decisively turn our backs on all the models that all the charlatans, cut from the same cloth, have tried to sell us for the past ... There can be no salvation without saying no to that. No development without breaking with that' (Sankara 2014: 61). Such severance will not be without price, even the ultimate price. New paths and designs will be met with resistance, rejection, superfluous acquiescence and outright intellectual snobbery. The capacity to self-express is not the exclusive preserve of any one group of people. This inalienable right to self-determination includes the willingness of the people to chart their destinies. In this way, the dangers of being singled-out, silenced and cut off are reduced. Resistance to imperialist models takes on a formidable form, audacious move and resonates as a collective statement of truth. This unwavering confidence in the ability of the people to revolutionise their existence is at the core of the consciousness Sankara personified.

Who Needs Debt?

What preceded the maxim that debt ought to be paid is the 'wisdom' that debt is essentially an escape route, or a safety valve, for the needy. In other words, the essence of debt is to 'help' the needy get on their feet. Yet, when the growth figures no longer speak for themselves; when the promises of improved living condition fall flat; when the people begin to 'protest' against the hardship occasioned on them by government's decision; and when the government begins to show signs or 'resistance' to the terms of debt and the need to 'negotiate' becomes rife, the concern becomes how to reschedule, restructure and rearrange payment patterns to avoid default (Alogoskoufis 2012; Skaperdas 2015).

The imperative to protect debt from the people it professes to 'help', even in the face of hardship from its constricting effects, indicates this notion of 'helping the weak' is part of the ideology of debt. Moreover, the proclivity to protect debt at all costs – a facet of debt that was clear in the recent case of Greece, where the welfare of Greeks was not considered – substantiates this assertion. During the modern Greek Debt Crisis, the troika (European Commission, the European Central Bank and the International Monetary Fund) was primarily concerned with guaranteeing the financial interest of the banks (Skaperdas 2015: 7). This 'morality of help' is all too familiar. In Madagascar over ten thousand people died because the money meant for malaria treatment was swapped for debt settlement (see Graeber 2011: 4; cf. Maurer 2013: 81). Debt remains *in service* regardless of the larger social, political and environmental circumstances.

Similarly, the right to determine one's life, as inalienable, is grossly undermined through debt. For Sankara, this is an anathema to democracy. Democracy, here, is taken to 'mean the freedom of expression of a conscious majority, well informed of the issues and of their internal and external implications, capable of verifying the fairness of electoral processes and in a position to influence their outcome' (Sankara, Twelve Hours with Thomas Sankara, 24 October 1983). When it comes to debt, the power to negotiate is usually thrown at the doorstep of government, handicapped as it is, the pendulum swings in favour of corporate lenders (Skaperdas 2015). Though governments claim to represent the people, governments come and go but it is the people who bear the burden of irresponsible state actions. Governments do not pay debt; people do. Thus, to deny the people the ability to actively partake in issue that touches so directly on their lives is to abrogate democracy. Sankara reasserted his belief in the resolve of the people and their economic and political right to determine their future within the ambits of the resources bestowed them by nature. Sankarism is a philosophy grounded by the imperative of self-sufficiency and sustainable development that emanates from within and not from without.

NOTE

1 Unless noted otherwise, quotations from Sankara in this chapter are available in Sankara (1988).

REFERENCES

Ake, C. (2012) Social Science as Imperialism. In H. Lauer and K. Anyidoho (eds), *Reclaiming the Human Sciences and Humanities through African Perspectives*, vol. 1. Ghana: Sub-Saharan Publishers.

Alogoskoufis, G. (2012) Greece's Sovereign Debt Crisis: Retrospect and Prospect. *Hellinic Observatory Papers on Greece and Southeast Europe* 54: 1–49.

Commons, J. R. (2005) *Institutional Economics: Its Place in Political Economy*, vol. 2. London: Transaction Publishers.

Davidko, N. (2011) The Concept of Debt in Collective Consciousness: a Socio-historical Analysis of Institutional Discourse. *Studies About Language* 19: 78–88.

Foucault, M. (1972) *The Archaeology of Knowledge and the Discourse on Language*. New York: Pantheon Books.

Graeber, D. (2011) *Debt: The First 5,000 Years*. New York: Melville House.

Grice, P. (1957) Meaning. *Philosophical Review* 66: 377–388.

Husserl, E. (2001) *Logical Investigations*. London: Routledge.

Iyoha, A. M. (1999) *External Debt and Economic Growth in Sub-Saharan African Countries: An Econometric Study*. Research Paper 90. Nairobi: African Economic Research Consortium.

Maurer, B. (2013) David Graeber's Wunderkammer, Debt: The First 5,000 Years. *Anthropological Forum* 23(1): 79–93.

Mauss, M. (1967) *The Gift: The Form and Reason for Exchange in Archaic Societies*. New York: W. W. Norton & Co.

Millet, D., Munevar, D. and Toussaint, E. (2012) *2012 World Debt Figures*. Liege: Committee for the Abolition of Third World Debt.

Saiag, H. (2014) Towards a Neo-Polanyian Approach to Money: Integrating the Concept of Debt. *Economy and Society* 43(4): 559–581.

Sankara, T. (1983) 'Twelve Hours with Thomas Sankara', Interview of Thomas Sankara by Mohammed Maiga in *Afrique-Asia* (Monthly Exclusive), October 24, 1983.

Sankara, T. (1988) *Thomas Sankara Speaks: The Burkina Faso Revolution, 1983–87*. New York: Pathfinders.

Sankara, T. (2014) *We Are Heirs of the World's Revolutions: Speeches from the Burkina Faso Revolution, 1983–87*. New York: Pathfinders.

Savadogo, K, Coulibaly, S. and McCracken, A. C. (2004) *Analysing Growth in Burkina Faso Over the Last Four Decades*. Growth Working Paper 4. Nairobi, Kenya: African Economic Research Consortium.

Skaperdas, S. (2015) *Seven Myths about the Greek Debt Crisis*. Working Paper, June. Irvine, CA: University of California, Irvine.

UNECA (1991) Financing Growth and Development in Africa: Outlook and Issues – A View from ECA. Paper presented at IMF/AACB Symposium on Structural Adjustment, External Debt and Growth in Africa, Gaborone, Botswana.

CHAPTER 13

Sankara's Political Ideas and Pan-African Solidarity

A Perspective for Africa's Development?

Felix Kumah-Abiwu and Olusoji Alani Odeyemi

INTRODUCTION

The publication of this volume marks the 30th anniversary of the death of Thomas Sankara. Part of this book project has been to explore the ways in which the legacies of Sankara continue to extend beyond the shores of Burkina Faso to other countries in Africa, Europe and the Americas as intellectuals and activists gather from time to time to discuss his ideas in our contemporary era (see also Harsch 2013). Sankara was assassinated in October 1987, but the accomplishments of his revolution in the social, economic and political spheres continue to generate interest. His political ideas on social progress were not only visionary in nature but transformative as well. Carina Ray captures this assertion very well when she argues that Sankara understood the central objective of the revolution and its role in transforming the Burkinabe society. For Ray (2007), the task of Sankara's visionary goal was to liquidate all forms of imperialism and neo-colonial exploitation across the African continent. Like other African revolutionaries of the past, Sankara's clarion call to dismantle imperialist influences is what Kumah-Abiwu (2016b) describes elsewhere as the struggles (e.g. economic exploitation and foreign debt challenges) for Africa's economic self-determination.

The legacies of European colonialism and the post-colonial challenges, including the political upheaval(s) and socio-economic problems that many African countries faced during the 1980s, were illustrative of precisely these struggles for self-determination, often expressed in the form of military takeovers and revolutionary movements. Captain Thomas Sankara's emergence on the political scene in Upper Volta (which he would later rename Burkina

Faso) did not only reflect the political trends of the era, but Sankara's particular political ideas and revolutionary ethos. This was an ethos based on anti-neocolonialism, economic self-sufficiency and Pan-African solidarity, which distinguished him from other leaders of his era. No wonder then, Sankara has often been described as the 'Che Guevara' of Africa (Harsch 2013; see Chapter 5, this volume).

For many observers, Sankara's display of charisma was similar to other African leaders such as Kwame Nkrumah, Sekou Toure, Modibo Keita and Patrice Lumumba (Skinner 1988). These leaders stood against colonialism and neo-colonialism, and promoted strong African identities and Pan-African solidarity. Although Sankara's regime was short-lived (Harsch 2013; Ray 2007), his core ideas on critical issues of economic self-reliance, African dignity and Pan-African solidarity continued to be admired beyond the African continent. While recognising the importance of Sankara's ideas, we also need to be cognisant of the fact that his political ideas were partly shaped by the Cold War geo-politics of the 1980s, including the East–West rivalry. It is for this reason that some have contested whether Sankara's political ideas are still relevant in the current and seemingly 'uniformed globalised' system, in which Western-backed neoliberalism dominates the development discourses. In spite of this apparent uncertainty, we argue that Sankara's ideas are relevant for contemporary considerations of the discourses on Africa's development. How, then, might Sankara's political ideas be adapted in practice as a distinctive model for Africa's development? This chapter explores what a contemporary application of Sankara's policies, strategies and ambitions might look like in our era of 'uniformed globalisation'.

The first part of the chapter examines the evolution of Sankara's political ideas within the context of external and internal influences, especially the influence of European colonialism and neocolonialism in Africa. The next part extends the analysis by highlighting the political ideas of Sankara and how his ideas evolved over time. Political ideas such as economic self-reliance, African dignity and the collaborative efforts against systemic oppression of African people are examined. The final part underscores the usefulness of Sankara's political and philosophical ideas for the existing challenges of Africa's development. The chapter concludes by advancing the argument that the political and philosophical ethos of Sankara is not only relevant to our contemporary era, but the tenets of his ideas are necessary for Africa's economic self-sufficiency and overall development.

THE EVOLUTION OF SANKARA'S IDEAS: EXTERNAL INFLUENCES

Like other African revolutionaries, Sankara's revolution sought to transform his country from decades of socio-economic difficulties. Many of Upper

Volta/Burkina Faso's problems of the period were the manifestations of complex legacies of colonialism alongside the mismanagement by Burkina's own political elites for several decades (Harsch 2013; Wilkins 1989). Given the complex nature of European colonial history in Africa and the devastating legacies of this historical relationship, the nature of this colonial relationship and its influence on political leaders such as Sankara is imminently valuable.

Africa's contact with Europe not only altered the continent's social progress, but the long-lasting consequences are perceived prominently on two interrelated economic fronts: (a) trade exploitation and (b) resource extraction (human and natural). The first includes the forceful integration of the continent into unequal global trading system that was designed to serve European interests at the expense of Africans (Webster and Boahen 1967). As Webster and Boahen (ibid.) have argued, Africans traded valuable goods such as gold and other precious minerals with less valuable European goods during the pre-colonial era. The second centres on the conquest and control of Africa through the system of colonialism and exploitation of its human and natural resources. Brett's (1973) observation on the impacts of colonialism on Africa might help explain the influence of these historical events on the evolution of Sankara's political ideas. According to Brett (ibid.), as Rodney (1974) has also argued, European colonialism did not only hasten the exploitation of Africa's resources, but Europe used these resources to develop while Africa was left underdeveloped. In fact, Brett's (1973) *hastened exploitation* idea typified the colonial influence of France in Upper Volta/Burkina Faso, for example, and there seem to be significant overlaps between the articulation of 'hastened exploitation' and Sankara's knowledge about the roles of European neocolonial powers in Africa.

It is therefore not surprising that colonialism became the rallying point for anti-colonial and nationalist leaders such as Nkrumah, Kenyatta and Nyerere as the political ideas of these leaders evolved around strategies they could adopt to dismantle the system of colonialism in Africa. The demise of colonialism in the 1950s throughout the 1960s was a welcome new era, but decolonisation did not entail a total independence for African countries (Brett 1973). While Africa's newly independent states maintained a façade of political control, their former colonial powers continue to exert influence over their socio-economic lives. Some examples include, unfair trade agreements, high interest rates on foreign loans, low reinvestment of profits from foreign capital and other neoliberal policies, which are mostly unfavourable to African countries. Former president Kwame Nkrumah describes this scenario as neocolonialism.

Like our former nationalist leaders whose political ideas were influenced by colonialism in terms of their strategies to end its existence, we argue that neocolonialism also created the incentive for the emergence of revolutionary leaders who were determined to confront the forces that continue to exploit

Africa's natural and human resources. This is where Sankara, the fearless revolutionary leader of the 1980s, fit into a larger picture of post-colonial revolutionary leaders whose ideas were largely shaped by these injustices. In effect, we argue that the manifestations of injustices such as abject poverty, underdevelopment and the extreme human suffering created the motivation for the emergence of revolutionary ideas that could denounce and eliminate neocolonialism.

THE EVOLUTION OF SANKARA'S IDEAS: INTERNAL INFLUENCES

In addition to these external influences, Sankara's ideas were simultaneously shaped by the internal manifestations of neocolonialism, exploitation and underdevelopment of Upper Volta/Burkina Faso, especially the post-colonial influence of France. In this chapter, we show how important historical issues across Africa (external) and within Upper Volta/Burkina Faso (internal) simultaneously shaped Sankara's knowledge and philosophies before and during the revolution (see Figure 13.1 later in this chapter). In order to better understand the internal influences on the formation of Sankara's political ideas, it would be useful to examine his formative years as well as the socio-economic conditions in the country prior to the revolution. The next section explores the dynamics of these issues.

Sankara's Formative Years

Sankara was born in the northern town of Yako on 21 December 1949 into a Silmi-Mossi family. His father served as a gendarme in various parts of Upper Volta, where the young Thomas was exposed to other cultures and severe conditions of poverty and underdevelopment of his country (Ray 2007). His parents wanted him to become a Roman Catholic priest but he instead chose a military career (ibid.). Sankara spent part of his military officer training in the early 1970s in Madagascar, where he witnessed the popular uprising of workers and students who succeeded in toppling the government of that country. He was later sent to France for further military training where he became exposed to Left-wing political ideologies (ibid.). On his return to Upper Volta/Burkina Faso, Sankara became aware of the social injustices and the conditions of extreme poverty across his country. Not only did he blame French colonial influence for his country's underdevelopment, but he was also convinced that his country's socio-economic problems were the direct consequences of two main factors: (a) the continuous influence of France, the former colonial power over the very fabric of the society and (b) the forced labour system, which drained the country's workforce to Côte d'Ivoire and other prosperous former French colonies (Wilkins 1989: 376). As Ray (2007) observes, the country's socio-economic difficulties before the revolution were characterised by high infant mortality, poor education and abject poverty. Basic infrastructure to provide social services was woefully inadequate with an average yearly income of about US$150 per person (Ray 2007).

At the same time, Sankara's Left-wing ideological orientation had advanced to the point where he identified himself as a Marxist (Harsch 2013; Wilkins 1989) following the failure of his country to develop on the ideals of neoliberal economic policies and the strong neocolonial connection to France. The political elites of the country were also blamed for the socio-economic problems. For example, the government of the first president, Maurice Yameogo, was not only full of French advisers, but the government was considered by the people to be incompetent in terms of its mismanagement of the country (Brittain 1985). The successive military regime of Sangoule Lamizasa (1966–1980) was also characterised by mismanagement (ibid.). The educational system under Lamizasa's regime, for instance, was neglected to the point where approximately 95 per cent of the population did not know how to read during the era. The health sector was faced with many problems (see Chapter 16, this volume) with no investment in the transportation sector as well (ibid.). It became clear, given these continuous socio-economic and governance difficulties, that the post-independent state of Upper Volta/Burkina Faso was facing serious problems. Lamizasa's regime was toppled by Colonel Saye Zerbo, but Zerbo's government failed to resolve the socio-economic problems of the country (Brittain 1985; Wilkins 1989). In short, Upper Volta/Burkina Faso faced major socio-economic and political crises in the late 1970s to the early 1980s (Ray 2007). While Sankara's was not oblivious to the internal factors responsible for his country's underdevelopment, he also knew that external factors such as neocolonial forces of exploitation were equally responsible for the socio-economic woes of Burkina Faso and the rest of the African continent (Ray 2007; Harsch 2013), which have become known as the Afro-pessimism narrative of Africa (more on Afro-pessimism is discussed later in the chapter).

Sankara served in Zerbo's government as a Minister of Information but he eventually resigned from his position on the basis of ideological differences with the government (Wilkins 1989: 381). He would later serve as Prime Minister under Jean-Baptiste Ouédraogo's government and this propelled his popularity with grassroot groups such as students across the country (Williams 2014). While serving as Prime Minister, Sankara took advantage of his position to intensify his anti-imperialist stance and to publicly denounce neocolonialism. The Ouédraogo regime, as Wilkins (1989) has observed, deemed that Sankara was becoming a threat not only to the regime's internal survival, but also externally due to his rising disapproval by France (again because of his growing popularity and Marxist-leaning postures). In response to these apprehensions, he was arrested in May 1983 with several other army officers and charged with treason, but Sankara's popularity with his fellow soldiers and among the general public helped free him from detention (Brittain 1985). Not long after, the murky military situation developed into the 5 August 1983 revolution of which Sankara would become the leader (Wilkins 1989; Brittain 1985).

As revealed in the preceding discussion, the complex interactions of external and internal issues of concern on the continent, especially in Upper Volta/Burkina Faso not only shaped Sankara's political ideas, but these issues were more likely to have created the incentive for the revolution. More importantly, these complexities, as this chapter argues, guided Sankara's development-focused blueprint for the transformation of his country. Notwithstanding, Sankara's political ideas, as some observers have suggested, are also characterised by contradictions (particularly regarding his blending of Marxist–Leninist Pan-Africanism) and other nuanced particularities, including his courageousness and charisma as well as his sustained critiques of Afro-pessimism.

CONTRADICTIONS OF SANKARA'S IDEAS: SANKARA'S MARXISM

One of the central debates regarding Sankara focuses on his ideological orientation of Marxist political thought. Harsch (2013) argues that Sankara identified himself as a Marxist and the influence of Marxist ideas was apparent not only through his speeches but his actions as well. Sankara was careful not to impose a Marxist label on the actual revolutionary process (ibid.: 362). Although Harsch (ibid.) notes that Sankara 'took care not to impose' his Marxist ideas on the revolutionary process, a critical analysis of the statement, including an attention to the reasoning behind the argument, could be problematic and misleading. The literature on Sankara has shown that he was a modest man by all standards and strongly believed that political power should belong to the people. In fact, what distinguishes Sankara from other revolutionary leaders of his era, as Amber Murrey articulates, was his trust in the capabilities of the ordinary people to the extent that he did not consider himself to be a special messiah (Murrey 2012), although he could have taken advantage of his charisma and popularity and done so. Sankara made these ideas known when he addressed the United Nations (UN) General Assembly in 1984. He asserted:

> I make no claim to lay out any doctrines here. I am neither a messiah nor a prophet.
> I possess no truths. My only aspiration is … to speak on behalf of my people … to
> speak on behalf of the 'great disinherited people of the world', those who belong to

the world so ironically christened the Third World. And to state, though I may not
succeed in making them understood, the reasons for our revolt.

(Sankara quoted in Murrey 2012: 2)

On one level, we could agree with Harsch's (2013) reading of Sankara's
carefulness not to impose his Marxist ideas on the people. On another level,
it might be problematic, as earlier stated, to make such an argument since the
'organising principles' around most of the populist revolutions of the era (1970s
and 1980s) were largely influenced by Marxist populist ideas with the strong
mantra of anti-capitalist tendencies. What is clear with less contradiction is
the fact that Sankara's political ideas were shaped by Marxist ideology. What
is unclear is the extent to which his Marxist political thoughts influenced his
strategies for political mobilisation and/or governance. In other words, the
debate is whether Sankara's populist outlook, especially his conceptualisation
of political power, socio-economic injustices and neo-colonialism put him
in a Marxist ideological framework or not. According to Williams (2014: 13),
Sankara, like Rawlings was 'burdened with the monumental task of defining
his regimes' ideological orientation to appease the domestic forces that brought
him to power, while carefully navigating the global politics of the Cold War'.
On Martin's (1987) part, as Williams (2014) also shares, Sankara seems to reject
the notion that the 1983 revolution was 'inspired by or patterned after any past
or present foreign ideology, experience or model', despite his very well-known
attraction to Marxist ideas. For Skinner (1988), Sankara and his compatriots
wanted to allay any fears of potential counter-revolutionary forces that might
have threatened the survival of the regime. This might also explain why Sankara
and his regime declared that they did not subscribe to the revolutionary Marxist
thought espoused by other political leaders such as Fidel Castro, Jerry Rawlings
and Muammar Qaddafi. Rather, they insisted that their revolution was based
on local realities (Skinner 1988: 441).

In spite of Sankara's attempt to define or frame the revolution through a
localised lens, he still maintained ties with the Marxist-influenced governments
of Qaddafi in Libya, Rawlings in Ghana and Kerekou in Benin (Skinner
1988). Sankara, like other radical leaders of the 1980s, faced the problem of
ideologically defining his regime (Williams 2014) and perhaps tried to shield
his regime's public image from Marxist leaning principles. However, we are
of the view, as other scholars have articulated, that Sankara's ideas were not
only nourished by the global geo-politics of the era (East–West rivalry), but the
bipolar ideological nature of the period shaped his political ideas from Marxist
leaning principles. Sankara's Marxist ideas were therefore rooted in the rhetoric
of anti-imperialism and the exploitative nature of capitalism. This rhetoric
might have helped considerably in terms of his success in rallying his people to
resist oppression and unite as one Burkina Faso – we turn our attention now

to another aspect of Sankara's presidency that earned him wide appeal: his charisma.

SANKARA'S COURAGEOUSNESS AND MAGNETISM

Now that we have characterised some of the (internal and external) dynamics that gave rise to Sankara's particular brand of Pan-African anti-neocolonial Marxism in 1980s Burkina Faso, we situate his legacy alongside those of other revolutionary African leaders so as to draw out some of the similarities and differences between these political legacies. As previously argued, the radical ideas of revolutionaries of the 1980s (such as Sankara and Rawlings) can be compared to the transformative ideas of past nationalist leaders (such as Nkrumah and Nyerere). The determined efforts of these leaders with popular support helped put an end to colonial domination of Africa. While the anti-colonial movements differ in focus and democratic orientation compared to the populist military regimes of the 1980s (Hutchful 1986), these eras shared three main commonalities. First, leaders of both eras had a well-defined objective. For example, while the goal of the anti-colonial nationalists was to end European colonialism, the revolutionaries of the 1980s focused their energies on tackling issues of neocolonialism, mismanagement and corruption by Africa's political elites and their external counterparts. Second, both eras witnessed popular support from ordinary citizens and some members of the political classes. Third, political leaders of both eras were the calibre of leaders that Saaka (1994) describes as strong and decisive in personality with personal magnetism. Leaders such as Nkrumah, Rawlings and Sankara appear to fit Sankara's (1994) conceptualisation of personal magnetism or charisma.

Skinner's conceptual insight into the magnetism idea might be useful to reiterate. To Skinner (1988), Sankara's charismatic power shows precisely the ways in which his political persona encapsulated a sort of charismatic personhood through the mixture of physical appearance and the craft of leadership. In the words of Skinner:

> Charisma has come to mean, especially in politics, of leadership that captures popular imagination and inspires unwavering allegiance, confidence, and devotion. Whether deliberatively or not, Sankara did present the picture of a young 'charismatic' leader of a small country, challenging a large complex, corrupt, and often brutal world. He was handsome, dashing, personable, and very much on stage.

> (Skinner 1988: 437–438)

We concur with Skinner's interpretation of how Sankara's charisma captured the essence of confidence, devotion and the courage to challenge a complex, corrupt and often brutal world system. These are useful lessons for our contemporary African leaders.

A REVOLUTION TO COUNTER AFRO-PESSIMISM

Of particular interest here is the discourse on the relevance of Sankara's ideas to Africa's development. The question of how Sankara's ideas might be adopted in practice as a distinctive model for Africa's development is another aspect of the ongoing debate that needs further scholarly scrutiny. Before we discuss the significance of Sankara's ideas, it would be useful to briefly examine the achievements of Sankara's regime. We draw on Harsch's (2013) ideas to examine Sankara's achievements from two standpoints. First, we categorised the likely causes of the revolution into internal and external factors as earlier discussed. Second, we also categorised the achievements into five typologies. Figure 13.1 provides a schematic illustration of our re-categorisation.

As can be seen in Figure 13.1, the complex interactions of internal and external factors were more likely to have created the incentives for the revolution to occur. One of Sankara's goals was to counter a mainstream Afro-pessimism narrative about his country and the rest of Africa. By definition, Afro-pessimism is the negative portrayal of Africa as a region confronted with problems that could not sustain good governance practices and high economic growth (Gordon and Wolpe 1998). Afro-pessimism was popular in Western countries, including France, a country that has exploited Africa's resources for several decades.

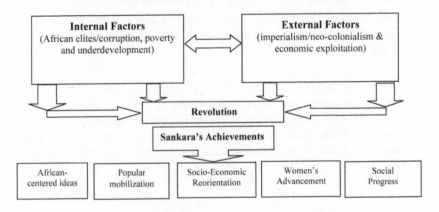

13.1 Schematic illustration of ideas put forth by Ernest Harsch (2013).

While countering such negative portrayals of the continent, Sankara also promoted African-centred philosophies with a strong flair for African identity and solidarity. For example, Sankara spoke against the ills of imperialism, neocolonialism and the exploitation of the continent by major European powers. He disregarded all of the niceties of Eurocentric diplomacy and criticised the foreign policy position of France in the presence of the French President (Francois Mitterrand) during his visit to Burkina Faso (Harsch 2013). Another important aspect of Sankara's anti-imperialist campaign was when he urged his fellow African leaders not to pay the continent's growing foreign debt owed to the so-called donor countries that exploit the resources of the continent (Harsch 2013; see Chapter 12, this volume). Sankara's decision to change his country's name from Upper Volta to Burkina Faso was another display of his commitment to his strong ideas on African identity. As Miles (2006) notes, Sankara saw the name Upper Volta as too colonial, but Burkina Faso, which means 'land of upright people' as African-centred.

The successes of the revolution in the socio-economic spheres were equally impressive. In the health sector, for instance, the country became the first African country to run huge measles vaccination campaigns in the 1980s with increase in access to healthcare in local communities (Harsch 2013). School attendance also increased from 12 per cent to about 22 per cent in two years. Other initiatives such as affordable housing, job-creation programmes, water and sanitation campaigns, reforestation programmes and access to transportation increased across the country (Ray 2007). Sankara's emphasis on the emancipation and dignity of women represents one of the high points of his achievements. As Harsch (2013: 366) observes, 'Sankara emphasised the emancipation of women as one of his central social and political goals – a rarity for any president in Africa at the time', especially in a patriarchal society like Burkina Faso and other African societies.

USEFULNESS OF SANKARA'S IDEAS AND AFRICA'S DEVELOPMENT

As the preceding discussion has shown, Sankara achieved a considerable number of successes, especially within the socio-economic sphere for Burkina Faso although his regime was short-lived. Besides the socio-economic successes, we argue that Sankara's elevation of the political philosophy of African-centredness, identity and self-sufficiency are lasting legacies of his ideas – ideas that remain relevant for Africa's development. But the question of how these ideas might be adopted is less clear. As we have previously noted, our fundamental question is to explore how African countries might draw on Sankara's ideas for development. Proposing concrete answers to these questions is complex, but we believe that it is important to start somewhere. We also want to caution that the attempt to advance the argument of adopting the core ideas of Sankara as a distinctive model for Africa's development is certainly not to suggest that his ideas are a panacea for Africa's development. While mindful of this aspect of the debate, we are also of the strong view that Sankara's African-centred idea of development within the context of self-sufficiency constitutes a viable option. Sankara's strong leadership, personality traits and his joining of ideological conviction with innovative policy ideas offer three useful guides in applying his ideas to contemporary development.

A good starting place (first useful guide) is the courageous voice of Sankara against internal and external forces that limit the continent's development. Sankara spoke vigorously against public sector corruption and the extravagant standard of living adopted by government officials. He understood the impacts of public sector corruption on the development of Burkina Faso and the rest of Africa. He stated that corruption is often encouraged and nurtured by imperialism and neocolonialism (Prairie 2007; Harsch 2013). Yet, three decades after his death, public sector corruption is still one of the major problems facing many African countries, including Burkina Faso. A recent study on corruption by Transparency International and Afrobarometer in 28 sub-Saharan Africa countries reveals that public sector corruption continues to not only increase, but corruption is having devastating effects on Africa's growth and development. The study estimates that nearly 75 million people have paid a bribe in the past year to either escape punishment by the police or courts and/or to access basic services (Transparency International 2015).

Harsch (2013) observes that Sankara's anti-corruption campaigns and personal examples of modesty would continue to draw admiration across Africa. A recent demand in South Africa for President Jacob Zuma and other leaders of the African National Congress (ANC) to give up their mansions and lavish lifestyles and live by the same standards as ordinary people represent a good case in point. Interestingly, the demand was made by a South African black consciousness group (Economic Freedom Fighters) that draws inspiration from Sankara's political ideas (Harsch 2013: 363). We advance the argument that our contemporary Africa needs strong and courageous leaders as Sankara to sound the alarm on the devastating impacts of corruption. Ordinary people, civic society groups and the media have vital roles to play in demanding accountability from public officials as well as political leaders while speaking against corruption.

Second, the African-centred idea of development and economic self-sufficiency that Sankara promoted constitute another useful aspect of his ideas in discussions of development. African leaders and policymakers in our era need to rethink the idea of foreign aid. One of Sankara's active campaigns was against the continent's foreign indebtedness due to the over reliance of many countries on foreign aid for development (Harsch 2013). Although the position Sankara took when he urged his fellow African leaders not to pay the debt owed to the donor countries might seem impractical to adopt in our modern neoliberal era, we suggest the need to rethink the idea of foreign aid to Africa's development. Another aspect of rethinking the issue on foreign aid must be focused on ordinary Africans whose endless taste for the consumption of foreign goods (Mazrui 1986) continues to increase the debt burdens of countries. Rather than seek external solutions, Sankara popularised the use of domestically produced fabrics and locally manufactured products during his era in Burkina Faso. Not only did he wear locally produced clothing, but he also encouraged his people to patronise them (Prairie 2007). Civil servants were required to wear traditionally designed cloth instead of Western-style suits with the purpose of boosting indigenous culture as well as to create a domestic market for clothes made from local cotton (Harsch 2013). While the idea of a mandatory requirement for public servants to wear only traditional cloths to work might be too limiting in our contemporary era, policies can still be initiated to encourage citizens of African countries to patronise locally produced products.

Finally, Sankara's strong leadership traits just as Rawlings (Kumah-Abiwu 2016a) might be useful to our modern era. There is no doubt that Sankara's political ideas and conviction to defend the interest of marginalised people against oppression and exploitation partly contributed to his successes and other achievements. Sankara would like a world in which the voiceless and the oppressed are not only given a voice and recognition, but are given the chance to chart their own path of development without unnecessary external influence, control and exploitation. Unfortunately, the African continent in our modern era appears to lack visionary and courageous political leaders who are willing to publicly speak against the exploitation of the continent.

Sankara was brave to stand against the forces of oppression and the global exploitative system, which was precisely why he was assassinated. Any development policies that seek to follow his example must take these risks and dangers seriously. At the same time, Africa needs brave and selfless leaders who are willing to stand up against injustices on the continent as a sacrifice for our future generations. Harsch (2013) reminds us that Africa needs a far-reaching vision for radical transformation and Sankara had that vision for Africa. Sankara underscores this point by noting that, 'you cannot carry out fundamental change without a certain amount of madness' (quoted in Harsch 2013: 371). A madness that comes from some levels of nonconformity and the courage to turn one's back on the old formulas as well as the courage to invent future possibilities (Harsch 2013; Prairie 2007).

While Sankara's political ideas for radical transformation of his country and the rest of Africa were nourished by the geo-politics of the Cold War era, the ascendancy of Western hegemony forecloses the development alternatives for the radical Left. However, the rise of China, India and other Asia tigers open another opportunity for Africa to collaborate with countries in the global south for development. Given the massive economic challenges, mass poverty and perilous youth migration to Europe in recent era, it is imperative for our Africa nations to initiate and implement development plans that will draw on Sankara's political philosophy and ideas.

CONCLUSION

Africa is currently at a crossroad in terms of its future economic independence given the growing exploitation by the old Western neocolonial actors and emerging actors from the East, including China. Given these predicaments as well as the possibilities for self-sufficiency and development, scholar-activists, policy experts and ordinary citizens have revived the debate on the value of Sankara's ideas and praxis as a distinctive framework for Africa's development. In this chapter, we have advanced the argument that key aspects of Sankara's political ideas – his core ideas on African-centredness, African identity, solidarity and economic self-sufficiency – remain relevant in the quest for Africa's development. In terms of self-sufficiency, Nigeria, for instance, spends billions of dollars on the importation of rice (just as many other African countries). The Nigerian Minister of Agriculture and Rural Development, Audu Ogbeh, recently noted that Nigeria spends about $20 billion a year on the importation of food from other countries (Anwar 2016). Sankara demonstrated the possibility of food self-sufficiency with his dramatic intervention in agriculture, which yielded huge increase in wheat production for Burkina Faso during the revolutionary era. Nigeria and other African countries might achieve food self-sufficiency if Sankara's endogenous development policies are adopted.

While it is possible for African leaders to draw lessons from Sankara's ideas, this is certainly not to suggest that his ideas, as previously noted, are the entire solution for the continent's development challenges. Two reasons inform our reasoning on this assertion. First, the era of Sankara's revolution, as earlier argued, was characterised by the geopolitics of East–West rivalry with the option for a regime to pursue Marxist leaning ideas in order to receive economic assistance from Eastern communist countries. Anti-imperialist pronouncements paid off well for many of these revolutionaries. While this chapter intends not to undervalue the uniqueness of Sankara's revolution, we are also of the view that the trajectory of Sankara's ideas was nourished by the dualistic pattern of the geopolitics of the era. In other words, some African leaders of today might be able to achieve what Sankara did for Burkina Faso and the rest of Africa, but they are likely to encounter many challenges in the current 'uniformed globalised' system with the dominance of Western neoliberal development ideas and strategies.

Also, the praises sometimes lavished on the achievements of Sankara's revolution should not be seen or interpreted as an endorsement of military coups or forceful takeovers of democratically elected governments. Nonetheless, Sankara's African-centred ideas of respect, dignity and economic self-sufficiency which epitomised his revolution will continue to inspire the next generation of scholars and African leaders. To this end, the revolution led by Sankara moved many parts of the Burkinabè society towards social progress before his untimely death on 15 October 1987. We are certain that Sankara's Africa-centred ideals, Pan-African unity and solidarity will continue to ignite our public and scholarly discourses for another 30 years to come.

REFERENCES

Anwar, A. (2016) Nigeria Spends US$20b on Food Importation Yearly. *The Guardian.* Retrieved on 3 March 2017 from https://guardian.ng/news/nigeria-spends-20b-on-food- importation-yearly-says-ogbeh.

Brett, E. A. (1973) *Colonialism And Underdevelopment In East Africa: The Politics Of Economic Change 1919–1939.* New York: NOK Publishers.

Brittain, V. (1985) Introduction to Sankara and Burkina Faso. *Review of African Political Economy* 32: 39–47.

Gordon, D. and Wolpe, H. (1998) The Other Africa: An End Of Afro-Pessimism. *World Policy Journal* 15(1): 49–59.

Harsch, E. (2013) The Legacies of Thomas Sankara: A Revolutionary Experience in Retrospect. *Review of African Political Economy* 40(137): 358–374.

Hutchful, E. (1986) New Elements in Militarism: Ethiopia, Ghana and Burkina Faso. *International Journal* 41(4): 802–830.

Kumah-Abiwu, F. (2016a) Leadership Traits and Ghana's Foreign Policy: The Case of Jerry Rawlings' Foreign Economic Policy of the 1980s. *The Round Table: The Commonwealth Journal of International Affairs* 105(3): 297–310.

Kumah-Abiwu, F. (2016b) Beyond Intellectual Construct to Policy Ideas: The Case of the Afrocentric Paradigm. *The Journal of Pan African Studies* 9(2): 7–27.

Martin, G. (1987) Ideology and Praxis in Thomas Sankara's Populist Revolution of 4 August 1983 in Burkina Faso. *A Journal of Opinion* 15: 77–90.

Mazrui, A. (1986) *The Africans: A Triple Heritage.* Boston, MA: Little Brown & Company.

Miles, W. F. (2006) Letter from Ouagadougou. *The Antioch Review* 64(1): 99–116.

Murrey, A. (2012) The Revolution Cannot Triumph without the Emancipation of Women: A Reflection on Sankara's Speech, 25 Years Later. *International Journal of Socialist Renewal.* Retrieved on 7 March 2017 from http://links.org.au/node/2969.

Prairie, M. (2007) *Thomas Sankara Speaks: The Burkina Faso Revolution, 1983–87.* New York: Pathfinder Press.

Ray, C. (2007) True Visionary Thomas Sankara (1949–1987). *New African* 468: 8–9.

Rodney, W. (1972) *How Europe Underdeveloped Africa.* London: Bogle-L'Ouverture Publications.

Saaka, Y. (1994) Recurrent Themes in Ghanaian Politics: Kwame Nkrumah's Legacy. *Journal of Black Studies* 24(3): 263–280.

Skinner, E. (1988) Sankara and the Burkinabe Revolution: Charisma and Power, Local and External Dimensions. *The Journal of Modern African Studies* 26(3): 437–455.

Transparency International. (2015). People and Corruption: Africa Survey 2015. Retrieved on 11 March 2017 from www.transparency.org/whatwedo/publication/people_and_corruption_africa_survey_2015.

Webster, B. and Boahen, A. (1967) *The Revolutionary Years: West Africa Since 1800.* London: Longman Publishing Group.

Wilkins, M. (1989) The Death of Thomas Sankara and the Rectification of the People's Revolution in Burkina Faso. *African Affairs* 88(352): 375–388.

Williams, J. (2014) New Africa in the World Coming to Harlem: A Retrospective Comparison of Jerry Rawlings and Thomas Sankara. *Journal of Pan African Studies* 7(7): 7–25.

CHAPTER 14

'Revolution and Women's Liberation Go Together'

Thomas Sankara, Gender and the Burkina Faso Revolution

Namakula E. Mayanja

The revolution and women's liberation go together. We do not talk of women's emancipation as an act of charity or out of a surge of human compassion. It is a basic necessity for the revolution to triumph.
Thomas Sankara, speech on International Women's Day, 8 March 1987[1]

INTRODUCTION

In this chapter I explore the gender basis of Thomas Sankara's political philosophy and its potential for reconstructing statehood in Africa. Sankara's political philosophy and leadership challenged patriarchal politics and societies that fail to appreciate and integrate women's contributions to statehood and state-making. Despite post-independence national constitutions, the African Union's gender policy and international conventions (which recognise women's agency, political and civil rights, state decision-making and societal administration) remain male-dominated with patriarchal orientations. Sankara believed in the contribution of ordinary people in state construction. He knew that Burkina Faso's revolution would be incomplete without the participation and emancipation of women.

REVOLUTIONARY TURNING POINT

On 4 August 1983, a revolutionary government was established in Upper Volta under the leadership of Thomas Sankara. With the citizenry acting as agents of social, cultural, political and economic transformation, Sankara advanced a fight against imperialism and neocolonialism for a genuine independence. Following African tradition (in Ghana, Zimbabwe, Tanzania, Burundi, for example), he renamed the country Burkina Faso (land of upright people) – a change that marked a new identity based on revolutionary ideals.

Sankara's political philosophy considered women's emancipation to be a key component of the revolution. In his 1987 speech during a women's rally outside Ougadougou, he observed that the 'system of exploitation' relegated women to the third place, just like the 'Third World' is arbitrarily held back, dominated and exploited (Sankara, on International Women's Day, 1987). For Sankara, women's predicaments parallel the systemic oppression, exclusion, enslavement and denials characteristic of imperialism, which prevented and remains pivotal in hampering African nations' advancement to sovereign statehood. Sankara's political philosophy was anchored in confronting the hegemonic political philosophies that, for over a century, oppressed Africa's nations. He understood the hegemony of patriarchy that oppressed and suppressed women. At independence, when many African leaders assumed leadership, the implementation of statehood followed imperial templates that normalised, for example, women's oppression and made politics a male-dominated prerogative.

Unlike some other African leaders, when Sankara became the president he formed the National Council of Revolution (CNR) and he recognised women as equal players in the battles against neocolonialism and for state reconstruction. Currently only Rwanda, Senegal, South Africa and Namibia have more than 40 per cent women representation in parliament. During the four years of his presidency, he transformed Burkina Faso's politics and economy through an agenda of social well-being. Unlike the majority of other African nations at the time, Sankara's government prioritised the well-being of women and the majority of the population.

Since then, there have been international efforts to promote women's rights, including the Millennium Development Goals (MDGs). Goal Three of the MDGs aimed to 'promot[e] gender equality and empower women' while Goal Five sought to 'improv[e] maternal health'. Since the MDGs were not realised by 2015, the Sustainable Development Goals (SDGs) have subsequently been designed to further implement developmental initiatives. Goal Five of the SDGs focuses on 'achieving gender equality and empowering women and girls' and Goal Sixteen aims to 'promot[e] peaceful and inclusive societies'. Continentally, the African Union declared 2015 to be the Year of Women's empowerment and development (under the auspices of Africa's Agenda 2063). Meanwhile,

2016 was declared the African year of Human Rights, with a particular focus on the Rights of Women. Despite these grandiose initiatives, a visit to Africa's rural communities today quickly demonstrates that little has changed for the majority of women and girl children on the continent.

In this chapter, I explore Sankara's political philosophy, its gender basis and its potential for reconstructing Africa's statehood. I use gender and feminist lenses to examine how politics, power relations, institutions, policies and practices impact women and reinforce or reduce their gendered subjugation. Feminist theories seek to expose, understand and challenge 'the often unseen androcentric or masculine biases in the way that knowledge' and state power are constructed to propagate unequal gender relations (Tickner 2005: 3). I argue that women's emancipation is the *sine qui non* (the essential) feature for reconstructing Africa's statehood in a way that ensures social and ecological well-being, yet it remains a missing link. Women's agency in radically transforming African nations, communities, politics, economics and the generation of knowledge is not a theoretical option, but a practical priority for survival and well-being. Because women are the first educators of children, the main food providers on the continent and endangered during conflict, they have powerful perspectives on the needs of society.[2]

FEMINISM, GENDER AND WOMANISM

Feminists oppose and are critical of male dominance. According to Amina Mama (2001: 59), 'feminism signals a refusal of oppression, and a commitment to struggling for women's liberation from all forms of oppression: internal, external, psychological and emotional, socio-economic, political and philosophical'. Feminism seeks to create a consciousness based on new attitudes, beliefs and lifestyles that are open to and encouraging of women's agency (Mwale 2002). In other words, feminism takes a critical stand that challenges and questions the taken-for-granted patriarchal *status quo*.

Gendered unequal power relations and socially constructed roles and behaviours are rendered opaque through 'naturalisation and normalisation'.[3] Thus, shifting these relations requires a dramatic change or revolution: it requires an overhaul of social systems, beliefs, and values starting from the nuclear family to the highest state levels. For example, it may be considered 'normal' that women keep silent and let men make all domestic decisions, or that housekeeping and caring for the children and elderly are women's tasks while men watch TV or socialize, or that girl children do household duties while boys play, or that politics and the military are men's prerogative – but these are patriarchal attitudes cultivated through social norms and, as Sankara (1987: 345–349) asserted, they need to change. Differences between men and women are socially normalised and thus societies become insensitive to oppressive structures and systems (Freedman 2015).

A gender lens adopts the feminist standpoint, which positions 'men as the perpetrators of female oppression and discrimination' in patriarchal societies, where the discrimination of women is engrained in social, political, economic and religious structures and relationships (Mwale 2002: 116).[4] Oyewumi (2002: 1) argues that today gender is 'one of the most important analytic categories' to describe the world. In seeking to find solutions, leading feminist researchers use gender as the parameter through which they account for women's global oppression and subordination.

Some African intellectuals advocate for a more contextualised understanding of gender and feminism. Some have suggested the use of 'womanism' rather than feminism. The challenge is that often feminism in Africa fails to tackle issues affecting women and fails to engage men at the grassroots (Chidam'Modzi 1994/5). Instead, womanism identifies with the African men in the struggle for social, political and economic emancipation, unlike the 'middle-class white feminist who ignores the fact that racism and capitalism are concomitants of sexism' (ibid.: 45), a social reality acknowledged by Sankara in his 1987 speech on women's emancipation. Thus, the womanist's approach might be more inclusive and refrains from stereotyping in engaging and relating with men knowing that men are important in life and lasting solutions must be devised by both men and women (ibid.: 46). *Ipso facto*, men should be included in women's emancipation. Thus, Sankara appears to have been a 'womanist.' He encouraged men towards cultural transformation, to recognise women as counterparts in the liberation struggle.

WOMEN AND STATEHOOD IN AFRICA

While gender practices are often context-specific, I contend that there are notions that are appropriate across the continent. In this chapter, I adopt a Sankarist focus on statehood issues by looking at those issues that affect ordinary women and not the elite. Basil Davidson (1992: 188) argues that Africa's problems spring from 'the social and political institutions within which decolonised Africans have lived and tried to survive. Primarily this is a crisis of institutions'. The nation state (and its sense of nationalism often characterised as 'Europe's last gift to Africa') is a *burden*, frustrating Africans and women in particular, so thoroughly subjugated by colonialism (Davidson 1992). Cheikh Anta Diop (1959) and Mohammad Al-Kiki (1997) observe that, while African matriarchal states survived and were sustainable for over three thousand years, patriarchal capitalist states have been highly unsustainable. For Diop, patriarchy is an imported social system. Al-Kiki saw patriarchy as an effort to rob women's wealth by destroying matriarchal systems, replacing them with patriarchal colonial systems responsible for continental underdevelopment. It is now widely accepted that the origins of the structural and institutional weaknesses of post-colonial African nations lies in their creation (Araoye 2014): they were failed by design at the moment of decolonisation.

Examining conflict in Africa, Robinson (2010) offers an understanding of war as 'gender wars' that benefit Western nations (especially with regards to using the war strategy to exploit Africa's resources with effects such as rape and environmental degradation that affect women's livelihood) and elite individuals. The latter includes the African rulers who substitute the common good with personal aggrandisement, loyalty to ones sovereign nations with loyalty to exploiters and national power with personal power. This system is a 'highly efficient imperial weapon' (Robinson 2010: 103), propelled into African societies at the scale of the home. Robinson asserts, 'the West spreads patriarchy as a prophylaxis [i.e. a preventative measure] against its own implosion' (ibid.: 116). Sankara's formidable efforts stand as powerful example for African countries as a framework to establish state-people relationships that honour, support and create space for women.

SANKARA'S GENDERED POLITICAL PHILOSOPHY: LESSONS FOR STATE BUILDING

Sankara combined the feminist and womanist approach to construct his gendered philosophy, inviting men and women to collaborate in altering a normalised and naturalised *status quo* that enslaves and oppresses women, preventing them from playing their role in politics and economics and therefore not realising their individual and collective potential. For him, both men and women are 'victims of imperialist oppression and domination' and must wage the same battle for genuine liberation and women's emancipation (Sankara, on International Women's Day, 8 March 1987).

Gender Inequality as Systematic

On 2 October 1983, in the Political Orientation Speech, Sankara declared that women would be engaged in battles to break 'various shackles of neocolonial society', including decision-making and the implementation of projects for establishing 'a free and prosperous society' where women are free. Their emancipation was not considered a favour but 'a basic necessity for the revolution [for Africa's liberation] to triumph' (Sankara, Political Orientation Speech, 1983). Moreover, he encouraged women to take the initiative for their own liberation: 'Let our women move up to the front ranks! Our final victory depends essentially on their capacity, their wisdom in struggle, their determination to win' (ibid.). Sankara understood that the oppression of women is systemic. During the Political Orientation Speech, he said:

> Posing the question of women in Burkinabè society today means posing the abolition of the system of slavery to which they have been subjected for millennia. The first step is to try to understand how this system functions, to grasp its real nature in all its subtlety, in order then to work out a line of action that can lead to women's total emancipation.
>
> (Sankara 1983: 202)

In a globalised world, women's subjugation is endemic to patriarchal and racialised capitalism, which grows on the exploitation of the vulnerable. For Sankara, the struggle of Burkinabè women is inextricably linked to women's global struggle. According to Sankara, imperialism, capitalism and bureaucracy are tethered together to reinforce women's subjugation. He emphasised the importance of women knowing that colonialism was the root of their oppression and that Burkina Faso's revolution was incomplete without the women as active partners in change not passive victims or spectators but as comrades in struggle who by right should assert themselves as equal partners in the revolution. He invited all African women to acknowledge their irreplaceable roles in reconstructing African societies and challenged them to be active in playing their roles.

CELEBRATING WOMEN IN SOCIETY

Sankara's gendered political philosophy is inextricably linked to his charismatic and Pan-Africanist leadership. Unlike those African rulers who hardly associate with the people they (appear to) lead, he was comfortable in the direct presence of the people he represented. I use the term ruler here deliberately because rulers dominate, govern states as personal businesses and are not accountable to people. Over the years, leadership in Africa has suffered profound setbacks. There is little fidelity to ethics and the law partially due to corruption and the high tolerance of the African people improper leadership practices. Looking back at post–independence leaders – Kwame Nkrumah and Julius Nyerere – and, more recently Sankara and Nelson Mandela, we see that their leadership was inspired by love, service and liberation of the people and not personal aggrandisement and accumulation of wealth. Great leaders long to establish nationhood build on ethics and integrity, thus the name Burkina Faso, the 'Land of Upright People'

Sankara rallied thousands of women in Ouagadougou to commemorate the International Women's Day on 8 March 1987. In his speech, he addressed women's oppression at a great length, highlighting the historical origins of women's oppression and how it was perpetuated in contemporary Burkina. This powerful speech highlighted the pains and joys, loneliness, isolation, and humiliation that women face.

> She remains voiceless and faceless; first to rise and last to retire; she collects water yet is the last to quench her thirst; cultivates and gathers wood to prepare the food, yet may only eat if there are leftovers. She is not paid for her domestic duties. Referred to as 'house wife' [meaning] they have no job … they are not working [although women are] putting in hundreds of thousands of hours for an appalling level of production.
>
> (Sankara, speech on International Women's Day, 8 March 1987)

Again, unlike most of the world's leaders at the time, his recognition and applause for women as mothers, companions and comrades in the struggle went beyond acts of speech to the assertion of women's transformative roles in society. He celebrated women as sources of happiness, affection and inspirational models. Sankara referred to women as the anchors for familial well-being: 'the midwife, washerwoman, cleaner, cook, errand-runner, matron, farmer, healer, gardener, grinder, saleswoman, worker.' Because of these roles, Sankara argued that women must affirm themselves as equal partners in the success of revolution – in order for the revolution to be successful. He argued that it was paramount to restore the dignity of women by ensuring freedom from the exclusions and differentiations. He sought to terminate the hypocrisy that shamelessly exploit women:

> Imbued with the invigorating sap of freedom, the men of Burkina, the humiliated and outlawed of yesterday, received the stamp of what is most precious in the world: honour and dignity. From this moment on, happiness became accessible. Every day we advance toward it, heady with the first fruits of our struggles, themselves proof of the great strides we have already taken. But the selfish happiness is an illusion. There is something crucial missing: women. They have been excluded from the joyful procession … The revolution's promises are already a reality for men. But for women, they are still merely a rumour. And yet the authenticity and the future of our revolution depends on women. Nothing definitive or lasting can be accomplished in our country as long as a crucial part of ourselves is kept in this condition of subjugation – a condition imposed … by various systems of exploitation.
>
> (Sankara, speech on International Women's Day, 8 March 1987)

Sankara was convinced that 'the genuine emancipation of women should entrust them with responsibilities and involve them in productive activities inherent to the liberation struggles that people face' (ibid.). For him, 'a development project without the participation of women is like using four fingers when you have ten' (Sankara 2007: 51).

For Sankara, the reconstruction of Upper Volta was *with* and *for* all people, with an emphasis on women. In contrast, for many African heads of state, collaboration of the leadership with the masses does not appear to be a high concern, particularly when political legitimacy does not come from the population. When there is the nominal call to elect leaders, political campaigns are marred with corruption. Politicians instrumentalise poverty by buying votes. During my time as an election observer in DR Congo, Uganda, Burundi, Tanzania and Kenya, it was a common phenomenon for politicians to lure voters with beer, sugar, salt, T-shirts, matches and so on. Consequently, those who get into leadership positions are not necessarily those with leadership qualities, but are sometimes the most corrupt. Politics is a lucrative business for personal aggrandisement and not service and collaboration with the population. To use the African analogy, politics therefore becomes 'like employing a lion to look after the goats'.

ACKNOWLEDGING THE COMPLEXITY OF WOMEN'S SUBJUGATION

Acknowledging that some oppressive structures are part of African cultures, during the interview with the Cameroonian historian Mongo Beti, Sankara indicated that, for the revolution to move forward, it was necessary to

> stifle all the negative aspects of our traditions. This is our struggle against all retrograde forces, all forms of obscurantism, a legitimate and indispensable struggle to liberate society from all decadent domains and prejudices, including the marginalisation of women ... We are fighting for the equality of men and women, not of a mechanical, mathematical equality, but by making women equal to men before the law and especially before wage labour.
>
> (Sankara, interview with Mongo Beti, 1985)

Sankara asserted that the emancipation of women would require sustained attention to education and economic power. One of Sankara's first initiatives was to ensure that the Ministry of Education made 'women's access to education a reality' (Sankara 2007: 52). Sankara considered education as a tool for emancipation, yet education for the girl child remains an urgent contemporary prerogative of human rights activists and feminists. This stands in opposition to contemporary politicians, many of whom do not trust educational institutions and are not bothered to improve their standards. Their children are most often educated abroad or domestically in the British, French or American systems. It is not that it is wrong to educate children abroad; the problem is failing to address educational injustices domestically. Great leaders like Julius Nyerere of Tanzania and the present John Magufuli educated their children in Tanzanian schools.

In Burkina, the Ministries of Culture and Family Matters were to collaborate with women towards social transformation for new paradigms that would establish new social relationships and practices. The practice of the woman's family providing a bride price at the marriage was suppressed. Sankara held that the practice of the bride price reduced women to commodities to be traded.

Women were to play central parts in the revolution. Mothers and wives were catalysts of 'revolutionary transformation' by educating children and family planning. This patriotism had the impulse to establish 'revolutionary moral values and an anti-imperialist lifestyle' (ibid.: 53). To this effect, those ministries in charge of culture and family affairs were to stress a holistic paradigm shift towards better social relationships. Women were not to be limited to the kitchen and the home: men and women *shared* home tasks. To reinforce equality between men and women, he destroyed neocolonial state apparatuses and systems that perpetuated women's oppression by entrusting women with responsibility, remunerating them like men when they do the same job and compelling men to respect women.

A FOCUS ON CONCRETE ACTIONS: HEALTH AND THE ENVIRONMENT

Unlike many rulers and leaders, who merely 'pay lip service' to gender equality, Sankara honoured International Women's Day, appointed women into government positions and in the revolutionary army, created the Ministry of Family Development and the Union of Burkina Women (UFB) and amended the constitution making it mandatory for presidents to have at least five women as ministers in cabinet. With these established policies, he banned the practice of female circumcision, polygamy and forced marriage. He established education programs to teach home economics, parenting and HIV/AIDs prevention.

He went further to eliminate the conditions that prevent women's emancipation. Sankara purged corruption to ensure that national resources benefit all people, prosecuted the 'enemies of the people' who used their powerful positions to enrich themselves through 'bribery, manoeuvres, and forged documents', becoming shareholders in different companies, confiscating peoples land, owning mansions, financing businesses and receiving approval in the name of the state.

Sankara's fight against environmental degradation, which impinges on women's livelihood and threatens social well-being at all levels in a predominantly rural country fed by small-scale farming, was ahead of many other international leaders. Widespread deforestation was (and is) leading to desertification in Africa. It threatens the water sources and species on which women depend for natural medicines, food and firewood. Women walk longer and longer distances in search of fertile land for farming and to gather water and wood. Diseases are on the rise. Even today, environmental destruction threatens Africa's societies, politics and economy, aggravated by violent multinational resource extraction and political elites concerns with personal economic gains and not the well-being and future of the continent (Bassey 2012).

He increased access to health care so as to reduce discrimination in the medical system. This is a discrimination that denies women and their children access to medical care, including during pregnancy, all the while offering 'VIP' treatment to political officials (an inequality Sankara spoke of often). African rulers have the practice of seeking medical treatment abroad while the hospitals in their home countries fail to offer even basic malaria treatments. The massive sums spent on foreign treatments would suffice to establish functional hospitals on the continent.

He embarked on improving conditions for food security through an integrated system of food justice, which affects women's lives in particular (Murrey 2016). Three decades after Sankara's death, famine remains a continental challenge with millions surviving on food aid. For Sankara, depending on imported food is 'imperialism on the plate' (Sankara 2007: 62). Liberation is incomplete when people hunger daily. Environmental protection and sustainability were therefore crucial to Sankara's strategic thinking. Today, the continent faces serious environmental and climatic challenges that affect food production, access to water and public health. These challenges include water pollution, deforestation, soil erosion, droughts, floods, desertification, insect infestation, and wetland degradation. Environment protection is inextricably linked to social security, poverty eradication, and health and is liable to increase wars, thus exacerbating women's insecurity. Persistent war and political unrest in Africa curtail women's emancipation and instead makes them victims of violence, rape, poverty and suffering.

Sankara understood the essential relationship between women's emancipation and national state building and social-economic development. Women have an organic capacity for collaboration and practical innovation. He knew that educating women would translate into healthier families, educated children, supported workers, environmental commitment and dedicated politicians. Investing in women was therefore investing in social and economic development, not merely individual wealth.

LOVE AS CENTRAL TO SANKARA'S RADICAL POLITICS

What enabled Sankara to establish and implement this gendered political philosophy? I submit that he loved his country and people. I use the verb 'love' deliberately as a component of Sankara's philosophy and politics because he was *more* than patriotic. He was motivated, at least in part, by love – unlike some African revolutionary leaders who claim to be patriotic but are driven to serve personal interests, amass wealth, cling to power and suppress rights, particularly for women. This part of his motivation was central to his politics and everyday life.

He collaborated with people as equals and not with the 'I know it all' attitude prominent among leaders who dictate rather than collaborate with the people in reconstructing the nation.[5] He encouraged people to become protagonists of social and political transformation and to serve the needs of the oppressed and the exploited. He adopted a simple lifestyle (see Introduction, this volume). Journalist Paula Akugizibwe (2012) notes that as a president, Sankara 'rode a bicycle to work before he upgraded, at his Cabinet's insistence, to a Renault 5 – one of the cheapest cars available in Burkina Faso at the time. He lived in a small brick house and wore only cotton that was produced, weaved and sewn [locally]'. While Sankara lived a modest life, too many contemporary African presidents live lavishly, with expensive jets, houses, cars and offshore accounts. It is a common phenomenon in East Africa's parliament to spend the first sessions discussing salary increases for parliamentarians even as the people they represent cannot afford a meal a day, have no access to clean water and are dying due to malaria or HIV. Sankara's politics of love stands in opposition to such selfishness.

Sankara deeply appreciated the role of women in society by staying close to the people in his military position and as a president. Social needs and human potentials were not abstract concepts for him, rather he could see and feel that women were central to social well-being, including the economy. His policies exhibited an innovation that women and families – and therefore the nation – needed for genuine emancipation.

CONCLUSIONS

There are many lessons we can take from the Burkinabè experience and the leadership of Thomas Sankara so as to create policies that advance women's authentic emancipation today.

First, sustainable revolution starts by the liberation and decolonisation of the mind. If the mind is conquered, emancipation is implausible. The question we need to ask ourselves is: what type of education is needed for Africa today to foster liberation? If women are to contribute towards Africa's statehood, they must learn to think creatively, and to do so critically.

Second, while women must demand their emancipation, achieving it requires the overhaul of the systems that reinforce women's oppression. Effective women's emancipation should start from the nuclear family, the schools, churches, local communities and playgrounds where children are socialised. Respect for the woman's equality with men and their liberation starts in places and institutions where women's oppression, exclusion and discrimination starts, and only then will women's emancipation and agency contribute to reconstructing African statehood.

Third, and drawing from the previous point, the emancipation of women must become part of mainstream education. Respect for women must be inculcated at an early age in schools for boys and girls, within families, in places of worship and in the highest levels of society. Even if a woman becomes a president, when other women remain battered or dominated in their homes and harassed in the streets and places of work, women's emancipation is incomplete.

These efforts require commitment, love for women as mothers, sisters, daughters and wives. In Sankara's words, 'You cannot carry out fundamental change without a certain amount of madness. In this case, it comes from nonconformity, the courage to turn your back on the old formulas, the courage to invent the future. It took the madmen of yesterday for us to be able to act with extreme clarity today. I want to be one of those madmen. We must dare to invent the future' (Sankara 1988: 144). Men and women must name and struggle together against the forces that alienate, abuse and oppress.

NOTES

1 Unless noted otherwise, quotations from Sankara in this chapter are available in Sankara (1988).

2 War is a common phenomenon in many African nations. In my examination of the history of war in post-independence Africa, I note that since 1960, few African nations have not experienced war or armed conflict: Botswana, Gabon, Malawi, Mauritius and Madagascar.

3 Gender concerns all people, although much of the research on gender tends to focus on women because they are the victims of gendered inequalities within cultural, political, economic and academic power structures.

4 Of course, not all men perpetrate female oppression and not all women advocate for women's emancipation.

5 For example, during the African Union conference summit in 2016, President Mugabe said, 'I will be [here] until God says come, but as long as I am alive, I will lead the country.' The simple analysis is that he does not consider Zimbabweans as capable of leading or as partners in national development (see O'Grady 2016). President Kagame seems to consider himself to be the only Rwandan leading national economic progress, ensuring Rwandans to vote for his rule until 2034 (see McVeigh 2015). President Yoweri Museveni claims that all of Uganda's problems have been solved by him and that the citizens are like 'passengers on a bus'. He does not acknowledge them as equal contributors to national progress (see Bwire 2015).

REFERENCES

Akugizibwe, P. (2012) 'Debt Is A Cleverly Managed Reconquest Of Africa' – Thomas Sankara. Retrieved on 7 November 2016 from http://Thisisafrica.Me/Debt-Cleverly-Managed-Reconquest-Africa-Thomas-Sankara.

Al-Kiki, M. (1997) *Taking Gifts From Women Where The Fair Ruler Is Absent* (ed. A. Tawfiq). Beyreuth, Lebanon: Dar Al-Gharb Al Islami.

Araoye, A. L. (2014) *Sources of Conflict in the Post-Colonial African State*. Nairobi: Africa World Press.

Bwire, J. (2015) All Ugandan Problems Have Been Solved by Me, Says Museveni. *Daily Monitor*. Retrieved on 23 May 2017 from www.monitor.co.ug/SpecialReports/Elections/All-Ugandan-problems-solved-Museveni/859108-2968156-j4n6h5z/index.html.

Chidam'Modzi (1994/5) Addressing African Feminism. *Journal of Humanities* 8(9): 43–53.

Davidson, B. (1992) *The Black Man's Burden: Africa and the Curse of the Nation-State*. New York: Three Rivers Press.

Diop, C. A. (1959) *L'unite Culurelle De L'afrique Noire; Domaines Du Patriarcat Et Du Matriarcat Dans L'antiquite Classique*. Paris: Presence Africaine.

Freedman (2015) *Gender, Violence and Politics in the Democratic Republic of Congo*. Abingdon: Routledge.

Mama, A. (2001) Talking about Feminism in Africa. *Agenda: Empowering Women for Gender Equity* 50: 58–63.

McVeigh T. (2015) Rwanda Votes to Give President Paul Kagame Right to Rule until 2034. *The Guardian*. Retrieved on 23 May 2017 from www.theguardian.com/world/2015/dec/20/rwanda-vote-gives-president-paul-kagame-extended-powers.

Murrey, A (2016) 'Our Stomachs Will Make Themselves Heard': What Sankara Can Teach us About Food Justice Today. Retrieved on 23 May 2017 from http://Africanarguments.Org/2016/04/22/Our-Stomachs-Will-Make-Themselves-Heard-What-Sankara-Can-Teach-Us-About-Food-Justice-Today.

Mwale, P. N. (2002) Where Is the Foundation of African Gender? The Case of Malawi. *Nordic Journal Of African Studies* 11(1): 114–137.

Nnimmo B. (2012) *To Cook a Continent: Destructive Extraction and the Climate Crisis in Africa*. Cape Town: Pambazuka Press.

O'Grady, S. (2016) Robert Mugabe: The Dictator Bucking Zimbabwean Life Expectancy Rates. *The Independent*. Retrieved on 23 May 2017 from www.independent.co.uk/news/world/africa/robert-mugabe-the-dictator-bucking-zimbabwean-life-expectancy-rates-a6885376.html.

Oyewumi, O. (2002) Conceptualizing Gender: The Eurocentric Foundations of Feminist Concepts and the Challenge of African Epistemologies. *Jenda: A Journal of Culture and African Women Studies* 2(1): 1–9.

Robinson, M. R. (2010) Gender Wars: Patriarchy, Matriarchy and Conflicts. In T. Falora and C. Rahael (eds), *War and Peace in Africa*, 101–128. Durham, NC: Carolina Academic Press.

Sankara, T. (1988) *Thomas Sankara Speaks: The Burkina Faso Revolution 1983–87*. New York: Pathfinder Press.

Sankara, T. (2007) *Women's Liberation and the African Freedom Struggle*. New York: Pathfinder Press.

Tickner, A. (2005) What Is Your Research Program? Some Feminist Answers To International Relations Methodological Questions. *International Studies Quartely* 49: 1–21.

PART III
LEGACIES

CHAPTER 15

Balai Citoyen

A New Praxis of Citizen Fight with Sankarist Inspirations

Zakaria Soré[1]

INTRODUCTION

Three decades after his assassination, Thomas Sankara remains popular among African youth. Youth movements, most often drawing from the sound bites of the ideal of Sankara, have emerged that draw powerfully on Sankara's legacy and political philosophies. Among these, Balai Citoyen or 'Citizen Broom', a popular and grassroots movement of Burkinabè civil society, stands out as one of the most remarkable.

The movement was born at a turning point in the country's political life, in a context marked by President Blaise Compaoré's efforts to change the constitution to expand presidential term limits, a change that would allow him to remain in power after 27 years of rule. From the beginning, the intentions of the regime materialised in the proposed establishment of a Senate. The Balai Citoyen spoke out quickly against this plan. It also denounced the lack of justice in the country, pointing to numerous pending cases of gross miscarriages of justice, including the assassination of Sankara and the death of Norbert Zongo (see Chapter 23, this volume), and the misappropriation of national wealth by a minority close to the government.

The movement is called 'Citizen Broom' to denote the desire to rid the country of 'dirt', including the greed of political corruption. Activists often hold the broom as a symbol of this action of cleaning house and refer to themselves as 'Cibal'. Composed of the contraction of the words 'citizen' and 'broom', the neologism signifies any person engaged in the triumph of the values of integrity, honesty, social justice and accountability in public governance. Claiming a Sankarist ideology, Balai Citoyen animates youth through a bottom-up Africanist discourse. Its calls for mobilisation are inspired by the political philosophies outlined in the speeches of Pan-African combatants, including Thomas Sankara.

Regarding themselves as the 'heirs' of Thomas Sankara, members of Balai Citoyen draw on Sankara's revitalisation of the political philosophy of *burkindlum* and advocate for the integration of the values of integrity, accountability and social justice in the management of public affairs. The movement was officially launched on 25 August 2013 at the Place de la Nation. However, the movement's earlier history dates back to 2011, during an informal discussion on the country's political situation, among journalists, students and human rights activists. These young Burkinabè were inspired by the initial successes of both the Arab Spring and Senegalese youth movements like Y'En a Marre (We are Fed Up), which addressed and struggled against socio-political challenges similar to those faced by Burkinabè youth. In this way, a reflection with international roots was initiated, particularly among youth. At the same time, the project has much longer roots: the representatives of civil society movements had already been mobilising against poor political governance, corruption and the lack of alternatives for youth. Examples of such organisations include Cadre de Réflexion et d'Actions Démocratiques (CADRe), Generation Cheick Anta Diop, the Movement of the Voiceless, REPERE, Réseau Barke and the Club Rousseau. Balai Citoyen is an umbrella organisation uniting all democratic associations and sincere patriots, committed to a significant pro-people changes and consolidation of democracy. It is made up of artists, journalists, lawyers, merchants, farmers and other stakeholders.[2]

In this way, the Balai Citoyen is a mass movement. It has both a national coordination and regional coordination, whose representatives are elected by General Assembly for a term of one year. To better reach people, Balai Citoyen, like the August 1983 Revolution that had implanted the Revolution Defense Committee (CDR) throughout the territory, set up Cibal Clubs in each district. Cibal Clubs are considered to be the basic cells of the movement. Once a Cibal Club has been created at the grassroots level, one person is designated by the Club to liaise with the regional and national coordinators. Outside the territory of Burkina Faso, Cibal embassies represent the movement. Hence, Balai Citoyen has an international orientation and scope.

In this chapter, I draw from interviews conducted in 2016 among leaders, activists and supporters of the Balai Citoyen movement.[3] Drawing from original fieldwork during an important moment in Balai Citoyen's formation, I argue that Balai Citoyen's entry into political activism caused a transformation of the protest movement landscape in Burkina Faso. The movement came with a new spirit of struggle. The Balai Citoyen, from its original organisational structure – from the way it finances activities and it relationship with other structures – and its ideological orientation, breaks with those movements that were already part of Burkinabè protest landscapes. The Balai Citoyen mobilised through a series of public actions: street occupations to express poiltical messages, organising debates and initiating awareness caravans. To put pressure and to provoke change, the movement combines traditional approaches with what Norris (2002) calls 'unconventional practices'. These unconventional practices include legal demonstrations and strikes as well as illegal protest actions such as the sequestration of administrative officials and the blocking of roads.

LE BALAI CITOYEN: YOUTH GATHERING WITH SANKARIST INSPIRATIONS

The Balai Citoyen is often represented as a homogeneous protest movement, but it is built on a collective of people from diverse political affiliations and backgrounds who share Sankarist ideals, including the power of public action. In its call to action, Balai Citoyen takes as its central reference the history of political struggle during the August Revolution, led by Thomas Sankara. When Balai Citoyen entered the political landscape of Burkina Faso, they drew inspiration from the direction of the preceding revolutionary context of 1983:

> When in 1983, against the ambitions of imperialism and its local lackeys who to exploit the country, the patriotic youth of Upper Volta rebelled, deserting classrooms, lecture halls, workshops and tea groups to [formulate] a strong resistance to these reactionary forces. In a remarkable unity of action, civilian and military dealt the final blow to imperialism by establishing the Revolution, allowing the people to write glorious pages of its history.
>
> (Extract from press kit release on the official launch of the movement, at the Place de la Révolution, 25 August 2013)

The tone was set. Balai Citoyen established Thomas Sankara as a sort-of compass. The speeches, key phrases and actions of Sankara are discussed at each Balai Citoyen meeting. Sankara was given the status of Supreme Cibal, again signalling the ideological line of the movement. These references to Sankara are not surprising given that, among the members of the movement, many hail from anti-globalisation, leftist and Marxist-leaning movement backgrounds (including the Alumni Association Nationale des Étudiants du Burkina, or ANEB, in which the leader of the Revolution of 4 August still has a strong presence). Nonetheless, the movement activists whom have come to be known as 'Sankara's heirs' have vastly different trajectories as well as different commitments to the movement. To understand the characteristic of the militant movement, it is useful to get an idea of the trajectories of these different individuals' backgrounds and commitments.

The majority of militants were born in the 1980s. These are people whom have known Thomas Sankara only through books and film. The strong commitment of this generation to Sankara's ideals is explained, in part, by the sympathetic tone of many authors of texts on Sankara. Many hold Sankara's logic of conducting public affairs to be the best and, therefore, this logic is held up as the one most likely to encourage development. These are highly committed young people who have ambitions to live the ideal of Sankara, but often lack the access to spaces to do so.

Sankara's heirs have long commitments against injustice, including commitments to human rights. In this way, the militancy of the Balai Citoyen was the culmination of long personal histories of struggle for change, which were coming together under the new umbrella of Balai Citoyen. Eric Ismael Kinda, a member of the national coordination team, explained some of this long history of struggle for a more equitable management of public funds:

> The management team is composed of people who have a history in the struggle. We come from different backgrounds and have many experiences. Many have experienced militant life before arriving at Balai Citoyn. Activism for many of us did not start with the Balai Citoyen. I myself am a member of workers union, the Federation of National Trade Unions of Workers of Education and Research (F-SYNTER). I was trained in the union mould. Before the teachers' union, I was in the student union. Guy Hervé Kam has long led a syndicate of magistrates.
>
> (Eric Ismael Kinda, interview with Mikaël Alberca on 9 May 2015 in Ouagadougou)[4]

Long militant trajectories were also characteristic of professional people in the movement, including artists.

The two main headliners of the movement, Karim Sama (a.k.a. Sams'K le Jah) and Serge Martin Bambara (a.k.a. Smockey), both had considerable political engagement and experiences prior to the Balai Citoyen. They were among those who had long called for justice for Thomas Sankara. Sams'K le Jah, indeed, was one of the first Burkinabè artists to dedicate an album to Thomas Sankara. Their joining together was part of a search for unity and cohesion to better lead the struggle against corruption as well as the struggle for justice for Sankara and Zongo. Karim Sama, a member of the national coordination of Balai Citoyen, explained this search for justice:

> Initially, everyone was commitment [to Norbert Zongo]. Smockey was into rap and I was into reggae. We ended up on the ground and moved closer in the Norbert Zongo case with Semfilms and the Burkinabe Movement for Human Rights and Peoples (MBDHP) who wanted to mark the 10th anniversary of the assassination of Norbert Zongo through a CD.
>
> (Karim Sama, interview with author, 13 October 2016)

By tracing the histories of the members of the Balai Citoyen, it becomes apparent that they were Sankarist before the actualisation of the movement. These are activists who were already engaged in struggles for justice, social justice and democracy.

These deep individual commitments by members of Balai Citoyen signal an important communal coming together of activists similar to that described by the political sociologist Birgitta Orfali (2011: 47–48): 'When it comes to opting an opinion, choosing an attitude, the individual does not want to be alone. He [*sic*] wants to know that others think like him [*sic*]. He [*sic*] therefore seeks out groups whose ideology he [*sic*] assumes are close to his [*sic*] own.'[5] As Orfali outlines in *L'Adhésion: Militer, S'Engager, Rêver*, members of Balai Citoyen gravitated toward a collective organisation to concretise an ideology.

Another commonality between members is a distrust of political parties. This distrust includes even those parties that are Sankarist in inspiration since Balai activists consider that they do not incarnate Sankara's ideals. Bruno Jaffré (1997) argues that Sankara was himself similarly suspicious of party politics. Jaffré explains:

> The history of the Upper Volta and the history of Right-wing parties taught him that [political parties] were unreliable. As for those whom he learned to visit with on the left, [those] who claimed to be Marxist, he was wary of their tendency towards hegemony. While he appreciated the skills and qualities of PAI activists, he feared that at one time or another their organization, whose structuring and discipline he admired, would occupy so much space that they would control the entire state apparatus ... [Sankara] refused to submit to any organization.[6]
>
> (Jaffré 1997: 175; see also Chapter 5, this volume)

Similar tensions occurred between Balai Citoyen and political parties. A public statement from the Club Cibal Thomas Isidore Noel Sankara, asserts:

> With political parties, we understand that [their] ideology is to fight for oneself and not for common causes. Politicians seek their own interests ... see how there are the large number of parties who claim to be Sankarist [but fail to embody Sankarist ideals].
>
> (Club Cibal Thomas Isidore Noel Sankara, October 2016)

Balai Citoyen activists do not believe in parties for several reasons, principal among them were accusations of corruption, collaboration with the Congress for Democracy and Progress (Compaoré's party), selfishness and, especially, a desire for separation from previously established entities.

Activists' individual commitments to Sankara's legacy and philosophies created the foundation for the consolidation and establishment of the movement, whose main reference continues to be Thomas Sankara. Movement activists founded a collective through shared ideals and orientations – a shared orientation that is based on their own, often long-standing, political commitment to Thomas Sankara. While an older generation pioneered a revolutionary period, a younger generation discovered Sankara in the books and stories retold by those who experienced the revolution. In this way, Balai Citoyen is a common house where activists gathered to declare a collective disappointment with Sankarist political parties and to articulate a credible activism based on Sankara's philosophies. The militant movement emerged to fill a dual purpose: to live in tune with Sankara's ideas and, hopefully, thanks to the strength of the group, to reintroduce Sankara's political philosophies in public governance.

While movement initiators share ideological orientations, it was a struggle to find a shared formula or praxis to drive action. Indeed, the emergence of Balai Citoyen was marked with some internal tensions and uncertainties. During the initial stages of the movement, a governing body emerged that was made up of two spokespersons. In the first march of the movement, one spokesperson, Hyppolite Doumboué, was suspected by some members to be too closely affiliated with established political groups (including some political bosses who had reached considerable power under Compaoré). For the members of the movement, it was feared that this proximity could eventually undermine the independence of Balai Citoyen and threaten their objectives for political transformation. Further, Doumboué was criticised for his charisma and eloquence. To the latter point, the movement needed a person with some of the vivacity and charisma characteristic of Sankara's leadership style to lead the fight (for more on Sankara's leadership, see Chapter 5, this volume). Beyond these initial conflicts, Doumboué might also have been a victim of his past as an ANEB activist. Indeed, this group has never hidden its proximity with the Parti Communiste Révolutionnaire Voltaïque (the Voltaic Revolutionary Communist Party or PCRV), which remained an underground party and which remained critical of Sankara during the years of the Revolution. The PCRV has maintained that the August 1983 was a coup and not a revolution (see Chapter 6, this volume).

In addition to these internal arguments, some of the other members were likewise criticised for their proximity to established political parties. Beyond being historical reminders that exposed the opposition between different trends within the movement, proximity to existing political parties would, it was believed by many, likely undermine the cohesion within the group and might influence the management of coming struggles. The accusation of proximity of the first spokesman of the movement with the political parties was confirmed during the first meeting of the People's Movement for Progress (MPP) in Bobo Dioulasso, where young people dressed in Balai Citoyen T-shirts went to welcome officials policies. Some members of the movement, products of their fresh success – including ousting Compaoré – saw these associations with established political parties as unacceptable. The movement subsequently made a clarification on the subject for the public, reaffirming its independence vis-à-vis political parties (NetAfrique 2014).

These differences of political-ideological positioning between players lead to a kind of crisis. The need to adopt a sufficiently distant leadership from political parties was essential, especially as Balai wanted to be the preeminent organisation of the struggle. The members agreed on the establishment of a set of crisis resolution mechanisms that would enable the movement to achieve its objectives. Idrissa Barry, the communications manager and member of the national coordination of Balai Citoyen explained the importance of this shift,

> After the departure of [Doumboué and other members of the trend of ANEB], the movement had become more homogeneous. It is now composed of young people claiming Sankara['s] ideologies and do not identify themselves with the Sankarist political parties.
>
> (Idrissa Barry, interview, 19 September 2016)

A meeting was organised in Kombissiri a town near Ouagadougou. Following this meeting, there was a reorganisation of the governing body. An artist, Serge Martin Bambara, and a lawyer, Guy Hervé Kam, were designated as spokespersons. Their appointment may have been prompted due to their commitment in justice for Thomas Sankara and their outspokenness (for which they had already achieved a national renown).

In their latter form a more strategic approach was taken, this included efforts to persuade intellectuals through the parole of Guy Hervé Kam, a human rights attorney with a distinguished record as well as through the parole of people known in popular circles, including a number of important musicians who are members of Balai Citoyen. Members of the movement wanted people to speak in a straightforward manner and these new spokespersons met these requirements. This reframing has allowed the movement to maintain internal cohesion while gathering 'Sankara's heirs' in the struggle for the creation of '*burkindim*': the country of honest people. So, with Thomas Sankara's heirs now moving in the same direction, Balai Citoyen began afresh in April 2014. More central to this new orientation than ever, Sankara retained his place as a Cibal leader in the movement. The subsequent slogans were inspired by his behaviour, his positions and his political orientations.

RESTORING *BURKINDLUM*: INTEGRITY

A year after becoming president and well on the way toward realising his vision of creating a better functioning of society, Thomas Sankara renamed Upper

Volta. On 4 August 1984 the country was named Burkina Faso: the country of honest or upright people. With this new name for the country, Sankara engaged in an anthropological-ideological construction. Of particular importance is the word 'Burkina', which is associated with the values and attitudes that people should display in their daily behaviour. Ouédraogo (2014) demonstrates that the concept draws from the term *burkindlum*, which has its roots in a political and moral philosophy of social groups in Burkina Faso and encourages action. The anchoring of this concept in the daily lives of Burkinabè connotes an on-going engagement against all forms of injustice.

The spirit of sacrifice is another important aspect of *burkindlum*. Sankara continues to be appreciated in youth circles because he consistently put forward the people's interests at the expense of his own interests or enrichment. Translating this value for the governance of the country meant Sankara needed to develop initiatives to improve the living conditions of the population. His presidency was not a race for personal enrichment. The proof: even as head of state, he kept his officer's salary from the army and personal gifts to the President of Burkina Faso were donated to the treasury to enable to carry out projects for the population. Jaffré describes Sankara's lifestyle:

> In February 1987, before the *Commission du Peuple* in charge of preventing corruption, [Sankara] declared as personal property: a villa that he acquired through a loan and which he repaid month by month, undeveloped land in a village, a 1976 car and various other household items or items of little value. On this occasion, he listed all the gifts he had received, mostly money that was then transferred immediately to various state financial institutions and cars that were then given to the government's fleet of vehicles.[7]
>
> (Jaffré 1997: 191)

Behaviours that deviated from *burkindlum* include embezzlement of public funds, illicit enrichment, corruption, laziness in performing administrative tasks and more; the actions, then, should be subject to criminal and administrative penalties. During the four years of the revolution, several people in public administration, politics and the business community were brought before the tribunal for the mismanagement of public funds. Bamouni (1986) indicates that one of the first acts of the revolution – before even the beginning stages of social transformation outlined by the revolutionary political line – was to 'settle a twenty-three year old dispute with crooked politicians who had appropriated [communal or state] properties' (ibid.: 109).[8]

These values that Thomas Sankara had held up for the Burkinabè disappeared with him. Cases of corruption and embezzlement became the norm: the 'business' of corruption increased and the struggle for development dissipated because of the behaviour of political leaders. Sanctions became rare and Sankara's spirit of sacrifice disappeared from public leadership.

Unlike Sankara, Compaoré put in place a system of governance in which he was wilfully blind to the mismanagement of public affairs. He let family members invest in significant areas of social life: economics and politics especially. Mathias Ollo Kambou, a member of the Balai Citoyen national coordination of movement, explained:

> Since 1987, we saw the emergence of another political class; we have seen political and institutional leaders that monopolise wealth [and] the country's land. This contrasts with Sankara's way of seeing. For Sankara, the ruler must be an example to people at all levels, there must be honesty, an example of integrity, an example of accountability.
>
> (Mathias Ollo Kambou, interview with author, 14 October 2016)

Indeed, for the members of Balai Citoyen, reference to Sankara was important given that he was such an important figure of the political landscape of Burkina Faso.

BALAI CITOYEN AND *BURKINDLUM*

Members of Balai Citoyen were outraged to see the values of dignity and integrity erode so dangerously after Sankara's assassination. In the movement's manifesto, they denounced the efflorescence of corruption and the development of a culture of impunity as one axis of their struggle. The movement's critical points of struggle and mobilisation include the fight against mismanagement, the fight against cronyism in public promotions and the struggle for access to basic social services. According to this logic, the movement has opposed the promotion of all those considered reactionary and has worked to facilitate the teaching of the people in the philosophy of *burkindlum*. In the formation of the first government after the fall of Blaise Compaoré, Balai Citoyen mobilised against the nomination of Adama Sagnon because he was considered to have worked to prevent justice in the case of Norbert Zongo. They also mobilised for the dismissal of the former Minister of Infrastructure, Moumouni Djigemdé, who was accused of mismanaging public funds.

Fraternity is an important feature in the philosophy of *burkindlum*. Members are committed to promoting this value everyday through two important means: participation in the work of mutual interest and cooperation with various social and professional groups. One member of the Cibal Club explained,

> [We] participate in all aspects of community life: we cleaned schools, health centres, we cleaned the markets in neighbourhoods [and] we cleaned cemeteries.

We donated to vulnerable persons in health centres. We donated blood. We
donated bins to participate in the beautification of people's living environment.
(Member of Cibal Club, interview with author, October 2016)

These activities are initiated in the various clubs and in national and regional
coordination to achieve a cohesion of people working together. For these
efforts, Balai Citoyen was considered to be a major force in the success of
the struggle for development. Football matches between the activists of
the movement and young neighbourhoods are organised. One of the most
symbolic acts of cooperation – and one that is also directly a reflection
of the group's selection of Sankara as inspiration for course of action – is
the association between personal defence and security forces. Military and
paramilitary bodies are seen as only components of society and, therefore,
Balai Citoyen discourages that civilians fear of the military. Observing
the popular uprising of October 2014 and gathering first-hand accounts
through interviews with leaders of the movement reveals the group's
acknowledgement of the need for proximity with defence and security forces
as a form of protection. Idrissa Barry, communications manager and member
of the national coordination of Balai Citoyen, said:

We wanted to break the walls between civilian youth and young soldiers – this is
the spirit of Sankara. This is what Sankara did in Pô and it marked the inhabitants
of the city [back then]. When there was work, when there were problems in the
city, the soldiers became involved and this created a symbiosis. We found these
values [of cooperation] with the young policemen, young police officers, young
soldiers [and] we have stock in them and our speech is the same. We ask people
not to insult them during the marches because they are our brothers. We changed
paradigms through this process. During the struggles of the collective – when we
went to the camps – we booed them, we whistled at them ... but with the steps
we've taken since 2013, when we went to the headquarters of the armed military,
we applauded the police that were lining the steps. [We] applaud[ed] to say that
we are together. We asked people not to attack the police and when we look at the
popular uprising [and] there were few [instances] of violence against them.
(Idrissa Barry, interview with author, 19 September 2016)

Using this logic, Balai Citoyen also initiated reforestation projects in the
enclosures belonging to the police, gendarmerie and army. It supports the
elements of the defense and security forces that ensure safety on the roads.
Balai Citoyen conducted these activities because they are convinced that the
development, which Sankara believed in so deeply, is possible only if the various
sections of the population hold hands.

This spirit of sacrifice is in the image of Sankara. To forgo his rightful salary
as President, Sankara worked fully to improve his country by changing the

living conditions of the people. Jaffré explains, 'for him, the revolution [was] first [and foremost to] work for the good of the people and the improvement of living conditions' (Jaffré 1997: 183). President Sankara was a leader who led by example and his example has since been held up and emulated, including by members of Balai Citoyen.

DEVELOPMENT THROUGH PERSONAL ACTION

Sankara thought that people were responsible for their own destiny in the struggle for change. He exhorted the people to fight for their own good: 'people of Burkina Faso, rise up as one ... to defend your violated dignity and snatch your freedom'. In his political orientation speech, delivered on 2 October 1983 (in which he outlined the revolution), he declared that the most obvious demonstration of the truth was when people stand up to imperialism and when the social forces allied to make imperialism tremble.

This feature of Sankara's political philosophy was turned into a practice within Balai Citoyen, whose approach demands civic education and the awakening of political consciousness to bring people together in the fight for democracy. This focus on consciousness is also reflected in Article 3 of the Statute of the Balai Citoyen, which aims 'to make effective the responsible and conscious involvement of the population in the management of public affairs'. Such involvement can only be achieved if people are aware of their responsibilities and duties in national governance. Thus, the movement is part of a desire to educate the population so that the people themselves will address the political, economic and developmental concerns of the country. This is what Canivez (1995) calls 'citizen education'. In the logic of Canivez, the citizen must be able to think, to go beyond the expression of his purely particular interests, to reach a universal point of view and to thus address problems by considering the interest of the community as a whole (ibid.: 155). This is the reason why activities such as awareness caravans, video projections of political and economic debates as well as awareness-raising musical concerts are frequently organised by the movement. Through such processes, Balai Citoyen wants to help make people understand that it is up to them to fight for their happiness. Balai Citoyen wants to assist in the creation of conditions that allow people to stand up and stand as one to bring about significant political and social change.

It is for the Balai Citoyen to get people to rely on themselves as Sankara always wished. Having accepted this logic of Thomas Sankara, the framework of Bali Citoyen is one in which the organisation insists on its own agency and actions for its activities. For most of the activities implemented, funding is provided by members of the movement through contributions in goods or cash. Through observing the organisation and conducting interviews with the militants and leaders, it seems that for each of the organisation's activities a budget is proposed and everyone is asked to contribute in the area in which s/he is competent. Idrissa Barry explained:

> When we have activities, we do the budget and we ask for input from all of us, including our key people. Key people are people of a certain level, people who have responsibilities in public or private administration who have a [access to different] means. We minimise financial contributions. For activities, each of us brings what we have. If I have a video projector, I bring it; Sams'K can give the sound system; Smockey can give a podium or a generator. We work like this and it minimises costs.
>
> (Idrissa Barry, interview with author, May 2016)

This mode of operation seeks to maintain the independence of the group through small steps that do not overwhelm the members; this approach does not mean that the group dictates slogans or firmly held positions on problems in society. Rather, it is a way for the movement to remind its members that commitment is a matter of conviction and sacrifice and, importantly echoing Sankara, that everything begins with the mobilisation of oneself. One of the strongest slogans of the revolutionary period was 'rely on ourselves'. For Balai Citoyen, mobilising the resources collectively is the first step in realising this aspiration of the Revolution.

Balai Citoyen has a network of intellectuals from various scientific disciplines that it also mobilises for the animation of conferences and public projects. Among the partners, there are private individuals who can also contribute to the realisation of activities without waiting for counterparts. The broadcast of biographical films on the life of Thomas Sankara and the use of awareness-raising films is a favoured method of public engagement. Indeed, many artists and producers involved in Semfilms Burkina, a film association that has the objective of defending and promoting human rights and freedom of expression, are members or sympathisers of the movement.[9] In its way, the movement organises activities with partners that share interests in specific areas of public life, including social justice and human rights. With the support of actors like Diakonia,[10] Independent National Electoral Commission (CENI), Oxfam, Balai Citoyen has carried out numerous awareness-raising activities on the need to participate in elections and even agricultural challenges. Because many journalists and media officials are members of Balai Citoyen, the movement has access to media outlets and has achieved a public profile in Burkina Faso.

A TWO-PRONGED APPROACH TO JUSTICE FOR SANKARA

Within Balai Citoyen, one particular idiom from Thomas Sankara has been retained and repeated over and over during my conversations with leaders and militants: I want people to remember me as a man who has fought for my nation. For this wish to be realised, the 'heirs' of Sankara are committed to celebrating his actions and preserving his memory. Sankara's 'heirs' do not want the assassination of the 'father of the Revolution' to be a pretext for forgetting what he did for Burkina Faso (see Chapter 20, this volume). The Cibal seek to make death the beginning of immortality, much like the French Revolutionary Robespierre thought.

Working against forgetting Sankara's important role in Burkina Faso, members of Balai Citoyen are committed to building a memorial in his honour. This memorial will be a place of remembrance and recollection in which the history of Sankara will be exposed: his ideologies, his discourses, his material possessions, his approaches, his acts, his singularity, his relations with populations, his books that have consecrated his life throughout the world and so on. For the members of the movement, this is the best way to do justice to and honour the 'father of the Revolution'. This memorial will preserve Sankara's memory and will show who Sankara the person and Sankara the President was and what he did – this will be for the benefit of future generations and will have an international appeal. Karim Sama (Sams'K le Jah), a member of the national coordination, explained:

> In the case of Sankara, justice must be done at two levels: [the first is] a moral justice that will materialise in the rehabilitation of Sankara in the minds of the people. The other justice is criminal. Tomorrow in justice, we condemn the guilty for the assassination of Sankara, [but] is that enough for us? No, that's not enough. There is another aspect of justice that is the rehabilitation of the man and his ideals through a memorial where we can gather testimonies to build up youth, where we can group books that young people can consult [and] can group the objects that Sankara used. I think that the greatest justice that can be done in Sankara is that first.
>
> (Karim Sama, interview with author, 13 October 2016)

Karim Sama argued that a memorial of this sort is the best way to communicate Sankara's life and legacy for young people. Sankara wished that we keep of him the image of a person who led a useful life for all. For members of Balai Citoyen, this cannot be done without the memorial. Toward these ends, members of the movement returned individually to the organising committee for the launch of this memorial. Considering the erection of the memorial as a moral duty, the militants of Balai Citoyen have committed themselves to its realisation.

For them, the memorial has a double objective: to perpetuate the ideals of Sankara on the one hand and, on the other hand, to bring about a sort of psychological justice. For those working toward the memorial, the museum itself will create an additional pressure for justice for Sankara. The memorial will be a place of memory that can also encourage the search for truth. In the struggle for the memorialisation of Sankara's life and ideals, the choice of places and dates was highly important as there was a desire to stay true to key moments in his own political life. Thus, the memorial was launched on 2 October 2016, the date of Sankara's political orientation speech and will be built within the Council of the Agreement, which is where Sankara had an office and also were he was assassinated. Abdul Salam Kaboré, a former companion of Thomas Sankara, said:

> We believe that the Council of the Agreement is the best place for the memorial. On 4 August 1983, we moved to the Council. Sankara had a table and an office in the Council, where he always gathered his close collaborators for important decisions. The Council [was] an important place in the life of the Revolution and [in] Sankara['s life as well]. For all these reasons, the Council is the most appropriate place to erect the memorial.
>
> (Abdul Salam Kaboré, interview with author, October 15, 2016)

The memorial will be an important milestone in achieving justice for Sankara and will stand in honour of his life and legacy in Burkina Faso. The struggle for justice for his assassination continues (see Afterword, this volume).

CONCLUSION

Thomas Sankara was an exceptional man who was remarkable for seeking positive change in many areas of social life: economic relations, the education of the population, the management of public goods, the transformation of the social relations between men and women and more. For Balai Citoyen, Sankara was an undisputed example of a positive force in the political scene. This is why, thirty years after his death, he continues to be popular among African youth. For Balai Citoyen, reference is so often made to him, particularly in regards to restoring the principles and philosophies of *burklindlum* to public life, which deteriorated after Blaise Compaoré's twenty-seven years as president. The logic of the movement is not only a logic of protest, but also one of recognition of the values elevated by Sankara and which have been forgotten in recent years. The members of Balai Citoyen seek, through citizen education, to sweep the society clean of the defects of greed, misappropriation and corruption in politics.

The birth of the Balai Citoyen movement was considered by its actors as the realisation of a prophecy stated originally by Thomas Sankara: 'To kill Sankara today, tomorrow there will be thousands of Sankaras'. Members of the movement regard themselves as 'Sankara's heirs' and work to actualise the ideals of Sankara in public governance. Thus, they seek to give a revitalised human face to public management inspired by Thomas Sankara's political revolution. They want a public governance in which the governors leave the 'four prisons' in the meaning of Olivier de Sardan (2016) and invest themselves in the development of the country. Members of Balai Citoyen are invested in the development of the country through a grassroots figuration of power.

They want to set an example like Thomas Sankara by putting themselves at the forefront of the struggles. This chapter has shown that there have been internal limitations and struggles within the movement (particularly in regards to maintaining its autonomy from political parties). Moreover, some aspects of Sankara's life are difficult to replicate today. Social change and shifts in the political, technological and ideological contexts have rendered inapplicable certain wishes articulated by Sankara. Thus, while at the collective level, the movement is largely inspired by Sankara, at the individual level, it sometimes seems almost impossible to do as he did. The leaders of the movement remind members and sympathisers that they should make efforts to go in the direction of Sankara. Having built its popularity on reference to the ideals of Sankara, Balai Citoyen is today continuing this momentum for progressive social change and for sweeping out corruption, greed and misappropriation.

NOTES

1 Translated from French by Seydou Drabo, a doctoral Candidate at University of Oslo.
2 'Stakeholders' here refers to people who, because of their position in society, cannot commit publicly, but bring their support in other ways to the movement.
3 I conducted individual interviews with movement leaders and held focus groups with members of Cibal Clubs in Ouagadougou. I conducted participant observation during activities of national and regional coordination in Ouagadougou as well as during activities of different Cibal Clubs.
4 The full interview is available at www.youtube.com/watch?v=PNjGH7x8fFE&t=46s (accessed 10 August 2016).
5 This passage was translated from French by Amber Murrey (all faults in translation and meaning are her own).
6 In-text translation by Amber Murrey.
7 In-text translation by Amber Murrey.
8 In-text translation by Amber Murrey.
9 The association also has a film collection and a webtélé (a website where video can be streamed) dedicated to human rights. Access their website at: http://www.semfilms. org.
10 A Swedish humanitarian organisation working for an equitable and sustainable world without poverty.

240 I *Zakaria Soré*

REFERENCES

Bamouni, B. P. (1986) *Burkina Faso: Processus de la Révolution*. Paris: L'Harmattan.

Canivez, P. (1995) *Éduquer le citoyen*. Paris: Hatier.

Jaffré, B. (1997) *Biographie de Thomas Sankara: La patrie ou la mort*... Paris: L'Harmattan.

NetAfrique (2014) Meeting du MPP à Bobo: La Mise au Point du Balai Citoyen. Retrieved on 13 October 2016 from http://netafrique.net/meeting-du-mpp-a-bobo-la-mise-au-point-du-balai-citoyen.

Norris, P. (2002) *Democratic Phoenix: Reinventing Political Activism*. Cambridge: Cambridge University Press.

Olivier de Sardan, J. P. (2016) Niger: Les quatre prisons du pouvoir. Retrieved on 13 June 2016 from www.marianne.net/debattons/tribunes/niger-les-quatre-prisons-du-pouvoir.

Orfali, B. (2011) *L'adhésion: militer, s'engager, rêver*. Brussels: De Boeck.

Ouédraogo, N. B. (2014) *Droit, Démocratie et Développement en Afrique. Un parfum de Jasmin souffle sur le Burkina Faso*. Paris: L'Harmattan.

CHAPTER 16

La Santé Avant Tout
Health before Everything
T. D. Harper-Shipman

While revolutionaries as individuals can be murdered,
you cannot kill ideas.
Thomas Sankara, 'A Tribute to Che Guevara', 8 October 1987

The current international development paradigm is one predicated on notions of country ownership of development – a country's ability to manage its own development policies and strategies, and co-ordinate development stakeholders. The need for country ownership, heretofore ownership, grows out of criticisms over the limited progress gained under structural adjustments, the World Bank and International Monetary Fund (IMF) proposed country ownership of development as the answer to past and future development quagmires (Smith 2006; Pender 2001). In 2005, the rest of the international community of bilateral and multilateral donors co-signed and further entrenched the principle of ownership as the pinnacle of development with the Paris Declaration on Aid Effectiveness. The dominant document that international donors and institutions use to define articulate ownership is aptly titled, Poverty Reduction Strategy Papers (PRSPs). Consequently, ownership ostensibly marks a paradigmatic shift in the practices and expectations surrounding donor-recipient relations and development in the global South. The ownership principle, by allowing for a more comprehensive and country-specific approach to development, should lead to more quantifiable indicators of progress in aid-dependent countries (Booth 2012; Faust 2010). In essence, the current development paradigm depends heavily on this notion of country ownership to legitimate contemporary development interventions on the part of international donors into countries in the global South. *Prima facie*, this version of ownership appears to illustrate a fundamental shift in the historical power dynamics that have long characterised foreign aid and development in the global South, and especially Africa. However, the Burkinabè experience with ownership in the health sector illustrates the continuities and clandestine ways in which the concept plays out.

There are a plethora of actors contributing to the Burkinabè health system: faith-based organisations, nongovernmental organisations, international nongovernment organisations, community based organisations, and associations, just to name a few. Under the ownership paradigm, these actors should participate in elaborating the sector-wide strategy for the health sector and aid government in implementing the projects and programmes tied to national health policies. With a decentralised health system based on the Bamako Initiative, local actors are heavily incorporated into the health framework; but whether or not they in fact exercise power or have autonomy is an altogether different question.

The data in this chapter come from fieldwork that I conducted in Burkina Faso from June until August of 2015. While in Burkina Faso, I interviewed thirty-eight development stakeholders working primarily in the health sector. I focused exclusively on government officials in the Ministry of Health, Ministry of Finance and Economics, donor organisations including the World Bank, US Agency for International Development (USAID), the United States Peace Corps, the United Nations Population Funds (UNFPA), and civil society associations. The interviews took place in Ouagadougou, Koudougou, and Tenkodogo. I also draw from a range of government and donor policy documents and participant observations in Burkina Faso.

I argue that with respect to strategies for health development, and development in general, what remains of Thomas Sankara is the understanding of what it means to 'own' development. This rendering runs contrary to the dominant model of country ownership that comes from international donors, which I argue leads to more underdevelopment and donor dependency in Burkina. Where Sankara's version of ownership drew from cultural contexts, the donor model seeks to make culture conform to its version of health development.

SANKARA'S DEVELOPMENT

The notion that Burkina is a resource-poor country remains a haunting ghost of the colonial era. Donors, civil society, and public servants all mentioned how Burkina is lacking resources as an explanation for the country's dependence on foreign aid. This was not always the prevailing sentiment. Sankara's approach to development constitutes an alternative to the current neoliberal model of development prevailing in Burkina. His model rejected the teleological ends of development that the West espoused in favour of more culturally specific renderings of development. By being culturally specific, Sankara's model involved operating within the realm of Burkina's cultural, agricultural, and economic resources. In this way, the Burkinabè revolution was an attempt to rupture epistemologically and ontologically from Western notions of progress. Indeed, I am particularly interested in the ways in which Sankara's ownership of development challenges neoliberalism as well as how some of his philosophies linger in contemporary Burkinabè understandings of development ownership, particularly in public health.

Sankara promoted a national identity of self-reliance and social solidarity and with it, an anti-charity sentiment across the social and political sectors (Sankara 1985; Martin 1987). This is not to suggest that the country was not receiving external aid during this period. However, aid from international donors only targeted projects (Harsch 2013; Wilkins 1989). This very targeted aid was a consequence of both Sankara's development philosophy being one of self-reliance and dominant donor opposition to these same philosophies. For example, once France, the US, the World Bank, and other major international donors became aware of Sankara's anti-charity, anti-debt, anti-structural adjustments, and anti-neo-imperialist politics, these donors became anti-Thomas Sankara. Consequently, France and the World Bank ceased offering budgetary support to the Burkinabè government during Sankara's tenure (Gabas, Faure and Sindzingre 1997). Where donors did remain present, the Sankara government created a consultation table that required donors to sit down and work with the Burkinabè government around a model of development that allowed the people to determine what development was and how to bring it to fruition (Harsch 2013; Zagré 1994).

Sankara's self-reliance model meant that the national economy would operate based on domestic interests. The needs of subsistence farmers and rural communities would take precedence over exports that served international interests (Zagré 1994). The government departed from a top-down approach in allocating resources and focused instead on the needs of people and institutions at the grassroots level. To this end, the government relied on social mobilisation and community self-help projects to promote development. These community self-help projects were essential to maintaining the Sankara model of development during periods of economic hardship (from 1983 to 1984, in particular). A staunch anti-neoliberal, Sankara refused to accept the neoliberal structural adjustment packages that the World Bank and IMF were demanding of other indebted nations throughout the 1980s. In the context of my own fieldwork, while having a conversation with an older Burkinabè man about the recent political uprisings of the early 2000s, as with most political conversations in Burkina he began to talk about his time in the military under Sankara. More specifically, he recounted how opposed Sankara was to structural adjustment. The man recalled that during one of his speeches to the military, Sankara told the soldiers never to accept the structural adjustment packages that the World Bank and IMF were imposing across the rest of the continent. Sankara told the soldiers that accepting SAPS would be akin to selling out your family so that only a few members could eat. Instead, he advocated for a collective tightening of belts. Everyone, he proposed, should 'tighten their belts' until the period of economic hardship had passed because once the country accepts the SAPs, it can never pull out. As we spoke, the old man went on to lament how Burkina sits today exactly where Sankara predicted it would. As soon as former president Blaise Compaore took office after Sankara's death, one of the first things he did was implement World Bank and IMF structural adjustment policy reforms (see Chapter 7, this volume).

In unpacking the narrative that the older gentleman gave, one dominant theme of Sankara's development approach is evident: the country must develop using the resources at its disposal. In asking that Burkinabè make do with the resources that the country had available, Sankara was imposing a different type of adjustment programme, distinct from the type that spread hardship across all groups (Savadogo and Wetta 1991). In relying primarily on domestic resources, the government was still able to spend more on the health and the social sectors than in previous years (Harsch 2013). Although the country was experiencing challenging economic conditions during this time period, the Sankara government was still able to make noticeable changes in the public health sector. By 1986, the government built 7,460 primary health posts (almost one per village) throughout the country (Harsch 2014). Public health spending also increased by 27 per cent between 1983 and 1987 (Savadogo and Wetta 1991: 60). Furthermore, 2.5 million children received vaccinations (Smith 2015). Under Sankara, Burkina Faso also became the first country to acknowledge the HIV/AIDS epidemic (Falola and Heaton 2007).

After Sankara's death in 1987, the country implemented a host of reforms to the economy and health sector. Scholars have linked the macroeconomic reforms under World Bank and IMF-instituted Structural Adjustment Programmes (SAPs) to the stagnant progress in public health sector (Kanji 1989; Ridde 2011; Konadu-Agyemang 2000; Sahn and Bernier 1995). Because of the currency devaluation, drug prices became too exorbitant for the average Burkinabè to afford. After the currency devaluation, drug prices increased by 76 per cent and medication represented about 80 per cent of the cost for visiting health professionals (Haddad et al. 2006). Because of the required liberalisation, fees for consultation increased between 100 and 150 per cent, while fees for delivering a baby increased by 20–30 per cent (ibid.). After these economic reforms and their impact on the health sector, health care in Burkina Faso became more expensive than in neighbouring countries like Mali and Côte d'Ivoire (Bodart et al. 2001). The population remained generally dissatisfied with health services and the inefficient allocation of resources. These lingering lacunae from the BI implementation and SAPs is attributed to donors and NGOs in the health sector promoting an overemphasis on efficiencies and little focus on equity in health (Ridde 2008).[1]

THE ANTI-OWNERSHIP MODEL

Under the neoliberal model, ownership operates through a series of national policy documents that articulate the country's development strategy. The Plan National de Développement Sanitaire (PNDS) is the national strategy that articulates the national plan for developing the health sector in accordance with the priorities outlined in the Programme National d'Assurance Qualité en Santé (PNS), which corresponds with the country's larger economic development objectives in La stratégie de croissance accélérée et de développement durable (SCADD) – the Burkina's variant of the PRSPs. These documents do not remain stagnant at the national level. In fact, government and donor institutions alike use local level organisations to carry out the objectives by financing the relevant activities under the Programme d'Appui au Développement Sanitaire (PADS). Civil society members play a critical role in implementing the policies and programmes tied to either the national health strategy or to donor health programmes and projects that circumvent that government's strategy. For example, in order to implement the PADS and the PNDS, donors and government fund large NGOs. The NGOs, in turn, will find local associations throughout a particular region in order to implement the different activities and sensitise the population based on the articulated directives from the PADS. These community-based organisations are responsible for working with a certain number of villages and their agents de santé (health promoters) to carry out grassroots health promotion in the village. In this way, civil society members become essential for implementing the health policies created under the ownership model, in a top-down fashion. These actors reflect the ways in which ownership is not an innocuous concept that state actors and donors employ with little consequence. Instead, these actors breathe life into the concept through their implementation of PADS and other national health strategies produced under the ownership framework. I was able to experience this process first hand in Tenkodogo.

While in Tenkodogo, I was able to participate in a meeting hosted by the NGO Renforcement de Capacités (RENCAP), which funds ten different associations working in the Tenkodogo district. The PADS is composed of multiple targets based on the PNDS. Donors pay the NGO, who pays the associations, who pay the village agents, to implement the related programme. Donors include the *panier commun* (community basket), which is a compilation of various donors, the World Bank, UNFPA, DBC, and Gavi vaccinations. The meeting I attended in July 2015 functioned to gather ground-level data from the various associations with respect to their implementation of key activities. At the meeting, representatives from the ten different associations presented their reports from the previous trimester of activities to the NGO representatives. The NGO then gathered the data for a larger report to transmit to the donors and government funding the different strategic activities. There were four major strategic activities that donors funded: improving governance and leadership in health; reinforcing communication for changing behaviour; improving the delivery of health service and promoting health and the fight against diseases.

The tone and orientation of the meeting was illustrative of the impact that donor priorities and knowledge structures have in dictating how policies are executed and subsequently turned in to reports that suggest progress in development. The number of community awareness-raising activities or sensibilisations that each association carried out, along with whether or not they were successful in completing the tasks assigned, weighed heavily in whether the NGO thought the associations would continue to receive funding. In another instance, the head of the NGO at the helm of the consultation questioned how all of the associations could have 100 per cent completion of all of the assigned activities; he in turn suggested that he would corroborate reports with the various CSPSs. The general tone was not one of full participation in the decision-making process with respect to the health activities or some 'partnership' between these local associations and the more politically endowed NGO, donors, and the state. Rather, it appeared as if the associations were to function mainly as the sensibilising mechanisms for the larger health policies that came from the capital, Ouagadougou. Not to mention, much of their data and motivation for the activities seemed purely financial. Many of the members noted in their interviews how their organisation could not continue functioning without the funds from the PADS. As one of the association members stated:

> When financing falls, it's not something to play with. They tell you, look, you respect our clause. We want to intervene in Tenkodogo's health district. And look, we are waiting for these, these, and these results. So, it's the donors who have the last word. Us, we do nothing but execute their desires.[2]
>
> (anonymous interview with author in Tenkodogo, 29 July 2015)

Ownership of development in the Burkinabè contexts operates to further entrench the problematic elements of the development enterprise. More specifically, the donor version of ownership attempts to keep states locked into a neoliberal development paradigm through the act of sensibilisation at various levels. Despite donors contending that ownership is evident where governments are financing the majority budget for development, this does not mean that donors do not see a continued need for their presence in Burkina's health sector. Instead, donors are moving to position themselves as technical and epistemic sources of power. By promoting their contribution as less financial and more knowledge-based under this framework of development partners, donors have the potential to become permanent advisors on development without the financial burden. This manoeuvre places the responsibility for failed health policies on the state and civil society, while absolving donors of any direct responsibility.

CREATING THE UNDERDEVELOPED

The ownership paradigm situates poverty reduction and development as key problems that the international community and domestic actors in 'developing' nations must address. The belief in the country's struggle or incapacity to develop without donor assistance is also evident in its PRSP and PNDS. Much of the belief that countries like Burkina remain works in progress, with respect to development, is also evident in the explicit aims of MDGs. By investing in this model, development's underlying process of creating the underdeveloped does not cease. Instead, it is further entrenched in national actors' imaginaries.

At the state level, the Burkinabè government has, in fact, tangibly bought into the notion that the country is underdeveloped or developing by producing PRSPs and using them as a measure of ownership. With this process comes the reinforcement of being underdeveloped in popular consciousness as well. One government official noted, 'Burkina is an underdeveloped country. So when one speaks of development, get out of being underdeveloped. It's to be totally independent. Actually, we depend a lot on outside aid' (anonymous interview with author in Koudougou, 1 July 2015). No government official would disagree with this statement. In fact, these sentiments resurfaced at the MOFE and MoH alike, government officials describing Burkina Faso as 'un pays pauvre' (a poor country) or 'un pays sous-développé' (an underdeveloped country).

Despite the government's efforts to remediate problems such as high infant and maternal mortality, decreasing the number of fatal malaria cases, and increasing the number of CSPSs, Burkina still remains unable to achieve MDGs and satisfy the global agenda for development in health (Ministry of State for Planning, Land Use and Community Development, and United Nation System in the Burkina Faso 2012). In fact, using the measurements provided by the UN, over 80 per cent of low-income African countries were off track for meeting the 4th and 5th Millennium Development Goals (on reducing mortality in children under five years old and improving maternal health), although they made significant progress in these areas (Cohendet et al. 2014).

Civil society actors were also keen to point out how poor and underdeveloped Burkina is. Health workers in the different associations articulated a very similar sentiment to that voiced by government officials: 'We can't actually say that Burkina is actually developing. But, there are efforts being made at least towards development' (anonymous interview with author in Tenkodogo, 3 August 2015). Beyond just the actors working directly with civil society organisations, my personal encounters with Burkinabé also reflected this understanding of Burkina as poor and not having enough resources to develop in isolation. On several occasions, my status as an American solicited request for money and help with visas to the US because 'All Americans are rich and the Burkinabè are poor'. This persistent reference to Burkina not as 'developing' or 'developed' but 'underdeveloped' speaks to the critiques that scholars like Gustavo Sachs (1992) and Sylvia Wynters (1996) have of the development industry. There are psychological and tangible consequences for the underdeveloped subject. Situating oneself on a teleological spectrum of progress predicated on the unique histories of only a handful of the world's population requires that one perpetuate and reify the myth of development. Oddly enough, the most pervasive donors (i.e. the World Bank and USAID) in Burkina's health sector were also the ones to note that the ways in which one defines development are in some ways based on a Eurocentric model and international norms.[3] Nevertheless, the feelings of being underdeveloped and too poor to develop without donors percolate from the government level to the level of society.

INDISPENSABLE DONORS

The above solutions for resolving Burkina's health problems under the ownership model lead to the indispensable donor. For many of the state and local stakeholders working in the health sector, donors are essential for maintaining Burkina's health system. Government officials were very clear that the Burkinabè government elaborates its own health development strategies in collaboration with other stakeholders (both local and international). Again, this exemplified ownership for many of the respondents in the MOFE and MOS. However, they also made it very clear that developing and executing the strategies would be especially difficult without donors' financial and technical assistance (anonymous interview with author in Ouagadougou, 22 July 2015).

For example, nurses at the CSPS in Koudougou were vocal about the role that they think donors play in keeping the health system a float: 'It's donors that come and relieve so much of the Burkinabè population' (anonymous interview with author in Koudougou, 16 July 2015,). More often than not, the health workers suggested that donor influence and presence was not only positive but essential for providing subsidised medicines and services to the Burkinabè population. The building and aesthetics of secteur cinq (sector 5), a typical CSPS, were by no means welcoming. Parts of the ceiling were rotted out. All of the walls were covered with more dirt than paint. The floors, cracked slabs of cement, were equally layered in dirt. Each wall displayed health propaganda that bore the mark of an international donor. One sign stated, 'You want your wife to help you work? Support her in choosing a contraceptive' paid for by USAID. Each of the consultation rooms contained boxes of Plumpy Nut and sacks of cereal from World Food Programme, staples of food relief. Given the amount of tangible goods the nurses at the CSPS receive from donors and the ubiquitous presence of donor-sponsored health fliers, it is no wonder they feel that donors maintain the health system.

Associations at the local level find that their work would be especially difficult to carry out without donor support. As the director of one association noted, 'We are in a system where financing is necessary. One needs financing to be able to function' (anonymous interview with author in Tenkodogo, 27 July 2015). Or, as another member of a different association stated, 'Today, things evolve with money' (anonymous interview with author in Tenkodogo, 28 July 2015). This sense of financial necessity guides much of the reverence for donors and their contributions to the health sector. It also leaves the majority of the organisations unable to say that they are autonomous. As a number of workers in grassroots health promotion organisations commented in interviews, many of their important health activities depend on donor funding to continue. This is also not particular to just the health sector. The majority of community-based associations and NGOs in Burkina depend on donors to finance not only their activities, but also their over-head costs (Engberg-Pedersen 2002). Such financial dependence on donors and the state calls into question whether these organisations fall into the traditional understanding of civil society. At the same time, they demonstrate how these groups are brought directly into the ownership paradigm to maintain it, not subvert it.

LEGACIES OF SANKARA

What remains of Thomas Sankara in the Burkinabè health sector is an alternative understanding of what it means for a country to 'own' its development. Burkinabè stakeholders in the health sector relate ownership to an understanding of the role that individuals within the community have in bringing about development at the country level: 'Development should be a problem or a question for everyone. And everyone should involve himself or herself so that the state can develop. It's not a problem for only government leaders, but all citizens involve themselves so that we can achieve development' (anonymous interview with author in Ouagadougou, 3 August 2015). These sentiments reflect the dominant understanding of development amongst members of civil society. 'Ownership of development means that each one of us has development in mind. He shouldn't wait for someone elsewhere to come to tell you; you must do it this way in order to be developed. That's not a development that is just for you personally' (anonymous interview with author, Tenkodogo, 28 July 2015). For many Burkinabès, notions of ownership are thus shaped both by the need to understand the policy itself and by a felt sense of responsibility for implementing it.

There is a direct lineage between Sankara's ownership and the one that the Burkinabè harbour today. What the revolution attempted to instil in the population was a sense of responsibility and involvement in the direction of the country. This is especially pertinent with respect to health development. For example, at the behest of donors like the World Bank, Bill and Melinda Gates Foundation, USAID, and UKAID, the Burkinabe government is implementing aggressive family planning policies to address a purported population crisis (Burkina Faso Ministry of Health n.d.). And despite using local associations to sensibilise Burkinabè men and women to increase their consumption of modern contraception, consumption of modern contraception methods remains low in Burkina (ibid.). The reason for low prevalence of modern contraception is often attributed to their being a dearth of understanding about the importance of family planning and cultural impediments (World Bank 1993; Burkina Faso Ministry of Health n.d.). At this point, culture becomes an obstacle to progress, which begs the question, how then can this type of development be context-specific? The Sankara administration, on the other hand, although sceptical of the Malthusian arguments surrounding family planning, did promote women's control of their own reproductive health (Sankara 1985). Contraceptives were made available but not imposed on Burkinabè women. Through examining the influence that Sankara's ownership has over the Burkinabè today, low prevalence of family planning, may demonstrate a level of agency not allotted Burkinabè men and women under the neoliberal ownership paradigm.

Nevertheless, the dominant findings from my time examining ownership in Burkina's health sectors indicate the country now sits politically and economically where Sankara had feared. The country is operating under a model of ownership that gives legitimacy to Western control and intervention under the guise of development. This neoliberal model of development also acts to perpetuate the 'underdeveloped' Burkinabè. These findings are the antithesis of the goals of the Burkinabè revolution. Along with the promotion of sharing hardship across the different groups, the revolutionary model of adjustment also pushed Burkinabè to buy locally. In a conversation on the history of imperialism in Burkina that I had with a young man who was not yet born during Sankara's time in office, his words were again marked by invocations of the revolutionary spirit of Sankara. The young man recalled Sankara's words that the African was so busy trying to fight the imperialists but that he should look down at his plate: imperialism was sitting on the plates as he consumed rice and other imported foods from Western countries, despite producing these same foods in his own country. Stories such as these serve the dual purpose of illustrating the impactful legacy that Sankara left in Burkina, as well as the alternative path of development that Burkina was in the process of undertaking during Sankara's short time in office. These narratives also demonstrate how the revolution was not merely political or economic, but it was also mental. Sankara thoroughly understood how colonialism was a process that could not take hold in any other sphere if it did not first capture the heart and mind. To this end, as Ngugi Wa Thiong'o (1994) once noted, there is need for a decolonisation of the mind for the rest of the revolution to take hold.

CONCLUSION

In many respects, the story of ownership in Burkina is the narrative struggle and sacrifice for the chimera of development. The World Bank, IMF and international community writ large proposed ownership of development as the catholicon for poverty reduction and all around progress, when, in fact, it proves to be one more nostrum that serves only to further entrench development in its neoliberal state.

Donors continue to assess levels of ownership (whether at the locus of government institutions, CSOs or community level) based on indicators of economic development. And, although donors are very influential in the health sector (so much so, many respondents in my interviews believed that the health system would collapse without donors), the responsibility for failed health policies, projects and programmes falls squarely on the government's shoulders. The donor version of ownership is grounded in the assumption that there are no alternative approaches to, or understandings of health and progress that emanate from Burkinabès themselves. A secondary assumption is that Burkina will attain a certain level of socio-economic progress not based on the resources that the country has at its disposal but commensurate with the level of outside support it receives. Based on this model, any substantial progress will remain elusive; superficial success will come at the expense of alternative knowledge/ approaches to development.

As bleak as this assessment may sound, it exists within a historical context that adds necessary layers to l'appropriation de développement in Burkina. The ways in which government and CSO stakeholders define ownership differ drastically from the donor/international community's conceptualisation, because local perceptions of ownership have been significantly shaped by the legacy of Thomas Sankara. Evident in the recent political uprisings across the country and the intimate political conversations I had in interviews conducted behind courtyard walls are the lingering spirit of Sankara's revolutionary approach to development in Burkina. Thus, I propose Sankara's model as an example of an alternative to the current ownership paradigm – an alternative derived from Burkina's cultural history. Although many Burkinabè stakeholders are invested in, and believe in, the telos of Western-style development, they are not blind to the power and influence that donors wield over the process. In fact, their frank admission of this fact echoes Sankara's own assessment of development. However, these contemporary stakeholders feel that bending to the will of the international community and absorbing external expertise is more of a Faustian bargain they are willing to strike in exchange for development.

Sankara's model of development called for a type of ownership from the various facets of Burkinabè society that is ontologically different from the version of ownership that donors have created and continue to proffer today. Ownership under this alternate model meant individual sacrifice for collective progress along with a deep-rooted understanding of the individual's position and responsibilities within the collective for furthering development. The sacrifice pertained to the need to thrive with the resources that the country had available and to forgo the Faustian-type bargain that came with the development that the West was promoting through SAPs and foreign aid. Although its application is difficult in the context of the current aid paradigm, the spirit of Sankara's 'ownership' remains embedded in Burkinabè notions of ownership today. However, civil society members and government officials in the Burkinabè health sector have bought into the dominant (neoliberal externally-funded) philosophy of development, and thus feel that donors are necessary for achieving this end because, as many respondents note, Burkina is a poor country with no resources. Thus, there is no more imagining an alternative that aligns with what the country has to offer, but rather an unyielding view of Burkina and Burkinabès as lagging in development and struggling to catch up.

NOTES

1 There is considerable scholarship that addresses the ways in which the quest for efficiency through neoliberal policies led to inequality in the delivery of social services outside of Africa as well – see Abouharb and Cingranelli (2008), Chapman (2016) and Easterly (2005).

2 Translation by author.

3 One of the USAID respondents gave an example of how with respect HIV/AIDs Burkina could be considered more developed than places like Washington DC in the US, where nearly 1 in 5 people is infected with the virus versus in Burkina where seroprevalence is around 1 per cent. A World Bank official explains how we do not label Cuba as developed although it has a health system comparable to Canada.

REFERENCES

Abouharb, R. and Cingranelli, D. L. (2008) *Human Rights and Structural Adjustment.* Cambridge: Cambridge University Press.

Bodart, C., Gerard, S., Yansane, L. M. and Bergis, S. (2001) The Influence of Health Sector Reform and External Assistance in Burkina Faso. *Health Policy and Planning* 16(1): 74–86.

Booth, D. (2012) Aid Effectiveness: Bringing Country Ownership (and Politics) Back in. *Conflict, Security and Development* 12(5): 537–558.

Burkina Faso Ministry of Health (n.d.) *National Family Planning Stimulus Plan 2013–2015.* Burkina Faso Ministry of Health.

Chapman, A. (2016) *Global Health, HR and the Challenge of Neoliberal Policies.* Cambridge: Cambridge University Press.

Cohendet, P., Grandadam, D., Simon, L. and Capdevila, I. (2014) Epistemic Communities, Localization and the Dynamics of Knowledge Creation. *Journal of Economic Geography* 14(5): 929–954.

Easterly, W. (2005) What Did Structural Adjustment Adjust? The Association of Policies and Growth with Repeated IMF and World Bank Adjustment Loans. *Journal of Development Economics* 76(1): 1–22.

Engberg-Pedersen, L. (2002) The Limitations of Political Space in Burkina Faso: Local Organizations, Decentralization and Poverty Reduction. In N. Webster and L. Engberg-Pedersen (eds), *In the Name of the Poor: Contesting Political Space for Poverty Reduction*, 157–182. London: Zed Books.

Falola, T. and Heaton, M. (2007) *HIV/AIDS, Illness, and African Well-Being.* Rochester, NY: University Rochester Press.

Faust, J. (2010) Policy Experiments, Democratic Ownership and Development Assistance. *Development Policy Review* 28(5): 515–534.

Gabas, J., Faure, Y. A. and Sindzingre, A. (1997) The Effectiveness of French Aid-Burkina Faso. In G. Carlsson et al. (eds), *Foreign Aid in Africa: Learning from Country Experience*, 36–64. Uppsala: Nordic Africa Institute.

Haddad, Slim, Nougtara, A. and Fournier, P. (2006). "Learning from Health System Reforms: Lessons from Burkina Faso." *Tropical Medicine & International Health* 11 (12):1889–1897.

Harsch, E. (2013) The Legacies of Thomas Sankara: A Revolutionary Experience in Retrospect. *Review of African Political Economy* 40(137): 358–374.

Harsch, E. (2014) *Thomas Sankara: An African Revolutionary.* Athens, OH: Ohio University Press.

Kanji, N. (1989) Charging for Drugs in Africa: UNICEF'S 'Bamako Initiative'. *Health Policy and Planning* 4(2): 110–120.

Konadu-Agyemang, K. (2000) The Best of Times and the Worst of Times: Structural Adjustment Programs and Uneven Development in Africa: The Case of Ghana. *The Professional Geographer* 52(3): 469–483.

Martin, G. (1987) Ideology and Praxis in Thomas Sankara's Populist Revolution of 4 August 1983 in Burkina Faso. *Issue: A Journal of Opinion* 15: 77–90.

Ministry of State for Planning, Land Use and Community Development, and United Nation System in the Burkina Faso (2012) *Burkina Faso: Accelerating Progress Towards the MDGs: Eradicating Extreme Poverty and Hunger.* New York: United Nations.

Paris Declaration on Aid Effectiveness (2012) Accra Agenda for Action. (Paris, ocDe). Retrieved on 1 June 2017 from www.oecd.org/dac/effectiveness/34428351.pdf.

Pender, J. (2001) From 'Structural Adjustment' to Comprehensive Development Framework': Conditionality Transformed? *Third World Quarterly* 22(3): 397–411.

Ridde, V. (2008) 'The Problem of the Worst-Off Is Dealt with after All Other Issues': The Equity and Health Policy Implementation Gap in Burkina Faso." *Social Science and Medicine* 66(6): 1368–1378.

Ridde, V. (2011) Is the Bamako Initiative Still Relevant for West African Health Systems? *International Journal of Health Services* 41(1): 175–184.

Sachs, W. (ed.) 1992. *The Development Dictionary: A Guide to Knowledge as Power*. London; Atlantic Highlands, NJ: St. Martin's Press.

Sahn, D. and Bernier, R. (1995) Health Sector Reform in Developing Countries: Making Health Development Sustainable Have Structural Adjustments Led to Health Sector Reform in Africa? *Health Policy* 32(1): 193–214.

Sankara, T. (1985) The 'Political Orientation' of Burkina Faso. *Review of African Political Economy* 12(32): 48–55.

Savadogo, K. and Wetta, C. (1991) The Impact of Self-Imposed Adjustment: The Case of Burkina Faso, 1983–1989. Retrieved on 1 July 2017 from https://ideas.repec.org/p/ucf/iopeps/iopeps91-43.html.

Smith, D. (2015) Burkina Faso's Revolutionary Hero Thomas Sankara to Be Exhumed. *The Guardian*. Retrieved on 1 June 2017 from www.theguardian.com/world/2015/mar/06/burkina-fasos-revolutionary-hero-thomas-sankara-to-be-exhumed.

Smith, M. (ed.) (2006) *Beyond the 'African Tragedy': Discourses on Development and the Global Economy*. Burlington, VT: Ashgate.

Thiong'o, N. (1994) *Decolonising the Mind: The Politics of Language in African Literature*. Nairobi, Kenya: East African Publishers.

Wilkins, M. (1989) The Death of Thomas Sankara and the Rectification of the People's Revolution in Burkina Faso. *African Affairs* 88(352): 375–388.

World Bank (1993) *World Development Report 1993: Investing in Health*. Washington, DC: World Bank.

Wynter, S. (1996) Is 'Development' a Purely Empirical Concept or Also Teleological? A Perspective from 'We the Underdeveloped. *Contributions In Afroamerican And African Studies* 169: 299–311.

Zagré, P. (1994) *Les Politiques Économiques Du Burkina Faso: Une Tradition D'ajustement Structurel*. Paris: Karthala Editions.

CHAPTER 17

Social Movement Struggles and Political Transition in Burkina Faso

Bettina Engels

This chapter provides an overview of social movement struggles in Burkina Faso, outlining the claims raised by social movements and their organisations, and how these claims are framed and enforced by the popular classes. This comprehensive overview demonstrates that the tradition of popular class struggles in Burkina Faso dates long before Thomas Sankara's time. In this way, Sankara was himself a product of this rich history. Although Sankara has become an iconic figure and is frequently referred to by many political actors across Burkinabè society, his precise ideologies and programmatics are nowadays virtually absent from the political agendas of many contemporary resistance movement actors. Herein, offer an original periodisation of Burkinabè resistance, which can be conceived of through six historical phases from independence until today:

1 From independence in 1960 until the late 1980s, including Sankara's 'revolutionary' era, Burkina Faso's national political development was shaped by a repeated alternation of strikes, military coups and constitutional referendums.
2 During the first phase of the Compoaré era, from the late 1980s to the late 1990s, trade unions, students and other youth were jointly engaged in the struggle for democratisation and, after the first structural adjustment programme (the Programme de facilité d'ajustement structurel renforcé) was signed in 1991, protested against economic liberalisation, including the privatisation of state-owned firms.
3 From the late 1990s to the mid-2000s, demands for human and civil rights were in the focus of the activities of the social struggles; socio-economic topics (in particular those related to structural adjustment and its impacts) never disappeared from the agenda.

4 In the second half of the 2000s, responding to the global food and fuel price crisis, material issues (notably the high cost of living) were again in the forefront of the popular class struggles, in Burkina Faso as in many other African states.

5 From 2011 onwards, civil rights claims and democratisation were linked to each other. The alliance of oppositional actors was enlarged and the conflict accelerated rapidly, finally resulting in the dismissal of Blaise Compaoré from the presidency on 31 October 2014. When the Presidential Guard (Régiment de sécurité présidentielle, RSP) launched a *coup d'état* on 16 September 2015, civil society massively resisted against it and obliged the putschists to surrender after one week.

6 The new government was elected in November 2015 and contemporary social movements are focusing on the political crimes of the last two decades, including the death of those who have been killed during the most recent protests of 2014–2015.

SOCIAL MOVEMENT STRUGGLES FROM INDEPENDENCE TO THE LATE 1980S

Social movements have a long tradition in Burkina Faso, reaching back to colonial times. The first two decades in the history of Upper Volta following its independence in 1960 were characterised by a repeated alternation of strikes, military coups and constitutional referendums (Englebert 1996). The first president of Upper Volta, Maurice Yaméogo, was overturned in 1966 following mass demonstrations by the trade unions against the suppression of workers' rights, particularly the 1964 ban on strikes. A general strike in January 1966 was followed by a military putsch, after which Lieutenant Colonel Sangoulé Lamizana took over the office of president. A constitutional referendum in 1970 established the Second Republic. A further wave of strikes began in November 1975 right after Lamizana announced the creation of the party (and thus the creation of a single-party government), Mouvement pour le renouveau national. Other segments of the popular classes joined the strikes, and in January 1976, mass protests led to the government's dissolution by Lamizana and to a further referendum. A new government was formed in February 1976. The Third Republic existed for only two years: in 1980, teachers throughout the country went on strike. This was followed by a military coup, the suspension of the constitution, and the formation of a military junta under Saye Zerbo. Zerbo was replaced by Jean-Baptiste Ouédraogo following a further coup in November 1982. Ouédraogo appointed Captain Thomas Sankara as prime minister. When Sankara was arrested a few months after taking office – due in part to his critique of Ouédraogo's regime – strikes by students and trade unions forced his release (Hagberg 2002: 228–229). In the following year Sankara led a coup; he was supported by Blaise Compaoré, among others, who was also an army captain at the time. Thomas Sankara was killed in a subsequent military putsch in October 1987. Following the putsch, Sankara's companion, Blaise Compaoré, became president and held the office until he was forced to give it up in late October 2014 – again after massive popular protests.

A glamorous and charismatic figure, Sankara rapidly became an icon comparable to Che Guevara – not only in Burkina Faso, but throughout Africa, Europe, and the Americas (Harsch 2013). However, among Burkinabè social movement activists, Sankara's role is contested, some even remember the 'revolutionary' phase as an obstacle for social mobilisatio, as people were intimidated and felt repressed by Sankara's local committees of the revolution's defence or Comités de défense de la revolution (CDR; anonymous activist, personal communication with the author, 10 September 2016).

STRUGGLES FOR DEMOCRATISATION (THE LATE 1980S TO EARLY 1990S)

In the late 1980s and early 1990s, mass strikes and other protests – particularly by students and civil servants – urged formal political liberalisation in Burkina Faso and many other African states (Bratton and Walle 1992: 423). The multiparty system was introduced in 1990 and a constitutional referendum in the following year led to the founding of the Fourth Republic. In the first multiparty elections, which were boycotted by the opposition, Compaoré was confirmed in office. The first 'structural adjustment' programme immediately followed formal political liberalisation (see Chapter 7, this volume) and was accompanied again by strikes and trade union protests against the liberal economic policy oriented towards the global market (Federici and Caffentzis 2000; Harsch 1998). Comprehensive cuts in public spending and the privatisation of state-owned firms resulted in increased unemployment and decreased wage levels (EI 2009). In January 1994, under pressure from the IMF, the West African CFA franc was devaluated. This weakened purchasing power further and significantly enlarged the gap between prices and wages, even for privileged workers with regular employment.

The activities and claims of the social movements from the late 1980s to the early 1990s were shaped by processes at the transnational and global scale. After the end of the Cold War, going hand in hand with political transformations all over the world and particularly in Eastern Europe, states in the former Soviet Union and sub-Saharan Africa pushed demands for multi-party elections and other democratic reforms (Bratton and Walle 1992). In the first half of the 1990s, the politics of International Financial Institutions (IFIs) included the liquidation of state-owned firms, wage and personnel cuts in the public sector, and the devaluation of the franc CFA, leading to demonstrations and strikes in Burkina Faso and other countries in the Global South (Walton and Ragin 1990; Walton and Seddon 1994). In Burkina Faso, the trade unions and the student movement joined together as the main players in both waves of protests.

The federation of trade unions Confédération générale des travailleurs du Burkina (CGT-B) originated from the French Confédération générale du Travail (CGT). It is the biggest trade union federation in Burkina Faso in terms of membership figures. Apart from the CGT-B, five other trade union federations exist: The Confédération Nationale des Travailleurs du Burkina (CNTB), the Confédération Syndicale Burkinabé (CSB), the Force Ouvrière – Union Nationale des syndicats libres (FO-UNSL), the Organisation Nationale des Syndicats Libres (ONSL) and the Union Syndicale des Travailleurs du Burkina Faso (USTB). The trade unions in Burkina Faso are organised along ideological lines. The CGT-B is oriented towards a Marxist–Leninist ideology and understands itself as 'revolutionary', whereas the other federations are, all in all, oriented towards more reformist and/or social democratic ideas. In Burkina Faso, as in many other countries, university and secondary school students' organisations understand themselves also as 'trade unions'. Overlaps in personnel among the civil society associations are commonplace; virtually all functionaries of the CGT-B and its member organisations were previously organised in the student movement, notably in the Union Générale des Etudiants Burkinabè (UGEB) and Association Nationale des Etudiants Burkinabè (ANEB), which are ideologically close to the CGT-B.

Pressure from the protests in this period led to the introduction of multi-party elections and the establishment of the Fourth Republic – a first step towards political liberalisation that paved the way for further waves of contentious collective action.

FOCUS ON HUMAN AND CIVIL RIGHTS (THE LATE 1990S TO MID-2000S)

From the late 1990s onwards, social struggles in Burkina Faso were led by student and human rights organisations and trade unions, and shaped by demands for human and civil rights. The prominent position of human and civil rights on the civil society agenda from the late 1990s to the mid-2000s was triggered by the murder of journalist Norbert Zongo on 13 December 1998. Zongo had conducted research on the death of David Ouédraogo, the former driver of Blaise Compaoré's brother, François Compaoré. The journalist was found shot dead in his burned-out car. The government declared his death an accident (in a manner resembling the state reaction to the death of

Thomas Sankara). The next day thousands took to the streets and demanded an investigation into the circumstances surrounding Norbert Zongo's death and an end to impunity (Frère 2010; Harsch 1999). Trade unions, human rights organisations, students and political opposition parties joined forces in the Collectif d'organisations démocratiques de masse et de partis politiques (Collective of the Democratic Mass Organisations and Political Parties, or 'Collectif') in order to unite their struggles. The 'Collectif' still exists today, and in December 2014, to mark the anniversary of Zongo's death, the collective mobilised thousands of people for a central demonstration in Ouagadougou, as it has done regularly in the 16 years since his murder. The death of Norbert Zongo triggered protests against impunity and for civil rights such as freedom of the press and freedom of assembly. The 'Collectif' was led by the Mouvement burkinabè des droits de l'homme et des peuples (MBDHP), one of the most active human rights organisations in West Africa. The MBDHP, the trade union federation CGT-B and the student union UGEB had already collaborated since the late 1980s. However, the 'Collectif''s base was significantly larger, as it included also the other trade union federations and political parties. Between political parties and civil society organisations, tensions quickly emerged. Civil society representatives complained that party politicians would use civil society action for individual power purposes. The most prominent example is Hermann Yaméogo, President of the Union nationale pour la démocratie et le développement (UNDD), who attempted to use the 'Collectif' to seize power, as activists see it (author interview with anonymous activists from human rights organisations, Koudougou, 8 December 2011).

As a consequence, they stated, political parties were excluded from the alliance established in the protests against the high cost of living over the course of the global food and fuel price crisis from 2008 onwards (interviews, Ouagadougou, 16 November 2011, and Koudougou, 8 December 2011). Notwithstanding, this alliance built heavily on the network established through the 'Collectif'. The experience protest actors made, and the alliance and networks they built in this period were, and are still, central for enabling protests in the following phases.

PROTESTS RELATED TO THE GLOBAL FOOD AND FUEL PRICE CRISIS (LATE 2000S)

Since the early 1990s, Burkinabè trade unions have mobilised against the disparity between increasing prices and stagnating incomes (EI 2009; Englebert 1996; Federici and Caffentzis 2000). These protests peaked in response to the global food and fuel price crisis in January and February 2008 that led to price increases in Burkina Faso by 30 per cent for meat, 44 per cent for corn, and 50 per cent for cooking oil (Mission Conjointe Gouvernement et al. 2008: 5). The world market crisis struck Burkina Faso and other African states particularly hard because of long-term structural causes, in particular a focus on commercial agricultural production for the world market instead of emphasising local food security (although Sankara had worked to challenge this trend by focusing on agro self-sufficiency, his efforts were swiftly co-opted in the name of economic liberalisation following his assassination; see Chapters 5 and 7, this volume). With a history going back to colonial agricultural policies, this tendency deepened from the 1970s onwards in the context of the debt crisis, structural adjustment, and world trade liberalisation (Amin 1973; McMichael 2009). In the course of the 2007/2008 price crisis, protests against the high cost of living took place in more than 20 cities worldwide, most of them in Africa (Amin 2012; Harsch 2008; Janin 2009; Maccatory et al. 2010; Schneider 2008). Burkina Faso was among the African states in which protests were particularly intense and continuous.

Protests started in late February 2008 with shopkeepers at the local markets of Bobo-Dioulasso and Ouahigouya marching against the implementation of a communal development tax (taxe de développement communal, or TDC). The planned duty on mopeds, motorcycles, cars and trucks had been approved several years earlier, but it would come into force at a time when prices for consumer staples were rising enormously. Within a few days, food riots occurred in several cities (including Bobo-Dioulasso and Ouadougou, Banfora, and Ouahigouya) throughout the country. Public buildings, shops and petrol stations were damaged. Road blockades were erected and set on fire between 20 and 28 February, namely in Bobo-Dioulasso and Ouagadougou. Numerous people were injured and hundreds arrested (*Ouestaf News*, 28 February 2008). The CGT-B immediately called for other civil society groups to assemble and, on 12 March 2008, all major trade union federations and single unions, consumer and professional associations, human rights organisations, and the student and youth movements set up a new alliance: the Coalition nationale de lutte contre la vie chère, la corruption, la fraude, l'impunité et pour les libertés (Coalition against the High Cost of Living, Corruption, Fraud, Impunity and for Freedoms, or CCVC; CCVC 2008a). This new alliance initiated a first central demonstration in Ouagadougou on 15 March 2008 and a countrywide general strike on 8–9 April and 13–15 April 2008. Several more mass rallies in Ouagadougou followed, including those on 15 May 2008, 8 April 2011 and 26 May 2012. Led by the trade unions, namely the CGT-B, the CCVC was – and still remains – the main force in mobilising against the high cost of living in Burkina Faso.

From 2008 onward, the Burkinabè government adopted various measures, such as temporary price fixing, the suspension of import duties and value added taxes (VAT) on staple goods, and the establishment of shops for subsidised foodstuffs (called 'boutiques témoin'; Africa Research Bulletin 2008; AN 2008; Chouli 2012b; Zahonogo et al. 2011). In 2011, the government suspended the communal development tax and reduced wage taxes while increasing salaries in the public sector (*L'Observateur Paalga*, 28 April 2012).

The CCVC became the leading alliance in protests against the high cost of living from March 2008 onwards. It is striking to note, however, that the protests started with spontaneous riots in late February 2008 and the protagonists of these riots were people hardly represented in the social movements and their organisations: the marginalised, urban sub-classes, mostly youth without regular, gainful employment. The range of people involved also included artisans and petty traders and, once the riots broke out, students and workers joined them. However, the informal sectors of society were the largest group. The riots proceeded through informal networks within the urban neighbourhoods by passing information from person to person and via text messages without any formal organisational structures. In contrast, many activists in the social movements are wage-dependent employees or university and high school students. Although most activists of the CCVC member organisations could be considered part of the urban middle classes, most of them are equipped with middle-class expectations and formal education rather than material wealth. The CCVC's demands reflect the dominant role of trade unions within the alliance, which count public service employees as their largest clientele group by far. For instance, the first demand in the CCVC's central declaration is 'a rise in the salaries and pensions of state employees and workers in the private sector' (CCVC 2008b). Consequently, one of the central achievements of the CCVC's protest was that the government reduced wage taxes and increased salaries in the public sector (*L'Observateur Paalga*, 28 April 2012; also confirmed through interviews with representatives of CCVC member organisations, Banfora, 24 November 2011, Ouagadougou, 3 December 2011 and 2 September 2012). 'The new premier has taken dynamic measures that really pay attention to our claims', a trade union leader stated, 'the TDC was suspended … [and] there were measures taken in the health sector' (author interview, Ouagadougou, 2 September 2012).

It is no coincidence that protests related to the global food and fuel price crisis were so intense and continuous in Burkina Faso. The global food price crisis and the prompt and rapid price increase in the local markets triggered protest in Burkina Faso by opening a window of opportunity for the social movements to mobilise (Engels 2015). Since the high cost of living had already been on the trade unions' agenda for some years, they were able to take up the price increase issue promptly in February 2008 on the grounds of their previous struggles. Moreover, the CCVC was able to successfully mobilise on short notice because of its heavy administrative and personnel overlaps with the 'Collectif'. The protests related to the price increase from 2008 onwards put further pressure on the president and government, and it took only three years until the next mass protests began.

STRUGGLES FOR REGIME CHANGE AND THE REMOVAL OF BLAISE COMPAORÉ (2011–2014)

Since the 1990s, the political regime in Burkina Faso has persistently come under pressure from trade unions and other civil society organisations (Chouli 2012b; Federici et al. 2000; Harsch 2009; Hilgers and Mazzocchetti 2010; Hilgers and Loada 2013; ENREF_29 Loada 2010). The protests reached a peak in 2011, when massive demonstrations arose after the death of Justin Zongo, a young man who died in the town of Koudougou on 20 February after being detained several times by the gendarmerie. These protests triggered one of the most severe political crises in the country since Blaise Compaoré seized power in 1987 (Chouli 2012b; CNP 2011; Hilgers and Loada 2013). The 2011 crisis also revitalised protests against the high cost of living: major protests in 2008 gave way to relatively low mobilisation in 2009 and 2010, but after the struggles related to Justin Zongo's death, one of the largest demonstrations against the high cost of living and against impunity was organised on 8 April 2011 (Chouli 2012a). This is hardly surprising against the background of the overall high level of social tensions and popular mobilisation in Burkina at this moment. A year later, when petrol prices increased by 50 per cent and caused local transportation fares to rise by 25–35 per cent, thousands of people again marched in Ouagadougou on 26 May 2012.

In 2013 and 2014, tens of thousands of people took to the streets on numerous occasions, protesting Compaoré's attempt to revise Article 37 of the Burkinabè constitution, which would enable him to run for a fifth term (Loada and Romaniuk 2014). At the same time, the CCVC continued to mobilise: the alliance organised a mass demonstration on 20 July 2013 against the high cost of living and 'bad governance' and another one on 29 October 2014 against the disastrous conditions in the education system (*Jeune Afrique*, 20 July 2013; *Sidwaya*, 29 October 2014). The trade unions alliance, Unité d'Action Syndiale (UAS), announced a 24-hour strike for 11 November 2014, and if the government did not agree to its substantial demands, another 48-hour strike on 25–26 November (UAS 2014). However, both strikes were suspended after Blaise Compaoré stepped down from the presidency on 31 October (*Le Pays*, 9 November 2014).

The National Assembly's passage of the proposal to revise the constitution was announced on 21 October 2014. The protests escalated on 28 October with a massive opposition that led demonstrations around the country. Within the labour, human rights, student and youth movements, activists were surprised by the intensity of the protests and the high numbers of people joining them. On 30 October, the vote for the constitutional amendment was scheduled in parliament and what had been protests turned into a popular insurrection (Chouli 2015; Frère and Englebert 2015). State security forces used tear gas, truncheons and guns against the demonstrators. At least 30 people were killed in the confrontations. Protestors broke through the police line to occupy the parliamentary building and, shortly afterward, the national television station in Ouagadougou. President Compaoré was forced to dissolve the government and, that same evening, withdrew his proposal to revise the constitution. At first, however, he did not intend to resign from office. The military forced him to do so the following day. For two weeks a senior military officer, Lieutenant Colonel Yacouba Isaac Zida, assumed the role of the head of state. On the basis of a transitional charter signed by representatives of the military, political parties, traditional authorities and civil society, the former diplomat Michel Kafando was appointed transitional president on 17 November 2014. He immediately appointed Zida as Prime Minister. National elections were planned for October 2015.

In view of the history of Burkina Faso since the 1960s and the experiences in other West African states, it is hardly surprising that the military took over temporarily after Blaise Compaoré was forced to resign. Nevertheless, some civil society activists were disappointed. They felt that the military had exploited the demonstrations. 'The military are stealing our revolution' said an activist on the day following Compaoré's resignation (personal communication with the author, 1 November 2014). 'Give the civilians what belongs to them', demanded another activist in the news portal lefaso.net (5 November 2014). The army had conducted a coup d'état, declared the MBDHP chairman, Chrysogone Zougmoré, who is also vice-president of the civil society alliance 'coalition against the high cost of living', at a press conference on 2 November 2014. The military had 'once again usurped the fruits of the heroic struggle of the people' (CCVC 2014). This 'paves the way for antidemocratic endeavours, as the history of our country has taught us' (ibid.). The civil society organisations continued their mobilisation. A general strike against the high fuel prices was held on 17–18 February 2015, and a nation-wide protest day was organised on 8 April 2015. From the civil society organisations' perspective(s), a major achievement of the transition phase was the re-opening of investigations into the assassinations of Norbert Zongo (in December 1998) and of Thomas Sankara (in 1987). In so doing, long-standing core grievances of national and international civil society actors have been, finally, addressed. These grievances had long been blocked by influential parts of the military.

It is, however, important to note that protestors are not a homogenous bloc. Without doubt, activists from the CGT-B, the MBDHP, UGEG, and the Youth movement, were very engaged in the 2013-2014 protests that led to the end of Blaise Compaoré's presidency. However, the base of these protests was significantly broader than previous waves of protest (those led by the 'Collectif' and the CCVC, for instance). This is also due to the fact that the claims of the 2013–2014 protests, all in all, were focused on stopping the constitutional referendum and hindering Compaoré from running for a fifth term. Other than the struggles against neoliberal structural adjustment and against the high cost of living, where the trade unions were at the forefront, the recent protests against the constitutional referendum were driven by more moderate actors, notably political (opposition) parties. The Sankarist Party, the Union pour la renaissance/parti sankariste (UNIR/PS), was among them, but did not play a major role. The main actor was the Mouvement du peuple pour le progrès (MPP), a political party founded in January 2014 by core politicians who quit Blaise Compaorés Congrès pour la démocratie et le progrès (CDP) related to the conflict over the fifth presidential term.

In the course of the protests against the constitutional referendum, a new civil society group came into existence in July 2013, the Balai Citoyen (literally 'citizens' broom' Chouli 2015; Frère and Englebert 2015, 301-303; see Chapter 15, this volume). The founders and frontmen of Balai Citoyen are the reggae musician Sams'K le Jah and the rapper Serge Bambara aka 'Smockey' (*Radio France Internationale*, 20 July 2014). They used their popularity as musicians to mobilise large numbers of people for the protests against Compaoré. Rhetorically, at least, they place themselves in the tradition of Thomas Sankara: the broom is a symbol for the wish to 'sweep out' Compaoré and his ruling élite, Sams'K le Jah declared to the press (*BBC News*, 30 April 2014).

AFTER THE FALL OF BLAISE COMPOARÉ (2014–2016)

Presidential elections were initially scheduled for 11 October 2015. On 7 April, a new electoral law passed and on 5 June a law was adopted that demanded military personnel quit the army before they were allowed to hold a political office. There was uncertainty as to whether candidates who had previously come out in support of the disputed revision of article 37 of the constitution should be allowed to run for the office of the president. The transitional government decided against and, as a consequence, several confidents of former president Compaoré were excluded from announcing their candidature.

This, on 16 September 2015, resulted in a coup by the RSP, led by its commander, General Gilbert Diendéré. The RSP entered a cabinet meeting of the transitional government, and took President Kafando, Prime Minister Zida and two ministers as hostages. The news spread quickly and protestors mobilised immediately, burning barricades in Ouagadougou and attempting to enter the Presidential Palace. The following day, Diendéré declared the transitional government dissolved and himself President (interview with *France 24*, 17 September 2015). Immediately, the trade unions declared a general strike and virtually all civil society groups mobilised to resist the putsch. In Ouagadougou, the RSP responded with brute force against the protestors. Between 16 and 23 September 2015, 14 protestors were killed and more than 250 were injured. National and international media were intimidated with threats of violence. The RSP destroyed the station of the national phone company in Ouagadougou so that phone and Internet access was temporarily unavailable in the capital city. However, this did not stop the protests and, after initial hesitation, the national army prepared to intervene. Finally, six days after the coup, on 23 September, Diendéré gave up and handed himself in.

Presidential elections were held seven weeks after their initial scheduling, on 29 November 2015. Roch Marc Christian Kaboré, Chairman of the MPP, succeeded in the first ballot (ICG 2016; ISS 2015) and was inaugurated officially to the presidential office in late December. From the point of view of most observers, this does not indicate a significant change in political orientation: Roch Marc Christian Kaboré had previously been Minister, Prime Minister, and Chairman of the National Assembly during the presidency of Blaise Compaoré. According to the civil society groups that had hoped for a fundamental change after Compaoré's fall, the transition ultimately amounted to one fraction within the CDP succeeding against another. Currently, there is virtually no serious opposition to the MPP and their allies in the spectrum of licensed political parties in Burkina Faso: even the UNIR/PS supports the MPP.

CONCLUSION

This chapter has depicted social struggles in Burkina Faso since independence. From the late 1980s onwards, the mobilisation of workers, students and other activists paved the way for the civil rights struggles of the late 1990s and protest related to the 2008 food price increase, which then reinforced pressure on the president and government. When civil society protests occurred again following the death of Justin Zongo in 2011, they facilitated a revitalisation of the CCVC's activities. The global food and fuel price crisis of 2007/2008 opened a window of opportunity for the trade unions and other civil society organisations. Though they had relatively limited material resources at its disposal – not only in international comparison but also against the backdrop of structural adjustment policies, which left many activists impoverished – they compensated for material deficits by mobilising their organisational power and well-established networks. This was possible thanks to their past experience and networks from longstanding previous struggles. The efficiency of these networks again became obvious in the protests that led to the turnover of Blaise

Compoaré in October 2014 and in the immediate mobilisation against the RSP coup d'état in September 2015. Thirty years after his assassination, Thomas Sankara is still an icon and is frequently referred to rhetorically by protestors and activists, both from within civil society and the political scene. However, his political programmatic and ideas are virtually absent from agendas.

The challenges Burkina Faso is now facing are considerable In the 54 years since decolonisation, the political system has been characterised by putsches and military rule. Half of the post-independence period has been ruled over by Blaise Compaoré. Though hopes for a fundamental political transition are currently weak, 2015 was, nevertheless, a historically unique year in Burkina Faso: it is beyond example that a whole country opposed a military coup and therewith forced the putschists to resign. For the first time in the country's history, a president was elected into office by the people of Burkina Faso. Still, many representatives of the oppositional groups that protested against Blaise Compaoré and his planned renewed term are disappointed with the transitional phase. Central grievances – including impunity, corruption and political inaction after human rights violations – remain unaddressed and the achievements of the transition remain far behind the ambitious hopes of protestors and activists.

The new government must now ensure a legal reappraisal of cases of murder and 'disappearances' that, in all probability, were politically motivated – including the well-known cases of Thomas Sankara and Norbert Zongo, but also those of a number of activists from the student, human rights and trade union movements. Such a reappraisal will help to ensure that future governments in Burkina Faso do not use the same violent methods for eliminating opposition. Public reappraisal of these cases and legal proceedings against the perpetrators and those politicians and military figures responsible is needed to help ensure that the subsequent change of government in Burkina Faso does not result in dozens of deaths, as in the past.

REFERENCES

Africa Research Bulletin (2008) Burkina Faso: Food Riots. *Africa Research Bulletin: Economic, Financial and Technical Series* 45(2): 17735C–17736A.

Amin, J. A. (2012) Understanding the Protest of February 2008 in Cameroon. *Africa Today* 58(4): 20–43.

Amin, S. (1973) *Neo-Colonialism in West Africa*. Harmondsworth: Penguin.

AN (2008) *Rapport de la Commission ad hoc sur la vie Chère*. Ouagadougou: L'Assemblée Nationale du Burkina Faso.

Bratton, M. and Walle, N. van de (1992) Protest and Political Reform in Africa. *Comparative Politics* 24(4): 419–442.

CCVC (2008a) *Acte de naissance de la CCVC*. 12 March. Ouagadougou: CCVC.

CCVC (2008b) *Platform revendicative*. 15 July. Ouagadougou: CCVC.

CCVC (2014) *Situation nationale: La CCVC appelle la population à faire échec 'à ce énième coup d'Etat militaire'.* 2 November. Ouagadougou: CCVC.

Chouli, L. (2012a) *Burkina Faso 2011: Chronique d'un mouvement social.* Toulouse: Editions Tahin Party.

Chouli, L. (2012b) Peoples' Revolts in Burkina Faso. In F. Manji (ed.), *African Awakening: The Emerging Revolutions*, 131–146. Cape Town: Pambazuka.

Chouli, L. (2015) L'insurrection populaire et la Transition au Burkina Faso. *Review of African Political Economy* 42(143): 148–155.

CNP (2011) *Crise Sociale au Burkina Faso: Relure de Presse sur la crise consécutive au décès de l'élève Justin Zongo à Koudougou, période: février–mars 2011.* Ouagadougou: Centre National de Presse Norbert Zongo.

EI (2009) *Study on the Effects of Structural Adjustment Policies in Burkina Faso.* Brussels: Education International.

Engels, B. (2015) Social Movement Struggles against the High Cost of Living in Burkina Faso. *Canadian Journal of Development Studies* 36(1): 107–121.

Englebert, P. (1996) *Burkina Faso: Unsteady Statehood in West Africa.* Boulder, CO: Westview.

Federici, S. and Caffentzis, G. (2000) Chronology of African University Students' Struggles: 1985–1998. In S. Federici, G. Caffetzis and O. Alidou (eds), *A Thousand Flowers: Social Struggles Against Structural Adjustment in African Universities*, 115–150. Asmara, Eritrea: Africa World Press.

Federici, S., Caffetzis, G. and Alidou, O. (2000) *A Thousand Flowers: Social Struggles Against Structural Adujstment in African Universities.* Asmara, Eritrea: Africa World Press.

Frère, M.-S. (2010) 'Enterrement de première classe' ou 'leçon de droit': La presse burkinabè et l'affaire Norbert Zongo. In M. Hilgers and J. Mazzocchetti (eds), *Révoltes et oppositions dans un régime semi-autoritaire: Le cas du Burkina Faso*, 241–267. Paris: Karthala.

Frère, M.-S. and Englebert, P. (2015) Briefing: Burkina Faso – the Fall of Blaise Compaoré. *African Affairs* 114(455): 295–307.

Hagberg, S. (2002) 'Enough is Enough': An Ethnography of the Struggle against Impunity in Burkina Faso. *Journal of Modern African Studies* 40(2): 217–246.

Harsch, E. (1998) Burkina Faso in the Winds of Liberalisation. *Review of African Political Economy* 25(78): 625–641.

Harsch, E. (1999) Trop, c'est trop! Civil Insurgence in Burkina Faso 1998–90. *Review of African Political Economy* 26(81): 395–406.

Harsch, E. (2008) Price Protests Expose State Faults. Rioting and Repression Reflect Problems of African Governance. *Africa Renewal* 22(2): 15.

Harsch, E. (2009) Urban Protest in Burkina Faso. *African Affairs* 108(431): 263–288.

Harsch, E. (2013) The Legacies of Thomas Sankara: A Revolutionary Experience in Retrospect. *Review of African Political Economy* 40(137): 358–374.

Hilgers, M. and Loada, A. (2013) Tension et protestations dans un régime semi autoritaire: croissance des révoltes populaires et maintien du pouvoir au Burkina Faso. *Politique Africaine* 2013/3(131): 187–208.

Hilgers, M. and Mazzocchetti, J. (eds) (2010) *Révoltes et oppositions dans un régime semi-autoritaire: Le cas du Burkina-Faso.* Paris: Karthala.

ICG (2016) *Burkina Faso: transition acte II.* Briefing Afrique de Crisis Group no. 116, 7 January. Dakar: International Crisis Group.

ISS (2015) Burkina Faso Set for an Electoral Uprising? *ISS Today*, 24 November. Retrieved on 27 July 2016 from www.issafrica.org/isstoday/burkina-faso-set-for-an-electoral-uprising.

Janin, P. (2009) Les 'émeutes de la faim': une lecture (géo politique) du changement (social). *Politique étrangère* 74(2), 251–263.

Loada, A. (2010) Contrôler l'opposition dans un régime semi-autoritaire: Le cas du Burkina Faso de Blaise Compaoré. In M. Hilgers and J. Mazzocchetti (eds), *Révoltes et oppositions dans un régime semi-autoritaire: Le cas du Burkina-Faso*, 269–294. Paris: Karthala.

Loada, A. and Romaniuk, P. (2014) *Preventing Violent Extremism in Burkina Faso. Toward National Resilience Amid Regional Insecurity.* Goshen: Global Center on Cooperative Security.

Maccatory, B., Oumarou, M. B. and Poncelet, M. (2010) West African Social Movements 'Against the High Cost of Living': From the Economic to the Political, from the Global to the National. *Review of African Political Economy* 37(125): 345–359.

McMichael, P. (2009) A Food Regime Analysis of the 'World Food Crisis'. *Agric Hum Values* 4: 281–295.

Mission Conjointe Gouvernement, Agences du SNU and ONG Save the Children UK (2008) *Impact de la hausse des prix sur les conditions de vie des menages et les marcés de Ouagadougou et Bobo-Dioulasso: Rapport de synthèse de fin de mission.* Ouagadougou: Burkina Faso DGPSA CONASUR DN, PNUD, UNICEF, PAM, FAO and Save the Children.

Schneider, M. (2008) *'We Are Hungry!' A Summary Report of Food Riots, Government Responses, and States of Democracy in 2008.* Ithaca, NYL Cornell University.

UAS (2014) *Notification de préavis de grève (no. 2014-22 –UAS/CS-SA/PDM, 9 Octobre 2014).* Ouagadougou: Unité d'Action Syndicale.

Walton, J. and Ragin, C. (1990) Global and National Sources of Political Protest: Third World Responses to the Debt Crisis. *American Sociological Review* 55: 876–890.

Walton, J. and Seddon, D. (1994) *Free Markets and Food Riots: The Politics of Global Adjustment.* Oxford: Blackwell.

Zahonogo, P., Bitibale, S. and Kabre, A. (2011) *Etude sur la structure des prix des biens et services de grande consommation.* Ouagadougou: Ministère de l'industrie, du commerce et de l'artisanat.

CHAPTER 18

To Decolonise the World
Thomas Sankara and the 'Last Colony' in Africa
Patrick Delices

INTRODUCTION

At the time that the United States began to normalise its economic, political and cultural relationship with Cuba in 2014, the Institute of the Black World assigned me to visit the refugee camps of the 'last colony' in Africa on a fact-finding mission. The 'last African colony' is the Western Sahara, which is colonised by the Kingdom of Morocco. The last colony in Africa, as it has come to be known, had a special relationship with the global anti-colonial revolutionary movements of the 1950s and 1960s, including with the 1980s anti-colonial revolution led by Thomas Sankara in Burkina Faso.

This special relationship between Burkina Faso and Western Sahara started on 5 August 1960. On that particular date, the Republic of Upper Volta, under the leadership of its first president Maurice Yaméogo, gained its independence from France. Later, by 1984, Thomas Sankara, as the fifth President of the Republic of Upper Volta, would rename his nation Burkina Faso. Early on in his presidency, Sankara vowed to support anti-colonial and anti-imperial projects throughout the world, including the Polisario Front's revolutionary movement in the Western Sahara.

In this chapter, I contend that Burkina Faso and Western Sahara have several important commonalities and shared experiences that include colonialism and subsequent underdevelopment because of colonialism; both nations adopted some form of Pan-Africanism and social democracy; and both nations are similar in terms of landmass dimensions – geographically, Burkina Faso and Western Sahara are about the same size.

Herein, I provide some groundwork for a larger, and what I hope will be a sustained, conversation on the relationship between the Western Sahara and Sankara's Burkina Faso. This preliminary examination of the relationship between Thomas Sankara and the Polisario Front is significant as it is not well known in either academic or activist circles. This examination is important in the context of the current paucity of literature concerning Western Sahara's relationship to anti-imperial revolutionary movements, including that of Thomas Sankara's Burkina Faso. There is no existing literature regarding the political relationship between Thomas Sankara and the revolutionary movement in Western Sahara. This chapter considers the legacy of Thomas Sankara for contemporary and emerging anti-colonial and anti-imperial communities. More particularly, my focus here is on the intersections between Sankara's anti-imperial philosophies and solidarities and the rarely broadcast anti-colonial struggle of Western Sahara against Morocco. Drawing on my experiences in Western Sahara in 2014, this chapter, which includes a survey of the historical and political account of Thomas Sankara's influence and legacy, will outline aspects of Sankara's unique relationship to the transnational revolutionary movement for social justice and decolonialism in Western Sahara.

An expository analysis of Thomas Sankara's internationalist solidarities against oppression, as illustrated by his political advocacy and collaboration with the Saharawi people in Western Sahara, reveals not only his revolutionary geo-political range, but also his socio-political significance and influence on the last colony in Africa. Through an exploration of the anti-colonial movement of the Polisario Front in Western Sahara under the leadership of El-Ouali Mustapha Sayed and Mohamed Abdelaziz, I argue that Thomas Sankara's political philosophy, praxis and legacy influenced the socio-political climate and anti-colonial movement in Western Sahara. Thomas Sankara shaped and exposed the anti-colonial movement of Western Sahara to gain support from other nations and major non-governmental organisations.

In a comparative analysis of Western Sahara and Burkina Faso, the characteristics of Sankara's relationship with and impact on the anti-colonial movement of Western Sahara become apparent by examining five specific dynamics of colonialism as outlined by decolonial scholar Sandew Hira (2014). Since the fifteenth century, European powers colonised much of the world. At least 95 per cent of the world's landmass and people have been colonised by Europe at one time (Fisher 2015). The consequences of colonialism extend beyond colonising land and people. Decolonial scholar Sandew Hira (2014) outlines five major aspects of colonialism for a 'Decolonising the Mind' framework: geographic, economic, political, social and cultural dimensions. From a decolonial perspective, I will apply these five major aspects as the main theoretical framework for analysing Thomas Sankara's relationship with and impact on Africa's last colony.

GEOGRAPHICAL COLONISATION

The first aspect of colonialism deals with a geographical dimension. Geography is 'the rise of a global system where nations, states and people have been dislocated and rearranged in global space. In this process land has been colonised by the coloniser (companies, individuals, states) without payment of rent' (Hira 2014: 7). Within colonised geographical spaces, the coloniser often forcibly renames land and landscapes, performing an erasure of the people whom are and the culture that is of that place. Under French colonial rule, the area now known as Burkina Faso was named *Haute-Volta* (Upper Volta) by France (see the Introduction and Chapter 9, this volume, for a detailed description of this epistemic violence and re-naming). By 1898, France and Britain entered into an agreement known as the Franco-British Convention where the territorial borders of Burkina Faso were established. By 1904, the Volta basin territories became part of Niger, Mali and Senegal and became known as 'French West Africa'. Therefore:

> The map of Africa that exists today is largely a legacy of nineteenth century colonialism. Some of these borders are disputed and large sections of them have yet to be formalized. To this day the African Union has a 'Border Program' in charge of clarifying where the borders lie and of preventing and resolving disputes about them.
>
> (Englebert 2015)

Similarly, portions of the Western Sahara, under the colonial rule of Spain, were re-named. The Saguia el-Hamra (Red Canal) became part of the Spanish Sahara, called Río de Oro by Western colonial powers. The name was an adaptation of the earlier Rio do Ouro (River of Gold), which was the ambitious title applied by the Portuguese seafarer, Afonso Gonçalves Baldaia, in 1436. Baldaia, upon 'discovering' a dried out river (i.e. a wadi) named it for the Portuguese desire for gold and mineral wealth. No gold was ever found there. Hence, Hira's (2015) deconstruction of the erroneous perception regarding European 'discovery' as an instrument of not only colonialism, but also coloniality.

In addition to renaming African land, Europeans also re-mapped Africa by creating borders. Nigerian-American journalist Dayo Olopade in *The Bright Continent: Breaking Rules and Making Change in Modern Africa* states:

> European powers, led by the Portuguese, French, British, and Germans, decided to carve up the African continent using maps and borders of their own creation. At the Berlin Conference in 1884, they drew boundaries that had never existed on the continent, scrumming for natural resources from tobacco to peanuts to gold (oil would soon follow). Their boundaries preserved the gap between foreign perception and African reality that has been difficult to close ever since.
>
> (Olopade 2014: 3)

While 'boundaries that had never existed on the continent' and other parts of the world were enforced by the Papacy and Catholic Church along with competing European monarchies and nations, explorers, missionaries, merchants, enslavers and colonial administrations, Eurocentric perception of Africa was not one of a continent rich in natural resources with diverse and powerful peoples, but rather – drawing on earlier dehumanisations propagated during the Trans-Atlantic slave trade – was one of a continent maligned by poverty, ignorance, backwardness, 'witchcraft'/ 'black magic' and economic despair.

To achieve decolonisation, Africans must not only reclaim their lands, but they must also rename these lands and properly change old colonial borders as established by European nations – a practice adopted by Thomas Sankara and other Pan-African leaders of the twentieth century. However, the difficulty of full decolonisation is illustrated in societies across the continent, including (and perhaps especially) in the on-going colonial occupation by Morocco of Western Sahara. To understand this, it is useful to unpack the complex history of the geopolitical strategies and patterns of colonisation in that region.

The Kingdom of Morocco currently claims that the larger western section of Western Sahara originally 'belonged' to Morocco and was part of its territory until Spain and France, during the Berlin Conference, created boundaries along Northwest Africa that borders Morocco, Mauritania and Algeria. Thus, Western Sahara is sundered into two major regions: the larger western section which is known as the Southern Provinces, while the smaller eastern area is recognised as the Free Zone by Algeria, the African Union (AU), the Sahrawi people and the Polisario Front.

The Polisario Front was founded by El-Ouli Mustafa Sayed on 10 May 1973 to fight colonialism, first by Spain, then by Mauritania and then by Morocco. Nine years after the founding of the Saharawi Arab Democratic Republic (SADR) – better known as the Western Sahara – by the Polisario Front, Thomas Sankara visited the conflict-torn territory. Since 1976, SADR has declared Western Sahara as its sovereign territory. Nonetheless, Morocco continues to claim Western Sahara as its colonial possession. Currently, SADR governs 25 per cent of Western Sahara. Morocco governs the remaining 75 per cent of the territory. As stated earlier, SADR identifies its portion as the Free Zone or Liberated Territories. Morocco identifies its section as the Southern Provinces (what SADR identifies as an occupied territory). SADR is recognised and backed by the African Union (AU) and 40-member states of the United Nations (UN). However, since Morocco re-joined the AU in 2017, support for the independence and decolonisation of Western Sahara by various African nations has been insufficient – thus representing an enduring geo-political legacy of colonisation.

POLITICAL COLONISATION

Political colonisation is another of Hira's dimensions of colonialism. Political colonisation deals with the enterprise of managing, governing and controlling colonised people and their land by way of 'law and order'. Politically, under colonial rule, both Western Sahara and Burkina Faso had restrictions regarding freedom of speech and press. However, with the rise of Thomas Sankara to the presidency of Burkina Faso on 4 August 1983, restrictions on that particular freedom were lifted. Also, in 1983, Sankara took on the anti-colonial cause of Western Sahara. Under Thomas Sankara,

> the Burkinabè government officially recognized the SADR, and at the end of March 1984 Sankara became the first head of state to visit areas of Western Sahara under the control of the Polisario Front. He then pushed strongly within the OAU for wider recognition of the SADR. Before the year was out, the OAU did officially admit the Sahrawi republic, prompting Morocco's withdrawal from the organization and irritating France, which generally supported Morocco's claim to the territory.
>
> (Harsch 2014: 121)

In 1983, Sankara became the President of the West African Economic Community. In this role, he advanced not only Pan-Africanism and democratic socialism, but also economic democracy throughout the continent of Africa. In that same year, in New York City, Sankara pushed for an anti-colonial and anti-imperialist political order when he addressed the Thirty-ninth Session of the United Nations General Assembly. In this important address, he raised the controversial issue of colonialism in Western Sahara. Sankara said:

> This is why we hold the fate meted out to the people of Western Sahara by the Kingdom of Morocco to be unacceptable, and we unconditionally condemn it. Morocco is using delaying tactics to postpone a decision that, in any case, will be imposed on it by the will of the Saharawi people. Having personally visited the regions liberated by the Saharawi people, I am convinced that nothing will be able to impede any longer their march toward the total liberation of their country, under the militant and enlightened leadership of the Polisario Front.
>
> (Sankara 2007b: 76)

By publically addressing and exposing the colonial economic and socio-political realities of the Saharawi people at the United Nations, Sankara had a cross-cultural and worldwide impact on anti-colonial movements – not only at that time and space, but forever.

Hence, politically, a Fanonist Sankara understood that to achieve decolonisation, armed struggle and forming alliances along with media and public exposure were of central importance. As such, on 12 November 1984, while attending the Organisation of African Unity (OAU) summit in Addis Abada, Ethiopia, Sankara employed various forms of revolutionary Fanonism by announcing publically his support and recognition of the sovereignty of the Saharawi Arab Democratic Republic (SADR) in Western Sahara. In response to Sankara's repudiation of colonialism in Western Sahara, the OAU admitted SADR as a member state and Morocco rescinded its membership from the OAU. Prior to the OAU summit, in a 1984 press conference at Ouagadougou, Sankara clearly stated the political position of Burkina Faso on the issue of Western Sahara becoming a sovereign nation by declaring the following:

> We have recognized the Saharawi Arab Democratic Republic [SADR] and we feel there's no reason to hesitate on the question – when a people has decided to choose an organization, it's a duty to recognize it. So we feel there can be no OAU summit without the SADR. Someone would be missing. If someone is missing and the reasons for that absence aren't legitimate, Burkina Faso won't play along.
>
> (Sankara 2007a: 125)

From 1984 to 2016, Morocco remained the only African nation not a member of the African Union (AU). This fact alone speaks to the impact of Pan-African leaders who stood in solidarity with Western Sahara – Thomas Sankara among them – on the continent of Africa. However, recently, due to the deteriorating relationship within the Maghreb Arab Union and other economic factors, Morocco has made several political advances by way of public speeches and economic inducements to become again a member of the African Union (AU).

Thirty-three years after Thomas Sankara's speech to the OAU, King Mohammed VI of Morocco delivered a speech on 31 January 2017 at the 28th AU Summit which was held in Addis Ababa, Ethiopia. His speech to the AU can be characterised as a form of pandering. In it, he sought to appeal, appease, placate and win-over the AU by skilfully and cunningly expressing views that corresponded to the wishes and likes of that group. His speech indicated new efforts to win worldwide public support while failing to address underlying political, personal and economic motives (one of which is the on-going occupation of Western Sahara). Therefore, the policy of Morocco remains the same regarding SADR, but its larger political approach is different as it now elects to win-over various member states within the AU in hopes of weakening the political influence of SADR and its supporters (such as Algeria, South Africa, Burkina Faso and many others).

What is hidden in Mohammed VI's speech regarding Pan-African unity, consolidation, cooperation and brotherhood is Morocco's attempts to curry favour and continental support to ultimately disable the African and worldwide anti-colonial consensus that supports the Polisario Front and recognises SADR as a sovereign republic. The statements made by Mohammed VI ultimately wanted to expand and secure the interests of Morocco in Africa, especially in Western Sahara (Lamin 2017). These interests are currently seen in Moroccan banks, such as Attijariwafa, which installed approximately 3,500 bank branches throughout Africa (ibid.). These interests are demonstrated by the actions of major Moroccan corporations, such as OCP, the phosphate conglomerate that dictates the contracts that provide farmers throughout Africa with fertilisers (ibid.). Morocco, by joining the AU, penetrates the massive car insurance, agricultural and gas and oil industries along with telecommunication/telecom markets in Africa (ibid.). One major way to control a people and their culture is to dominate their economy, including through gaining market entry to their industries and by creating economic barriers to those markets – thus, making those economic markets impenetrable.

ECONOMIC COLONISATION

In the previous section, I described the significant historical, political context that shaped Thomas Sankara's engagements with Western Sahara. While Sankara made significant political statements in solidarity with the people of Western Sahara, these remained mostly symbolic in nature during his four years as president of Burkina Faso. That this relationship remained mostly symbolic was probably a reflection of the immense difficulties of decolonisation in all its dimensions, but as I show herein, particularly economic decolonisation in a context of on-going colonial and neo-colonial plunder.

Hira (2014: 7) argues that economics is the second dimension of colonialism, where 'the colonized world creates wealth for the world of the colonizer' by stealing 'minerals and other goods without payment while forcing people to work for free (slavery) or for little money (underpayment)' – cheap labour. As new technology emerged, particularly in the motive powers industries (steam and electricity), along with the introduction of the rifle and ironclad ships, Europe during the nineteenth Century was able to control (always with resistance) not only Western Sahara, but most of the African continent (Rodney 1972). In gaining control of Sahara, inter-regional trade between the Sahara and neighbouring northwest African nations were disrupted as Europe's market entry to various manufacturing sectors created cheap labour and products, as it disrupted the economic livelihood of the people in the Sahara (Rodney 1972; Ajayi 1998: 213).

One of the main dimensions characterising colonial trade in Western Sahara has been the shattering of 'the economic unity of Northwest Africa ... by the French occupation of Algeria which diverted trans-Saharan trade routes east and west of Algeria. By the end of the nineteenth century, the trans-Saharan trade had almost completely collapsed' (Ajayi 1998: 216). Thus, European colonialism in Africa interrupted the major trade routes and key economic activities from the Mediterranean Sea to the Niger Basin.

Spain, and later Morocco, would dominate the abundant fishing waters and phosphate reserves in Western Sahara where fishing and phosphate serve as the main source of employment. Under the Madrid Accords, Spain obtained the rights to offshore fishing and phosphates industries and licenses in Western Sahara. Even so, by 1974, Morocco controlled the key resource areas of Western Sahara, including territories that are rich and abundant in oil, phosphates, petroleum, coastal fishing, sand and salt. In turn, Western Sahara fuels the economy of Morocco by bringing in billions of dollars in exports per year for the king and his kingdom (Delices 2015).

Also, by 1974, OPEC ended its oil embargo; Richard Nixon became the first US president to resign from office; Emperor Haile Selassie of Ethiopia was removed from his post; and the Upper Volta was engaged in a war over a major colonial border dispute with Mali. Furthermore, by 1974, at the age of 24, Thomas Sankara was a Burkinabè lieutenant who had fought in that war with Mali, which gained him mass popularity and appeal as a war hero from the people in Ouagadougou. Nonetheless, as Thomas Sankara matured politically, he acknowledged that the war or the border dispute with Mali was wasteful, unwise and imprudent, particularly since both African countries were victims of European colonial cartography and geo-politics.

In 1974, while Sankara was engrossed in a war with Mali, Muammar Qaddafi hosted the Pan-African Youth Movement summit in Benghazi, Libya, where El-Ouali Mustapha Sayed represented the Polisario Front and led its delegation. Later in that year, Sayed was elected Secretary-General of the Polisario Front. Furthermore, by 1974, the Polisario Front (under the leadership of Sayed) gained control of Western Sahara's countryside and forced Spain to relinquish its colonial hold of Western Sahara in 1975. Therefore, 1974 served as a major turning point for the careers of both Thomas Sankara and El-Ouali Mustapha Sayed. Moreover, 1974 served as a major turning point for the countries of Burkina Faso and Western Sahara as their borders were reconfigured. Western Sahara would ultimately be under the colonial control of the Kingdom of Morocco. While Burkina Faso was exercising its economic sovereignty by way of international trade, Morocco would gain not only market entry to the lucrative fishing and phosphates industries of the Western Sahara, but also control the trading relationship of Western Sahara with other nations. Sankara's solidarity with Western Sahara was an important political force; however, it did not create the necessary conditions for economic empowerment. Politically, Sankara's solidarity with Western Sahara was a powerful socio-cultural, anti-colonial symbol, but lacked economic substance given their rich and abundant resources. In terms of abundant resources, such as fishing and phosphates, Western

Sahara is also rich in oil and petroleum. Morocco would soon dominate those markets, too. Indeed, 'Morocco has turned to Western Sahara for oil reserves and petroleum ... Morocco contracted TOTAL, a French company along with Island Oil and Gas, a company in Ireland, and Kerr-McGee, a company from the United States to drill and extract oil in Western Sahara' (Delices 2015). In December 2014, while I was on a fact-finding mission to the Saharawis' refugee camps in Algeria (commissioned by Dr Ron Daniels's Institute of the Black World), a US oil company, Kosmos Energy, commenced its drilling venture for oil in Western Sahara on 19 December 2014 (ibid.). At present, 85 per cent of Moroccan foreign investments is in Africa, where Morocco is exploiting the oil and petroleum in Western Sahara to develop a natural gas pipeline that will serve as the main access and market entry to energy from northwest Africa to the Mediterranean and Europe.

In Burkina Faso, the main natural resources are pumice, limestone, marble, salt, manganese and gold. Burkina Faso is the fourth largest producer of gold in Africa. Although Sankara had an endogenous and anti-colonial approach to economic development, he never developed a bi-lateral anti-colonial trade agreement with colonised Western Sahara. This was probably so given the challenges imposed on both countries by international trade, international laws and imperial forces. Accordingly, in *How Europe Underdeveloped Africa*, Walter Rodney contends:

> From the beginning, Europe assumed the power to make decisions within the international trading system. An excellent illustration of that is the fact that the so-called international law which governed the conduct of nations on the high seas was nothing else but European law. Africans did not participate in its making, and in many instances, African people were simply the victims, for the law recognized them only as transportable merchandise.
>
> (Rodney 1981[1972]: 77)

Thus, the long-term economic results of colonising the economy of Western Sahara and Burkina Faso have been extreme impoverishment, excessive debt, an exploited labour class, low income per capita, high imports, low exports, dependency on external (European and US) markets, poor domestic savings and capital formation as well as the foreign ownership of land, labour and resources.

To decolonise and jumpstart an economy, a nation must be more capital-intensive than labour-intensive where exports (selling) outnumber imports (buying) as infant industries are protected. A capital-intensive nation protects its industries by securing capital and investing it in the production and manufacturing of goods and services. A labour-intensive nation depends more on labour than capital to produce goods and services-thus, within a labour-intensive country, labour outweighs capital. Whereas Western Sahara and Burkina Faso represent labour-intensive countries; Western Europe and the United States represent capital-intensive nations. Furthermore, it is an economic fact that a nation that exports more than it imports has a trade surplus – a favourable or positive balance of trade; while, a nation with an unfavourable or negative balance of trade tend to import more than it exports which ultimately creates a trade deficit or a trade gap. Essentially, it is better for a nation to sell its goods and services than to excessively buy goods and services.

Hence, for the economy of countries like Western Sahara and Burkina Faso to 'take-off', economist Ha-Joon Chang (2002) identifies the state/nation as the main driver and guide for economic development, especially as it pertains to the balance of trade by why of how much a nation exports and imports its goods and services. Chang (ibid.) also advises against foreign aid and free trade liberalism in favour of protectionism and institutional building for economic growth.

As the President of Burkina Faso, Thomas Sankara understood the economic history of nation-building given the reality that he nearly eradicated bureaucratic and institutional corruption at the state/national level in Burkina Faso. However, the late president of the Sahrawi people's Polisario Front movement in Western Sahara, Mohamed Abdelaziz identify colonialism by Morocco as the main economic obstacle that impedes the economic growth and sovereignty of Western Sahara.

When I met and interviewed President Abdelaziz during December of 2014, he claimed that bureaucratic and institutional corruption in Western Sahara regarding the Sahrawi people and the Polisario Front did not exist given their loyalty and commitment to fighting colonialism, and whatever corruption that exist at the state/national level in Western Sahara comes from Morocco, not the people of Western Sahara. Moreover, when I asked President Abdelaziz, once Western Sahara becomes a sovereign nation what economic model would he incorporate – he stated a mixed economic system that is neither capitalist nor socialist. Therefore, unlike Sankara, Abdelaziz did not fully embrace nor was he willing to completely adopt the political economy of Karl Marx and a planned (socialist) market economy. However, Abdelaziz, like Sankara, tilted toward democratic socialism where workers would be united and not exploited as class would no longer exist. Yet, unlike Sankara, Abdelaziz was open to accepting foreign aid, especially aid (financial and otherwise) from the United States under the presidency of Barack Obama. But President Obama favoured capitalism by way of free trade liberalism. Moreover, President Obama favoured the first country that recognised the independence of the United States, Morocco. In 1777, Morocco recognised the United States as a sovereign nation and by 1786, the two nations signed a treaty known as the Moroccan–American Treaty of Peace and Friendship. And this enduring international bond between the United States and Morocco will not be interrupted nor jeopardised by Western Sahara's appeal to the United States to support and aid its anti-colonial cause.

Nonetheless, to decolonise a colonial economy, economic democracy must be in place, while economic dependency on colonial powers must be eradicated; foreign debt must be forgiven; ownership of resources and businesses should be in the hands of the indigenous population; job growth and creation must be implemented; wages should be fair and equitable; protectionism must be in place; privatisation should be avoided; land, labour, resources and people should not be commodified; distribution of wealth should be equal; the economy should be either planned or mixed; workers should be organised and form unions; and women should be part of the workforce not simply as labourers, but as owners and managers. However, there are challenges of bi-lateral trade between Western Sahara and Burkina Faso as the long-term economic results of colonialism have direct social consequences, such as a low prevalence of formalised literacy, food injustice as well as high infant mortality rates. As such, a colonialised economy causes not only economic despair, but also major sociological ills.

SOCIAL COLONISATION

The third aspect of colonialism, according to Hira, is its social dimension(s). In a colonial society, the development of human social relations is structured, organised and institutionalised to fortify not only colonialism, but also racism and sexism. In such a system, race, ethnicity, colour and gender are categorised in the domain of superior and inferior or, according to decolonial thought, in the zone of being and non-being as illustrated in the colonial history of Western Sahara and Burkina Faso.

In *Black Skin, White Masks*, world-renowned psychiatrist Frantz Fanon (2008) provides a psychoanalysis of racism, colonialism and dehumanisation. Fanon, in his psychoanalysis, determines that racism and colonialism are power structures based on domination and dehumanisation. As such, for Fanon, the anatomy of racism and colonialism divides human beings into two unequal, discriminatory lines of demarcation: the zone of being and non-being. In the zone of being, humanity is acknowledged, respected and cherished where conflicts are often handled peacefully (ibid.). In the zone of non-being, humanity is not recognised and is therefore disrespected and despised where conflicts and differences are handled by using force and violence (ibid.). Put simply, the zone of being belongs to white people whose lives matters due to their race and racial privilege; while, the zone of non-being belongs to non-whites whose lives don't matter due to their race and lack of racial privilege. Therefore, in the zone of being, whites are humans who must be valued; whereas, in the zone of non-being, non-whites are not humans and must be devalued and dehumanised. However, the zone of being and non-being is a model based on race not gender; even though gender is considered where white women are often oppressed and exploited by white men, but due to their race they are still privileged as they thread the zone of being (ibid.).

In terms of gender, under colonial rule, non-white women under the zone of non-being were not allowed access to formal education and were positioned in political, economic and social subordination to all men in spite of the zone and being of their male counterparts. Indeed, a major social challenge, more so perhaps in Burkina Faso than in Western Sahara, was gender inequality. Despite the promotion of democratic socialism and gender equality in both nations, a patriarchal colonial sexist culture remains the norm – creating serious limitations for decolonisation.

In recognising such challenges and limitations, approximately one year before his assassination, in a speech commemorating International Women's Day on 8 March 1987, Sankara said:

> Starting now, the men and women of Burkina Faso should profoundly change their image of themselves. For they are part of a society that is not only establishing new social relations but is also provoking a cultural transformation, upsetting the relations of authority between men and women and forcing both to rethink the nature of each.
>
> (Sankara 2007c: 22)

In that same speech, Sankara also stated:

> in order to win this battle common to men and women, we must be familiar with all aspects of the woman question on a world as well as a national scale. We must understand how the struggle of Burkinabe women today is part of the worldwide struggle of all women and, beyond that, part of the struggle for full rehabilitation of our continent. The condition of women is therefore at the heart of the question of humanity itself, here, there, and everywhere. The question is thus universal in character.
>
> (Sankara 2007c: 24–25)

Sankara's words regarding the fair and equal treatment of women might have influenced the first President of the Sahrawi Arab Democratic Republic (SADR), Mohamed Abdelaziz, who served as President of SADR from 1982 until his death in 2016 (after a long illness). President Mohamed Abdelaziz, given his motion toward democratic socialism and adoption of Pan-Africanism, believed in a revolutionary socio-political philosophy similar to Sanakra's, especially his belief that the liberation of a nation depends on the liberation of its women.

President Abdelaziz selected several important women as members of his executive cabinet. Under the presidency of President of Mohamed Abdelaziz, I met with the sister leadership representing the anti-colonial revolutionary movement in Western Sahara. According to one delegation member, famed Ugandan journalist and editor in chief of the *Black Star News*, Milton Allimaldi:

> we met two very articulate female ministers, Kheira Boulahi, minister of Professional Training, and Khadija Hamdi, the minister of culture; they both outlined their visions of a free and liberated Western Sahara. The women developed their independence over the years as they took care of homes when men were out fighting for the country's liberation; some women also became guerrilla fighters.
>
> (Allimaldi 2015)

Allimaldi's words echo Sankara's repeated insistence that women could and would hone their own agency in pursuing independence and radical social transformation. As such, Sankara developed a Ministry of Women. Western Sahara, under the leadership of the Polisario Front, created various ministries for women in addition to the National Organization of Sahrawi Women, which served as the military and political counterpart of the Polisario Front. El-Ouali Mustapha Sayed and Mohamed Abdelaziz of Western Sahara, much like Sankara in Burkina Faso, employed significant socio-political reforms and economic measures to empower the most impoverished people, including a focus on women. Indeed, women served in armed revolutionary struggle in both Western Sahara and Burkina Faso. Both countries made educating women a top priority.

To decolonise social relations, both societies retained a focus on educating and empowering women. To combat infant mortality, both countries developed strong ties with Fidel Castro's Cuba for healthcare and other social services, including those with a focus on gender. By 1983, Cuba had extended its hand to Sankara by sending about twenty-four doctors and healthcare professionals to Burkina Faso (Harsch 2014: 116). Similar to Burkina Faso under Sankara, the 'Sahwaris believe education is the key to building their nation and send many of their daughters and sons for university education overseas to countries that offer scholarships. They have a special relationship with Cuba, which has trained more than 5,000 engineers, doctors, teachers and other professionals through the years, at no cost' (ibid.). During my fact-finding mission, I was overcome with a deep sense of Pan-African pride as I met and interviewed Cuban doctors in Saharawi's refugee camps. The majority of doctors at Saharawi refugee camps hailed from Castro's Cuba.

In the 1980s, both societies had some of the highest rates of infant mortality. However, in Burkina Faso, infant mortality rates dropped from 208 to 145 for every 1,000 infants born (Sankara 2007c: 16). Furthermore, both societies had some of the lowest prevalence of formalised literacy in the world (at the time, Burkina Faso had a 1 per cent formalised literacy rate, followed by Western Sahara's 10 per cent literacy rate). Moreover, in Burkina Faso, under the leadership of Thomas Sankara, literacy programs based on indigenous languages were implemented.

By 1976, as the people of Western Sahara sought protection at refugee camps from several aerial bombings by the Moroccan air force, the formalised literacy rate of the Sahrawi people was about 10 per cent. Currently, it is about 90 per cent (Allimaldi 2015). For El-Ouali Mustapha Sayed, the nationalist leader of the Sahrawi people (the Father of the Sahrawi Nation) and the co-founder of the Polisario Front, 'Morocco and Mauritania were tiny enemies in comparison to illiteracy' (FamPeople.com 2012). Even in a context of on-going and neo-colonial economic and socio-political struggles, both Sayed and Sankara were attentive to the social dimensions of decolonisation. Unfortunately, in 1976, as he was developing a relationship with Sankara, Mustapha Sayed was killed in combat while fighting for the economic, political and cultural decolonisation of Western Sahara.

CULTURAL COLONISATION

Culture is Hira's final dimension of colonialism. Also related to psychology, culture includes mental state, makeup, character and behaviour. In colonised societies, these are often based on a colonised education and religious ethos. For Sankara (2007b: 53), 'culture in a democratic and popular society, should have a three-fold character: national, revolutionary, and popular' where 'our culture extols dignity, courage, nationalism, and the great human virtues'. However, under colonial rule, a main feature of culture is to impose the cultural ethos of the coloniser on the colonised by making the indigenous culture not only unpopular – sometimes illegal – but also inferior. In cultural imperialism, the coloniser's language (be it French, Spanish, Portuguese, English or Arabic) is enforced as the collective rubric for intellectualism and the quality of being (which is labelled as refined and sophisticated). Simply put, the way of life, way of knowing, speech, language, dress, taste, customs and religion of the coloniser are deemed superior and must be adopted, often for the 'well-being' of the colonised people. The culture of the colonised is 'inferior' in the colonial hierarchy and is rejected, devalued and disrespected.

In Burkina Faso, the colonial culture was French. French language and style dictated significant aspects of cultural life in Burkina Faso. However, Sankara retained the cultural focus to decolonising the African mind. This focus addressed foremost education as pedagogy, now taught in indigenous languages rather than French. Sankara radically transformed the literacy rate by making indigenous African languages the norm and an acceptable – even valued – way of communicating. In Western Sahara, cultural imperialism remains apparent: an African-Arab Islamic monarchy controls another African-Arab Islamic state. The Saharawi people, because of their historical experience with colonialism, speak mainly three colonial languages: French, Spanish and Arabic (some Saharawi people also speak English). However, to achieve decolonisation and to put an end to cultural imperialism, the people of Western Sahara adopted the three-fold character of culture similar to that delineated by Sankara, where their character extols a dignified Saharawi nationalism along with a popular anti-colonial revolutionary movement that has not only courage, but also great human virtues and an appreciable indigenous African cultural legacy, where according to Sankara (2007a: 128), 'there is only one colour – that of African unity'.

CONCLUSION

European nations grew rich and powerful as they captured African markets by exploiting African natural resources and destroying indigenous social relations by way of forced and low pay labour. Walter Rodney (1981[1972]: 33), in his classic tome, *How Europe Underdeveloped Africa*, states that 'Africa today is underdeveloped in relation to Western Europe and a few other parts of the world; and that the present position has been arrived at, not by the separate evolution of Africa on the one hand and Europe on the other, but through exploitation' of the socio-economic life and material basis (land, labour and resources) of African societies. Rodney's words remain relevant for today's global geopolitical and cultural positioning of many African societies, Burkina Faso and Western Sahara included. Drawing on Hira's five dimensions of colonialism illustrates the multidimensional layers of destruction effected by colonialism, including those of the social and economic fabric of Burkina Faso and Western Sahara, which created internal political strife over border disputes, religious differences and gender disparities that still exist. These disputes over geography (and interrelated issues of politics and economics) are seen in the cases of Western Sahara and Morocco as well as in Burkina Faso and Mali. Sankara had the revolutionary vision and political will to critique some of the internal conflicts in Africa as senseless disputes that benefit former colonial powers. Even today, the conflicts that we witness in Africa have roots in colonialism and neo-colonial relations, geographies and politics, with the reformation of capitalism in the guise of neo-imperialism and neoliberalism. In our contemporary epoch, decolonisation of each of the five major dimensions of colonialism remains a top priority, particularly in a time when capitalism has taken neo-imperial and neoliberal forms. What we need is democratic socialism and a decolonisation as we hold the '1 per cent' (i.e. the world's super-rich) accountable for their actions or inactions.

Sankara warned against colonial imperialistic 'booby traps'. He linked politically and culturally with the anti-colonial revolutionary movement of Western Sahara. By exposing Morocco's exploitation of Western Sahara along with its oppression of the Saharawi people, Sankara called for the death of colonialism and imperialism. Sankara urged the restoration of humanity (being) and the independence of Western Sahara. The depth of Sankara's internationalism is apparent in this sustained struggle against colonialism and imperialism, including his efforts for the independence of Burkina Faso. He was a vocal critic of apartheid in South Africa and supported the anti-imperialist revolutionary movements of Nicaragua, Palestine, Angola and Namibia (Sankara 2007b: 17). That is why, in 1984, the people of Harlem, New York welcomed Sankara enthusiastically (ibid.). Sankara's popular and social democratic revolution touched the core of working-class people not only in Africa, but also in Asia, Europe, the United States, Latin America and the Caribbean (ibid.). It is our job not to let his vision of a decolonised world be lost to history. Morocco continues to colonise Western Sahara, while the United States and other European nations continue to colonise our minds.

REFERENCES

Ajayi, J. F. A. (1998) *Africa in the Nineteenth Century until the 1880s, General History of Africa Volume VI.* Paris: UNESCO.

Allimaldi, M. (2015) Africa Last Colony: Sahwaris Want Barack Obama's Help. *The Huffington Post,* 16 January. Retrieved from www.huffingtonpost.com/milton-allimadi/africa-last-colony-sahwar_b_6479078.html.

Chang, H.-J. (2002) *Kicking Away the Ladder.* London: Anthem Press.

Delices, P. (2015) Sovereignty and Decoloniality: From the United States to Western Sahara. *Black Star News.* Retrieved from www.blackstarnews.com/us-politics/policy/sovereignty-and-decoloniality-from-the-united-states-to-western.

Englebert, P. (2015) The Real 'Map' of Africa: Redrawing Colonial Borders. *Foreign Affairs,* 8 November. Retrieved from www.foreignaffairs.com/articles/2015-11-08/real-map-africa.

FamPeople.com (2012) El-Ouali Mustapha Sayed: Biography. Retrieved from www.fampeople.com/cat-el-ouali-mustapha-sayed_2.

Fanon, F. (2008) *Black Skin, White Mask.* New York: Grove Press.

Fisher, M. (2015) Map: European Colonialism Conquered Every Country in the World, but These Five. *Vox,* 25 February. Retrieved from www.vox.com/2014/6/24/5835320/map-in-the-whole-world-only-these-five-countries-escaped-european.

Harsch, E. (2014) *Thomas Sankara: An African Revolutionary.* Athens, OH: Ohio University Press.

Hira, S. (2014) *Decolonizing the Mind: 20 Questions and Answers about Reparations for Colonialism.* The Hague: Amrit Publishers.

Hira, S. (2015) Scientific Colonialism: The Eurocentric Approach to Colonialism. In M. Araújo and S. R. Maeso (eds), *Eurocentrism, Racism and Knowledge: Debates* on *History and Power in Europe and the Americas*, 136–153. New York: Palgrave Macmillan.

Lamin, H. M. (2017) What's on Morocco's Agenda as it Rejoins African Union? *Al-Monitor*, February. Retrieved from www.al-monitor.com/pulse/originals/2017/02/morocco-agenda-join-african-union.

Olopade, D. (2014) *The Bright Continent: Breaking Rules and Making Change in Modern Africa*. New York: Houghton Mifflin Harcourt.

Rodney, W. (1981[1972]) *How Europe Underdeveloped Africa*. Washington, DC: Howard University Press.

Sankara, T. (2007a) *Thomas Sankara Speaks: The Burkina Faso Revolution 1983–1987* (ed. M. Prairie). New York: Pathfinder Press.

Sankara, T. (2007b) *We are Heirs of the World's Revolutions: Thomas Sankara Speeches from the Burkina Faso Revolution 1983–87*. New York: Pathfinder Press.

Sankara, T. (2007c) *Women's Liberation and the African Freedom Struggle*. New York: Pathfinder.

CHAPTER 19

'Daring to Invent the Future'
Sankara's Legacy and Contemporary Activism in South Africa
Levi Kabwato and Sarah Chiumbu

INTRODUCTION

South Africa was one of the last countries in Africa to gain political independence when it did so in 1994, two years after the prison release of Nelson Mandela. The country was praised for its peaceful transition. The 'Rainbow Nation' – a concept coined by the country's prominent Archbishop Desmond Tutu – has been used as a trope to denote the supposed unity of the many cultures, identities and nations in the post-apartheid context. Rainbow Nationism, manifested in many symbolic and discursive interventions (for example the South African flag represents a Rainbow Nation by sporting six different colours), is designed to encourage a sense of belonging and unity (Puttick 2011).

However, more than two decades since the end of apartheid, the country struggles with mounting poverty, inequality and race, class and gender divisions. Scholars have argued that the neoliberal economic policies adopted by the government over the years have entrenched inequalities and poverty by creating a policy environment that has generally favoured the privatisation of basic services (Bond 2014; McDonald and Smith 2004), thus hitting the poor the most. The result of this has been a sustained period of struggle and protest concerning socio-economic rights by the poor – both on the streets and in the courts. South Africa, known colloquially as the 'protest capital' of the world, is home to hundreds of community protests (against poor housing, unemployment as well as water and electricity provision and cut-offs) annually (see Alexander 2010).

In addition, the incumbent governing party, the African National Congress (ANC), has been accused of corruption and ignoring the concerns of the poor. Young people have been at the forefront of articulating the growing sense of disillusionment concerning the slow pace of transformation, persistent economic inequalities and on-going racism in the country. In 2015, two interlinked student movements emerged: #RhodesMustFall and #FeesMustFall,[1] both of which call for the decolonisation of universities, the removal of symbols of oppression and colonialism from campus, a revision of the curriculum and a re-imagination of intellectual life on post-apartheid South African campuses (Naicker 2016). These struggle repertoires (of marches, rallies and sit-ins): (a) are reminiscent of apartheid-era resistance and anti-apartheid tactics, (b) are expedited through the use of new technologies of social media and (c) draw inspiration from an awareness of international movements and Pan-African figures, including Thomas Sankara.

In the last three years, young people have expressed a sense of common identity and critical consciousness as they challenge the established order. It is in this context of disillusionment and political re-awakening that a youth-led political party, the Economic Freedom Fighters (EFF), emerged in 2013. The EFF is a self-declared Marxist-Leninist-Fanonist political party that was formed in opposition to the dominant ANC. Led by former ANC Youth League President (ANCYL), Julius Malema, in only three short years, the party has managed to tip the balance of power in the country and shift the political landscape. In 2014, it participated in the national and provincial elections as a six-month old party and received more than one million votes, translating into a 6 per cent representation in the parliament. Two years later, in the 2016 local and municipal elections, the party received 8.1 per cent of the vote and gained 761 council seats nationally (Morken 2016).

In this chapter, we examine the ideology and political praxis of the EFF, with a particular attention to its re-introduction of radical political philosophies into mainstream discourse. We show that key components of these radical philosophies have been influenced, in part, by the revolutionary spirit of Thomas Sankara. We draw on decolonial theories to read EFF's political praxis against Sankara's ideologies and vision. Decoloniality is a project of epistemically, ontologically and materially de-linking from the colonial order (see also Chapter 8, this volume). A decolonial reading of Sankara demonstrates that his vision was centred on completing the process of decolonisation by liberating the people of Burkina Faso from coloniality. He was alive to the reality that although Africa had achieved juridical-political decolonisation, the continent continued to exist within a colonial power matrix. Similarly, EFF's focus on economic freedom highlights persistent colonial domination, asserting that more than 'twenty years after the attainment of formal political freedom, the black people of South Africa still live in absolute mass poverty ... and vestiges of apartheid and colonial economic patterns, ownership and control remain intact despite the attainment of political freedom by the former liberation movement' (EFF Founding Manifesto, cited in Smith 2014: 117).

Five decades after attaining independence, Africa remains economically enslaved to Western neoliberal capitalism. Forces of neoliberalism – from the structural economic adjustments programmes and the World Trade Organization (WTO) in the 1990s to the current Millennium Development Goals (MDGs) and Sustainable Development Goals (SDGs) – undermine the power of national governments and continental organisations such as the African Union (AU) to design policies divorced from global imperial designs. Ama Biney (2013) argues that since the murder of Sankara in 1987, African leaders have been locked in the Washington Consensus rationality and have lacked the courage to seek alternative policies that meet the needs of their people. The meta-narrative of 'Africa Rising' detracts from fundamental challenges facing the continent, including poverty, food insecurity, gender inequality, social exclusion and access to and control over land. Recent events, such as the 2008 global economic meltdown, Occupy Movements and the 2011 Arab Revolutions suggest that we may be entering a period of 'non-hegemony' and an era of significant transformation in the organisation and structure of world order (Cobbett and Germain 2012: 110). Robert Cox states the world is entering 'a time of gradual disintegration of a historical structure (neo-liberal hegemony), which not so long ago seemed to be approaching what Francis Fukuyama once called "the end of history"' (cited in Schouten 2009: 1).

We argue that these developments provide opportunities for counter-hegemonic articulations. Indeed, we have seen increased calls for 'decolonisation', not least in South Africa where the post-apartheid project is on trial. Young people especially are turning to writings and speeches of African political thinkers of the past such as Thomas Sankara, Frantz Fanon, Amilcar Cabral and Steve Biko to find inspiration to advocate for an alternative political future for Africa. The EFF is nestled in the midst of these wider debates on decolonisation.

Our chapter is divided as follows: First, we provide a theoretical lens in which to read both Sankara and the post-apartheid revolutionary politics in South Africa. Second, we outline the incomplete process of decolonisation in South Africa, despite the end of apartheid, and highlight similarities in this incompleteness of the decolonising project with Sankara's critique of neo-colonialism (through an analysis of Sankara's political speeches). This is followed by a discussion on the emergence of the EFF and an examination of EFF's ideologies and elucidations of an alternative political future for South Africa. Fourth, we examine the EFF's politics of performance and the significance of its political colours and associated emblems in its repertoires. We end the paper with reflections on emerging revolutionary spirits and political consciousness of young people across Africa, influenced by Sankara and other Pan-Africanists, who are 'daring to invent a future' beyond colonialism and coloniality.

THEORETICAL DEPARTURE: SANKARA AND DECOLONIAL MEDITATIONS

Thomas Sankara articulated his beliefs within what can loosely be termed a 'postcolonial discourse', which materialised out of resistance and critique of colonialism and its continuing legacies (Omeje 2015). While principally preoccupied with ending poverty and corruption and carrying out projects of nationalisation and of land redistribution in Burkina Faso, Sankara also cast an eye on the rest of the continent. He provided a powerful critique of international structures that continued to reinforce colonial legacies and asymmetrical power relations on Africa and tapped into the ideology of Pan-Africanism and the policy goal of African unity. Sankara invoked the leftist-historical materialism (Marxist political economy) of earlier political thinkers from the Global South – such as Frantz Fanon, Kwame Nkrumah, Amilcar Cabral, Cheikh Anta Diop and Walter Rodney – who also confronted imperialism.

The continuing imperial designs in all areas of modern life have been theorised as coloniality, which refers to 'long standing patterns of power that emerged as a result of colonialism, but that define culture, labour, intersubjectivity relations, and knowledge production well beyond the strict limits of colonial administrations' (Maldonado-Torres 2007: 243). Although written largely with Latin American context and background, these works have been highly influential in helping illuminate the 'continuity of colonial forms of domination after the end of colonial administration' (Grosfoguel 2007: 219). Coloniality exists in the realms of power, knowledge and being. Anibal Quijano (2000) states that the coloniality of power is a global hegemonic model of power that controls all aspects of life to favour the needs of capital. Coloniality of knowledge refers to the manner in which Eurocentric knowledge systems are privileged over other knowledges and epistemes (Mignolo 2007). Hegemonic narratives, often from the Global North, are thus projected 'as absolute while knowledges outside the bounds of Western modernity are ignored, marginalised or repressed' (Chiumbu 2015: 5). Coloniality of being refers to the colonisation of subjectivity, racialised embodiment and its relation to power (Maldonado-Torres 2007). Africa remains entrapped and entangled within these three aspects of coloniality and, as Ndlovu-Gatsheni (2012) argues, the independence that Africa celebrates is a myth. What the continent needs is not emancipation, but liberation. Emancipation has given Africa liberal democracy and realisation of individual human rights, whereas true liberation will 'lead to decolonisation, social justice and the birth of a new humanity divorced from colonial modernity' (ibid.: 74).

Decoloniality is the project of disrupting coloniality. Mignolo (2011) states that decoloniality has its historical grounding in the Bandung Conference of 1955, which brought together countries from Africa and Asia to promote

African and Asian economic coalitions and decolonisation. Thus the political and epistemic foundations of decoloniality have been in place for over five decades. Nelson Maldonado-Torres states:

> The decolonial turn does not refer to a single theoretical school, but rather points to a family of diverse positions that share a view of coloniality as the fundamental problem in the modern (as well as postmodern and information age), and decolonization or decoloniality as a necessary task that remains unfinished.
>
> (Maldonado-Torres 2011: 2)

Important African revolutionary and political thinkers (including those mentioned above), were concerned early on about the 'ideological deficiency' of the decolonisation movements. For example, Amilcar Cabral was concerned about the 'failure of African nationalist leaders to distinguish between genuine national liberation and neo-colonialism' (Ndlovu-Gatsheni 2012: 76). Kwame Nkrumah stated that neo-colonialism 'acts covertly, creating client states, independent in name but in point of fact pawns of the very colonial power that is supposed to have given them independence' (quoted in Banda 2008: 90). Although Sankara was a doer and was action-oriented rather than a theorist or prolific author, his practice was influenced by a strong decolonial ethos – long before such an ethos was identified within universities. Sankara was driven by a conviction that Africa was not yet free from imperialism. He advocated for the total dismantling of the neo-colonial development structure, arguing that this development structure rendered African states slaves to foreign masters:

> The transformation of our mentality is far from complete. There are still many among us who take foreign norms as their point of reference in judging the quality of their social, economic and cultural lives. They live in Burkina Faso yet refuse to accept the concrete reality of our country.
>
> (Sankara, 4 August 1987)[2]

Referring to the entrapment of Africa to colonial matrices of power through foreign aid, he said:

> Debt is a cleverly managed reconquest of Africa ... that turns each one of us into a financial slave ... welfare and aid policies have only ended up disorganizing us, subjugating us, and robbing us of a sense of responsibility for our own economic, political, and cultural affairs. We chose to risk new paths to achieve greater well-being.
>
> (Sankara, speech at Organization of African Unity conference, 29 July 1987)

This call was, and still is, a radical departure from how Africans view(ed) themselves after gaining independence. Indeed, Sankara's remarks at the

Organization of African Unity were met with laughter from the African Heads of State present, rather than the serious consideration and deliberation they warranted in light of neo-colonialism and the debt crises suffered across the continent. This call highlights Sankara's awareness of the need for collective action to pursue a path determined by the aspirations of African people, not colonialists acting in cahoots with proponents of neo-liberalism.

ELITE TRANSITION IN THE COLONIAL AFTERMATH

Postcolonial scholar Leela Gandhi argues:

> The colonial aftermath is marked by the range of ambivalent cultural moods and formations which accompany periods of transition and translation. It is, in the first place, a celebrated moment of arrival – charged with the rhetoric of independence and the creative euphoria of self-invention.
>
> (Gandhi 1998: 5)

'Self-invention', as articulated by Gandhi (ibid.), is necessitated by a recognition of the physical and psychological damage caused by the colonial encounter. Yet, the task is always harder than it seems and those presiding over the newly independent State – firmly rooted in colonial thought and practice – usually appear ill prepared to decisively deal with both the question and task of 'self-invention' (or had been hand-selected by departing colonial administrators to oversee the continued coloniality of the state). South Africa's 'Rainbow Nation' miracle confronted this reality in 1994 and it has been contested since. Under the dominant image of Nelson Mandela as president of the ANC and the country's first democratically elected leader, tensions emerged between the hopes, dreams and aspirations of the majority Black population against the uncertainties and fears of the minority white population (which had benefited under Apartheid). Therefore, as Meredith (2006) argues, 'the magnitude of the task of transforming South Africa into a fully fledged democracy after many years of white-minority rule was indeed haunting. The entire system that Mandela inherited had been designed largely to serve white interests' (ibid.: 647). The transition that ensued was thus conducted within a negotiated process between the white elite of the White National Party (NP) and the leadership of the new ruling party, the ANC. For the NP, they conceded political power, but largely retained economic power while for the ANC leadership concessions involved moving away from radical policies and aims that antagonised business (Sparks 2009: 199). The economic edifice remained intact, biased towards racialised capital. As a result, South Africa is very far from the 'revolutionary democracy ... in which poverty, want and insecurity shall be no more' that Mandela looked forward to in his 1964 speech from the dock during the Rivonia Trial[3] (Pithouse 2016: 126–127). Leela Gandhi (1998: 6–7) argues, 'postcoloniality as a historical condition is marked by the visible apparatus of freedom and the concealed persistence of unfreedom'. This is the case not only in South Africa, but most of the postcolonial world.

This 'unfreedom' is exactly what the project of decoloniality is attempting to undo. Unfreedom makes up a cornerstone of Thomas Sankara's political thought, as well. For example, when he gave his Political Orientation Speech in October 1983, two months after the revolution, Sankara elucidated the connection between the challenges that plagued Upper Volta/Burkina Faso since independence and the August 1983 coup, which brought him to power. Such a connection, informed by ever-increasing contradictions, could only result in a popular revolution that would capture the aspirations of masses in the midst of their discontentment. For Sankara, therefore, the popularity of the August 1983 revolution was not based on the appeal of the leaders but rather on its sincerity and commitment to respond to neo-colonial excesses – including a commitment to challenge these excesses and leverage State power to express popular will. As Sankara said in his Political Orientation Speech in October 1983:

> The enthusiastic adherence of the broad popular masses to the August revolution is the concrete expression of the immense hopes that the Voltaic people place in the rise of the CNR (National Council of the Revolution). They hope that their deep-going aspirations might finally be achieved – aspirations for democracy, liberty, independence, genuine progress, and the restoration of the dignity and grandeur of our homeland, which twenty-three years of neo-colonial rule have treated with singular contempt.

Needless to say, the Political Orientation Speech became the manifesto of the revolution and every citizen who believed in the revolution was expected to know its contents, and teach those who did not believe as yet. In part, Sankara knew that the revolution would not succeed if the people whom it was meant to serve were not aware of the history that gave birth to it and, more importantly, the ever-present threat of imperialism and neo-colonialism. Thus, the people had a direct stake in not only working to see their aspirations fulfilled but also to actively guard against threats to the country.

Frantz Fanon (1963) forewarned the nature of the political economy of post-colonial transitioning in his book, *The Wretched of the Earth*: the colonising presence/occupying power never relinquishes its central position in State affairs except when expanding its tentacles to reach those previously excluded (the colonised) and now willing to work – unwittingly in most cases – towards the entrenchment of European standards on development as prescribed by the colonial metropolis (Gatzambide-Fernández 2012). It is not surprising in this context of elite transition and renewal that, after 1994, the new South African government abandoned the socially oriented Reconstruction and Development Programme (RDP) introduced in 1994 in favour of the market-friendly Growth, Employment and Redistribution (GEAR) in 1996. This shift signalled a neoliberal turn that has influenced subsequent economic policies. Bond (2014) rightly argues that South Africa has witnessed the replacement of racial apartheid with 'class apartheid': a systemic segregation of the oppressed majority through structured economic, political, legal and cultural practices.

THE MASTER'S HOUSE IS BURNING: EMERGENCE OF THE ECONOMIC FREEDOM FIGHTERS

Due to growing inequalities and rising disillusionments, it was only a matter of time before the post-apartheid project exploded. The emergence, in July 2013, of the new youth-led party, the EFF (discussed earlier) symbolises some of this explosion. The EFF benefited from the intra-party tensions within the ANC, some of them affecting their leader, Julius Malema, who was expelled on the charge that he was bringing the party into disrepute in 2012. During his time as Youth League president, Malema amassed power within the party, exerted influence and advanced policy positions that were not consistent with the party's own. These included calls for the nationalisation of land and mineral wealth in South Africa for purposes of advancing 'economic freedom in our lifetime' and he also took foreign policy positions, endorsing Zimbabwe's Robert Mugabe while calling for the removal of Ian Khama in Botswana. And, despite having played a key role in former president Thabo Mbeki's recall, which ensured the ascendency of Zuma into the presidency, Malema had fallen out of favour with the latter by the time of his expulsion. In November 2011, as his disciplinary proceedings were underway, Malema spoke of a dying culture of open engagement and free expression in the ANC, although within the same breath, he vowed never to resign from the party. He later faced legal challenges, resulting in the loss of his plush suburban home, luxury vehicles and a farm.

Despite this, Malema's message of 'economic freedom in our lifetime' received overwhelming support from many young people across South Africa, especially the unemployed and those disillusioned with the promises of 1994. They repeatedly showed up at his disciplinary hearings and subsequent court appearances, forming a ready audience and prospective membership of the new political party. The EFF also managed to lure established ANC members, like Advocate Dali Mpofu, who later became the party's National Chairperson. On leaving the ANC, Mpofu said:

Now, the EFF is the only political formation which brings to the table cogent, understandable and practical alternatives to the status quo. Of course, mainstream media and sections of society are hard at work to trivialise the political and economic plan of EFF because of narrow class and unfortunately racial prejudices. Hence the vitriolic cartoons and racial caricatures betraying the general and understandable pandemonium and panic among the noisy classes about the emergence of the EFF.

(Mpofu 2013)

In saying this, Mpofu was confronting middle-class outrage, including the elite mainstream media, directed at him personally. As a Senior Counsel (SC) and former executive, he was the perfect symbol of black middle class aspirations in South Africa: highly educated, wealthy and politically connected. As such, dominant thinking at the time seemed to suggest Mpofu had no business associating with a pro-poor movement such as the EFF, a movement that could potentially get in conflict with the middle-class as represented by people like Mpofu himself. In acknowledging the EFF as offering 'practical alternatives to the status quo', Mpofu was also burying his intimate association with the ANC, a party he had been involved with since an early age.

The genesis of the EFF is rooted in an interlinked chain of events. The party also needs to be understood within the materialisation of transnational youth movements involved in radical activism from distinct but complementary perspectives. The party is made up of relatively young men and women – many of them involved in youth political activism. This activism fits within a larger African context of protest movements against corruption, poor service delivery and financial scandals. Across the African continent, alongside the more well-known events in Egypt and Tunisia, disillusioned young people have taken to the streets in anti-government protests for political, social and economic emancipation (Honwana 2014). Across francophone Africa (including Burkina Faso, Mali, Côte d'Ivoire, Benin, Togo, Senegal and Cameroon), networks of social movements have emerged, including Génération Cheikh Anta Diop and the Mouvement des Sans Voix ('The Voiceless'). On 25 August 2013, Le Balai Citoyen (the Citizens' Broom) was formed as a grassroots movement which brought together youth activists across Burkina Faso (see Chapter 15, this volume). These movements played a central role in the 2014 October Uprising, in which president Blaise Compaoré, an accomplice in Sankara's assassination, was toppled. In Senegal, the Y'en A Marre ('We are Fed Up') movement has also played a significant role in disrupting the status quo and it is credited with helping to mobilise Senegal's youth vote, whose electoral outcome saw the ouster of incumbent President Abdoulaye Wade (Gueye 2013). This youth activism is a powerful rejection of the forces of neo-colonial capitalism that Sankara so vociferously critiqued – what Henry Giroux (2003) has called the 'terror of neoliberalism' and the 'politics of greed'.

This violence of neoliberalism has also contributed to the shifting of the political landscape in South Africa and is, in part, the cause of the cracks in the post-apartheid edifice. This rupture started to show as early as the turn of the twenty-first century, when a loosely organised left – made up of social movement and community activist coalitions – repeatedly challenged the state and capital (through protests, picketing and legal action) against the commodification of most basic services, including housing, water and electricity. By 2013, when the EFF was formed, the 'rebellion of the poor', as Alexander (2010) calls it, had reached fever pitch, with the country witnessing hundreds of community protests a year against lack of service delivery. In the period, labour strikes also increased and these have come to characterise the daily lives of the working class, nonworking class and under-employed South Africans' (Lynch 2012, quoted in Chiumbu 2016). Coupled with this has been growing corruption and consolidation of political and economic power in the hands of a small elite. This segmentation of power has alienated a huge proportion of the low-income population and progressive movements. Therefore, the emergence of a radical and leftist political party is not surprising.

Internal politics of the governing party, the ANC, also produced a fertile ground for the emergence of an alternative politics outside the mainstream opposition party, the Democratic Alliance (DA).[4] By the time it turned 100 years old in 2012, the ANC was showing glaring weaknesses as a political establishment – the oldest in Africa. Intra-party tensions were visible and the party was in decline and operating within the realm of prophetic warnings by Fanon:

> Since the proclamation of independence the party no longer helps the people to set out its demands, to become more aware of its needs and better able to establish its power ... there no longer exists the fruitful give-and-take from bottom to the top and from the top to the bottom which creates and guarantees democracy in a party. Quite on the contrary, the party has made itself into a screen between the masses and the leaders. There is no longer any party life, for the branches which were set up during the colonial period are today completely demobilised.
>
> (Fanon 1963: 136–137)

Perhaps the moment of the ANC's 'demobilisation' and rupture was most palpable in the aftermath of the 'Marikana massacre' of 16 August 2012. In Marikana, in the North-West province, 34 mineworkers were shot dead by South African police for protesting against low wages and deplorable working conditions at London Mining's Lonmin platinum mine. The Marikana massacre exposed the economic interests of the ANC leadership – and broadly the State – through its violent collusion with capital. The EFF grew out of post-Marikana sentiment. The official launch of the party was held in Marikana, where a large audience gave it a good reception.

A separate radical movement emerged out of the EFF: Black First, Land First (BLF), a Pan-Africanist and revolutionary Socialist party in South Africa, founded in 2015 by former EFF Commissar, Andile Mngxitama, following his expulsion from the party. Largely made up of young people, BLF has adopted a Sankarist leadership ethos that compels each elected representative to sign the 'Thomas Sankara Oath', which demands that signatories follow Sankara's example of a public service that serves the people and not politicians or unscrupulous public servants. In its 'BLF Revolutionary Call', the movement stresses that land is the source of dignity for Africans. The call explicitly draws inspiration from Sankara's thought and practice:

> We pledge to build a revolutionary movement, that is Sankarist in belief and practice, following and honouring the revolutionary legacy of Thomas Sankara. We believe that for the movement to succeed it needs a servant leadership – an accountable, democratic, responsive leadership that puts black people first!
>
> (Black First, Land First 2015)

This Sankarist orientation is significant. Although BLF acknowledges the influence of key political figures (such as Steve Bantu Biko and Robert Sobukwe) in its ideology, it is Thomas Sankara who fully captures the ethos of what the movement stands for. This is not a negative reflection on Biko and Sobukwe. Rather, it is Sankara's ascendency to the highest national public office, while maintaining his commitments to social and economic injustice, that sets him apart. Sankara's leadership gives BLF – and other African youth – an example through which to imagine the possibilities of a State that is controlled by 'servant leader'.

DISRUPTING COLONIALITY: THE EFF VISION FOR AN ALTERNATIVE POLITICAL AND ECONOMIC FUTURE SHARES MUCH WITH SANKARA'S VISION

More than two decades since the end of apartheid, South Africa is still operating within the 'colonial matrix of power' (Quijano 2000). The structures of inequality that came with the imposition of the apartheid systems in South Africa remain intact. According to the 2014 Oxfam Global Inequality report, inequality is greater in South Africa today than it was in 1994 (Seery and Caistor Arendar 2014). The EFF confronts this reality and exposes the political 'miracle' of 1994 as a myth that never dealt with critical issues of dispossession and redistribution:

> The political power that was transferred to the black majority through inclusive elections in 1994 was never transformed into economic freedom as the majority of Africans remain on the margins of society as unemployed, underemployed or

discriminated-against in their employment, while those who held economic, social and political power since the colonial period continue to enjoy economic, social, and professional privileges.

(EFF Founding Manifesto, quoted in Smith 2014: 120)

In articulating the above statement, the EFF proclaims that it is drawing 'inspiration from developments around the world on what has been done to advance the development and betterment of people's lives in the aftermath of the defeat of colonialism and against imperialism' (ibid.). Further, the party states that it 'draws inspiration from the broad Marxist-Leninist tradition and Fanonian schools of thought in their analyses of the state, imperialism, culture and class contradictions in every society' (ibid.: para. 28). There are significant ideological similarities between Sankara and the EFF, with both pushing a pro-nationalisation, pro-land redistribution and anti-imperialist policies. Sankara's disruption of coloniality was demonstrated in his unwavering stance against any form of imperialism. For instance, he stressed the importance of self-reliance through local organisation and resource sharing. His revolutionary thinking and praxis was in many ways a reaction to the conditionality politics of Western governments – a politics that made adopting multi-party politics a condition of getting aid. Bryan Williamson argues that Sankara and his revolutionary compatriots wanted:

to free the Burkinabé from the torment posed by debts owed to French and Ivorian governments and private investors. They considered themselves the architects of a new politics aimed at fighting against 'imperialism'. Sankara opposed nations that used force to make people to serve their social, economic and political purposes.

(Williamson 2013: 38)

Sankara's radical vision for Burkina Faso and its partial success – set against scarce resources, dismal poverty, regional and international hostility and a waning ideology of socialism – showed that an alternative political and economic future for the continent is indeed possible. In a speech given in March 1983, Sankara asked: who are the enemies of the people?

The enemies of the people are both inside and outside the country … The enemies of the people inside the country are all those who have taken advantage of their social position, of their bureaucratic position, to enrich themselves illicitly … They claim they are serving Upper Volta. These are the enemies of the people. They must be exposed. They must be combated. We will combat them together with you.

(Sankara, 1988: 54)

Similarly, the EFF was formed on the back of a question: what is to be done? The response was captured in a Declaration that emerged from an EFF meeting, held on 26 and 27 July 2013 in Soweto, in south Johannesburg:

Economic Freedom Fighters ... should be an economic emancipation movement, which should be mass based, associate and relate constantly with the grassroots and community movements, anti-capitalist, anti-imperialist and most importantly contest political power. Economic Freedom Fighters will therefore be an independent economic emancipation movement which will contest political power in all spheres of government.

(EFF Founding Manifesto, quoted in Smith 2014: 118)

Significantly, the date for this declaration was not an accident:

We gather on the 26th of July 2013 because we are inspired and agitated by the Cuban July 26 Movement, which from the 26th of July 1953 launched a struggle that culminated in the victorious Cuban Revolution, which is still intact despite trade embargoes, isolation, natural disasters and terrorism against the Cuban people.

(EFF Foundin Manifesto, quoted in PolitcsWeb 2013)

For many Pan-African revolutionary movements, Cuba holds a special place and continues to inspire the fight against imperialism and promotion of international solidarity. The growth of Burkina Faso's international consciousness, for instance, became evident through the expressed solidarity with the 'disinherited of the world' in Africa and beyond. For Sankara, the influence of the Cuban Revolution and its Marxist-internationalist appeal in this regard is notable. For example, the Argentina-born Cuban revolutionary, Che Guevara, used the Marxist-inspired phrase 'disinherited of the world' in 1967 (Deutschmann 2003: 352) and it was also be used by Sankara in his maiden address at the United Nations General Assembly (UNGA) in October 1984 (Sankara 1988: 154). These revolutionary cross-fertilisations were many. In March 1983, Sankara attended the Non-Aligned Movement (NAM) Summit in India and met for the first time with presidents Fidel Castro (Cuba), Samora Machel (Mozambique) and fellow Prime Minister, Maurice Bishop (Grenada). He would later speak about all three with great affection. In September 1984, he received the Order of José Marti, Cuba's highest honour, awarded by Castro himself. In the same year, he spoke about his pain at the death by execution of Bishop and expressed regret at not having sent a letter he had written him. In October 1986, he delivered an impassioned speech on the occasion of Samora Machel's assassination by parcel bomb in Mozambique. Finally, in October 1987, a week before he was assassinated himself, Sankara paid tribute to Che Guevara on the anniversary of Che's execution by inaugurating an exhibition in Che's honour.

The character of the EFF fits within this framework of international solidarity. EFF's former Commissar, Andile Mngxitama (now with BLF, mentioned above), in outlining the party's international solidarity mission, stated that the EFF will stand with the oppressed, disposed and exploited people of the world from Cuba to Venezuela. In doing so, the EFF joins in the global fight against renewed imperialism and growing neo-liberalism. While the rhetoric of international solidarity has been strong, the EFF has not built effective transnational connections and, in most cases, the party has been inward looking. This failure to connect transnational movements can be explained by the fact that the EFF, now operating as a registered political party in liberal or constitutional democracy, is constrained in many ways from achieving some of the issues outlined in their founding manifesto.

PERFORMANCE, POLITICS AND PROTEST

The EFF has introduced a new and disruptive culture in South African constitutional democracy. It has adopted red overalls, hard construction hats and domestic worker uniforms as its attire in both the national and provincial parliaments (Goldhamer 2014). This attire is a form of radical politics and also symbolic attack on the bourgeois lifestyle and conspicuous consumption of the centrist ANC-led government – an attack on bourgeois lifestyles that echoes Sankara's earlier rejections of government-issued limousines and insistence on wearing the faso dan fani (locally made clothing). According to the EFF, the jumpsuits express solidarity with the country's manual labourers and the red colour represents a connection not only to communist parties of the past but also to the blood of labourers, including miners who were killed by police in Marikana in 2012 (Goldhamer 2014). On many occasions, the EFF has been chased out of parliament for 'inappropriate dress' and, in response to this, the party has stated:

> The EFF will never be bossed around to abandon the worker overalls in parliaments across the country because this is who it represents ... Legislature is a place of work and it must represent the people: EFF is there to say the regalia of workers is also welcome in the Houses of Parliament as part of respectable and honourable decorum. Workers keep South African moving and there is nothing dishonourable about the clothes they wear when they keep our lives moving.
>
> (SowetoLive 2014)

Historically, the colour red has been a symbol of radicalism and revolt (Sawer 2007). The EFF have combined the party's blue-collar worker red attire with a red beret, invoking the red beret worn by Thomas Sankara. Sankara wore the beret not only because he was a military man but also for its symbolic linking of his politics and ideologies to Cuba's Che Guevara. Sankara articulated this connection:

> Che Guevara called his beret la boina. He made that beret and its star known almost everywhere in Africa. From north to south, Africa remembers Che Guevara ...

Che is Burkinabè. He is Burkinabè because his ideas inspire us and are inscribed in our Political Orientation Speech. He is Burkinabè because his star is stamped on our banner.

(Sankara, A Tribute to Che Guevara, 8 October 1987)

The EFF has also introduced the 'politics of the spectacle' in Parliament, effectively disrupting the decorum that has always characterised the South African National Assembly. The combative approach that they have used in the National Assembly as well as the use of military imagery and ranks symbolises the party's fight against coloniality, poverty and dispossession of the poor. The performativity of its politics is linked with the speaking of truth to power – one of the lasting virtues of Sankara, a man renowned for his charismatic presence and speaking style (see Chapter 5, this volume). The aim of this combative project therefore is to promote, to use Benita Parry's words, the 'construction of a politically conscious, unified revolutionary self, standing in unmitigated opposition to the oppressor' (quoted in Gandhi 1998: 11). Similarly, Sankara never observed Western-informed notions of diplomacy nor the practiced and often artificial politeness inherent in liberal and constitutional democracy. For instance, when Francois Mitterrand, the then French President visited Ouagadougou in 1986, Sankara 'greeted his guest not with the usual diplomatic niceties and ceremonial toast … he offered a "duel" of ideas and oratory' (Harsch 2014: 15). Sankara disrupted the status quo and simply did not fit into the established political rules of the game and often used theatrical symbolism to disdain the pomp and ceremony that came with his office (ibid.). The EFF demonstrates many of these brave and avant-garde approaches to politics, governance and assembly.

CONCLUSION: YOUTH DARING TO INVENT AN ALTERNATIVE FUTURE

Contemporary Africa is facing a leadership crisis. The revolutionary zeal of former political leaders and thinkers – including Patrice Lumumba, Amilcar Cabral, Steve Biko, Eduardo Mondlane and Samora Machel – seems to be so seldom evoked in the politics of today's leaders. Sankara's legacy for conscious African citizens is more relevant today than ever before. The Burkinabé revolution is a significant model in Africa for raising the critical consciousness needed to battle the tyranny of neoliberalism and continued forms of coloniality. South Africa is acting as an incubator for a Sankaraist anti-conformist, anti-capitalist and pro-revolutionary stance, not only through the EFF but also other radical formations such as Black First, Land First (BLF). The emergence of the EFF is a manifestation of the radicalisation currently taking place in

South African society. No other opposition party since the end of apartheid has made such an impact. Perhaps we can argue that the revolutionary energy emanating from the EFF has contributed, in part, to the growing radical student movement which is fighting against colonised and commodified education.

Just as Sankara threatened the established order and attracted many disenchanted youth from the streets to rally behind his idealism, the same is happening in South Africa. There is an enormous thirst for Pan-Africanist and decolonial ideas and a genuine desire for revolutionary change among the youth. Similar radical movements are mushrooming across the continent. For example, in Namibia, a new political party, the Namibian Economic Freedom Fighters (NEFF), was born in 2014, using the same red berets and military ranks and also describing itself as a radical left, anti-capitalist and anti-imperialist movement. The various youth-led movements present real possibilities for the deepening of anti-racist and anti-imperialist revolutionary struggles across sub-Saharan Africa. Thirty years after his assassination, Sankara remains an inspiration for many young people across the continent. His life is proof that 'another world is possible' for Africa.

NOTES

1 The Rhodes Must Fall Movement targeted Cecil John Rhodes's statue at the University of Cape Town and this movement expanded into a broader student movement, #FeesMustFall, which demands decolonisation of the curriculum, free education and social transformation in South African Universities.
2 Unless otherwise noted, all quotations from speeches of Thomas Sankara in this chapter are available in Sankara (1988).
3 The Rivonia was a trial that took place in South Africa between 1963 and 1964, in which ten leaders of the African National Congress, including Nelson Mandela were tried for various acts of sabotage designed to overthrow the apartheid system.
4 The Democratic Alliance (DA) is main official opposition political party to the governing African National Congress (ANC). The modern day DA is in large part a product of the white parliamentary opposition to the then ruling National Party during apartheid.

REFERENCES

Alexander, P. (2010) Rebellion of the Poor: South Africa's Service Delivery Protests – a Preliminary Analysis. *Review of African Political Economy* 37(123): 25–40.

Banda, F. (2008) African Political Thought as an Epistemic Framework for Understanding African Media. *Ecquid Novi: African Journalism Studies* 29(1): 79–99.

Biney, A. (2013) Revisiting Thomas Sankara, 26 Years Later. *Pambazuka News* 651 (Special Issue: Thomas Sankara and Inventing Africa's Future: 26 Years Later). Retrieved on 4 July 2016 from www.pambazuka.org/pan-africanism/revisiting-thomas-sankara-26-years-later.

Black First, Land First (2015) Revolutionary Call. Retrieved on 1 December 2017 from https://blf.org.za/policy-documents/blf-revolutionary-call.

Bond, P. (2014). *Elite Transition: From Apartheid to Neoliberalism in South Africa* (2nd edition). London: Pluto Press.

Chiumbu, S. (2015) *Interrogating Media and Democracy in Southern Africa: Decolonial Perspectives*. Paper presented at CODESRIA General Assembly "Creating African Futures in an Era of Global Transformations: Challenges and Prospects".

Chiumbu, S. (2016) Media, Race and Capital: A Decolonial Analysis of Representation of Miners' Strikes in South Africa. *African Studies* 75(3): 417–435.

Cobbett, E. and Germain, R. (2012) Occupy Wall Street' and IPE: Insights and Implications. *Journal of Critical Globalization Studies* 5.

Deutschmann, D. (2003) *Che Guevara Reader: Writings on Politics and Revolution*. Melbourne: Ocean Press.

Fanon, F. (1963) *The Wretched of the Earth*. Ontario: Penguin Books.

Gandhi, L. (1998) *Postcolonial Theory: A Critical Introduction*. New York: Columbia University Press.

Gatzambide-Fernández, R. A. (2012) Decolonisation and the Pedagogy of Solidarity. *Decolonisation: Indigeneity, Education and Society* 1(1): 41–67.

Giroux, H. (2008). *Against the Terror of Neoliberalism: Politics Beyond the Age of Greed*. Boulder, CO: Paradigm Publishers.

Goldhammer, Z. (2014) The Coded Clothes of South Africa's Economic Freedom Fighters. *The Atlantic*. Retrieved on 13 October 2016 from www.theatlantic.com/international/archive/2014/08/the-coded-clothes-of-south-africas-economic-freedom-fighters/375366.

Grosfoguel, R. (2007). The Epistemic Decolonial Turn: Beyond Political-Economy Paradigms. *Cultural Studies* 21(2–3): 211–223.

Gueye, M. (2013) Urban Guerrilla Poetry: The Movement Y'en a Marre and the Socio-Political Influences of Hip Hop in Senegal. *Journal of Pan African Studies* 6(3): 22–42.

Harsch, E. (2015) *Thomas Sankara: An African Revolutionary*. Johannesburg: Jacana Media.

Honwana, A. (2014) Enough is Enough: Youth Protests and Political Change in Africa. In Kadya Tall, Marie-Emmaneul Pommerolle and Michel Cahan (eds), *Collective Marginalisation in Africa: Enough is Enough*, 43–66. Brill: Leiden.

Maldonado-Torres, N. (2007) On the Coloniality of Being: Contributions to the Development of a Concept. *Cultural Studies* 21(2–3): 240–270.

Maldonado-Torres, N. (2011) Thinking through the Decolonial Turn: Post-continental Interventions in Theory, Philosophy, and Critique – An Introduction. *Transmodernity: Journal of Peripheral Cultural Production of LusoHispanic World* 1(2): 1–23.

McDonald, D. A. and Smith, L. (2004) Privatizing Cape Town: from Apartheid to Neo-liberalism in the Mother City. *Urban Studies* 8(41): 1461–1484.

Meredith, M. (2006) *The State of Africa: A History of Fifty Years of Independence*. Jeppestown: Jonathan Ball Publishers.

Mignolo, W.D. (2007) Delinking. *Cultural Studies* 21(2/3): 449–514.

Mignolo, W. (2011) Epistemic Disobedience and the Decolonial Option: A Manifesto. *Transmodernity: Journal of Peripheral Cultural Production of the Luso-Hispanic* 1(2): 44–66.

Morken, B. (2016) South Africa: The Local Government Elections – a Shift in the Political Landscape. Retrieved on 10 October 2016 from www.marxist.com/south-africa-the-local-government-elections-a-shift-in-the-political-landscape.htm.

Mpofu, D. (2013) Why I Left the ANC. *Radical Voice* 9(9). Retrieved on 10 October 2016 from http://effighters.org.za/Dali_Mpofu_V9.html.

Ndlovu-Gatsheni, S. J. (2012) Fiftieth Anniversary of Decolonisation in Africa: A Moment of Celebration or Critical Reflection? *Third World Quarterly* 33(1): 71–89.

Omeje, K. (2015) *The Crises of Postcoloniality in Africa.* Dakar: Codesria.

Naicker, C. (2016) From Marikana to #feesmustfall: The Praxis of Popular Politics in South Africa. *Urbanisation* 1(1) 53–61.

Pithouse, R. (2016) *Writing the Decline on the Struggle for South Africa's Democracy.* Auckland Park: Jacana.

PoliticsWeb (2013) Declaration of the EFF National Assembly July 26 to 27 2013. Retrieved on 13 October at www.politicsweb.co.za/documents/declaration-of-the-eff-national-assembly-july-26-t.

Puttick, K. (2011) First year students' narratives of 'race' and racism in post-apartheid South Africa. Unpublished MA thesis, University of the Witwatersrand, Johannesburg, South Africa.

Quijano, A. (2000) Coloniality of Power, Ethnocentrism, and Latin America. *NEPANTLA* 1: 533–580.

Sankara, T. (1988) *Thomas Sankara Speaks.* New York: Pathfinder Press.

Sawer (2007) Wearing Your Politics on your Sleeve: The Role of Political Colours in Social Movements, *Social Movement Studies: Journal of Social, Cultural and Political Protest* 6(1): 39–56.

Schouten, P. (2009) Robert Cox on World Orders, Historical Change, and the Purpose of Theory in International Relations. *Theory Talk* 37. Retrieved on 13 October 2016 from www.files.ethz.ch/isn/155098/Theory%20Talk37_Cox.pdf.

Seery, E. and Caistor Arendar, A. (2014) *Even It Up: Time to End Extreme Inequality.* Oxfam International Campaign Report. Retrieved on 26 Jan 2018 from https://policy-practice.oxfam.org.uk/publications/even-it-up-time-to-end-extreme-inequality-333012.

Smith, J. (2014) *The Coming Revolution: Julius Malema and the Fight for Economic Freedom.* Johannesburg: Jacana Media.

SowetoLive (2014) EFF condemns 'mindless removal' of members. Retrieved on 13 October 2016 from www.sowetanlive.co.za/news/2014-07-02-eff-condemns-mindless-removal-of-members.

Sparks, C. (2009) South African Media in Transition. *Journal of African Media Studies* 1: 195–220.

Williamson, B. (2013) From Upper Volta to Burkina Faso: A Study of the Politics of Reaction and Reform in a Post-Colonial African Nation-State, 1960–1987. Unpublished MA thesis, University of South Florida. Retrieved on 13 October 2016 from http://scholarcommons.usf.edu/cgi/viewcontent.cgi?article=5809&context=etd.

PART IV

CONTESTATIONS AND HOMAGES

CHAPTER 20

The Academy as Contested Space
Disappearing Sankara from the 'Acceptable Avant-Garde'
Nicholas A. Jackson

As covered throughout this volume, while Compaoré and his military associates (mercenaries?) brought about the immediate physical death of Sankara and of his comrades, Sankara died at the behest of many corporate entities and people who administered or sustained these entities. In this chapter, I look briefly at the corporate academy, which I see as the key contested space for production of those baseline narratives that legitimise inter-governmental organisation governance policies that then justify often-coercive corporate exploitation. Once one accepts the existence of the corporate academy as a contested space, Bourdieu's feudal hierarchy of 'homo academicus', it is not surprising that Sankara's ideas were rather successfully wiped from the governing documents of neoliberalism (Bourdieu 1988).[1] As described in my earlier chapter in this volume on reducing Sankara's legacy to 'improved incentives' (Chapter 7, this volume), this disregard for material reality fits comfortably within corporate economics departments where administrators strive for 'a virtual reality, seemingly real but dependent upon the conceptual apparatus and outlook that generates it' (Carrier 1998: 8).

Furthermore, it makes sense that central administrators of corporate political science shoehorned Sankara's legacy into the conventional social science categories of anti-hegemonic resistance, populism and totalitarianism (Kandeh 2004: 158; Englebert 1996: 58ff; Otayek 1989: 13–30). 'Populist' has been a favourite word of those who narrate neoliberal democratisation as the process of 'aggregating interests and mobilizing consent' in order to 'organize stable political rule [whether in a democratic or authoritarian manner] ... in the modern context of broad social mobilization and complex economic systems' (Haggard and Kaufman 1995). To be a populist means to 'irresponsibly' attempt to redistribute wealth and power from the coteries of privilege to the margins without filtering it through the narratives and governing organs of legitimisation. Huntington's broadside against the 1960s movements, *Political Order in Changing Societies*, is the classic work in this genre (Huntington 1968).

'Totalitarian' rulers are those who seek social transformation without first compromising with those already in power, accommodating familiar habits, and advocating incrementalism. In this, Kirkpatrick's classic piece joined Huntington and early advocates of modernisation theory in promoting the codes of 'legitimate' social and political-economic change:

> [Revolutionary Communist regimes] claim jurisdiction over the whole life of the society and make demands for change that so violate internalized values and habits that people flee by the tens of thousands in the remarkable expectation that their attitudes, values, and goals will "fit" better in a foreign country than in their native land.
>
> (Kirkpatrick 1979)

The emotive coding in these pieces makes any anti-hegemonic resistance movement (i.e. any movement against the interests of present-day corporate exploitation) 'totalitarian' and therefore by definition should be disregarded or eliminated.

More surprising and concerning is the erasure of Sankara from the more critical literature that focuses directly on 1980s neoliberal interventions and associated resistances, in Africa as well as more generally. Sankara is not only ignored in many of these pieces but, more importantly, his legacy is erased from the diagnoses and therefore prescriptions. Scholars have therefore tended to posit narratives concentrating on heads of state moving from state-led industrialisation to debt-led export of primary commodities. According to these narratives, only after state government leaders have instituted structural adjustment do populations begin to protest. Colin Leys's brilliant treatment of the 1980s 'development impasse,' *The Rise and Fall of Development Theory*, is a classic example. Leys emphasised the need to interrogate both theory and practice, focusing especially on the African experience. However, even in 1996 his book makes no mention of Sankara's project, which was unique in so many ways, including through Sankara's willingness and ability to effectively confront, on the ground, the burgeoning neoliberalism that was assumed to cause the impasse in development theory (Leys 1996). This absence leads Leys and subsequent critical scholars to offer much more one-dimensional narratives of corruption, venality and submission on the part of leaders in Africa, focusing on countries such as Ghana, Nigeria, Zimbabwe, Kenya and Côte d'Ivoire. In doing so, such literature seems to run the risk of masking agency and thus reproducing that Orientalism which Said exposed and confronted (Said 1978).

Even among books dealing specifically with 'class struggle' and 'Africa Uprising', the resistance movements tend to begin immediately after Compaoré overthrew Sankara:

> Africa's long exclusion from Western narratives ... is entirely unjustified ... The two previous major protest waves – those of the late colonial period and of the late 1980s to early 1990s – preceded the most important continent-wide political transformations of the last one hundred years.
>
> (Branch and Mampilly 2015)

Zeilig operates according to the same template in his otherwise truly important project, *Class Struggle and Resistance in Africa*. Patrick Bond is correct in describe it as 'cutting edge' (Zeilig 2002). However, through two editions of this book Zeilig and his associates fail to address Burkina Faso in any capacity, including the long history of movements within that country and Sankara's four-year Marxist–Leninist-inspired revolutionary project, even though, like Branch and Mampilly, Zeilig ironically introduces the book by deploring the fact that, 'from the late 1980s Africa underwent a political revolution hardly noticed in the West' (ibid.: 15). In recent years, Zeilig has examined Sankara's legacy in more detail, and this work is valuable even as he is highly critical of Sankara in ways that mirror not only academic treatments but even some of Compaoré's post-coup justifications. For example, Zeilig excoriates Sankara in a blog post for the autocratic nature of what Zeilig dismisses as his '"revolution" (i.e. top-down politics)' (Zeilig 2016).

When Sankara's existence is acknowledged, then scholars have the responsibility and opportunity to examine his legacy and Sankara's analysis of his own decisions. Was Sankara right to distrust the Ki-Zerbo-led teachers unions, given that they repudiated him immediately after he took power? How best can one separate grassroots movements from faux-destabilisation? Why did Sankara have tense relations with the established communist and socialist movements in Burkina Faso (see Chapter 17, this volume)? How do we distinguish Zeilig's argument about an 'autocratic' Sankara from the political science literature and from Compaoré's justifications?

IMAGINING AN ACADEMY THAT INCLUDED SANKARA

The far-reaching edited volume by Manji and Ekine, *African Awakening*, offers an exception that helps to imagine what academic scholarship would look like with Sankara's legacy included. Sankara features prominently throughout this book, including the introduction and a chapter on Burkina Faso by Chouli (2011: 131–146). In the introduction, Manji and Ekine begin with early post-colonial states that struck a 'social contract' wherein they met the social welfare needs of citizens in commendable, if inconsistent, ways. This changed with the rise of neoliberalism in the 1980s. 'Where progressive developments occurred – as in Burkina Faso under Thomas Sankara – assassinations, support for military coups and economic isolation were some of the weapons used to prevent citizens having the audacity to construct alternatives to the crass policies of neoliberalism' (Manji 2011: 6). The scholarly narrative immediately changes from simply being about protests against authoritarian states to an impactful revolution crippled only through brutal and internationally-assisted repression. It throws subsequent tentative steps in Latin America and Europe into a very different light.

What if critical scholars of development throughout the 1990s and early 2000s had more systematically engaged Sankara's ideas and experiences? How might this have improved Veltmeyer and Petras's *The New Extractivism: A Post-Neoliberal Development Model or Imperialism of the Twenty-First Century* (2014), concentrating as it does on Latin American state-led accommodation of multinational extractive industry corporations? Unlike Ecuador's Correa, Bolivia's Morales and others, Sankara did not shrink from confronting global corporate capitalism but rather promised a new way of organising material control and then tried to deliver on it. What of the Greek fiasco, where Alexis Tsipras took the debt discussion to Greek citizens and they overwhelmingly voted to stop the grinding debt poverty that the European Union required without negotiations or agreed-upon conditions? Then, after the referendum, Tsipras felt it necessary to unconditionally surrender to global debt-driven corporate exploitation. Early in 2015, Vashna Jagarnath proposed a way forward for Greece through the lessons afforded by Sankara (Jagarnath 2015). These represent important steps – but they are baby steps, constrained by the lack of long-term engagement and contextualisation of Burkina Faso's experience.

The possibility should be raised that even critical scholars missed or disregarded Sankara's importance because, embedded within the 'acceptable avant-garde' of Bourdieu's 'homo academicus', they are unwilling to entertain ideas about revolution that did not originate in European academic spaces (Bourdieu 1988). Sankara was quite critical of such scholars originating in Africa. '[The educated petty bourgeoisie of Africa and beyond] forgets that any genuine political struggle requires rigorous, theoretical debate ... A passive and pathetic consumer, the petty bourgeoisie abounds in terminology fetishized by the West, just as it abounds in Western whiskey' (Sankara 2007: 157). Scholars should never become comfortable in their learned spaces – like little more than 'potted plants in greenhouses' – and should take on at least some of Sankara's courage so as to transform academia (from outside if necessary, inside if possible) into contested spaces and thus confront corporate exploitation wherever the administrators reside or how much they portray their work as 'common sense' (Nyamnjoh 2012). Speaking about academic marginalisation in particular, Giroux suggests that '[m]aybe the space of exile is one of the few spaces left in neoliberal societies where one can cultivate a sense of meaningful connections, solidarity and engaged citizenship' (Giroux 2014).

NOTE

1   Much has already been written about corporate exploitation, including in the time of neoliberalism, operating through deceits and frauds. See particularly valuable treatments in Susan George's *A Fate Worse Than Debt* (1988), Susan George and Fabrizio Sabelli's *Faith and Credit: The World Bank's Secular Empire* (1994); David Harvey's *A Brief History of Neoliberalism* (2005) and Richard Peet's *Unholy Trinity: The IMF, World Bank, and WTO* (2009).

REFERENCES

Bourdieu, P. (1988) *Homo Academicus.* Stanford, CA: Stanford University Press.

Branch, A. and Z. Mampilly (2015) *Africa Uprising: Popular Protest and Political Change.* London: Zed Books.

Carrier, J. G. (1998) Introduction. In James G. Carrier and Daniel Miller (eds), *Virtualism: A New Political Economy*, 1–24. Oxford: Berg.

Chouli, L. (2011) Peoples' Revolts in Burkina Faso. In F. Manji and S. Ekine (eds), *African Awakening: The Emerging Revolutions*, 131–146. Oxford: Fahamu.

Englebert, P. (1996) *Burkina Faso: Unsteady Statehood in West Africa.* Boulder, CO: Westview Press.

George, S. (1988) *A Fate Worse than Debt.* New York: Grove Press.

George, S. and F. Sabelli. (1994) *Faith and Credit: The World Bank's Secular Empire.* Boulder, CO: Westview Press.

Haggard, S. and R. R. Kaufman. (1995) *The Political Economy of Democratic Transitions.* Princeton, NJ: Princeton University Press.

Harvey, D. (2005) *A Brief History of Neoliberalism.* Oxford: Oxford University Press.

Huntington, S. P. (1968) *Political Order in Changing Societies.* New Haven, CT: Yale University Press.

Jagarnath, V. (2015) Why What Sankara Had to Say about Sovereignty Still Resonates. *The Conversation*, 22 July. Retrieved on 28 September 2016 from www.theconversation. com/why-what-sankara-had-to-say-about-sovereignty-still-resonates-22864.

Kandeh, J. D. (2004) *Coups from Below: Armed Subalterns and State Power in West Africa.* New York: Palgrave Macmillan.

Kirkpatrick, J. (1979) Dictatorships and Double Standards. *Commentary Magazine*, 1 November. Retrieved on 19 January 2017 from www.commentarymagazine.com/ articles/dictatorships-double-standards.

Leys, C. (1996) *The Rise and Fall of Development Theory.* Nairobi: Eaep/Bloomington, IN: Indiana University Press.

Manji, F. (2011) African Awakenings: The Courage to Invent the Future. In F. Manji and S. Ekine (eds), *African Awakening: The Emerging Revolutions*, 1–18. Oxford: Fahamu.

Nyamnjoh, F. B. (2012) 'Potted Plants in Greenhouses': A Critical Reflection on the Resilience of Colonial Education in Africa. *Journal of Asian and African Studies* 47(2): 129–154.

Otayek, R. (1989) Burkina Faso: Between Feeble State and Total State, the Swing Continues. In D. B. C. O'Brien, J. Dunn, and R. Rathbone (eds), *Contemporary West African states*, 13–30. Cambridge: Cambridge University Press.

Peet, R. (2009) *Unholy Trinity: The IMF, World Bank, and WTO*. London: Zed Books.

Said, E. W. (1978) *Orientalism*. New York: Pantheon Books.

Sankara, T. (2007) *Thomas Sankara Speaks: The Burkina Faso Revolution, 1983–1987* (trans. Michel Prairie). New York: Pathfinder Press.

Veltmeyer, H. and J. F. Petras (2014) *The New Extractivism: A Post-Neoliberal Development Model or Imperialism of the Twenty-First Century?* New York: Zed Books.

Zeilig, L. (2002) *Class Struggle and Resistance in Africa*. Cheltenham: New Clarion.

Zeilig, L. (2016) Burkina Faso's Second Uprising: Review of African Political Economy. 7 June. Retrieved on 7 October 2016 from http://roape.net/2016/06/07/burkina-fasos-second-uprising-2015-military-coup.

CHAPTER 21

Art and the Construction
of a 'Sankara Myth'
A Hero Trend in Contemporary Burkinabè
Urban and Revolutionary Propaganda Art
Sophie Bodénès Cohen

C'est ma génération
qui fera changer les choses
génération arc en ciel
génération qui s'oppose

It is my generation
who will change things
rainbow generation
generation that resists

With this lyric in his song, 'My Generation' (which features in his 2015 album, *Prevolution*), Smockey, the leader and co-founder (with Sams'K Le Jah) of the resistance association Le Balai Citoyen describes his generation. Smockey was part of the Burkinabè youth leadership that came together to protest against the oppressive regime of Blaise Compaoré in October 2014. Youth mobilised for civil rights, freedom of expression and democracy. This generation, as described in the song, is 'connected' to one another and the wider social world through technology, is well informed, and, for the most part, lives in economic uncertainty. This generation, Smockey's generation, revolts against oppression and injustice. Smockey's song captures some of the impulses of the protestors, organisers and resistors of the 2014 movement and also points to the larger role of artists in the movement (see Figure 21.1).

Indeed, artists played an important role in the revolution of 2014. One of the unifying trends amongst artists was their use of the figure of Sankara in their fight for democracy. Sankara became the personification of change. His figure was a catalyst for ideas and concepts to which the young generation could identify. Many artists associated themselves with Sankara as a human being who lived closely with the people. In the streets of Ouagadougou, protestors held his portraits and, marching in procession, accumulated a sort of collective energy – a power. Through these acts, Sankara was reincarnated symbolically as the main opponent to Compaoré (see Chapter 23, this volume). He provided and inspired some of the necessary strength for the revolution.

The iconic figure of Sankara is seen widely in many forms of contemporary urban popular art, which exists on the margins of the mainstream Burkinabè contemporary art scene. In this chapter, I explore some of the recent engagements with Sankara's memory and image by Burkinabè artists, particularly considering how and when artists make use of the figure of Sankara in their art and larger struggle. Indeed, popular urban art in the city of Ouagadougou has an almost obsessive reference to the figure of Thomas Sankara. This popular urban art includes graffiti, photomontage, painting, theatre, music, poetry, film, photography and even T-shirt art. Popular urban art is also widely shared on social media networks, most prominently Facebook. I refer to these artworks as 'popular' because they are realised by a young generation of artists who are most often self-taught, by contrast to a more 'elite' urban artistic cadre who appeals to mostly European audiences and consumers. Johannes Fabian (1996) sees in popular art the possibility of a space for contestations between 'traditional' art and more elite forms. Indeed, popular art in Burkina Faso develops in parallel to the official system and it is a place for resistance and engagement. These 'popular' artists also actively took part in the Revolution of 2014 and many of their works were created during or just after the revolution. For instance, the activist photographer Vivien Sawadogo took photographs while protesting. The intention was not merely an artistic endeavour to document the riot but also to galvanise and participate in the larger resistance energy.

In what follows, I first explore artistic production during the 1983 Revolution, emphasising both (a) Sankara's support for art and its possible influences from USSR and North Korea as well as (b) Sankara's own rejection of hero-worshiping during his lifetime. Next, I draw from original ethnographic research with popular urban artists in Ouagadougou to outline some of the ways in which Sankara has become a powerful artistic and political symbol for contemporary social movements in Burkina Faso.

21.1 Smockey (in the centre) and Sam's ka le Jah (on the right) stand in front of a wall-painting of Sankara. Source: Smockey official Facebook page.

SANKARA, REVOLUTION AND ART

Place de la Revolution was a gathering place for protesters during the 2014 movement. As of late 2016, a marble stone remained marked in red graffiti with the words, 'Blaise Ebola Dégage' ('Blaise Ebola, Get Out!'): the ultimate trace of the 2014 insurrection. Indeed, Place de la Revolution was already a deeply symbolic place: it was constructed during the revolutionary regime of Sankara in 1984. Its fresco, built in cooperation with North Korea during the Cold War, is typical of the international Soviet style but adapted to a Burkinabè identity. On the fresco, we can see four characters representative of the 'people', including the soldier with the military jacket and red beret, which clearly refers to Thomas Sankara. At his right, in the centre, a woman and a man are carrying the hammer and sickle, emblems of communism. The woman carries a typical cloth from Burkina Faso and the man carries a book (to refer to cultural and intellectual reform and policy) and a scythe (to symbolise agricultural reform). The landscape in the background, with palm trees and its red-orange tonality, creates a socialist-realism style version of 'Africa'. In order to promote the 'popular and democratic revolution', Sankara created social and economic policies of auto-sufficiency and Burkinabè authenticity. He had visionary ideas regarding women, for whom he created a special day, and encouraged the people to produce for and consume in African markets.

Sankara also implemented policies to promote art and culture. These included the so-called 'genius' fellowships for artists to travel and to promote their culture internationally. Four national theatres were built. The FESPACO (Festival Panafricain du Cinema et de la Television de Ouagadougou) became an important and internationally recognised film festival (see photos from these festivals by June Givanni after the Foreword, this volume). Enormous monuments were erected, including the Place des Cinéastes, the Place de la Révolution and le Monument de la Bataille du Rail. An official national orchestra, les Colombes de la Revolution, was also part of this national art.

Some of Sankara's support for culture, art and monument building was probably inspired by the propaganda art of the USSR and North Korea. Sankara, guided by the anti-colonialist and Pan-African ideologies of the post-colonial years, worked to foster economic, social and cultural partnerships with the USSR and North Korea. During the Cold War, the USSR developed diplomatic and friendly relationships with countries of the so-called 'Third World' to create a Soviet-friendly or socialist-leaning intelligentsia. USSR cultural propaganda programmes included the free shipping of books by Marx, Lenin and Engels, as well as the opening of Soviet cultural centres, where exhibitions of communist figures, including Lenin, were showcased and Soviet dance was celebrated. Photo reports of Sankara standing in front of Soviet monuments in North Korea contributed symbolically to this propaganda.

During his life, Sankara was opposed to the tendency to establish cults of personality for political figures. No statue of him was erected in the city. This was unlike the statue of Kwame Nkrumah in Ghana, for example. Officially, the national art promoted by the new revolutionary state was said to be dedicated to the people, to educate the masses. This national revolutionary art was supposed to educate the 'new person'. In this revolutionary consciousness, art was also a weapon to fight imperialism and neo-colonialism. Although the official state art was called 'popular', it was created to support the goals of the state.

Despite his personal dislike for iconography, his figure was sometimes used in art with ideological and political aims. This personality cult was less obvious than in some other socialist countries, including The Popular Republic of Bénin, Ghana or Ethiopia, for instance. One example of this iconography is the image printed on a widely recognised stamp, in which a close-up image of Sankara's face occupies half of the composition. In the image, he faces a crowd carrying banners with slogans of the party (see Figure 21.2).

Its composition is simple and efficient – this makes it easily understandable by most people, including those who do not know how to read. Due to its nature as an object that circulates widely, the image communicates Sankara's power and influence worldwide. This stamp was criticised by the French government and was called propagandist. It was even used to make the argument that Sankara was a megalomaniac (as S. Nikiema, an artist and sculptor, told me in a 2015 interview in Ouagadougou). However, Nikiema indicated that Sankara was unhappy with this promotion of his image. According to Nikiema, the artist

21.2 Artist unknown, *Stamp Thomas Sankara*, 1984.

Source: Google

who created the stamp said, 'One day, Sankara told me to come to his office. He was really upset. He told me to destroy the stamp'. In the country's national newspaper, *Carrefour Africain*, similar iconography was prevalent: Sankara's face loomed near large crowds throughout the newspaper's photomontages.

Stamps and photomontages in the press were widely circulated. This art was part of a bigger movement to honour Sankara. In addition, poems were regularly published in dedication to Sankara, often in elaborately celebratory and flattering styles (see Figure 21.3). Sankara was described as the 'messiah for his people'.

Sankara organised sizeable demonstrations and discourses in public places. He also enjoyed playing football with ordinary people. C. Dupré (2012) argues that Sankara was the 'real star' of the FESPACO festival. In the pages of *Carrefour African*, one issue shows him with Kim-Il Song in front of massive monuments like the Dutche Tower, which was the model for the Place de la Révolution in Ouagadougou. It seems likely that Sankara learned some tactics to elevate his image during his trips to North Korea. Sankara had charisma, a great sense of humour and he often used metaphorical images to garner increased attention for his political and economic messages. He used popular symbolic images in his speeches that were easily understandable by crowds of people.

The diffusion of a standardised iconography of propaganda (mainly in the press and during public demonstrations during which all people were to assist,

21.3 Photomontages showing Thomas Sankara on a trip to North Korea and in front of the monument of the Dutche (left), in *Carrefour Africain.*

Source: photo by author

and where traditional dances were performed and military parades performed) a near-mythology of Sankara was created. Sankara was seen as an exceptional politician, humble and loyal, funny, close to the people, a Pan-Africanist and anti-imperialist who was incorruptible and dedicated to his mission.

Only four years after the launch of the revolution, Sankara was assassinated and Blaise Compaoré set out to 'rectify' the revolutionary policies of Sankara's government. Sankara become a martyr, a hero and a prophet in the collective conscious and unconscious of Burkina Faso. His figure passed through memory (in some ways forcibly, see Chapters 20 and 23, this volume) and was transformed over time in the collective memory. This symbolic and mythical figure of Sankara passed through collective memory at a time when it was forbidden to talk about him and all references to him were destroyed. People nonetheless informally discussed Sankara and kept personal archives of newspaper articles during his presidency. Over time, his image reappeared progressively because of the work of the political opposition and those intellectuals and artists who re-read and spread word of Sankara's speeches, including through video archives. His presence slowly became a recurrent motif in contemporary, engaged popular Burkinabè art.

HOW DO CONTEMPORARY URBAN ARTISTS USE THE FIGURE OF SANKARA IN THEIR FIGHT FOR CIVIL RIGHTS, FREEDOM OF EXPRESSION AND DEMOCRACY?

After the assassination of Thomas Sankara in 1987, Blaise Compaoré and his government instigated what was called the 'rectification period'. Until 1998, references to Sankara were forbidden, the archives of his years as president were hidden and the 'Place de la Revolution' was renamed 'Place de la Nation'.

But in 1998, in reaction to the assassination of Norbert Zongo (the investigative journalist and leading opponent to Compaoré Regime), massive protests and riots lead to a crisis and the younger generation started to demand information. Sankara's figure reappeared and Compaoré was forced to proclaim Sankara a national hero. At this moment, the archives (both videos and photography) started circulating unofficially.

Along with political opponents, artists have played a crucial part in the reconstruction of the memory of Thomas Sankara. With the creation of Balai Citoyen by Smockey and Sam's Ka Le Jah, in songs like 'A Qui Profites Le Crime' and 'Capitaine Thomas Sankara', people rediscovered the story of the revolution and the figure of Thomas Sankara (although listening to the songs was forbidden in maquis and public places).

Young artists have rearticulated a vision of Sankara from two sources of memory. First is a visual memory that originates in the traces of artworks, photographs in newspapers and videos of speeches from the revolutionary period of Sankara. Second is a rearticulated image that comes from individual and collective memories. Some artists were alive in the period during which Sankara was president. Although they were children for most of the time, they might have attended some of the massive demonstrations. This type of event impacted strongly on their memories and sometimes had lasting impact. Sankara's figure also passed through the prism of the collective memory by way of narratives and memories, mainly transmitted by oral tradition.

Even if they collect all of the archives and watch all of Sankara's speeches, artists have a subjective and partial vision of Sankara. Any characteristics of dictatorship, oppression or authoritarianism are negated. Sankara appears in the artworks as a real hero. At the time of my writing this in mid-2017, I have not seen any artworks criticising the history of Sankara's revolution or the figure of Sankara in Burkinabè history.

The question remains: how did Sankara become an artistic icon?

21.4 Artist unknown, *Portrait of Thomas Sankara in a Workshop in Ouagadougou*, acrylic on canvas, 2016.

Source: photo by author

The canvas for the acrylic painting *Portrait of Thomas Sankara in a Workshop in Ouagadougou*, is made to human proportions. This painting is an example of one of the main features of revolutionary propaganda art in Burkina Faso and has common features of a hyperrealised memorialisation of leaders (see Figure 21.4). Some distinctive symbols are employed: Sankara's red beret and his military jacket and his recognisable smile. His eyes are looking, seeming beyond infinity: past, future or both. There is no background and a thick black frame takes him out of time, or beyond time. These features, together, create the portrait as iconic. The portrait was drawn from an archival photograph with details and a realistic style. This 'hyperrealism' (an artistic style resembling a high-resolution photograph) is a new tendency in urban contemporary Burkinabè art.

The first functions of this portrait are to honour, memorialise and immortalise Sankara. Beyond this, this type of painting might very well be used as a substitute for Sankara himself. Indeed, during riots, there are many documentary photographs of the protests where we can see the crowd holding these types of paintings of Sankara like banners. The visualisation of this iconic image within the 2014 protest crowd seems to re-enact the propagandist iconography of the revolution of 1984, including those images that featured Sankara's face among a mass of people (see Figure 21.5). Why would a young crowd protesting a dictator and fighting for freedom of rights, expression and democracy hold up the picture of an arguably authoritarian leader?

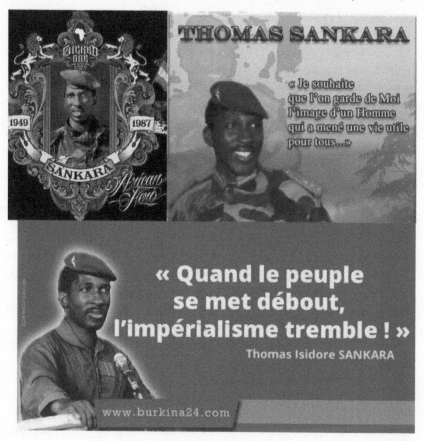

21.5 Anonymous popular art circulated on social media networks compiled by author.

The young protestors tend to ignore criticisms of Sankara. For these protestors, Sankara is remembered as the opponent of Compaoré, the post-colonial leader who was proclaimed himself 'for the people' and against neo-colonialism, including the françafrique (see Chapter 6, this volume). Some might wonder if there was a hidden force driving the use of the figure of Sankara during the resistance. That is to say, to fight a force, we need to oppose it with a force of the same or greater strength. If we use Sankara to oppose Compaoré, we can symbolically annihilate the force of the leaders against each other. So, to the power of the force of Sankara, we add the power of the strength of the protesting crowd, with all its protesting energy. In this case, instead of using violence, the work of art is used as a pacifist symbolic weapon.

The figure of Sankara also appears in some artwork as an iconographic element in a larger context – a context that enables us to understand how artists reconstruct the memory of the figure of Sankara. For example, many photomontages have flooded the Internet since the revolution of 2014. If we do a Google image search for 'Sankara' today, we see this phenomenon through the several dozens of new images in his honour (e.g. Figure 21.5). Young activists who want to honour Sankara and pay tribute to him have designed many of these photomontages. These sorts of photomontages are shared on the Facebook pages of Balai Citoyen or other civil associations, like Y'en A Marre and Lucha.

In such photomontages, extracts of Sankara's speeches are placed in front of Sankara in tribute; we might describe this positioning as mimicking the action of talking. Each of these phrases speaks to 'the people', to 'all Africans' or to the 'Burkinabè' and the fight against imperialism. Prior to the 2014 uprising, access to Sankara's speeches was not easy for young artists and activists in Burkina Faso. They had to collect such covert knowledge and information in informal ways, often through videos, some of which are sold in stands in Ouagadougou or through the collections of speeches that are sold during special events. In Ouagadougou, an independent centre called 'Generation Sankara' is the leading location for editing books on Sankara today (for more on Generation Sankara and Semifilms, see Chapter 15, this volume). Sculptors also make use of the figure of Sankara and often reference the two revolutions in their artworks.

Fernand Sawadogo, for example, is an eminent Burkinabè artist. A painter, he owns an independent studio and is in the process of creating his own gallery. Before the revolution of 2014, his main subject was love and social life. During the revolution, he took part in the riots and the electric atmosphere inspired him. He came back to his studio while listening to Smockey and he began to paint his most representative piece of the event: *L'Insurrection*. He began to collect papers to learn more about the period of Sankara. Once, he told me, he saw an old photograph in Black and White of Sankara, Cabral and Mandela framed against a map of Africa. He cut it because, to his mind, they represented 'inspiring figures' and 'remind[ed] me about what we have just lived'. By cutting out a newspaper clipping, he adopted a historian-archivist attitude. However, his photography is not entirely objective. This photography associates Africa to the figures of three major postcolonial leaders: Cabral in Guinée-Buissau, Mandela in South Africa and Sankara in Burkina Faso. This iconography evokes Pan-Africanism and the importance of African union – but also the idea that 'revolutions' are embodied by the figures of their leaders. At the time the image was created, these figures were already heroes. By incorporating this photomontage style in his art, Sawadogo combines history, memory, archive, myths and heroes.

Returning from protests, he would start his canvas using his personal method: the background was always composed by an abstract layer of colours invoking his current state of mind. From this, he elaborates, layer-by-layer, a series of figurative images. In his work, *The Revolution of 2014*, the three main characters have their mouths open (see Figure 21.6). Sawadogo cut extracts of phrases out of newspapers and in the piece, these become the screams of the protesters. By using text, he wants to immortalise and fix in history the complaints and motivations for the protests: 'Où est passée l'Afrique?' ('what happened to Africa'?) or 'l'impossible réforme agraire' ('agrarian reform is impossible'). In the background, Sawagodo paintings often feature brick walls, representing oppression, the feeling of being locked up in an unfair social and economic situation as well as a fear that justifies the fight for freedom and democracy.

All those walking in Ouagadougou in 2014, 2015 or even 2016 would have noted the graffiti calling for 'Justice pour Thomas Sankara' and 'Fuck Blaise' on the walls of buildings and fences in the city. At one crossroad, an emblematic graffiti declares, 'Justice pour Thomas Sankara' in capital letters with a little portrait of the bust of Sankara. This type of portrait is a 'logo' made with the technique of stencilling (pochoir). Linear and expressive, such graffiti testified to the situation of emergency in which it was grafted on the wall: aerosol bombs were used because they are quicker. The walls of the city were transformed into an open art exhibition for the largest audience possible. Anyone could see it and understand its significance, regardless of the level of education. These were prints of a situation of crisis, written down – illegally – in an emergency.

21.6 Fernand Sawadogo, *The Revolution of 2014*, acrylic on canvas, 2014–2016.

Source: photo by author

Another artist, Deris, was the pioneer of street art in Ouagadougou. He has been animating the 'Burkigraff' event since 2014, an event that brings together a collective of Burkinabè graff artists to promote and create art that raises political and cultural consciousness. Deris told me that he created this graffiti with an anonymous collective of graffiti artists. He insists that they were made 'collectively'. In this way, urban art is collective in the same way that you cannot organise a riot alone. Similarly, 'our number is our strength' ('Notre nombre est notre force') is in the same spirit the slogan of the Balai Citoyen: 'we can succeed only if we are several. If one of us dies, another will replace him'.

Although there is a strong spirit of collectivism, there are yet few graffiti artists as this art is as new as it is dangerous. For Deris, graffiti is the 'art of drawing, doodling on a wall, made by freelance artists'. Before the 2014 revolution, he drew a huge portrait of Sankara near a little river, in a safe place

21.7 Deris, *Self Portrait in Front of His Graff Thomas Sankara*, photography on Facebook, 2016.

21.8 Anonymous, *Graffiti 'Justice for Thomas Sankara'*, Ouagadougou, 2016.
Source: photo by author

that was mostly hidden from view because he needed more time to execute the portrait and he had to keep from being arrested by the police. This is not graffiti, this is a 'graff': a huge drawing on the wall. Deris had been drawing portraits of revolutionary leaders since 2004. Indeed, the early 2000s saw a trend spread, not only in Burkina Faso, but in West Africa and across the whole continent: the glorification of postcolonial leaders on portraits, T-shirts, iconic plastic works of art and jewellery. Like Bob Marley, Hailie Selassie and the King of Judas are the heroes of Rastafari-style politics we can now observe Qaddafi stickers, Sankara T-shirts, N'krumah photos, photomontages in honour of Lumumba and Cabral, and so on.

If we consider that these works are reproduced and therefore have a lack of singularity, we might question that they really are works of art, some might wonder if they have lost their aura. On the contrary, however, it seems that the presence of these images of Sankara give back to the leader a new aura, as if he were resurrected.

This is part of a larger question: do we exclude photomontages or the fashionable T-shirts from the category of art? We could say that in this case, photomontages and T-shirts are activist art, engaged art. They have roots in urgency and they have to be produced very quickly and to be spread on a massive scale to achieve political and emancipatory goals. However, there is still a commercial opportunity that is seized by some artists. For example, I requested a batik of Sankara, or a wood lamp engraved in Sankara's image to bring back home, as a tourist fascinated by the fascination of the Burkinabè for their cherished leader. The woodworker who crafted the lamp wore a Mandela T-shirt. He was also part of the Smockey's 'engaged generation'.

CONCLUSION

The riots of October 2014 in Burkina Faso had several aims: to fight for justice, freedom, civil rights, ask for the demission of Compaoré and, at the same time, to create a new radical social identity. The question of narrative is important in contemporary African art. Bogumil Jewsiewicki (1990) explains that, in the case of popular urban painting in Zaire, narration is often an important political element in the creation and imagining of a collective identity. Similarly, the figure of Sankara emerged as a powerful component of the new narrative of Burkinabè during the revolution. His image has transfigured through the prism of time and collective and individual memory. Following his assassination, references to and images of Sankara had been forced from public reference and public space. His memory was repressed, silenced, hidden and forced to remain in the collective unconscious. But, step by step, his image reappeared in popular urban art.

In art, the image of Sankara has reappeared like a ghost. There are important differences between the languages of history and the languages of memory—predominant among them is the perception of time. History is written linearly while memory, on the other hand, is cyclic, mythical. Memory is linked to affects, emotions. Symbols are linked to emotions and therefore establish the strongest connection to the human emotional intelligence. Art can generate idealisations of history, mythical figures and utopian possibilities. Memory is linked to imagination—much like art. For this reason, art has emerged as an ideal place for a popular reconstructing of the image of the memory of Sankara.

Why has the image of Sankara been deployed so widely, particularly by young people? Globalisation and the rediscovery of colonial and postcolonial history have generated new questions about identity and public consciousness. The young generation seeks to definite a new Burkinabè identity: a 'made in Africa' generation, as Smockey's musical lyrics indicate.

Sankara has become a symbol; indeed, he was perhaps already a symbol during his lifetime through his symbolic acts: his metaphor-riddled discourses, his art of speaking with humour and his charisma. Through this symbolism, he had an impact on people, including an impact on their *imagination*. This imaginative impact was retained in the collective subconscious and has survived through memory. Sankara's image, in the popular imagination, has become that iconic portrait of him with slight smiles, often mixed with portions of his most influential speeches. Thomas Sankara became and remains a personification and a catalyst for the Pan African ideas that young people identify with in today's Africa.

REFERENCE

Dupré, C. (2012) *Le FESPACO, Une Affaire D'états.* Paris: L'Harmattan.

Fabian, J. (1996) *Remembering the Present: Painting and Popular History in Zaire.* Berkeley and Los Angeles, California: University of California Press.

Jewsiewicki, B. (1990) 'Collective Memory and its Images: Popular Urban Painting in Zaire—A Source of "Present Past"' in Bourguet, M., Valensi, L. and Wachtel, N. (eds), *Between Memory and History,* 183-194. London: Routledge.

CHAPTER 22

Slanted Photography

Reflections on Sankara and My Peace Corps Experience in Burkina Faso

Celestina Agyekum

The photo of Thomas Sankara was one of the first things I noticed when I walked into my host family's home for the first time on 7 June 2013. It hung slanted on the wall. You might not notice it at first. It hovered over my father's self-assigned seat. No one touched it, even though it was clearly slanted. You might think the evidence of dust would prove its solitude but there was none to be seen. It was as if his framed caramel-edged photograph cleaned itself but forgot to straighten up. Maybe it was a metaphor for the country: its ability to appear renewed and robust, yet slanted. And perhaps it was simply that: a slanted photograph of the esteemed Thomas Sankara.

To my host dad, Thomas Sankara remained the only person who could have 'turned the country around'. He would sometimes tell me that Burkina Faso had yet to understand the gravity of Sankara's involuntary absence, and appreciate the vision he had for his people and all of Africa. It was refreshing to encounter this same sentiment my host dad felt in conversations I had with the people I met during my service. Our conversations about change were spirited as I could feel them yearn for a progressive and peaceful change – the kind of change Sankara embodied with pride and precision. As history would have it, it would be due to his very radical methods for social change that will eventually cause his assassination.

In this chapter, I discuss my personal experiences as a Peace Corps Education Volunteer in northern Burkina Faso alongside a consideration of Thomas Sankara's values of liberation through self-governance and the exclusion of Western influences and control. I draw upon examples and anecdotes from my service in this paradoxical framework, while staying true and transparent about my positionality and intersectionality as a Black, Ghanaian and American female in my small village North of Burkina Faso. I use the word 'my' to refer to my village because as a collective group, we worked together, celebrated and mourned together, ate together, cultivated and harvested together. Through this communal lifestyle, our relationship grew into one of stewardship, love, respect and duty towards each other.

THE PEACE CORPS IN BURKINA FASO

In 1986, Thomas Sankara revoked the Peace Corps' invitation in Burkina Faso and requested that the American government conclude its programme in the country, as it no longer complemented Burkina's development goals. He stood firm that the Burkinabé people were more than capable of governing their own affairs without Western influence, assistance or aid; and thus could stand on its own feet by use of its own resources. He articulated this best during his speech at the General Assembly of the United Nations in 1984 when he said, 'We must succeed in producing more, because it is natural that he who feeds you also imposes his will. He who does not feed you can demand nothing of you'. Sankara asserted that it was the discontinuation of aid that held the key to truly freeing Africans from their former colonisers. He referred to foreign assistance and aid as a (neoliberal) continuation of colonisation. He advocated for practices of self-governance by the masses in Burkina and encouraged all Africans to do the same. Towards the end in 1987, the remaining thirty Peace Corps Volunteers left the country and the ties between the Peace Corps and Burkina Faso halted until 1995, eight years after Thomas Sankara's assassination and the beginning of the rule of his friend Blaise Compaoré – who headed the coup d'état in which Sankara was assassinated. In 1995, Blaise Compaoré extended an invitation to the US to reinstate the Peace Corps programme, and it has remained since.

DILEMMAS, WHISPERS AND TENSIONS IN PEACE CORPS BURKINA FASO PROGRAMME

I arrived in Burkina the first week of June 2013. I was enthusiastically welcomed by the heat as I alighted from the plane. It was remarkable how still the air was and how strong the sun shone. It felt was as though the sun competed with another, because each day it shone brighter and more powerful. Those first moments and days were filled with a sense of optimism with no expectations, yet with confidence that I would play a positive role in my village.

Two months following my arrival I participated in what Peace Corps calls Pre-Service Training, PST. I underwent about three months of training in preparation for a productive service in my village as a volunteer who played the role of a catalyst, an observer, an educator, a mentor and any role the village requested of me. All of this was with an understanding that I was not there to take ownership but to rather be a cheerleader and devotee to the best of my capabilities as they drove their development in the direction they saw fit. However, this understanding was not mutual and over time there was tension between my village's expectations of my role and my training. In addition there was tension between what I could do and what I should not do because I did not want to perpetuate the very dependency cycle that went against Sankara's philosophy of self-sufficiency, autonomy and empowerment.

Volunteers are given a three-month period to integrate into their communities after training and relocation to their site. During these three months, we were to be participant observers as well as present and engaged in communal activities. In my three months, I learned the art of stenography and came to understand my intersectionality and positionality as a Ghanaian-American and a young single Black woman. The whispers in those three months in the village, as informed and translated by my Peace Corps counterpart were:

'What is she here to do for us?'

'When will she start?'

'She is black like us, I thought she would be white!?'

'She must speak the language then?'

'Wait, she doesn't understand what we were saying? How?'

Hearing this, I became anxious and burdened. I thought to myself, 'I am not *the* change they seek. I am not here to give them things. I thought they knew that this was a partnership and their interests were mine, not the other way around'. Regardless, I sought to work with the people of the village, in order to learn about existing challenges and how we might work together on them. However, my desire for a collaborative social change did not always match my village's desires. Their expectations that I deliver large-scale solutions perpetuated the cycle of dependency, poverty and exploitation and all of this was very difficult to convey. I recall times when, due to my title as an American I spoke with authoritative figures about the same issues a native pointed out but I was listened to more receptively, attentively and respectively; thereby continuing the notion that the foreigner knows better and holds a higher place. In this notion, the foreigner is given a higher and better seat than the native. I remember another instance when my counterpart asked me to speak to the headmaster (i.e. principal) of the school about permitting the older students to help us clean the preschool school closet. I asked her why *me*, and she replied, 'He will listen to you and not me'.

'Why?' I asked.

'Because you are the foreigner'.

I found myself in this role many times through my service and it was remarkable to see how my positionality opened doors that were closed to natives and consequently, how my intersectionality hindered me from the sort of solidarity work that I sought to do. Mentally exhausted from managing these unstable frictions, I withdrew and took less active roles in the community. My withdrawal subsequently triggered a new series of whispers. This time I was characterised as: upset, sad, ready to leave, uninvolved, an outsider who doesn't understand.

Sankara once said, 'Participation and control by the people are the best protection' from dependency and recolonisation. He asserted that 'our task is to decolonise our minds ... even though we'll have to endure some sacrifices' (CDR National Conference, 1986).[1] These words were then unknown to me but help to explain why I took a back seat in the journey to their development. My training and intersectionality told me to let people do it on their own with me as an assistant, thus my voice and role needed to be secondary. Although I used the participatory approach in my training and even though my village initiated the projects, I remained the gatekeeper for Peace Corps' project endorsement, money and resources. This dependency between us is precisely the one that Sankara fought so hard to abolish. This is the mental and economic slavery he died trying to eliminate. The idea that the Westerner holds the answers is destructive and hinders local innovation.

This dependency mind-set asserts that 'the outsider has the knowledge/ answers/keys/skills, and until s/he arrives, we will wait. And when s/he arrives, we will watch with arms folded (because we have no autonomy in this dependency paradigm and history has conditioned us to expect to receive without contribution)'. My presence created space for conversation about self-sufficiency, however these were characterised by my refusal to 'give', which brought about frustration. I did not play the role of a 'donor' although this history of the ideologies of the Peace Corps clothed me as one. I began to question the Peace Corps programme and to think how I could be of help without losing my sanity in the process of understanding people's choices. Did I reinforce dependency and reiterate the 'Western Saviour' epidemic? Importantly, I asked if my presence and that of the Peace Corps indirectly (or directly) inhibited people's self-development. Was I promoting or stifling the national emancipation that Sankara died for?

CONFRONTING THE PROBLEMS OF AID

Our country produces enough to feed ourselves. We can even exceed our level of production. Unfortunately, due to lack of organisation, we're still forced to hold out our hand to ask for food aid ... [this aid] is an obstacle in our path, creating and instilling ... these instincts of beggars.
Thomas Sankara, CDR National Conference, 1986

Dust rose as the brooms touched the floor. Lizards and insects hurriedly escaped as we emptied the pre-school closet. It was amazing to see all of the items the closet held and what we could work with. One by one we brought out playground equipment, books, blocks, puzzles, stationery, chairs, tables – but wait! 'Why are all these things looking new?' I thought to myself and later asked my counterpart. Her responses were:

'We don't know what they [i.e. puzzles] are so we never used it'.

'The kids will ruin them [i.e. stationery and playground equipment] so we do not use them'.

'We went on break so we kept the rest of the food because we are afraid of what CRS [Catholic Relief Services] would do if we gave the food away'.

My jaw dropped lower at each response with sadness and confusion. I was also informed that the teachers had not received training on how to use any of the materials and thus kept them in the closet in hopes that when and if I came, I would teach them. I nodded my head to her explanations and asked how long the equipment and materials had been sitting in the closet.

'Two years', she said.

I was struck by this and asked for clarification. My counterpart assured me of the year by pulling out the signed documents showing delivery dates. She added that each year more items are brought in but they usually do not know how to use them or why they were receiving them so they were again stored in the closet. Without practical training for the teachers, this 'aid' is useless. Then, in attempt to rectify the situation, 'aid' in human form (such as a Peace Corps volunteer) is sent. More 'aid' was poured into these preschools without equipment and managerial training, yet there was the expectation that the teachers use the materials to adequately educate students. This is but one anecdote from my time as a Peace Corps volunteer that suggests that the very thing Sankara was afraid of remains true in 'aid' work in Burkina today. This was happening across the Faso and I had unknowingly joined the circus halfway and now seemed powerless to alter its course.

In the face of these problems, I decided to train the teachers rather than teach to the children (directly or to co-teach). At the end of my service, my counterpart was familiar with and capable of planning and executing lesson plans. She had the tools and practise to continue without me – just as she had done flawlessly when I was away for some days during my service. Yet when my service was over, the school fell apart until another volunteer was sent to my village *against my recommendation to the Peace Corps*. It seemed that the teachers and pre-school board desired to be helped in a permanent capacity. This mentality was relayed to me in indirect and direct ways throughout my service. Sankara feared that aid would foster aid-seeking and prolonged or permanent dependency and I was witnessing it.

I did not initially see the Peace Corps as a perpetuator of dependency. However, I began questioning the level and quality of assistance that volunteers brought to the table and what would happen when they left. Although the Peace Corps employs sustainable and participatory approaches, it was still a challenge for people in my village to understand that I was not there to 'give' aid but to exchange ideas, work, learn and grow together. Somehow, our relationship became constrained through patterns of dependency thinking: I found myself being shunned because of my stance and what they heard and knew was done between Peace Corps volunteers and my friends. My effort to rectify this was to work only when the village desire. This was met with hesitation and resistance. New rumours emerged of my false promiscuity; parents withdrew their children from the school for reasons unknown to me. My counterpart encountered more challenges from her husband and his family; this affected both of our mental, emotional and physical states as our relationship went beyond the merely professional and because of the proximity of our houses. The more I stood my ground and refused to be a 'donor', the more unstable my place in the community became.

I left my village at dawn on my final day in deep conflict and melancholy. My turning to Sankara's life and philosophies has pointed to some of the roots of the uneven relationship that I experienced. His words confirmed my experience of the dependency-thinking that is built into the aid work that is the Peace Corps and other organisations. Not only are Burkinabè people left in the same dependency-mentality, the outsiders who seek to collaborate meaningfully are nonetheless shaped by local's expectations and history of dependency-thinking. 'True collaboration and self-reliance' is a struggle within this dependency-framework. This is why Sankara disbanded the programme during his presidency.

MADNESS, THEIR FREEDOM: *sankara vit!*

You cannot carry out fundamental change without a certain amount of madness. In this case, it comes from nonconformity, the courage to turn your back on the old formulas, the courage to invent the future. It took the madmen of yesterday for us to be able to act with extreme clarity today. I want to be one of those madmen. We must dare to invent the future.
Thomas Sankara, interview with Jean-Philippe Rapp, 1985

We spent our nights by the fire, after our long days in the farms in the village. The cities of Burkina Faso burned with decades of anger and hope. Thomas Sankara was sought after, but was nowhere to be found. His image and bits of his speeches appeared on walls, shirts and social media.

'Sankara vit!' (Sankara lives!) People yelled, marching forward in pride and resentment. My Burkinabè friends and family would say to me during the uprising, 'Ouaga est chaud' (Ouaga is hot) and indeed it was. The people burned down the Parliament House and Blaise Compaoré fled the country to Côte d'Ivoire. Thomas Sankara's name was sung in the streets with pride, anger, joy and hope. Sankara recognised the fate of the country long before this moment. People spoke of Sankara's earlier predictions with heads in hand. The upright people put their complaisance aside and roared. I stood with them in silent solidarity. Sankara was resurrected in our hearts and it was liberating to be in that moment.

NOTE

1 Quotations from Sankara in this chapter are available in Sankara (2007).

REFERENCES

Sankara, T. (2007) *Thomas Sankara Speaks: The Burkina Faso Revolution, 1983–87*. New York: Pathfinder.

CHAPTER 23

'We Are the Children of Sankara'
Memories as Weapons during the Burkinabè Uprisings of 2014 and 2015
Fiona Dragstra

INTRODUCTION

In this chapter, I highlight some of Sankara's political actions, focusing mainly on his now world-famous speeches and the ways in which select quotes from these speeches seem to live on in the revolutionary minds of many. Symbolisms and memories of Sankara persist(ed) through expressions of popular culture, including slam poetry, hip-hop, clothing, graffiti, spoken word and painting. We see evidence of Sankara in new forms of social and civic movements in Burkina Faso. These movements adopt symbolic names from memories and heroes of the past and act politically in the memory of past heroes, such as Thomas Sankara.

This chapter tells the stories of the mostly young activists that used all forms of expression (musical, artistic and other) to speak out against a regime that was no longer theirs. They sang, rapped and slammed against impunity and economic crimes committed by those in positions of political power (Hagberg 2002). They demanded justice and accountability while claiming a part of their national heritage. These popular expressions derived inspiration from key political heroes who inaugurated what it meant to be revolutionary and to be Burkinabè. This was a new conscious generation born through the use of memories as political weapons in their battle for socio-political change.

The stories retold in this chapter emerged during six months of fieldwork in Burkina Faso from March to September 2015. Interviews, informal conversations and observations during fieldwork are supplemented with online exchanges (on Facebook), blogs and news articles between October 2014 and October 2016. The identities of informants have been hidden and each has been designated an initial. I apply a reflexive perspective, meaning that the knowledge presented here is the result of multiple interpretations and systematic reflections on the implications of these interpretations (Alvesson and Sköldberg 2009). My interpretations emerge from the socio-economic and political contexts in which I, the researcher and author, was present. The knowledge I gained from interviews and informal conversations, and the 'truths' I aim to understand, are rooted in the meaning-making process of my informants within their own contexts. By employing 'a hybrid blend of investigative journalism and field ethnography' (Ross 2013), I came to understand some of the influences of past political heroes in the context of the Burkinabè uprisings. My informants told their 'truths' and experiences and I interpreted those in the light of my research and my understanding of this larger context. My study is guided by a desire to understand the ways in which the revival of past political heroes influenced the growth and outcome of the Burkinabè uprisings in 2014 and 2015.

MEMORIES AS 'WEAPONS'

In some countries, political elites are aware that memories are important in attaining and maintaining political power and political legitimacy (Igreja 2015). One of the ways in which this can be done is through the strategic use of the memories of those who are to be publicly forgotten or remembered (ibid.: 315). The naming of public institutions (such as universities and government buildings) and the role that the army plays in either forcing people to publically forget past actions (e.g. not remembering those who have lost lives) or forcing people to never publically forget past actions (e.g. constant threat of violence from the state), are important instruments in building a selective collective memory within society – one that reflects the views of the political elite. It is evident that the views of the (ruling) political elite might not always reflect those of the opposition and those of its people. Following Igreja (2013), when collective memories are either deliberately withheld from or forced upon public remembrance, memories of violence and past events can shape or give a new sense to the collective identity of a country. Long-term oppressions can foster fear through collective memories of past violence; in such contexts, people might start to feel powerless. Adebwani (2008) indicates that in post-independence Africa, national liberation struggles were often essentialised, whereas problematic memories – ones that could undermine their legitimacy to be in power – were removed from public memory and commemoration, so that public space and memory came to embody the new political order and regime. This process of in– and ex-clusion (of memories and events) cultivates contestations between social groups and potentially between the government and its citizens.

In times of political change, political elites use social memories as weapons (Igreja 2008) to gain votes and instigate contestation. They can be used to restrict or enlarge national unity, depending on which direction the state or the ruling political elite want the public opinion to go. On the other hand, social memories, when framed differently, can also be used by opposing (political) groups to enlarge unity among people who are already on their 'side' of the socio-political spectrum.

Collective memories as intersubjectively constituted by the shared experiences, ideas, knowledges and cultural practices through which people construct relationships to the past (Misztal 2003). Additionally, there is a group of people that share these memories of events and make these into (their version of) history. Thus there must be a process in which collective memories shape the collective identity of the group that adheres to these memories. Assman and Czaplicka (1995: 128–129) distinguish between 'communicative' memories and 'cultural' memories: communicative memories exist in the everyday communication of speech, texts and events, whereas cultural memories take place outside the everyday and have a fixed 'horizon'. These cultural memories have fixed points with which they resonate, such as monuments or institutional communications in the form of recitation and practices. Everyday communication exists within these fixed points on the otherwise changing horizon. These forms of expression crystallise collective experiences and attribute meaning to them, thus making them also accessible over time.

In this way, cultural memories comprise a body of reusable texts, images and rituals specific to a group or society in a certain age and time. They are reconstructions of the knowledge of a contemporary situation. However, by 'cultivating' these memories they stabilise and convey certain self-images, which are mobilised in the creation of collective knowledge. The creation of a collective identity based on cultural memories often focuses the knowledge from which a group derives awareness to a certain political tension or issue. This is reflected in the sense of 'this is *us*' versus 'they are *not* us'. The capacity to reconstruct refers to this process of memory-making, which does not replicate the past exactly. What remains of the past in memories is that 'which society in each era can reconstruct within its contemporary frame of reference' (Assman and Czaplicka 1995: 130).

Following Hodgkin and Radstone (2003), I contend that peoples' understandings of the past have strategic and political consequences. Contestation over the past spills over into the contestations of the meanings of the present and the visions for ways forward. The need to remain loyal to a certain group's account of events or the desire to tell their group's truth can be more important than reconciliation, result in forms of 'selective memory' (Gardner, Pickett and Brewer 2000).

In times of political transition, emerging governments or other groups within society try to (re)establish legitimacy, (political) inclusion and a sense of (national) unity. This means that there is a shaping or reshaping of collective identity during the process of democratisation or political transformation. Nationalism begins with the creation of a national identity, is bolstered by celebrated acts of heroism and struggles against oppression and unites the living members of the nation with the great cultural accomplishments of the past (Calhoun 2007: 86). Nationalism, as Calhoun (ibid.) suggests, is a subset of claims to identity and autonomy on the part of populations that have the size and the capacity to sustain themselves.

Calhoun (2007) suggests that, in times of revolution or political change, collectives derive meaning from their collective identity, which is shaped by collective memories. These memories, which are set on the 'horizon' of cultural memories, can be 'brought back to life' or invoked through the use of texts, speeches, events and institutional communication. Cultural memories can be used as weapons by politicians. At the same time, groups within civil society adhere to a memory-derived sense of collective belonging (Johnston 2013). In a society in which politicians reconstruct or give meaning to past events in ways that are contested by the wider society, contestation and conflict may arise which, in conjunction with other factors, can culminate into widespread protests, popular uprisings or revolution. When a ruling elite have deliberately concealed part of history but society is transitioning away from the elite's reading of history and from elite rule, memories can again be used to shed light on how society might be reshaped, who might or should be remembered and what stands as the 'truth'.

'ON PEUT TUER UN HOMME, MAIS ON PEUT PAS TUER SES IDÉES'

In the four years during which Thomas Sankara ruled Burkina Faso, his anti-imperialistic and Pan-Africanist philosophies gave rise to many famous speeches and provocative quotes but, above all, his philosophy was one of action. Even before he changed the name of the country in August 1984 in the service of its unification, he appointed representatives from different ethnic groups in his government to foster a sense of national unity.

He also attempted to break away from the economic dependence on France and other countries, by making Burkina Faso draw directly upon its own resources. In the search for sustainable, peaceful and systematic ways to preserve the environment, the population was asked to join in conservation activities, rather than to penalise those who cut trees. Sankara spoke of a 'democratic and popular struggle' to save the trees (Harsch 2014). Government inspired tree-planting initiatives became a regular practice at ceremonies, including family gatherings. This practice of collective tree-planting continues to the present day and has been taken over by, amongst others, the Balai Citoyen (a citizen movement that had an important role in the 2014 and 2015 uprisings) during inauguration ceremonies of new clubs.

As Sankara put in place radical policies to ensure the development of Burkina Faso as a country as well as a people, some of my older informants told me that he also had a bit of authoritarianism and stubbornness. And, as became evident after four years in power, his actions and anti-imperialist approach were not appreciated by everyone, especially not by the French. According to Manji and Ekine (2012: 35), Blaise Compaoré, Sankara's long-time friend and right-hand, is widely believed to be the person who intervened on behalf of the French and Western interests to bring the anti-imperialist, radical politics of Sankara to an end. In this account, Compaoré allowed Sankara to be killed: Sankara was pre-emptively declared dead 'of natural causes', buried in the middle of the night and his name and memory were removed from most public places. Comaporé took his place as president. In the 27 years that Blaise Comaporé ruled Burkina Faso, it was impossible to reopen Sankara's grave and investigate his bodily remains. 'Of course nobody believes that he died of natural causes, but what could we do? I guess many people were afraid to speak up about Sankara and demand justice', a friend told me. Finally, after Compaoré was ousted, the 'Sankara case' (as it is colloquially known) was reopened – 28 years after his assassination.

SYMBOLISM OR ACTION?

On a hot day in May 2015, a friend and I visited the tomb of Captain Sankara, which had been opened a couple of weeks before. After 28 years, the transitional government had consented to open the grave in search of Sankara's bodily remains. Was it the body of the former president? And if so, how did he die?

As we entered the cemetery, it was nearly empty, other than some stray dogs and three little boys. We asked the boys if they knew where the gravesite of Sankara was and they pointed to a pile of breezeblocks and heaps of sand.

During the exhumation ceremony on 26 May 2015, investigators found human remains, which they used to reconstruct the skeletons in order to determine whether or not the bodies found were actually those of Thomas Sankara and the twelve other soldiers (Thibault 2015). After the exhumation they left the former grave in shambles.[1] Seeing this disorder gave me an uneasy feeling – and not just me. My friend and the boys who showed us the way were upset too, one of them even shrieked, while others mumbled 'I don't understand'. Before I could even blink, they started digging in the sand. Together we dug out the pieces of the former tombstone that we could lay our hands on, sweeping away the sand that had buried most of the stones and digging out the remaining parts of the tomb. While digging, more boys joined, until we were six. Together we re-created Sankara's name and the flag of Burkina Faso. When we were done, the boys seemed content, giving each other high-fives and wanting to pose for pictures at the relocated stones. I, however, still felt uneasy, and shared my story about the abandoned gravesite with a friend of mine, a journalist and a member of the Balai Citoyen. I assumed he knew all along that the grave had been left like that but, to my great surprise, he was shocked. 'How could the authorities leave the tomb of our national hero shattered like that?'[2]

Apparently, nobody had gone back after the exhumation ceremony to verify the status of the tomb. These shattered pieces of the tomb of the national hero, abandoned like that, seemed to indicate that symbols and words from the past are more useful and powerful in protest, than as static remnants of stone.

Sankara's grave was only opened after Blaise Compaoré was ousted as president. Moreover, only recently was it officially reported that Sankara did, indeed, not die of so-called 'natural causes' as had been stated in his death report. Sankara was shot multiple times. Blaise Compaoré and General Gilbert Diendéré, the leader of the 2015 coup d'état and head of the presidential army RSP, are the prime suspects in the murder investigation. DNA tests, however, have yet to prove that one of the exhumed bodies is indeed that of the former revolutionary leader of Burkina Faso (Butty 2015).

23.1 Dagnoën Cemetery, Ouagadougou, 22 June 2015.

Source: photo by author

NORBERT ZONGO

Compaoré systematically tried to conceal the truth about the sudden death of Sankara in an effort to dismiss claims for justice. In the popular repertoire of Burkinabè heroes, Sankara is not alone. Norbert Zongo, journalist, publisher and editor of *l'Independent*, a local newspaper, likewise figures prominently as someone of whom people often say: 'I am proud to be Burkinabè, because he was, too'.[3] Zongo is a historical figure who inspires young people and generates a strong sense of pride. He died at the hands of the Compaoré regime after his newspaper began an investigation into the murder of a driver who worked for the brother of then-president, Blaise Compaoré.

The death of Zongo in 1998, classified by the government as a 'car accident', sparked massive demonstrations. For many, as Fessy (2014) indicates, the Zongo case was a turning point since it installed confidence in citizens about their own rights, particularly the freedom of speech. Moreover, as Hagberg (2002: 218) indicates, these massive demonstrations following the death of Zongo broke the silence surrounding impunity and the economic crimes committed by those in positions of political power and led to demands for justice and accountability. Until that moment, since the death of Sankara, the Burkinabè did not massively denounce impunity because people were given very little information (this was the pre-Internet days). Blaise made sure he had control. Nevertheless, even after these massive demonstrations and cries of 'Trop c'est trop' ('Enough is Enough!'; Hagberg 2002), it would take the Burkinabè another 12 years to oust Compaoré and, even then, the truth about both Sankara and Zongo's deaths has not been revealed.

Yet, the student protests and demonstrations after Zongo's death showed that the Burkinabè were quite capable of mobilising collectively in considerable numbers to demand justice and change. Burkinabès were fed up with the culture of impunity that existed among political power-holders and they would not be silent any longer (ibid.). Although one could argue that the silence and injustice around Sankara's death was not as important in the overall struggle of the Burkinabè considering there is still – up until the time of writing this chapter in late 2017 – no clear and official explanation given. However, I would argue that the decades of injustice combined with the outrage instigated by the emerging pieces of information on his death, the arrival of rapid ways of mobilising through social media and the building up of collective energy in uprising after uprising, led to the Burkinabè revolution and the ousting of Blaise.

Today, Sankara's face and quotes can be found on T-shirts, on pictures all over Facebook and on flyers and posters. Similarly, Norbert Zongo's face and quotes are similarly popular and illustrate the unabated outcry for justice and truth. He, too, continues to serve as an example for Burkinabès fighting for the freedom of expression. Commemorating him and his legacy, the national press centre in Ouagadougou is named after him. Since 12 December 2015, a street in the capital also bears his name. The Balai Citoyen and Semfilms (a film production company) urge justice and organise get-togethers to discuss 'who will be held accountable' and mobilise people on Facebook with the help of political discussion groups. Movements and organisations like the Balai Citoyen and Semfilms try to commemorate – in their view – national heroes. They urge the younger generation to understand where they come from and to use the thoughts and ideologies of revolutionary Burkinabè to work with their daily struggles and plans for their future, and that of Burkina Faso. I see this as a way of using the memory of Sankara and Zongo as a weapon to educate and to incite critical thought in the minds of young Burkinabè. Moreover, these young Burkinabè turn these memories into popular culture, making them accessible and contemporary weapons for social and political movements.

23.2 Public Facebook page of the Balai Citoyen and poster made by Semfilms. This poster was used for the commemoration of Zongo's death (17th anniversary) and for the baptism of the street in Ouagadougou that was named after him.

DABO BOUKARY

On 19 May 2015, the Université de Ouagadougou was covered with posters announcing the remembrance ceremony of Dabo Boukary. The ceremony was organised by the Union Générale des Étudiants Burkinabè (General Union of Burkinabè Students; UBEG) and the Mouvement Burkinabè des Droits de l'Homme et des Peuples (Burkinabè Movement for the Rights of Men and People; MBDHP[4]). Boukary was a medical student arrested during the student protests in 1990 and was later found dead. Amnesty International (1990) reported that he had been kept in detention, mistreated and eventually killed by security forces. As in previous cases, the government again failed to give information, stating that he 'simply disappeared'. Information about his death was not released until 1997, as a new wave of student demonstrations and massive strikes erupted (Manji and Ekine 2012).

Boukary and Zongo were two of the many who 'simply disappeared' in the era of Compaoré's rule. Yet, the more Compaoré and his ruling elite wanted the people to believe these victims had simply vanished, the more they were 'sawing the branch of the tree that they were sitting on'. People remember. Even though Compaoré made sure that investigations did not start on investigate the murders of Sankara, Zongo, Boukary and others, they lived on as camarades de la lutte and martyrs[5] in the minds, revolutionary hearts and spirits of the Burkinabè.

During the 25th anniversary of Boukary's death, an enormous university auditorium was filled to the brim with participants. The girl next to me, a student in law and political science, told me that many people had been mobilised to come via Facebook. She said that she was there because she thought it important to keep remembering those who had fallen. There were discussions on the current state of Burkinabè politics and the implications of Boukary's battle in the contemporary moment.

'Today we share the same battle. We must remember. We must understand the past events in our current times', the president of l'UGEB (Union Générale des Étudiants Burkinabè) said. 'In the past two years people were afraid to do something, to say something and to express themselves. Journalists did not know what to do with information because they were afraid. We did our discussions in the dark [online and face-to-face] and not in public because we were afraid. But now we are not afraid! Respect the march! How easy can it be?' Yet, even as Blaise had gone,[6] there was a sense that one should still be careful and never stop thinking critically. Amidst all this inspiring talk, the girl next to me whispered in my ear that she and her friends are still afraid.[7]

C,[8] a journalist, told me: 'For us demanding justice for Sankara, Zongo and Boukary means that we will not be left in the dark. We are not a horde of sheep that you can round up and leave for "stupid". We are one – we are Burkinabè-

and we demand justice for those that stood for our country and make us proud to be Burkinabè'.

THE REVIVAL OF PAST POLITICAL HEROES AND THEIR SIGNIFICANCE FOR THE BURKINABÈ UPRISINGS

During Ouaga Jazz 2015, Ouagadougou's yearly jazz festival, I was enjoying a concert with two friends when a group of young men started chanting along with the slammer who was taking the stage. At 3am they shouted, 'Nous sommes du pays des hommes intègres – c'est Burkina Faso d'où je viens – être intègre, être Burkinabè, est être révolutionnaire!'[9]

Phrases such as être intègre, être Burkinabè, être révolutionnaire symbolise some of the ways in which Sankara and his spirit live on in the minds and hearts of young Burkinabès. It speaks louder than many winding descriptions about where the Burkinabè get their sense of collective identity and unity from. This is the land of the honourable people. This is a land with a rich revolutionary heritage.

During Compaoré's rule, talking about Sankara was taboo. His legacy is now stronger than ever. Keita (2015) rightly indicates that immediately after Compaoré seized power and it became known that Sankara had died ('of which very little information was available in the pre-Internet days') the new

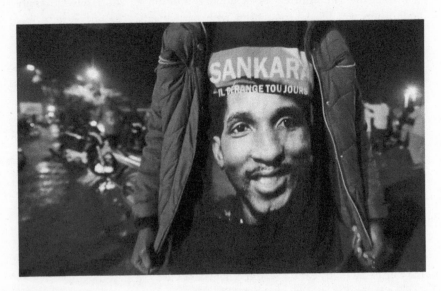

23.3 Sankara's image with the quote 'Il derange toujours' (freely translated to 'He is still disturbing things') during the protests in September 2015, following the failed *coup d'état* by the RSP.

Source: Reuters

regime launched a campaign to downsize Sankara's policies, character and image. The new ruling elite said that Sankara had been mentally unstable and that he was not to be trusted. They sought to undo many of his revolutionary programmes, such as the ban on polygamy and female circumcision. Compaoré later tried to claim that he helped to shape Sankara's revolutionary ideas and even – incredibly given that he most certainly had a role to play in Sankara's assassination (see Chapter 6 and Afterword, this volume) – that he had been the driving force behind Sankara's revolution. However hard Compaoré tried to become 'their' leader, he never succeeded in becoming as popular as Sankara. The cultural memory of Thomas Sankara as revolutionary leader was suppressed in order to create a Burkina Faso in the image of Compaoré. But he failed. During Compaoré's rule by impunity (Hagberg 2002), the revolutionary history of Burkina Faso (symbolised by Sankara, Zongo, Boukary and many others) nonetheless lived on in the memories of the Burkinabè.

The younger generation of Burkinabè draw inspiration from Sankara's image in many ways. They listen to his recorded speeches and sell, buy and promote T-shirts with his face and inspiring quotes. Most of these young Burkinabè were not born when Sankara was staging his revolution. Nevertheless, they take pride in being from the country of Sankara and even refer to themselves as 'des enfants de Sankara' ('we are the children of Sankara')[10] as a means of showing that they are part of Sankara's Burkina Faso, not that of Compaoré.

Burkina Faso has a past of popular discontent, including the 'Trop c'est trop' movement after Zongo's death in 1998 (Hagberg 2002; Manji and Ekine 2012) and the cost of living and food riots in 2008 (Engels 2015; Manji and Ekine 2012). However, these uprisings, often local as in Bobo-Dioulasso and Koudougou or Ouagadougou, did not lead to nationwide insurrections. When Compaoré introduced the referendum that would let the Burkinabè 'decide' whether or not the president was eligible for another mandate, it was the 'straw that broke the camel's back'. The build-up of anger, frustration, longstanding poverty and the impunity shielding the ruling elite, combined with the use of new media, cell phones and Facebook and people poured out into the streets.

During the mobilisation, the people I spoke with had a growing belief in the possibility of political change and even a major political uprising nationwide. Sankara was used as a rallying point through which the Burkinabè recalled a powerful past and forged an alternative path. The social movements, opposition groups and other collectives that rose up against the Compaoré regime used Sankara's legacy to create a sense of belonging and national unity. He became a means to mobilise the masses, especially the younger generation. Sankara and Zongo were revived as national heroes who died because of the Compaoré regime – they played powerful symbolic roles in mobilising the youth towards a possible future. Compaoré had tried to wipe out or change Sankara's memory and legacy. This history of silencing seemed to make Burkinabès even more determined to assert their former revolutionary leader as their example: 'Seul la lutte libère!' ('Only the fight will set us free!').

A friend and young activist summed it up for me: 'Sankara is seen as a symbol of freedom. He was one that listened to his people and respected the freedom and will of the people. He gave us the power to be what we wanted to be: a free people, proud and upright'. In more concise and politicised terms, she said: 'If they truly were the children of their Capitaine, only a revolution would free them from their oppressors'.[11]

NOTES

1 For the time being Sankara has a new symbolic grave, while his body is still under examination. There are plans to clear the Dagnoën cemetery and replace it with a housing project.
2 Field notes, 23 June 2015, Ouagadougou.
3 Field notes throughout the fieldwork period, but especially during press conferences of the Balai Citoyen in the press centre: Centre National de Presse Norbert Zongo.
4 The MBDHP were also one of the key organisers of the demonstrations that were held after the death of Norbert Zongo in 1998 (Hagberg 2002).
5 The word *martyrs* is used in public opinion to refer to those that died in the fight for freedom of repression.
6 He was in exile in Ivory Coast during this speech.
7 Field notes, 19 May, University of Ouagadougou.
8 For most of my informants I use the initial of their first or last name, because in some cases they do not wish to be public with their name and function or profession.
9 Text and performance by Valian. Translates to: 'We are from the land of the honourable man – it is Burkina Faso where I'm from – being 'honourable', being Burkinabè is being revolutionary!
10 Field notes during meetings and rallies and two interviews with young activists, April and May 2015.
11 Quotes from an informal talk with an activist and his friends, in Ouagadougou, 8 June 2015.

REFERENCES

Adebwani, W. (2008) Death, national memory and the social construction of heroism. *The Journal of African History* 49(3): 419–444.

Alvesson, M. and Sköldberg, K. (2009) *Reflexive Methodology: New Vistas for Qualitative Research*. Thousand Oaks, CA: Sage.

Amnesty International. (1991) Index number: AFR 60/002/1991. Available http://www.amnesty.org/en/documents/afr60/002/1991/en

Assmann, J. and Czaplicka, J. (1995) Collective memory and cultural identity. *German Critique* (65): 125–133.

Butty, J. (2015) Former Burkina Faso president wanted for killing of Thomas Sankara. *Voanews.com*, 22 December. Retrieved from www.voanews.com/content/former-burkina-faso-president-wanted-for-killing-of-thomas-sankara/3113160.html.

Calhoun, C. (2007) *Nations Matter: Culture, History and the Cosmopolitan Dream.* New York: Routledge.

Engels, B. (2015) Different means of protest, same causes: popular struggles in Burkina Faso *Review of African Political Economy* 42(143): 92–106.

Fessy, T. (2014) How Burkina Faso's Blaise Comaporé sparked his own downfall. *BBC.com,* 31 October. Retrieved from www.bbc.com/news/world-africa-29858965.

Gardner, W. L., Pickett, C. L. and Brewer, M. B. (2000) Social Exclusion and Selective Memory: How the Need to Belong Influences Memory for Social Events. *Personality and Social Psychology Bulletin* 26(4): 486–496.

Hagberg, S. (2002) 'Enough is Enough': An Ethnography of the Struggle against Impunity in Burkina Faso. *The Journal of Modern African Studies* 40(2): 217–246.

Harsch, E. (2014) *Thomas Sankara: An African Revolutionary.* Athens, OH: Ohio University Press.

Hodgkin, K. and Radstone, S. (eds). (2003) *Contested Pasts: The Politics of Memory.* New York: Routledge.

Igreja, V. (2008). Memories as Weapons: The Politics of Peace and Silence in Post-Civil War Mozambique. *Journal of Southern African Studies* 34(3): 539–556.

Igreja, V. (2013) Politics of Memory, Decentralisation and Recentralisation in Mozambique. *Journal of Southern African Studies* 39(2): 313–335.

Igreja, V. (2015) Amnesty law, political struggles for legitimacy and violence in Mozambique. *International Journal of Transitional Justice* 9: 239–258.

Johnston, H. (2013) *Social Movements and Culture* (vol. 4). New York: Routledge.

Keita, M. (2015) Why Burkina Faso's Late Revolutionary Leader Thomas Sankara Still Inspires Young Africans. *Quartz Africa,* 31 May. Retrieved from http://qz.com/415257/why-burkina-fasos-late-revolutionary-leader-thomas-sankara-still-inspires-young-africans.

Manji, F. and Ekine, S. (2012) *African Awakening: The Emerging Revolutions.* Cape Town: Fahamu/Pambazuka.

Misztal, B. (2003) *Theories of Social Remembering.* Maidenhead: McGraw-Hill Education.

Ross, A. (2013) Research for Whom? In N. Mirzoeff (ed.), *Militant Research Handbook,* 8–10. New York: Steinhardt School of Culture, Education, and Human Development, New York University.

Thibault, G. (2015) Exhumation de Thomas Sankara: un processus long et sous pression. *RFI.fr,* 26 May. Retrieved from www.rfi.fr/afrique/20150526-burkina-faso-exhumation-thomas-sankara-processus-long-sous-pression

Afterword

Aziz Salmone Fall

We salute the resistance of the people of Burkina Faso, particularly the progressive forces and those engaged youth of Burkina, who shouted 'Sankara lives', while overthrowing the regime of Compaore. We honour the martyrs.

Thomas Sankara knew the risks he ran, for he respected and was conscious of the long line of martyrs stretching back to the dawn of African decolonisation: Ben Barka, Mondlane, Moumié, Um Nyobé, Rwagasoré, Lumumba, Olympio and Samora Machel, to name just a few. Although the list was already long, it continued to grow after the assassination of Sankara: Dulcie September, Chris Hani and others.

It is said that behind every great man is a great woman. In the case of Thomas Sankara, that woman is Mariam Serme. The courage and resistance of this woman in the face of adversity is an example of resilience for all of Africa. As a First Lady, she was humble and undertook her professional obligations as a woman of the people. She remains convinced that social progress cannot occur without a radical change in the status of women. On the death of her husband and friend in the company of his comrades, she proved a model of dignified resistance. She supported the International Committee for Justice for Sankara (CIJS) in filing a complaint regarding the circumstances of Sankara's death. The CIJS has achieved a precedent in Africa against impunity (see below).

Nonetheless, much ground has been lost in the struggle for social justice during the thirty years that has followed Thomas Sankara's assassination. The disengagement and re-engineering of states has given rise to a new cast of plutocrats across the globe. With the connivance of a revamped imperialism, this cast of actors has monopolised the resources of the African continent. This unjust enrichment has not only reconstituted the *françafrique* fringe but has also fed the arrogance of the regime in Ouaga. The Compaoré government positioned itself at the heart of rewriting the mining codes, holding a 'fire sale' of state corporations and promoting the geopolitical re-composition of the sub-region. The Compaoré regime had a demonstrated capacity for both creating conflict (displayed by its bullying tactics) and profiting from conflict (by acting as mediator and/or fire fighter-pyromaniac). In addition, Compaoré's government corrupted many fringe elements of the left, including even those within the ranks of the Sankara-ites and the considerably dampened resistance. Despite all this, the resistance continued. We are confident that it will put the regime fully to rest by throwing out the contradictions that it has created. Confronting impunity and demanding justice played a key role in the success of the popular uprising of 2014 but both are as important now as ever before: securing justice for our martyrs will test the maturity of the army and the judiciary.

JUSTICE AND IMPUNITY: 20 YEARS OF STRUGGLE

In the case of martyrs like Cabral or Sankara, it was only the people in their inner circle who knew their secrets. There is a popular saying: 'too much trust breeds treason'. Despite it all, Sankara, like Cabral, never gave in to paranoia and potential crime. On the contrary, he followed his natural tendency towards tolerance and unity rather than divisiveness, and, in the end, that was what did him in (Fall 2013: 171).

Sankara was the last African head of state in the twentieth century who successfully endeavoured, without going through a stage of war for national liberation, to follow in Cabral's and Castro's footsteps. However, these efforts stopped abruptly when he was betrayed by his brother-in-arms, Blaise Compaoré, in collusion with the *françafrique* in an international plot. Compaoré was the sophisticated face of treachery: a willing steward of French machinations and sinister designs against the whole region. Following the popular uprising that saw him out of office, he was exfiltrated by France, granted asylum, elite status and offered citizenship in Côte d'Ivoire. While he was the Minister of Justice, he outrageously claimed that Sankara died of natural causes at the exact same time as a dozen of his colleagues. To this very day he refuses to allow the truth of the assassination to come out. As long as there is impunity and imperialist protection for it, treason will never end.[1]

Twenty years ago, the Group for Research and Initiative for the Liberation of Africa (GRILA, a Pan-Africanist group to which I belong) answered the call for justice by creating an international campaign with a two-pronged strategy that was both political and legal. It has been my privilege to co-ordinate a team of 22 lawyers defending Mariam and her sons, who put together a case for a full investigation into the murder of President Sankara and a dozen of his colleagues (Fall 2012).

From 1997 to 2001, the CIJS exhausted all of the legal recourses available to it in Burkina and was shamefully blocked at the level of the Supreme Court by a judiciary controlled by the Compaoré regime. The government of Burkina Faso, under the presidency of Blaise Compaoré, along with a highly compromised judicial system, blocked all efforts by the Campaign to bring the case to court locally. The absence of a public inquiry and legal proceedings to determine the identity and civil and criminal responsibilities of Thomas Sankara's assassins and the failure to rectify his death certificate constitute a serious denial of justice. The failure to establish the competence of the military courts was an obstruction of justice. The decision to charge an abnormally high deposit was an obstruction of justice. The case was subsequently dismissed due to the non-payment of a symbolic deposit on behalf of one of the plaintiffs, Auguste Sankara; as a minor, Auguste should have been exempted from paying such a deposit under the legislation in force.

After exhausting all possible legal recourses within Burkina, the Campaign brought the case before the UNHRC. In 2006, the UNHRC decided in favour of the International Justice for Sankara Campaign, demanding that the government of Burkina Faso take action to shed light on the circumstances of Thomas Sankara's death (Communication no. 1159/2003, UN Doc. CCPR/C/86/D/1159/2003 2006).

The UN Human Rights Committee, seized by the CIJS, deemed that, following judgment No. 46 of the Supreme Court of Burkina Faso of 19 June 2001 (rendering definitive decision no. 14 of the Court of Appeal, declaring the jurisdictions of common law incompetent) the authorities of Burkina Faso had effectively refused to send the case to jurisdictions of the Ministry of Defence, where judicial proceedings would have begun before the military tribunals (as provided by article 71(1) and (3) of the Code of Military Justice). It was concluded then that the prosecutor wrongfully stopped the procedure. The Committee concluded:

> The family of Thomas Sankara has the right to know the circumstances of his death ... the refusal to conduct an investigation regarding the death of Thomas Sankara, the official non-recognition of the location of his remains and the non-rectification of his death certificate, constitute inhumane treatment regarding Mrs. Sankara and her sons, contrary to article seven of the Pact.
>
> With respect to paragraph 3(1) of article 2 of the Pact, the State party is required to ensure a useful and effective remedy for Mrs. Sankara and her sons, consistent, notably, with the official recognition of the location of his burial site and damages for the pain and anguish that the family has undergone.
>
> The State party cannot explain the delays at issue and on this point. The Committee considers that, contrary to the arguments of the State, no ban can invalidate the action before the military tribunal, and from this point, the decision regarding non-denunciation of the matter before the Minister of Defense returns to the prosecutor ...

The Compaoré regime proposed different, less contentious recourses: the College of Elders, the Commission of national reconciliation, the Fund for the Compensation of Victims of Political Violence and the Mediator of Faso. These recourses were all non-binding. Although certain UN experts had been relatively complacent, the Compaoré regime now found itself confronted with the determination of our lawyers. We demanded the examination of an expert; we wanted an independent and respected forensic laboratory to proceed with the identification of the DNA of the body buried at Dagnoën Cemetery in Ouagadougou.

But the Human Rights Committee did not retain the right to demand an enquiry, nor did it demand compensation or recognition of Sankara's burial place. Burkina Faso has not provided any evidence to prove the authenticity of the burial site. The compensation offered to the family came to 430,445 FCFA – around 66,231 or US$65,000. Some experts estimate that the sum was more generous despite an obvious typo on the zero in the amount (US$650,000/434,450,000 FCFA) and that the State made an effort by crossing out the word 'natural' on the death certificate (which stated that Sankara had died of 'natural causes'). Despite the amendment of the figure by our lawyers and the fact that pilgrimages in honour of Sankara to a grave in the cemetery are not proof that he is actually buried there, the Human Rights Committee declared in April 2008 that it was satisfied with its findings and had no intention of taking the matter any further. The CIJS continued the fight against impunity, especially as Burkina Faso continued to rack up other prosecutable violations. Then President Compaoré, Sankara's suspected killer, became a mediator in a crisis in neighbouring Guinea. On Radio France International, he declared without missing a beat: 'We cannot tolerate that there are still discussions in Guinea about disappeared people whose bodies have not been found'.

All the while of course, Thomas Sankara's body was disappeared. One of our former lawyers, Me Nkounkou, introduced a confinement request procedure. The authorities never responded. Following the UN decision, CIJS waited years for the authorities to prove that the supposed grave of Sankara is indeed his. On 15 October 2009, the legal committee of the CIJS, represented by Me Nzeppa, filed a request for a subpoena and order for the DNA of the corpse in the sepulchre, erected by the Burkina Faso government, to be compared with that of Sankara's children. A procedural calendar was established on 9 February 2011. On 11 March 2011, the State of Burkina Faso raised an objection, noting that the Tribunal de Grande Instance de Ougadougou lacked the jurisdiction to proceed, rendering the demand inadmissible. Subsequently, the tomb was vandalised on 20 June 2011. The Compaoré regime claimed that it was someone with a mental disorder. The state responded by stationing police at the site to ensure the security of the tomb. Two years and four months later, the tomb was once again vandalised and a liquid was spilled all over it, in spite of the presence of police in front of the main door of the cemetery. Ultimately, on 30 April 2015, the complaint of the CIJS regarding DNA identification was rejected on the basis of the alleged lack of jurisdiction of the Tribunal. At the time, Blaise Compaore was also President of the Superior Court of the Magistrate. The Magistrate was so wracked by impunity that it was excluded from the process of transition.

For struggles against impunity to be effective, the judiciary must be made up of courts and tribunals that are impartial and vigilant regarding the protection of collective and individual rights. There were high hopes that after the popular uprising in 2015 a constitutional assembly could correct the distortions of the judicial system and lessen its dependence on the executive while reforming the army. Meanwhile, taking note of the courageous determination of the new regime to investigate Sankara's graves, our lawyers advised that this process be undertaken with forensic scrutiny and according to law.

We required forensic expertise and counter-forensic expertise. However, the judge never retained the international lab that we recommended for the expertise. The results of the DNA analysis revealed that the two analyses on the bodies of the victims were negative. The samples of genetic materials from the remains of ten of the victims of 15 October 1987 had decomposed so thoroughly that nothing could be identified. The legal-medical investigation in Burkina is limited by serious technical weaknesses. The scene of the crime was never sufficiently sealed off after 15 October 1987. We cannot confirm the quality of the process of sterilisation that followed the exhumation of the bodies.

At this time, the State undertook the tasks of supervising, recuperating and examining the presumed remains of the president (including his clothes and personal effects). Me Benwende Sankara requested a bailiff following the second act of vandalism of the tomb (when the unidentified liquids were spilled). We were not able to obtain any samples of the contaminated soil in order to determine if the liquid had a corrosive property. It remains unclear if a corrosive liquid was poured on all of the tombs. At this stage, the identification of a degraded DNA and the negative results cannot be allowed to prejudice the proceeding.

WHERE ARE WE NOW?

The political and constitutional crisis in Burkina unleashed an explosion of international indignation. While Compaoré was chased out of power in October 2014 by the popular uprising, he left behind his right-hand guards, the Regiment of Presidential Security (RSP), and some rogue terrorists from the Niger-Mali-Libya compact. By firing on the patriotic and unarmed youth, RSP aggravated impunity. They have been linked to atrocities within the sub-region. Several of its leaders, like other collaborators of the old regime, have comfortable pensions from the mining, transport and real-estate sectors. Many have become wealthy from the wars in Sierra Leone and Liberia, as well as by circumventing the ban on UNITA diamonds in Angola. The destabilising of Côte d'Ivoire during the mediation processes, ambiguous hostage-taking and terrorist exploitation in the Sahel were profitable for the Compaoré regime.

The RSP, in its persistent arrogance, claims to defend the interests of supporters of the former regime. General Diendere has long been a centrepiece of the *françafrique*, along with several in his entourage. In 2008, Gilbert Diendéré was honoured in France and received the legion d'honneur, one of the highest national honours in France. In Burkina Faso, as well as in France, the people who most probably killed Thomas Sankara are not just tolerated with total impunity but are celebrated and promoted by some prominent politicians and international figures. Diendéré was also a leading architect of the annual Flintlock exercises (between African, allied and US counterterrorism forces) and US-led counter-terrorism operations in the Sahel. He oversaw the expansion of secret bases for drones – including at Sand Creek and Ouagadougou airport – on behalf of Aztec Archer Intelligence Services and the Embassy of the United States.

After repeatedly disrupting the post-Compaoré political transition, the RSP is now attempting to obstruct the vision for society sought by the people of Burkina Faso. The RSP have failed for now, although they are still trying to undermine the army and much-needed judicial reforms. The Islamist terrorist cells allied to Compaoré are still active in the sub-region and there is ongoing political blackmail, which underpins the militarised management of the continent.

On Tuesday 29 September 2015 the regular army surrounded the camp of RSP. Gunfire was heard near the presidential palaces and the RSP barracks. Around 300 of the presidential guards estimated 1,200 soldiers had surrendered at a second camp in the capital. Regular army troops had taken control of strategic locations previously occupied by the renegades. Many of these soldiers and their supporters dispersed into the countryside. Their reputation as 'death squads' and their refusal to surrender have fuelled fears among the people. The government ordered an inquiry into the coup, and on Saturday 26 September 2015 the state prosecutor froze the accounts of Diendéré and 13 other suspected officers linked to the attempted coup.

Diendéré never accepted being dismissed from the leadership of the RSP and, like his sponsors, has not consented to the decision to ban representatives of the old regime from presidential candidacy. The coup, led by General Diendéré, occurred just hours before the scheduled hearing of the investigating judge in the Sankara case. The judge had convened attorneys of the International Campaign Justice for Sankara on 17 September to share the results of the ballistics and

DNA testing. It is very likely that findings from those tests might have helped to incriminate General Diendéré: he was long recognised as a member of the death squad that put a bloody end to the Burkina Faso revolution in 1987.

His coup aimed to redistribute the cards and change the balance of power. It is therefore not surprising that the Heads of States of ECOWAS, as provisional mediators, proposed softer crisis solutions than the African Union. As heads of state, they fear copycat uprisings in their own countries which are afflicted by many of the same problems. They do not intervene against neo-colonial plans, preferring to preserve the status quo (including ongoing re-colonisation). While perhaps their intention was to avoid civil war and to appear as neutral mediators, they have been far from impartial; indeed, they have reinforced the actions of the mutineers. An endemic culture of impunity, political destabilisation and economic and violent crime has come to characterise Burkina and, indeed, in the entire sub-region.

Balai citoyen (Citizen's Broom) again took courageously to the streets to end impunity. At the level of the grassroots, a fierce opposition emerged to resist the plotters and the regulatory measures of the ECOWAS mediators. Due to these efforts, Diendere was later arrested and charged. The Burkinabè military tribunal issued a warrant for the arrest of Blaise Compaoré. It indicted 13 suspects in connection with the assassination of Sankara and his comrades. While we were awaiting and preparing for the trial, the deaths in 2017 of Etienne Zongo, Valere Somé and Salif Diallo represented significant losses for those counting on the testimonies of crucial witnesses.

Air Force Lieutenant Etienne Zongo, Sankara's chief military officer, served at his side since the beginning of the revolution. After Sankara's assassination, he was captured, tortured and detained without trial for two years. After President Rawlings's mediation and intervention, he was released and, fearing for his life, sought asylum in Ghana. He was disconnected from his family for seven years, as described in his daughter's book (Zongo 2007). He had taken care to write down his version of events and was interviewed by Africa International in 2001 but his testimony would have been central to the case. The circumstances of his sudden death in Accra were ambiguous.

Valere Somé was a young ideologist of the revolution and was the leader of the Union of Communist Struggles. Sankara requested that he draft a programme for the unification of revolutionary organisations and factions. After Sankara's assassination, Somé sought asylum in Congo Brazzaville and later went back home and formed an opposition party, the Party for Social Progress. He had previously told me that there were things that he would only reveal the day of the trial. He died in France on 30 May 2017.

Salif Diallo died in France on 19 August 2017 while serving as the President of the National Assembly of Burkina Faso and head of the ruling party. A long-time member of government in various capacities, he re-surfaced on the waves of the transition after the 2014 upheaval despite the fact that he was one of Compaoré's closest allies, serving as Director of the Cabinet of Compaoré from 1987 to 1989, Minister of Environment and Water as well as Minister of Agriculture from 2000 to 2008. One year after the Sankara complaint was lodged in Ouaga, on the night of 27 November 1998, Salif Diallo claimed that sensitive, key documents related to the case were stolen from his room at the Hotel Bristol in France, while he was on an official visit with Ablassé Ouédraogo, the then foreign minister of Burkina Faso.

At the time, the Compaoré regime was nervous. On 23 March 1998, in order No. 06/98, the examining judge had decided, in contradiction to the prosecutor's decision not to open a judicial investigation, that the Ouagadougou Superior Court was the proper court of competence to examine the case. According to Blaise Compaoré's version, he and Salif Diallo were together when Blaise allegedly heard the gunshots that killed Sankara and 12 others on 15 October 1987. Diallo claimed that he 'barely' escaped death on the day because, a mere two hours prior to the assassination, he was sent to Compaoré's home to fetch a secret note to give to Sankara. Diallo recalled,

> I was at the home of Minister Blaise Compaoré. He was suffering [from an illness], he had a document that he had to hand over to President Thomas Sankara, and to tell you the truth, I was two fingers away from the meeting where Thomas Sankara died. I should have been at the meeting. I only barely escaped it ... Had it not been for the fact that Thomas Sankara sent me to [Compaoré's house to] retrieve the document, I would have been among the victims.
> (Interview with Salif Diallo, *L'événement*)[2]

High-ranking Liberian soldiers who were part of the plot denied this version, saying that Compaoré was indeed at the Conseil de l'Entente on that day (see Chapter 6, this volume).

Salif Diallo claimed that he was not part of the assassination plot and he maintained that the Bristol documents would have proven it. In 2004, Salif Diallo had fallen ill and was sent to France, where Compaoré visited him in the hospital and then reserved a suite at the very same Bristol Hotel. Following our victory at the UN in 2006, Salif Diallo sent a Cameroonian friend to bribe me to discontinue the struggle. In 2008, Compaoré dismissed him from his post as VP of the CDP, although he was later appointed as the ambassador to Austria. He continued to play various diplomatic and mediation roles for the regime before resigning from Compaoré's party on 6 January 2014. On 25 January 2014, Diallo joined Simon Compaoré and Roch Marc Kabore to found the People's Movement for Progress (MPP). Diallo was scheduled to visit Canada in June 2017, but our meeting was abruptly cancelled. I was expecting explanations about the attempted bribe as well as those famous Bristol documents. Diallo died two months later and those explanations are no longer forthcoming. The struggle against impunity is immensely difficult and our approach to it must be holistic.

HOPE GOING FORWARD: PAN-AFRICANIST SPIRIT TODAY

Sankara was a dedicated and organic intellectual, who spoke and worked on behalf of the masses as a leading figure of the so-called 'global South'. He inspires a non-aligned and Pan-Africanist spirit for the twenty-first century: the formation and crystallisation of intellectuals who are organic to the interests of the masses and the working class, those victims of imperialism.

There is a continued and urgent need for Pan-African and internationalist resistance as well as the re-politicisation of youth for a democratic future. It is important to build on the historical struggles that have been fought and to work more boldly on others, in order to realise the achievements of our people. There have been substantial but fragile gains for the Left in Latin America. The brakes have been placed on the uprisings in North Africa, as well as more recently in Burkina Faso. We need to work against the disarray of the Left and for a democratic re-politicisation of the people. A major portion of these populations has been rendered superfluous by global capitalism, which tries to contain their desperate migrations.

United against the oppression of nations, the potential to regain the path of self-reliance and to strengthen the Tricontinental front are the only exits possible against the crises in the global South (Bouamama 2017: 180). We must resist all foreign military bases settling in Africa.[3] But this radical reform is eminently political and must be realised through the rediscovery of internationalism and the defence of the common good of humanity. Such a democratic re-politicisation of our masses will aid in resisting the military momentum of collective imperialism.

We must pass this phase of indignation and engage more deeply. We must show, as Sankara did, even more audacity and organisation towards the development of a tricontinental internationalist political platform of convergence, until we reach a *transinternationalist* phase. The Bandung legacy is no longer one of neutrality. Today its spirit needs to build an anti-comprador social bloc, rooted in a tri-continental strategy within the so-called global South. I call this internationalist constellation, *TransInternationalism*, because change in the twenty-first century arises from the South.

The Pan-Africanist path forged by Sankara provides a roadmap for a societal project in a polycentric world – a multiply centred world in which the popular masses of the South and North are fed up with the dominant North-South monologue. Towards these ends, I offer a new concept, *Panafricentrage*, to describe the proposal to reorient globalisation towards a development that is truly about balance, that is to say *ma'at*: social justice, protecting Mother Earth, ensuring well-being and each person's upright conduct and attitude of integrity.[4] In our efforts to contribute to such a project, CIJS currently joins with progressive forces in recommending to the responsible leaders of Burkina Faso that they make commitments to:

- ensure the independence of the judiciary and allow prosecution of all pending cases;
- end impunity;
- prosecute those complicit in the terrorist destabilisation of the Sahel;
- prohibit travel and freeze the assets of all members of the so-called 'National Committee for Democracy' and anyone who has contributed to their terrorist enterprise;
- provide an audit of public funds of all stake-holders, politicians and senior government officials in charge of portfolios during the Compaoré era;
- revise the mining code (including its military and security component) signed by the Compaore regime and international development cooperation programmes;
- dissolve and disband the vestiges of the RSP by restructuring the national army and its neocolonial trusteeship under foreign forces; and
- convene a national conference on development focused on meeting the basic needs of the population and a implementing a fair redistribution of the resources and production of the country.

CIJS remains confident that the new regime in Ouaga will find the appropriate and impartial structures to ensure that our 20 years of work will end with some level of truth as we turn the page on impunity once and for all. CIJS repeats its plea to civil society in France, the US and Côte d'Ivoire, urging their assistance in opening up the files that can reveal the identity of anyone with a hand in Thomas Sankara's assassination. CIJS is thankful for the initiative, Justice Pour Sankara, Justice Pour l'Afrique, which is being simultaneously pursued by Bruno Jaffré and comrades. This initiative has gained the support of many Members of Parliament for declassifying the French archives regarding Thomas Sankara's assassination. Visiting Burkina Faso in November 2017, the current French President Macron promised that all documents will be declassified.[5] We are grateful to the Burkinabè people for their ongoing support and encourage them to be vigilant and keep up the struggle against impunity.

NOTES

1   '"Impunity" means the impossibility, de jure or de facto, of bringing the perpetrators of violations to account - whether in criminal, civil, administrative or disciplinary proceedings - since they are not subject to any inquiry that might lead to their being accused, arrested, tried and, if found guilty, sentenced to appropriate penalties, and to making reparations to their victims' (Orentlicher n.d.).

2   Available at www.evenement-bf.net/spip.php?article1662.

3   For more on this, watch the complete documentary film, *Africom Go Home: Foreign Bases Out of Africa*. Available at www.youtube.com/watch?v=-HLjrzVHWPM

4   For a more complete explanation of Panafricentrage, see www.youtube.com/watch?v=CTLT4-xC6VM.

5   For more on this emerging development, see www.francetvinfo.fr/monde/afrique/burkina-faso/qui-est-thomas-sankara-liconeanticolonialiste_2494741.html#xtor=EPR-502-%5Bnewslettervideo%5D-20171203-%5Bvideo4%5D

REFERENCES

Bouamama, S. (2017) *La tricontinentale, les peuples du Tiers-monde à l'assaut du ciel.* Genève: CETIM, Syllepse.

Fall, A. F. (2012) Postface. In N. S. Sylla (ed.), *Redécouvrir Sankara, Martyr de la liberté,* Douala: Africavenir.

Fall, A. F. (2013) The Cancer of Betrayal which We Must Uproot from Afrika. In F. Manji and B. Fletcher (eds), *Claim no Easy Victory, The Legacy of Amilcar Cabral,* 171. Dakar: CODESRIA.

Fall, A. F. (2015) Postface: Towards a New Movement: Aligned Trans-Internationalism, in Khudori, D. (ed.) *Bandung at 60: New Insights and Emerging Forces.* Yogyakarta: Pustaka Pelajar-ARENA, CIRFA, CODESRIA-Global U.

Orentlicher, D (n.d.) Promotion And Protection Of Human Rights: Impunity, Report Of The Independent Expert To Update The Set Of Principles To Combat Impunity Retrieved on 7 December 2017 from https://documents-dds-ny.un.org/doc/UNDOC/GEN/G05/109/00/PDF/G0510900.pdf?OpenElement

Zongo, N. (2007) *When Everything Has Fallen.* San Francisco: Booksurge Publishing.

Notes on Contributors

Celestina Agyekum is a Ghanaian-American scholar–activist and poet with interests in grassroots development, education, creative writing and photography. She combines her passions for development work and the arts to explore personal development journeys and the complexities of 'working in the field'. A published poet, she is currently working on a children's book as well as a collection of non-fiction that considers the experiences of Peace Corps volunteers in Burkina Faso.

Dr Ama Biney is an independent scholar with over 20 years of teaching experience in the UK. She has taught courses in African history (ancient and modern); Caribbean history; African American history; post-independence African politics; the history of Pan-Africanism and the history of black people in Britain. She is the author of *The Political and Social Thought of Kwame Nkrumah* (Palgrave Macmillan, 2011) and the co-editor (with Adebayo Olukoshi) of *Speaking Truth to Power: Selected Pan-African Postcards of Tajudeen Abdul-Raheem* (Pambazuka Press, 2010). Ama was the former editor-in-chief of the Pan-African weekly electronic newsletter, *Pambazuka News* (from 2012 to 2014) and is a regular contributor.

De-Valera N. Y. M. Botchway is currently an associate professor of history and African studies at University of Cape Coast in Ghana. His research interests include: the social and cultural history of West Africa, popular culture and the history of boxing in Ghana, African and global historical and cultural exchanges and experiences as well as African Indigenous knowledge systems. He has worked in and collaborated with more than five universities around the world, including as a fellow in the Centre of African Studies at the University of Cambridge in the United Kingdom, as a visiting scholar and global academic partner at the University of South Florida and as an exchange faculty at Grand Valley State University, Michigan.

Horace G. Campbell is a noted international peace and justice scholar and professor of African American studies and political science at Syracuse University in New York. Born in Montego Bay, Jamaica, he has been involved in Africa's liberation struggles and in the struggles for peace and justice globally for more than four decades and has published widely on Pan-Africanism, African politics and militarism in Africa.

Sarah H. Chiumbu is a senior research specialist in the human and social development research programme at the Human Sciences Research Council (HSRC) and senior visiting research fellow in the department of media and communication at the University of Witwatersrand. Her research interests include the following: media, democracy and citizenship, alternative media, social movements, race and transformation.

Sophie Bodénès Cohen's research focuses on socio-political art and the connections between art and revolution in Africa. She is a PhD candidate at the École des Hautes Études en Sciences Sociales in Paris, where she studies art history and social anthropology with a specialisation in the contemporary art of West Africa. She has a Masters in cognitive sciences and artificial intelligence.

Patricia Daley is Professor in the Human Geography of Africa in the School of Geography and the Environment, University of Oxford. She is of African-Jamaican descent. She has researched and published on aspects of refugee migration, militarism, and sexual and gender-based violence in East and Central Africa. She was a student in Oxford at the same time as Tajudeen Abdul-Raheem and a delegate to the 7th Pan-African Congress in 1994. She is the author of *Gender and Genocide In Burundi: The Search for Spaces of Peace in the Great Lakes Region of Africa*, published by James Currey.

Patrick Delices is a Pan-African scholar and public intellectual who specialises in decolonial revolutionary studies. Patrick has held academic posts at Hunter College in the department of Africana and Puerto Rican/Latino studies and at Columbia University, where he was a research fellow working under the late, Pulitzer Prize-winning historian Dr Manning Marable. Currently, Patrick is working on two books: a system analysis of the global impact of the Haitian revolution and a biography of his father, Georges Chardin Delices, Haiti's greatest football legend.

Fiona Dragstra holds a MSc in political communication from the University of Amsterdam, for which she researched new media and political engagement in Mozambique during the 2014 elections. She also holds a research MA in African studies from Leiden University. Her thesis, conducted within the 'Connecting in

Times of Duress' research programme, looks at the role that new media played in shaping political mobilisation, political agency and structural social change during and after the Burkinabè uprisings in October 2014 and September 2015.

Bettina Engels is junior professor for conflict and African Studies at the Otto Suhr Institute for Political Science, Freie Universität Berlin. Together with Kristina Dietz, she is head of the junior research group Global Change – Local Conflicts? Her research focuses on conflict over land and resources, resistance, urban protest and social movements in Africa.

Aziz Salmone Fall, Pan-Africanist and internationalist, teaches political science, anthropology and international relations at McGill University and at the Université du Québec à Montréal (UQAM) in Canada. Aziz is the president of the Internationalist Center (CIRFA), former coordinator of the Quebec anti-apartheid network and a founding member of GRILA (Groupe de Recherche et d'Initiative pour la Libération de l'Afrique). He coordinates the International Campaign Justice for Sankara (CIJS), a collective of lawyers that has set a legal precedent at the UN and is still leading the legal battle for justice for Sankara – a battle that has been 20 years long and continues. He directed the 2014 documentary film, *AFRICOM: Go Home, Foreign Bases Out of Africa*.

T. D. Harper-Shipman is a postdoctoral fellow in the Institute for Politics and Strategy at Carnegie Mellon University. Her research interests include international development, foreign aid, gender and human rights in Africa. She also has forthcoming publications on race and ethics in international relations and critiques of the World Bank's development strategy using the writings of Wangari Maathai.

Ernest Harsch is a long-time journalist and academic. He worked on African issues for more than 20 years at the United Nations Secretariat in New York. He is a research scholar affiliated with Columbia University's Institute of African Studies and was an Adjunct Associate Professor at Columbia's School of International and Public Affairs. He has published hundreds of newspaper and magazine articles and several books, including a biography *Thomas Sankara: An African Revolutionary* (Ohio University Press, 2014), books on the struggle against apartheid in South Africa and the Angolan civil war and *Burkina Faso: A History of Power, Protest and Revolution* (Zed Books, 2017).

Dr Nicholas A. Jackson is a scholar of international development and social movements. His current work examines the contested geographies of neoliberalism, corporate exploitation and resistance in Africa, Latin America and the Middle East. Nicholas's recent and forthcoming works draw from and incorporate neoliberalism as spectacle, fragmented stability in Cameroon and the rapid failure of the Chad–Cameroon Petroleum Development Project, social movement theory, and the corporate academy, as well as parallels between unconquered resistances in Egypt and Burkina Faso.

Bruno Jaffré has worn many hats over the years: he is a historian of the revolution of Burkina Faso (1983–1987); biographer of Thomas Sankara; former activist and organiser with Telecommunication CSDPTT (Coopération Solidarité Développement aux PTT), an NGO working to 'bridge the digital divide' in rural communities; member of SURVIE (http://survie.org), an organisation denouncing the françafrique; occasional journalist; former professor of mathematics and research engineer at a large company. The author of five books on Sankara, Bruno also coordinates the website thomassankara. net, a hub for information about politics in Burkina Faso, Sankara's life and the movements for justice following Sankara's assassination.

Levi Kabwato is a writer and social and political commentator. He is currently completing postgraduate studies at the Unit for Humanities at Rhodes University (UHURU) in Grahamstown, South Africa. He has been involved in various civil society initiatives across Africa, largely focusing on media and journalism, democratisation and technology. He maintains a weekly newspaper column, 'Levi's Notebook', published in Malawi by *The Sunday Times*. Follow him on Twitter: @LeviKabwato.

Felix Kumah-Abiwu is assistant professor of Pan-African studies at Kent State University. His research focus areas include: the politics of development, elections and democratisation in Africa, foreign policy, foreign aid, social movements of the African diaspora and global narcotics policy. He is the author of *The Dynamics of US Narcotics Policy Change: Implications for the Global Narcotics Regime* (Lambert Academic Publishing, 2012) and has recently published a chapter on the security challenges of drug trafficking in West Africa in a volume published by the UN University for Peace (UPEACE).

Patricia McFadden is a radical African feminist who lives and works on the African continent. She travels and teaches internationally, advocating and writing on women's rights and freedoms. Her work, which spans four decades of activist scholarship, has centred on the critical feminist challenges around sexuality, citizenship, and wellness as key to reproductive health and rights for women. Her published work can be found in books, articles, journals and other media forms, most of which are freely accessible in the open commons.

Namakula E. Mayanja is a PhD candidate in peace and justice at the University of Manitoba in Canada, where her doctoral research considers the mineral-related wars in South Kivu, eastern Democratic Republic of Congo. Evelyn holds an International Peace Research Association Foundation Scholarship. Her research agenda incorporates international systems and natural resource wars in Africa, peace leadership and governance for peace as well as security and development in Africa. She has published several peer-reviewed articles and book chapters and also writes frequently for online journals, including *Pambazuka News*.

Amber Murrey is a feminist decolonial geographer and anti-racist scholar. For the last decade, her research has elaborated the connections between resource extraction, race and international development and the knowledge-development nexus in contemporary African societies. She has published a dozen chapters, articles and reviews, some of which have featured in the pages of *Political Geography*, *Singapore Journal of Tropical Geography*, *Third World Quarterly* and more. She is currently a postdoctoral fellow at the American University in Cairo.

Olusoji Odeyemi is a lecturer in the social science department of Wesley University in Ondo, Nigeria, where he teaches courses in political science and international relations. His research focuses on African development, foreign policy and African relations in contemporary international systems. He is currently completing a PhD in international relations at Ekiti State University in Nigeria.

Brian Peterson is director of Africana studies and a professor of history at Union College in New York. He is a historian of colonial and post-colonial West Africa. His first book, *Islamization from Below: The Making of Muslim Communities in Rural French Sudan, 1880–1960* (Yale University Press, 2011), explored processes of religious change in southern Mali. He is currently completing a political and intellectual biography of Thomas Sankara entitled *Sankara: A Revolutionary Life in Late Cold War Africa* (Indiana University Press, forthcoming).

Craig Phelan is professor of modern history at Habib University in Karachi, Pakistan. His research focuses on trade unions around the world. Craig is the editor of *Labor History*, the pre-eminent journal on this subject, and also editor of the book series, 'Trade Unions Past, Present and Future', for Peter Lang. He has edited numerous books on the dilemmas facing contemporary trade unions worldwide and is currently focused on trade unionism in Francophone West Africa.

First to defend a doctoral thesis in sociology at Université de Ouagadougou, **Dr Zakaria Soré** teaches at Université Ouaga 1 Professeur Joseph Ki-Zerbo. He is also a civil society activist and author of several publications and lectures on the role of youth in political change in Burkina Faso. He has participated, on behalf of civil society, in several international meetings on the place of youth in the changes in Africa and the responsibility of youth in public governance. Navigating between the sociology of education and political sociology, his research focuses on youth political engagement, social movements and citizenship in Burkina Faso.

Moussa Traore is a senior lecturer at the department of English of the University of Cape Coast in Ghana. He teaches comparative literature, postcolonial studies and black diasporan studies. Dr Traore's broad research remit also includes bilingual translation and ecocriticism.

Sakue-C. Yimovie is currently pursuing a PhD in politics at the University of Sheffield. His broad research interests include political theory, postcolonial thought, democracy, public participation, political communication and engagement, international relations, policy-making and African politics. The core thread of his research is the correlations of knowledge and practice for the improvement of human condition – and this is in tune with Sankara's call for critical intellectual engagement as opposed to intellectual passivity.

Leo Zeilig is a writer and researcher. He has written extensively on African politics and history, including books on working-class struggle, the development of revolutionary movements and biographies on some of Africa's most important political thinkers and activists. Leo is also a novelist and has recently published *An Ounce of Practice* (Hope Road Publishing, 2016). Set in London and Harare, the book demands that readers confront the complexities and paradoxes of internationalism and political struggle in our contemporary moment. Leo is a senior research fellow at SWOP at the university of the Witwatersrand in Johannesburg as well as a senior fellow at the Institute of Commonwealth Studies at the University of London.

Index

Page numbers in **bold** refer to illustrations